Machine Translation Summit XVIII

Volume 2: MT Users & Providers Track

Online
16 – 20 August 2021

Editors:

Ben Huyck
Stephen Larocca
Janice Campbell
Jay Marciano
Konstantin Savenkov
Alex Yanishevsky
Stephen Richardson

ISBN: 978-1-7138-3920-0

Printed from e-media with permission by:

Curran Associates, Inc.
57 Morehouse Lane
Red Hook, NY 12571

Some format issues inherent in the e-media version may also appear in this print version.

Association for Computational Linguistics
209 N. Eighth Street
Stroudsburg, Pennsylvania 18360

Phone: 1-570-476-8006
Fax: 1-570-476-0860

acl@aclweb.org

Additional copies of this publication are available from:

Curran Associates, Inc.
57 Morehouse Lane
Red Hook, NY 12571 USA
Phone: 845-758-0400
Fax: 845-758-2633
Email: curran@proceedings.com
Web: www.proceedings.com

MT SUMMIT VIRTUAL 2021

Proceedings of Machine Translation Summit XVIII

https://mtsummit2021.amtaweb.org

Volume 2: MT Users & Providers Track

Editors:
Ben Huyck and Stephen Larocca (Government Track Co-chairs); Janice Campbell, Jay Marciano, Konstantin Savenkov and Alex Yanishevsky (Users & Providers Track Co-chairs); Stephen Richardson (General Conference Chair)

Welcome to the 18th biennial conference of the International Association of Machine Translation (IAMT) – MT Summit 2021 Virtual!

Dear MT Colleagues and Friends,

This year's MT Summit is hosted by the Association for Machine Translation in the Americas (AMTA). Every two years, the Summit is hosted on a rotating basis by one of the three sister organizations comprising IAMT: the European Association for Machine Translation (EAMT), the Asian-Pacific Association for Machine Translation (AAMT), and of course, AMTA. While each of these organizations holds its own conferences annually or biennially, the Summit is always held in odd-numbered years, and this year, AMTA is grateful to have that honor.

After a tremendously successful MT Summit XVII held in Dublin in 2019, we anticipated an equally successfully Summit in 2021 given the rapidly accelerating interest in and research and development of neural machine translation (NMT) in both academia and industry. But as you all know, the year 2020 brought a major surprise that no one anticipated. Our biennial AMTA conference, scheduled for the fall of 2020 in Orlando, Florida was transformed into a completely virtual conference after much consternation followed by a great deal of effort. We successfully rescheduled the MT Summit 2021 conference at the same venue for the following year, thinking that it would at least be a "hybrid" conference, but alas, here we are once again with a completely virtual conference. This decision was made late in the game last April when, based on the results of a survey of likely participants, it become obvious that the vast majority would not be attending in person. Recent spikes in the cases of COVID throughout the world have further justified our decision to go completely virtual.

There have been some silver linings to this COVID cloud, however, the main one being that our AMTA 2020 virtual attendance was double that of previous years, and we anticipate that attendance for the virtual Summit will be at least double what it was in Dublin. We are also grateful that once again, we were able to reschedule our intended venue in Orlando, Florida for AMTA 2022. We hope that many of you will join us there in person! And yes, we will still add a virtual component to the conference for those who are yet unable to travel.

But enough of this COVID-related confusion! We are very pleased with the response we have had to our calls for papers, presentations, workshops, tutorials, and exhibitions for MT Summit 2021 and we are sure you'll agree that the program is brimming with relevant, exciting, and useful information, not to mention the many opportunities to view the latest technology demonstrations and opportunities to network with colleagues both old and new from across the MT spectrum. The most unique aspect of these conferences is that they are truly global gatherings of MT researchers, developers, providers, and users. Academics, students, and commercial researchers and developers are able to share their latest results and offerings with colleagues, in addition to receiving and understanding real-world user requirements. Individual MT users, as well as those from language services providers, enterprises, and governments, benefit from updates on leading-edge R&D in machine translation and have a chance to present and discuss their use cases.

At this point, I need to give some serious thanks to many organizations and individuals who have made this conference possible. First, we have received amazing support from our sponsors, for which we are tremendously grateful! Our visionary sponsor, Microsoft, made it possible for the first 150 students to register for the conference at a very significant discount, and those students quickly took advantage of this generous offer. Our

Leader-level sponsors, who will be sponsoring our conference tracks, include: Apple, Intento, Lilt, Pangeanic, (RWS) Language Weaver, Systran, Vistatec, and Yandex Cloud. Our Patron-level sponsors are: Amazon (AWS), Facebook AI, Google, Kudo, Lengoo, Logrus Global, Star, and Welocalize. To all these companies we express our most sincere gratitude for their support of MT Summit 2021. Many of them will also give demonstrations of their systems and software during our Technology Exhibition Fair, and we hope that all our attendees will take advantage of this great opportunity to see the very latest commercial offerings and advancements in the world of MT. We are grateful to have three additional exhibitors in the Fair as well: CustomMT, KantanMT, and XTM.

Finally, I need to give special thanks and recognition to the members of our organizing committee, all of whom have worked very hard and given many hours and days of their time, for the most part voluntarily, to make MT Summit 2021 a success. Listing their names and official positions doesn't really seem to be an adequate reflection of their work and sacrifice, but it's the best I can do here, and I trust they know how much their efforts are truly appreciated.

Patti O'Neill-Brown, AMTA VP, Networking chair
Natalia Levitina, AMTA Secretary
Jen Doyon, AMTA Treasurer
Kevin Duh, Research Track Co-chair
Paco Guzman, Research Track Co-chair
Janice Campbell, Users and Providers Track Co-chair
Jay Marciano, Users and Providers Track Co-chair, Workshops and Tutorials Chair
Konstantin Savenkov, Users and Providers Track Co-chair
Alex Yanishevsky, Users and Providers Track Co-chair, Conference Online Platform Chair
Ben Huyck, Government Track Co-chair
Steve La Rocca, Government Track Co-chair
Ray Flournoy, Sponsorships Chair
Kenton Murray, Student Mentoring Chair
Elaine O'Curran, AMTA Counselor, Publications Chair
Alon Lavie, AMTA Consultant
Konstantin Dranch, Communications Chair
Kate Ozerova, Marketing Lead
Darius Hughes, Webmaster

Again, welcome one and all to MT Summit XVIII 2021! I look forward to "seeing" you online and hopefully, too, in person in the future.

Steve Richardson
IAMT President and MT Summit 2021 General Conference Chair

User/Provider Track: Introduction

The User/Provider Track at 2021 MT Summit features twenty-four presentations from individuals representing language service providers, machine translation services, universities, and other commercial enterprises.

We are privileged to have two esteemed keynote speakers. The first keynote of the conference is presented by Dr. Arle Lommel of CSA Research, who will speak on responsiveness to stakeholder requirements and touches on ethics as a part of "Responsible MT". Jane Nemcova, AI/ML Executive, is the second keynote speaker, and she discusses the importance of human knowledge in developing AI and the future needs of the market in "The Road to Infinity".

A recurring theme this year centers on evaluating, measuring, validating and improving MT quality in efforts to meet stakeholder expectations. Presentations focus on correlating various new auto-scoring metrics (e.g. hLEPOR, cushLEPOR, Prism, Laser, COMET) to human evaluations; evaluating productivity and quality of human translations versus machine-assisted translations; validating MTQE (MT quality estimation) in CAT workflows; and evaluating large volumes of post-edited data to determine confidence levels. Other topics focusing on quality improvement in NMT systems include data filtering methods and AI-enabled linguistic quality assessment of the source content.

We will hear about Canadian and European public agencies which have the need for many diverse language pairs that do not pivot through a high resource language. Different approaches to training low-resource languages are also being presented.

Another popular topic is MTPE (MT post-editing): how to measure translator productivity, its cost effectiveness, and how to incorporate MTPE training into translation pedagogy.

Important production pain points are addressed such as handling of inline tags, as well as terminology integration challenges, and glossary functionality in commercial MT systems.

Novel topics this year include sign language translation via a mobile app; MT-powered, real-time foreign news distribution; and using speech technology in translation workflows.

Finally, David Talbot, Head of Machine Translation at Yandex, serves as host and moderator for a roundtable featuring four commercial enterprises (NetApp, The Ford Motor Company, Autodesk and Salesforce) who explain each company's approach to building MT capacity and competence in-house.

We would like to thank the AMTA organizing committee for hosting this year's MT Summit and to the session and keynote speakers for their excellent presentations. We are especially grateful to the volunteer moderators for supporting the speakers, fielding the questions and keeping the presentations on schedule.

Sincerely,

Janice Campbell, Jay Marciano, Konstantin Savenkov, Alex Yanishevsky
The User/Provider Track Co-Chairs

Contents

AMTA
Edith Bendermacher
NetApp
NetApp 1 © 2021 NetApp, Inc. All rights reserved. — NETAPP CONFIDENTIAL —

NetApp

- Hybrid cloud data services and data management company
- We provide systems, software and cloud services
- 10,000 employees worldwide and sell into 150+ countries
- Headquarter is in San Jose, California

Globalization at NetApp

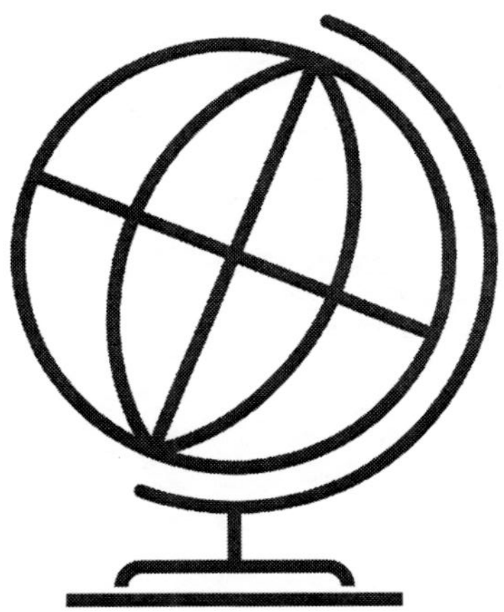

- Globalization team is Center of Excellence for the entire company
- Our mission is to drive globalization strategy and align with departmental roadmaps to lead in the global market, simplify the customer experience, and influence international revenue.
- We localize products, product manuals, marketing collateral such as presentation, videos, support content, tools.
- We localize into 10 languages and few other languages if requested
- Our globalization content strategy includes Human Translation, Neural Machine Translation with Post Edit and Raw, self-service and FastTrack translations.
- Our team is located across the world with HQ in Silicon Valley and offices in India, Japan, Italy, China and many more.

Utilizing Machine Translation since 2013

2013
Statistical Machine Translation for Knowledge Base Articles Japanese/Simplified Chinese

2017
Statistical Machine Translation for Product Manuals with Post Edit

Trained engines for Japanese/Simplified Chinese/German/French/ Spanish

2019
Statistical Machine Translation for Product Manuals without Post Edit Japanese/Simplified Chinese

Trained engines for Italian/Dutch/ Russian/Korean/ Tr Chinese

2020
Switch to Neural Machine Translation

Content Strategy via NMT: Digital Marketing, self-service, product GUI, Technical Reports

2021
GitHub Enterprise self-service

Digital Marketing and NMT

- Scope: localize .com into additional 5 languages using NMT
- Timeline: 1 months
- Scope: 150+ pages
- Main driver for NMT: speed, faster GTM
- Challenges:
  - engines not trained
  - new content
  - onboarding Post Editors and linguistic reviewers
  - spaced out content drops

- Goal accomplished: we delivered and launched on time

Thank you!

6

NetApp

Neural Machine Translation at Ford Motor Company

Nestor Rychtyckyj, Nelson Marcelino, Chandana Neerukonda, Josh Postel, Roshi Vojdan, Yao Ge

Artificial Intelligence Advancement Center
Global Data Insight & Analytics
Ford Motor Company

Background

- Ford started using MT in 2000 for translation of manufacturing build instructions
  - Controlled Language input
  - Customization
  - Confidentiality
- Increased scope of MT:
  - Warranty Claims
  - Dealer Feedback
  - Customer Feedback, etc.
- Migrated to statistical/hybrid MT
- Started developing NMT in 2018
- Deployed NMT in 2019 for 4 languages

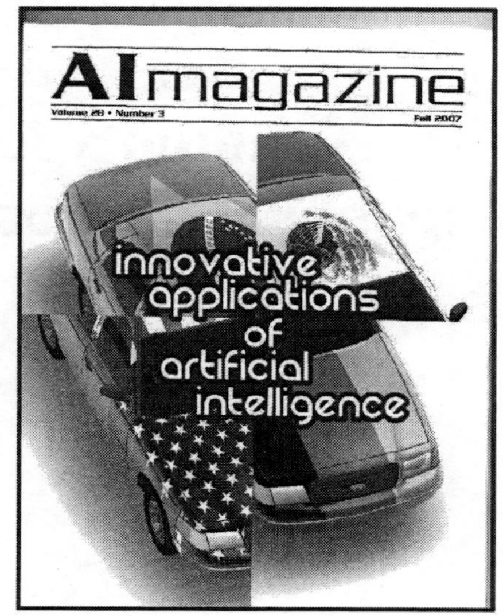

PROPRIETARY

NMT Current Status

- Deployed in October of 2019
- Supports 31 language pairs
  - From English to -> German, Spanish, Chinese, Portuguese, French, Italian, Thai, Turkish, Vietnamese, Romanian, Russian
  - From German, Spanish, Chinese, Portuguese, French, Italian, Thai, Turkish, Polish, Dutch, Norwegian, Finnish, Swedish, Danish, Vietnamese, Arabic, Tagalog, Hindi, Chinese (Traditional), Romanian to -> English
- NMT is a service that is available throughout Ford
  - User Interface (www.translate.ford.com)
  - High-Speed Table-Driven Batch Translation (Warranty, Customer Feedback)
  - Legacy Batch Translation through API (Call Center Feedback, Dealers, Manufacturing/Powertrain)
- NMT is trained on a combination of Ford-specific data and general-purpose data and is deployed on Kubernetes and the HPC

PROPRIETARY

Measuring Translation Accuracy

- Human Evaluation of Machine Translation
  - Bi-Lingual Speakers with Domain Knowledge
- Automated Evaluation
  - BLEU (Bilingual Evaluation Understudy)
  - Widely-used to compare MT models
  - Range between 0 to 1 (short phrases skew higher)
  - Compares similarity to human-translated text
- Issued with BLEU & other metrics
  - Shallow understanding of language
  - Does not take alternate translations into account
  - Does not always correlate to better translation quality

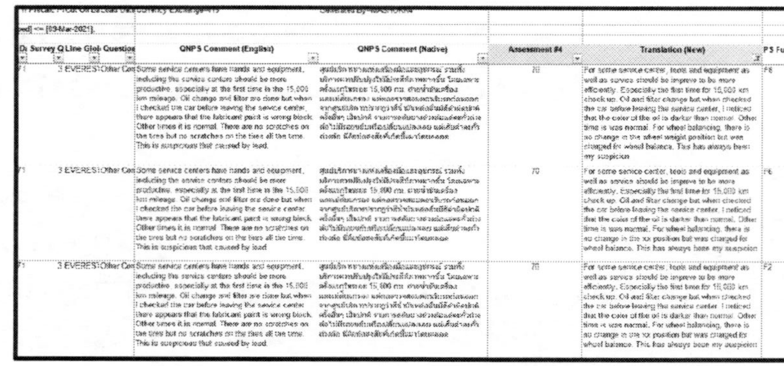

Assessment #4

Accuracy	Total	Accuracy %	B/(W)
ok	543	64%	4%
90	99	12%	0%
80	73	9%	-2%
70	44	5%	0%
60	5	1%	0%
50	47	6%	-2%
30	10	1%	0%
20			0%
ng	32	4%	1%
			-1%
Grand Total	853		
Acceptable		75%	4%

Assessment #3

Accuracy	Total	Accuracy %	B/(W)
ok	281	60%	11%
90	56	12%	-4%
80	49	10%	-9%
70	23	5%	1%
60	4	1%	1%
50	34	7%	2%
30	4	1%	
20	1	0%	
ng	14	3%	
n/a	5	1%	
Grand Total	471		
Acceptable		72%	7%

Assessment #2

Accuracy	Original	New	B/(W)
ok	30%	49%	19%
90	11%	16%	4%
80	12%	20%	7%
70	17%	4%	-14%
60	8%	0%	-8%
50	16%	5%	-10%
30/20	3%	5%	2%
NG	2%	2%	0%
Grand Total	1		
Acceptable	41%	64%	23%

Human Evaluation and Feedback

NMT Accuracy

- BLEU Scores – automated industry standard
- Manual human evaluation

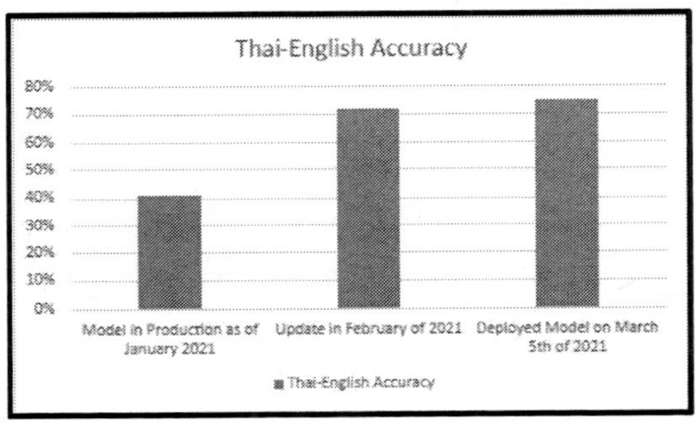

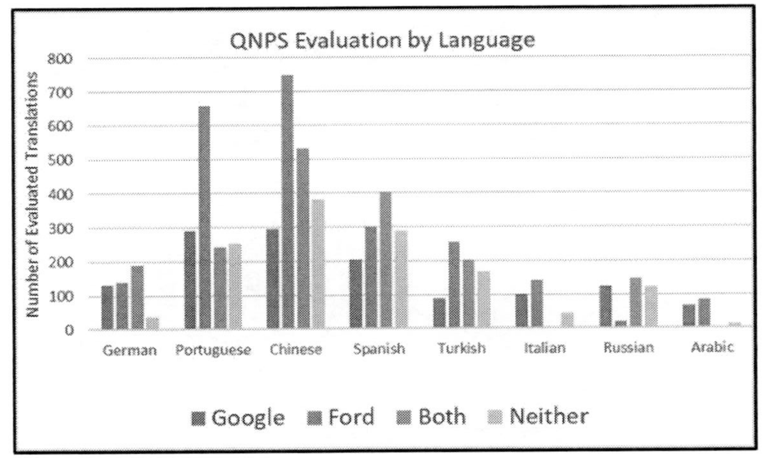

Compared our results vs. Google Translate on Ford internal QNPS (Quality Net Promoter Score) (2020)

Customer Feedback	Acceptable	Not Acceptable	PCT Correct
Chinese Feedback - Sep 2020	2484	386	86.55%
Thai Feedback - October 2020	2304	286	88.96%

PROPRIETARY

NMT Usage

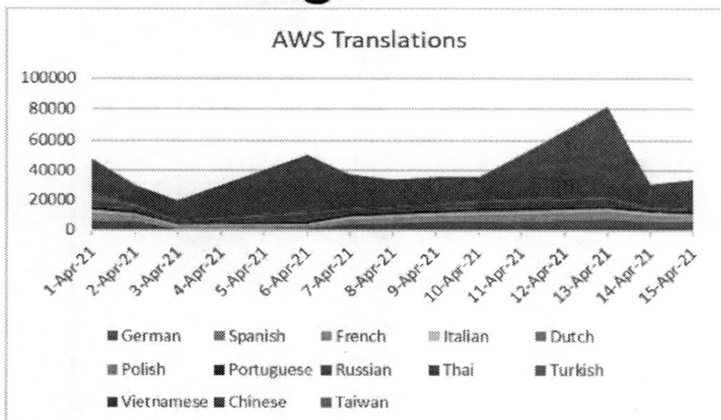

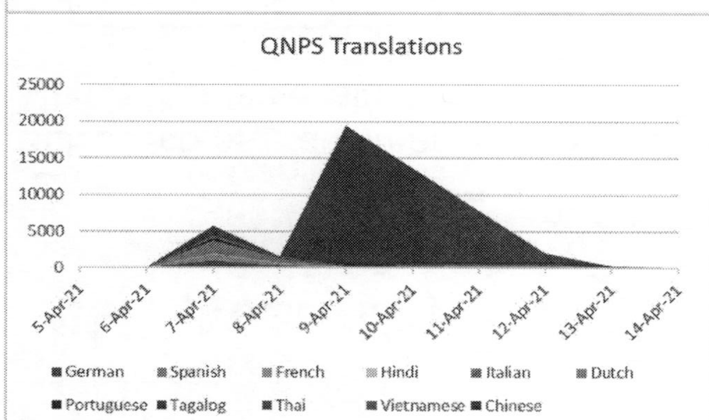

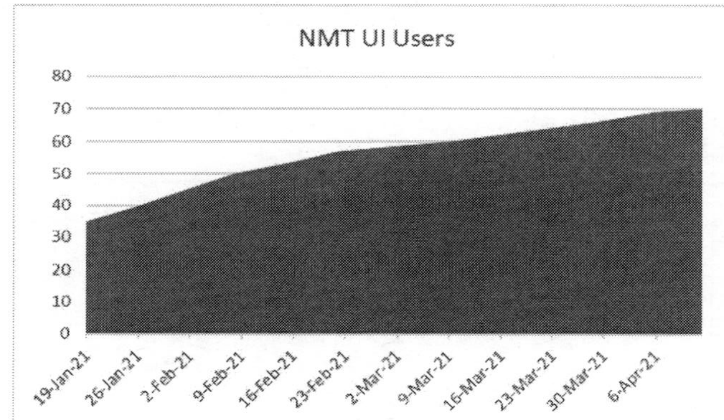

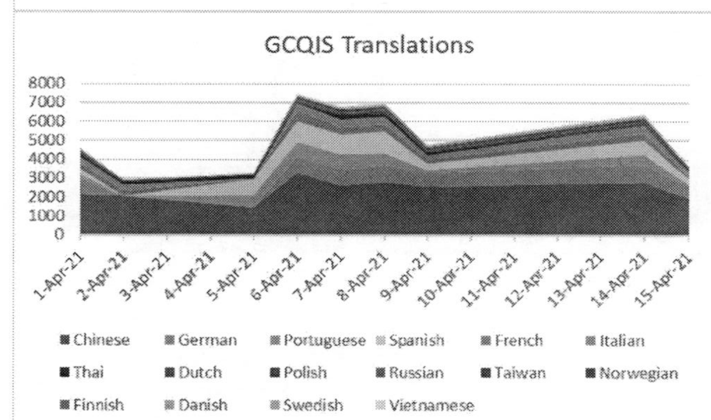

PROPRIETARY

NMT Architecture

Neural Machine Translation w/ OpenNMT-TF Architecture

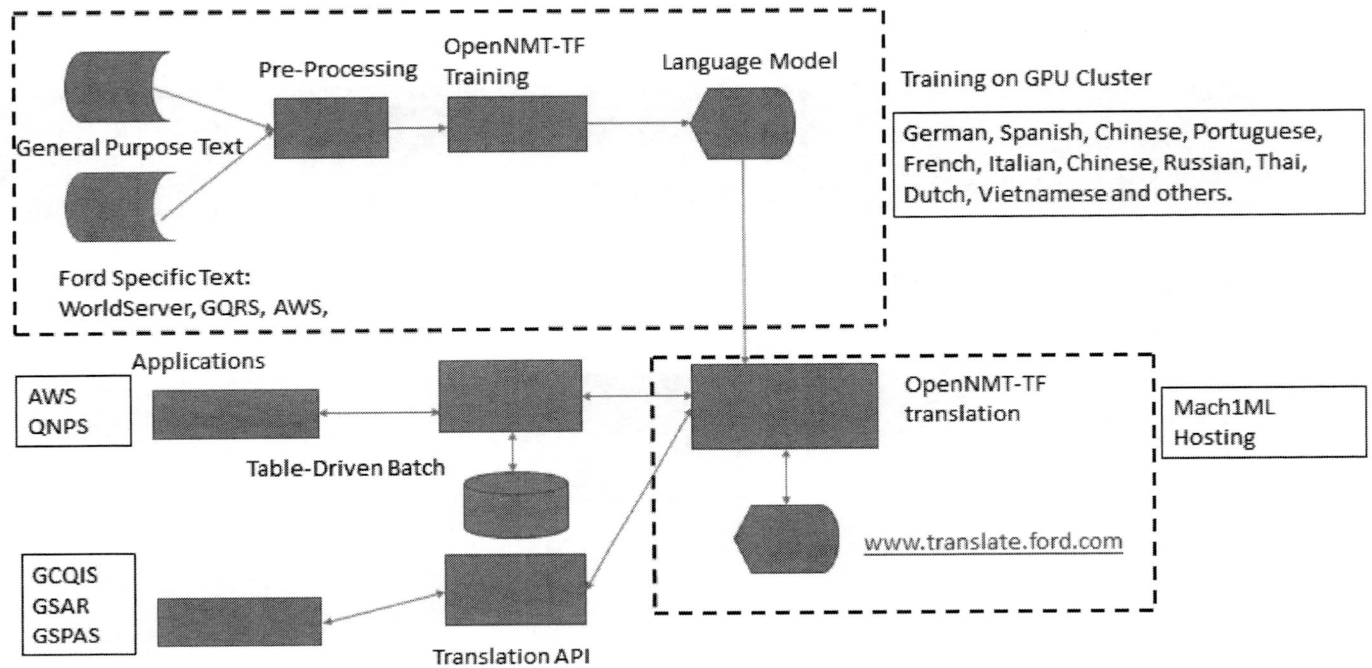

PROPRIETARY

Training Pipeline

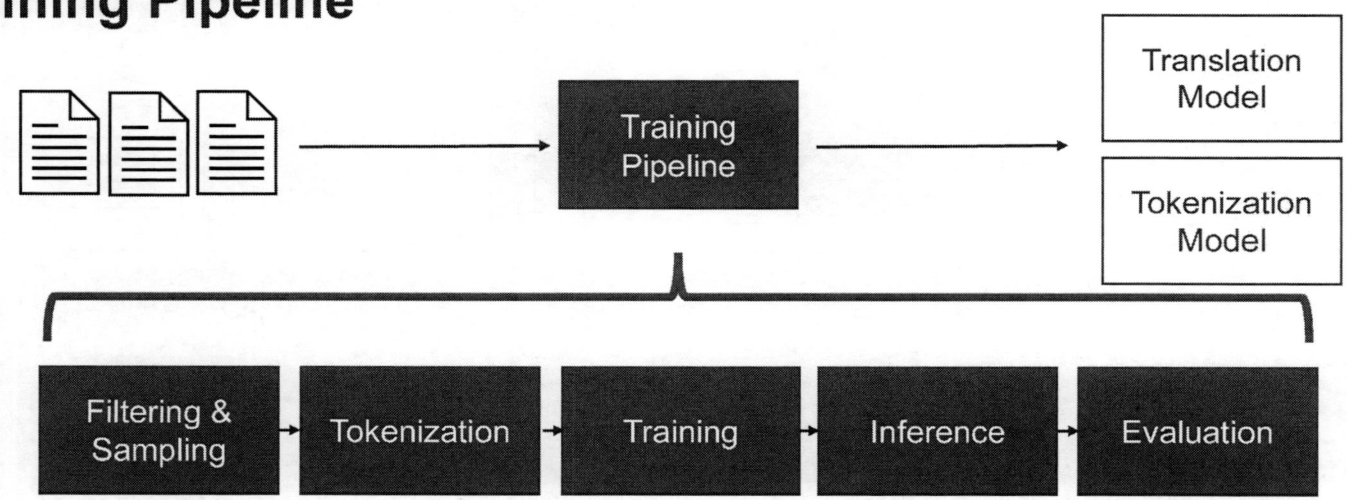

PROPRIETARY

Incremental Training

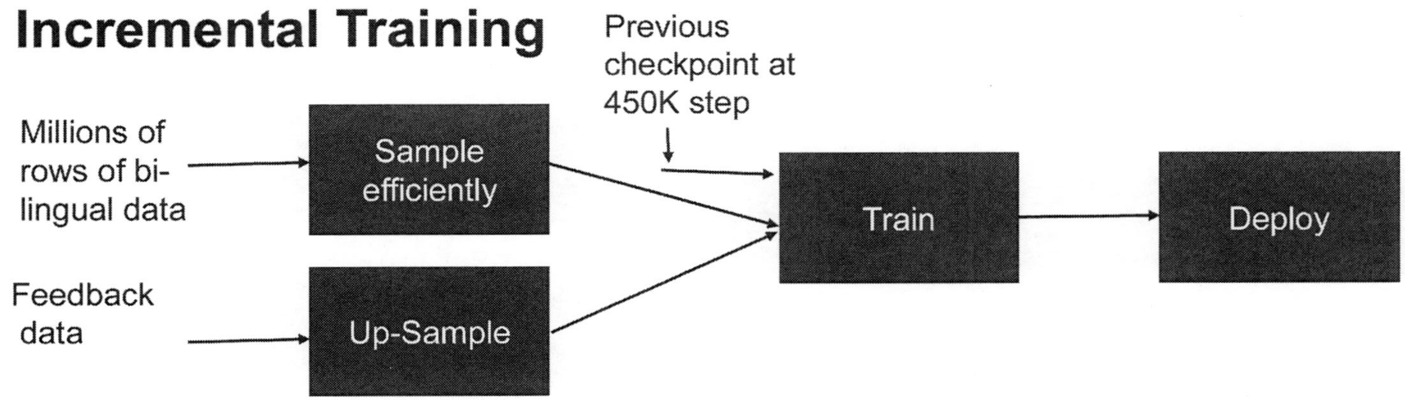

- Incremental training takes < 5000 steps i.e. 2-3 hrs on a single V100 GPU
- Even after searching through various sampling strategies and learning rates, model is available for deployment in a day.

PROPRIETARY

Q&A

Thank you!

salesforce
Salesforce NMT System:
A Year Later
Raffaella Buschiazzo
Director, Localization @ Salesforce
Virtual MT Summit 2021: Building MT
Capacity and Competence in-house

Agenda

- Salesforce MT Overview
- Primary Use Case
- What's Done
- MT Quality
- 2021 Roadmap
- Future Applications

Salesforce MT Overview

A 4-year collaboration between R&D Localization and Salesforce Research teams

NMT system:

- Built on Salesforce domain
- Language-agnostic architecture with models per language
- Leveraging Salesforce data and publicly available pretrained models (mBART, XLM-R, etc.)

Goals:

- Reduce translation time by enhancing translators' productivity
- Increase content accuracy/freshness by publishing updates on-time/more frequently > Increase case deflection
- For selected markets, eliminate translation cost by publishing raw MT or reduce cost through light PE
- Reinvesting savings into high-value content/products

US Patent No. 10,963,652 for "Structured Text Translation"

Primary Use Case: Salesforce Online Help

Languages

English
Français
Deutsch
Italiano
日本語
Español (México)
Español
中文（简体）
中文（繁體）
한국어
Русский
Português (Brasil)
Suomi
Dansk
Svenska
Nederlands
ภาษาไทย
Norsk

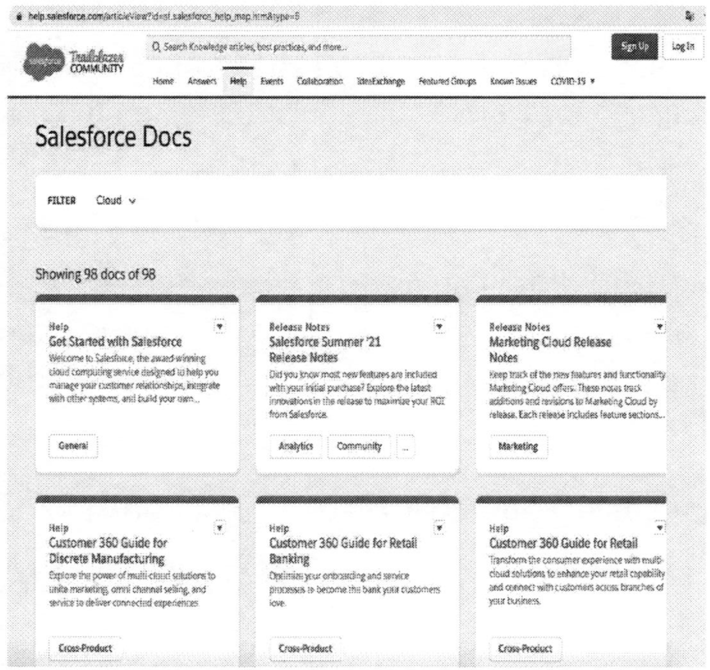

3 major releases

Translated 3 x year

New feature/product terminology per major release

Authored in DITA XML (200+ tags)

What's Done

Achievements in the last year

Implemented SF MT as a standard localization process for Core Help:

- 100% of Salesforce Help is MTed and PEd for all 16 languages.
- Developed plugin to track MT quality systematically.
- Trained our translators on MTPE best practices.
- Reduced training time for the MT models from 1 day to 2/3 hours per language.

MT Quality - Part 1

Manual

Initially

- BLEU score
- Conduct human evaluations at each MT system iteration. Translators evaluated 500 MTed strings using 1/2/3 categorization:
    - 1 - Translation is ready for publication
      2 - Translation is useful but needs human post-editing
      3 - Translation is useless
- Plus overall feedback provided by our translators after post-editing 100K new words + 300K fuzzies per major release.

MT Quality - Part 2

Automated

In 2020-21

- We started using **PEMp (Post-Editing Modification %)** on every PEd segment.
- Calculated using an algorithm respecting the 'Damerau–Levenshtein' edit distance
- Counts the minimum number of operations needed to transform one string into the other where an operation is defined as an insertion, deletion, or substitution of a single character, or a transposition of two adjacent characters.

MT Quality: PEMp Scores/5 Releases

Language	R1	R2	R3	R4	R5
ja-JP	64.22%	74.30%	81.60%	81.94%	81.35
da-DK		86.12%	89.87%	92.77%	91.67
de-DE		72.55%	82.76%	82.25%	82.71
es-MX		89.08%	95.74%	89.18%	89.55
fr-FR		81.84%	86.58%	86.12%	86.58
nb-NO		81.13%	84.39%	87.73%	88.51
pt-BR		86.67%	93.73%	94.15%	93.97
sv-SE		84.57%	90.18%	93.36%	94.61
ko-KR				81.84%	88.09
fi-FI				87.90%	77.71
it-IT					85.99
nl-NL					81.07
ru-RU					86.18
zh-CN					85.39
zh-TW					81.93

Average
all languages:
86.35%

MT Quality: Unedited Segments

Average for 5 releases

Language	Unedited segments
ja-JP	28.67%
da-DK	46.17%
de-DE	29.04%
es-MX	51.78%
fr-FR	29.28%
nb-NO	32.36%
pt-BR	47.60%
sv-SE	53.17%
ko-KR	41.32%
fi-FI	39.34%
it-IT	31.86%
nl-NL	28.39%
ru-RU	30.96%
zh-CN	26.87%
zh-TW	23.71%

Average
all languages:
36.03%

MT API for Continuous Localization

Publish **raw MT for Help in four Nordic languages**.

- Track page view #, MT disclaimer in H&T, thumbs up/down report, PE most viewed pages.

Test current model to MT **Help from acquisitions**

Knowledge Articles:
Increase number of translated KAs

Reduce cost

Video subtitles

Future applications

Internal to SFDC

- Extend MT to 34 languages
- MT for UI label testing (like pseudo loc)
- MTPE on software localization
- Other content (ex: developer's guides)

Customer-Facing/Product

- Case feed
- Experience Cloud
- Slacks apps

Make Salesforce MT API available for customers

- OOTB
- Trainable?

Thank You
Trail blazer
Trail blazer
Trail blazer

Neural Machine Translation – Localization and beyond

Emanuele Dias
Principal Machine Learning Engineer

AUTODESK

Autodesk – What do we do

Construction

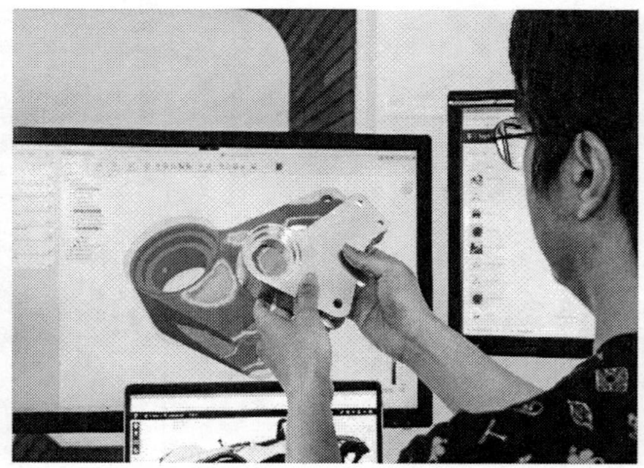

Manufacturing

Media and Entertainment

Our Localization Challenges

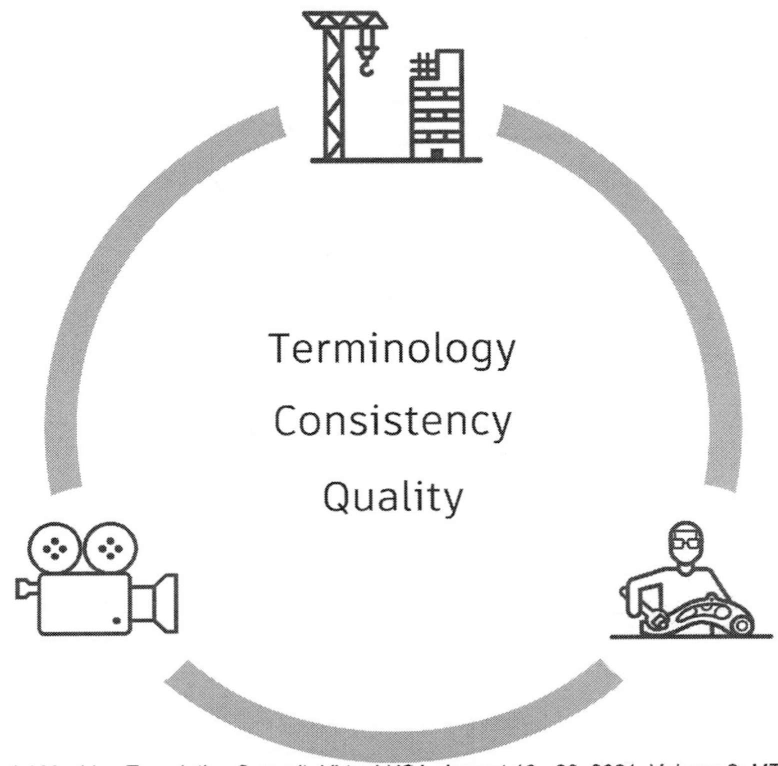

Autodesk's MT history

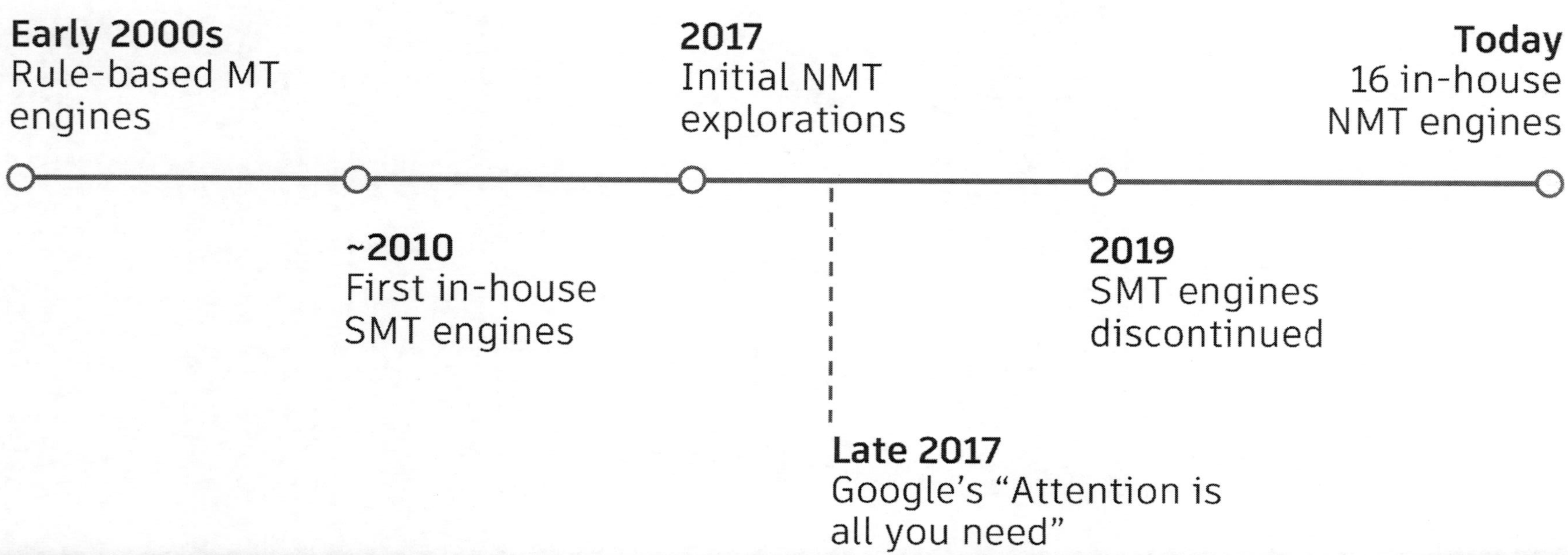

Why in-house?

Confidentiality
Privacy

Quality

Know-how

Quality

- Better overall quality and a more consistent handling of “external entities”
  - Less post-editing (PE) required
  - Better PE rates
  - More raw MT content
- Ability to fix problems quickly and with increased precision

Language	Difference (average rating points)	Autodesk	Best-Performing Competitor
Czech	2.46	78.56	76.10 (Google)
German	5.49	91.64	86.15 (Google)
Hungarian	9.17	73.80	64.63 (Google)
Chinese (Simplified)	5.71	87.68	81.97 (Google)
Japanese	1.72	89.21	87.60 (Google)
Portuguese (Brazilian)	2.32	89.30	86.96 (Google)
Spanish	5.16	90.12	84.96 (Google)

Know-how

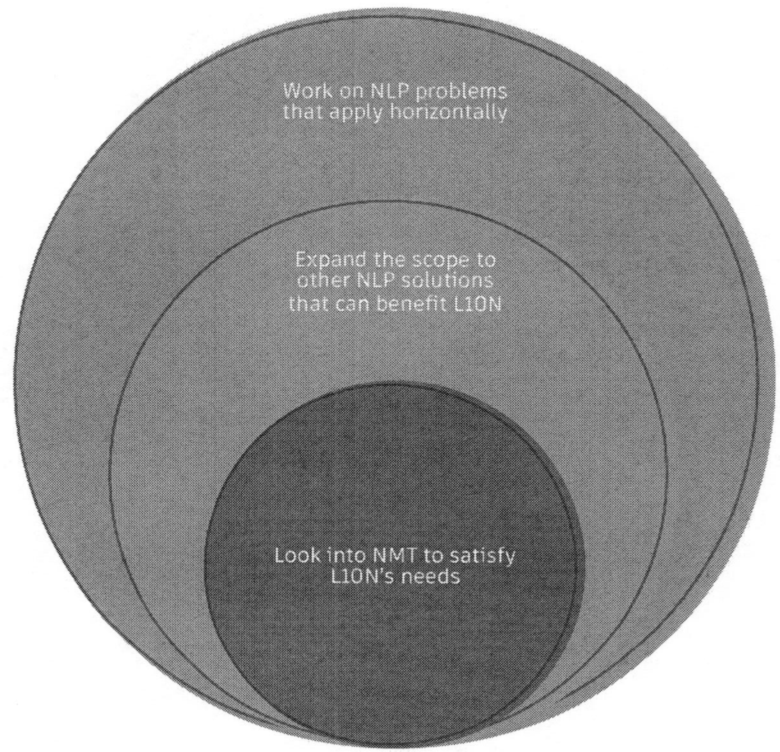

Work on NLP problems that apply horizontally
Expand the scope to other NLP solutions that can benefit L10N
Look into NMT to satisfy L10N's needs

NMT Beyond Localization

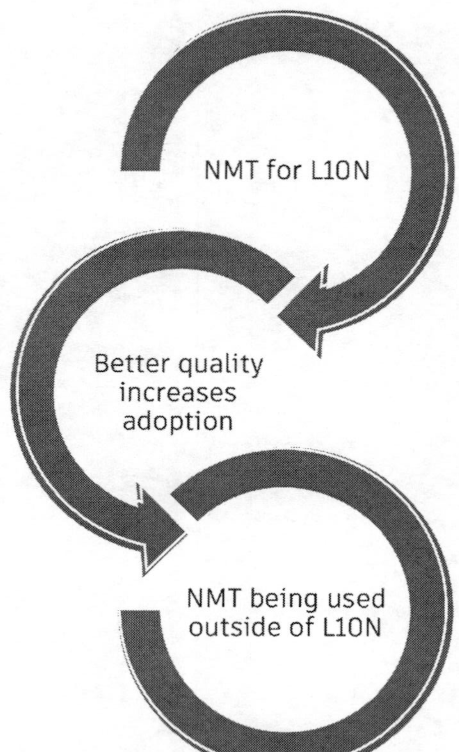

AUTODESK®

Make anything™

A Neural Translator Designed to Protect the Eastern Border of the European Union

Nowakowski Artur artur.nowakowski@amu.edu.pl
Faculty of Mathematics and Computer Science, Adam Mickiewicz University, Poznan, 61-614, Poland

Jassem Krzysztof jassem@amu.edu.pl
Faculty of Mathematics and Computer Science, Adam Mickiewicz University, Poznan, 61-614, Poland

Abstract

This paper reports on a translation engine designed for the needs of the Polish State Border Guard. The engine is a component of the AI Searcher system, whose aim is to search for Internet texts, written in Polish, Russian, Ukrainian or Belarusian, which may lead to criminal acts at the eastern border of the European Union. The system is intended for Polish users, and the translation engine should serve to assist understanding of non-Polish documents. The engine was trained on general-domain texts. The adaptation for the criminal domain consisted in the appropriate translation of criminal terms and proper names, such as forenames, surnames and geographical objects. The translation process needs to take into account the rich inflection found in all of the languages of interest. To this end, a method based on constrained decoding that incorporates an inflected lexicon into a neural translation process was applied in the engine.

1 Introduction

The Internet, even in its legal form, may be a source of criminal information. Government bodies all over the world search through Internet sites for potentially criminal texts, to prevent certain acts to which such texts may give rise. For example, the Polish State Border Guard, whose function is to protect the eastern border of the European Union, tracks texts that may concern criminal activities such as general smuggling, trafficking of drugs, medicines, alcohol and cigarettes, people trafficking, human organs trafficking, weapons and explosives, sex crime, document fraud, and trafficking of stolen cars and machines. Two factors make this task difficult for employees of the State Border Guard. Firstly, the texts of interest are sparse and not easy to detect. The problem of the detection of such texts is tackled in Nowakowski and Jassem (2021a). Secondly, criminal texts may appear in foreign languages, not known to a particular employee. In such cases a machine translation engine may be of significant help to the user.

This paper describes a neural translator designed for the needs of the Polish State Border Guard. The translator is a component of a system designed to search for and store criminal content. The system is being developed within a research project entitled "Advanced Internet analysis supporting the detection of criminal groups"[1] (the project's short name is AI Searcher). The architecture of the AI Searcher system is described in section 2. Section 3 reports on the data that was used for the training of language pairs applied in the system. Section 4 describes how the translation engine was adapted to the domain of criminal texts. Details on the lexicalized

[1] The project is financed by the Polish National Center for Research and Development.

translation methods applied in the adaptation are presented in section 5. Section 6 gives a few examples that show the difference between adapted and unadapted translation. We conclude the paper with some insights relevant to future work.

2 The AI Searcher project

The AI Searcher project was launched in December 2018. This three-year program has the aim of developing a system to support the protection of the eastern border of the European Union by searching the Internet for criminal texts that may be of interest to employees of the Polish State Border Guard. The user scenario is the following: The employee of the State Border Guard types an inquiry into an edit window. The Query Expansion Module expands the inquiry to a set of queries that are semantically related to the inquiry. The Translation Module translates the set of queries into Russian, Ukrainian, and Belarusian. The Crawler searches the Internet to find texts in Polish, Russian, Ukrainian, and Belarusian related to the queries. The Translation Module translates the foreign texts back to Polish. Finally, the Classifier analyzes the texts to return those with potentially criminal content.

3 Training data

The translator engines designed for the system are trained on the OPUS resources.[2] The sets for training, validation and testing are based on the Tatoeba Challenge[3] (Tiedemann 2020). Statistics on the bilingual corpora used in the project are given in Table 1.

Table 1: Bilingual corpora statistics

Corpus set	Polish–Russian	Polish–Ukrainian	Polish–Belarusian
training set	ca. 19.17m	ca. 1.68m	72,276
validation set	1,000	6,900	287
test set	3,543	2,500	287

The number of sentences for the Polish–Belarusian pair was too low to generate comprehensive translation. A multilingual (Polish–Russian–Ukrainian–Belarusian) model was designed to improve the Polish–Belarusian translation. Its statistics are given in Table 2.

Table 2: Multilingual corpus statistics

Corpus set	Russian–Belarusian	Russian–Ukrainian	Ukrainian–Belarusian
training set	72,870	ca. 1.52m	66,687
validation set	2,743	6,815	1,000
test set	2,500	10,000	2,355

Table 3 shows the BLEU scores of the AI Searcher Translator compared with Google Translate, calculated on the Tatoeba test set.

4 Translation of terminology and personal names

The State Border Guard expects that the translation engine should correctly translate proper names, such as surnames, forenames, geographical locations and objects, brands of cigarettes and alcohol, etc. The lists of such names were created semi-automatically: the names underwent

[2] https://opus.nlpl.eu/

[3] https://github.com/Helsinki-NLP/Tatoeba-Challenge

Table 3: Comparison of BLEU scores

Corpus set	pl -> ru	ru -> pl	pl -> uk	uk -> pl	pl -> be	be -> pl
AI Searcher	47.69	43.06	41.25	43.67	24.75	37.92
Google Translate	42.95	43.05	34.84	38.42	35.39	44.19
difference	+4.74	+0.01	+6.41	+5.25	-10.64	-6.27

automatic transliteration between the Cyrillic and Latin alphabets, and the most frequent names were carefully verified by native speakers. It is worth noting that all verified forenames and surnames were listed and checked together with their inflected forms (there exist 6–7 grammatical cases in all of these languages).

Forenames and surnames in their base Latin form were provided to us by employees of the State Border Guard, names of geographical objects were collected from the available OpenStreetMap resources, and criminal terminology, including brands of cigarettes, cars and alcohol, was gathered from various websites and forums.

Table 4 shows the numbers of base forms for verified proper names.

Table 4: Statistics of proper names

Proper Names	Polish–Russian	Polish–Ukrainian	Polish–Belarusian
male forenames	1,882	1,902	3,477
male surnames	16,142	29,628	17,421
female forenames	2,117	1,962	3,302
female surnames	19,898	26,114	20,170
geographical objects	5,092	7,613	9,460

The adaptation of the translation engine also took into account a lexicon of criminal terms, which consisted of 1203 entries in each of the language pairs.

5 Lexical constraints

The incorporation of lexicon in neural machine translation has been studied thoroughly in recent years (Arthur et al. 2016, Anderson et al. 2017, Hokamp and Liu 2017, Dinu et al. 2019, Song et al. 2019, Exel et al. 2020). The methodology used in the described experiments was based on a constrained decoding and "code-switching" approach. Our approach was focused on constrained decoding, which uses the Grid Beam Search algorithm introduced by Hokamp and Liu (2017) and extended by Post and Vilar (2018) and Hu et al. (2019). We designed an algorithm based on constrained decoding in order to take into account inflected forms of proper names. To evaluate the performance of the algorithm, we carried out experiments in two different scenarios: general and domain-specific. We compared our method with baseline translation, i.e. translation without lexical constraints, in terms of translation speed and translation quality. The lexicalized method resulted in a decrease in translation quality in the general scenario, which shows that augmenting general-domain texts with a specialized lexicon may impair the performance of a neural translator. In the domain-specific scenario the translation showed significant progress, with an increase of over 3 BLEU points. The cost of the algorithm is a decrease in the translation speed. The details of the experiment are reported in Nowakowski and Jassem (2021b). There, several manual metrics for the evaluation of terminology translation were introduced: Placement Rate, Duplication Rate and Inflection Rate. The metrics evaluated the proportions of output sentences in which the target lexicon terms were, respectively, properly placed, not duplicated unnecessarily and correctly inflected. The manual evaluation results showed that our method ensures terminological adequacy and consistency as well as linguistic correctness when translating into a morphologically rich language in domain-specific scenarios.

6 Examples of lexicalized translation

Tables 5 and 6 show examples of sentences translated with the unadapted and adapted translation engine into Russian and Ukrainian, respectively. The lexicon entries consist of a term in the source language with the equivalent in the target language along with a comma-separated list of its inflectional forms. For each sentence, a manual English translation is given for clarity.

Table 5: Examples of lexicalized translation into Russian

Lexicon entry	Georgy -> Георгий, Георгия, Георгию, Георгием, Георгии
Source sentence	**Georgy** Kuzmin przewozi fajki przez wschodnią granicę.
English translation	Georgy Kuzmin transports cigarettes across the eastern border.
Unadapted MT	Джорджи Кузьмин перевозит сигареты через восточную границу.
Adapted MT	**Георгий** Кузьмин перевозит сигареты через восточную границу.
Lexicon entry	szwarcować -> перебрасывать, перебрасываю, перебрасываешь
Source sentence	Zaczynamy **szwarcować** zioło klientom.
English translation	We are beginning to smuggle the weed to our customers.
Unadapted MT	Мы начинаем портить травы для клиентов.
Adapted MT	Мы начинаем **перебрасывать** траву клиентам.

Table 6: Examples of lexicalized translation into Ukrainian

Lexicon entries	Karpiuk -> Карпюк, Карпюка, Карпюкові, Карпюком hordenina -> горденін горденин гордеїн
Source sentence	Przyniesiemy **hordeninę** do **Karpiuka**.
English translation	We'll bring hordenine to Karpiuk.
Unadapted MT	Ми привеземо гордон до Карпіока.
Adapted MT	Ми принесемо **горденін** до **Карпюка**.
Lexicon entry	przećpać -> накачатись, накачатися, накачати, накачаться
Source sentence	Chcesz okazyjnie **przećpać** w promocyjnej cenie?
English translation	Do you want to get high at a discounted price?
Unadapted MT	Ви хочете побути в промоційній ціні?
Adapted MT	Ви хочете **накачатися** на промоційній ціні?

7 Conclusions

In this case study, a translation engine is part of a system that searches for criminal content in Internet documents written in the Polish, Russian, Ukrainian and Belarusian languages. The adaptation of the translation to the domain of criminal texts consists in the incorporation of lexicon into the neural machine translation engine. The criminal terminology is expected to be translated according to lexical constraints, and the lexical entries should be correctly inflected. An algorithm based on constrained decoding was designed to achieve this goal.

The project described here is ending in December 2021. Work in the near future will focus on further improving Belarusian translation and on increasing efficiency.

References

Anderson, P., Fernando, B., Johnson, M., and Gould, S. (2017). Guided open vocabulary image captioning with constrained beam search. In *Proceedings of the 2017 Conference on Empirical Methods in Natural Language Processing*, pages 936–945, Copenhagen, Denmark. Association for Computational Linguistics.

Arthur, P., Neubig, G., and Nakamura, S. (2016). Incorporating discrete translation lexicons into neural machine translation. In *Proceedings of the 2016 Conference on Empirical Methods in Natural Language Processing*, pages 1557–1567, Austin, Texas. Association for Computational Linguistics.

Dinu, G., Mathur, P., Federico, M., and Al-Onaizan, Y. (2019). Training neural machine translation to apply terminology constraints. In *Proceedings of the 57th Annual Meeting of the Association for Computational Linguistics*, pages 3063–3068, Florence, Italy. Association for Computational Linguistics.

Exel, M., Buschbeck, B., Brandt, L., and Doneva, S. (2020). Terminology-constrained neural machine translation at SAP. In *Proceedings of the 22nd Annual Conference of the European Association for Machine Translation*, pages 271–280, Lisboa, Portugal. European Association for Machine Translation.

Hokamp, C. and Liu, Q. (2017). Lexically constrained decoding for sequence generation using grid beam search. In *Proceedings of the 55th Annual Meeting of the Association for Computational Linguistics (Volume 1: Long Papers)*, pages 1535–1546, Vancouver, Canada. Association for Computational Linguistics.

Hu, J. E., Khayrallah, H., Culkin, R., Xia, P., Chen, T., Post, M., and Van Durme, B. (2019). Improved lexically constrained decoding for translation and monolingual rewriting. In *Proceedings of the 2019 Conference of the North American Chapter of the Association for Computational Linguistics: Human Language Technologies, Volume 1 (Long and Short Papers)*, pages 839–850, Minneapolis, Minnesota. Association for Computational Linguistics.

Nowakowski, A. and Jassem, K. (2021a). Detection of criminal texts for the Polish state border guard. In *MIS2-KDD 2021 : The Second International MIS2 Workshop: Misinformation and Misbehavior Mining on the Web*. Association for Computing Machinery. to appear.

Nowakowski, A. and Jassem, K. (2021b). Neural machine translation with inflected lexicon. In *Proceedings of Machine Translation Summit XVIII: Research Track*. Association for Computational Linguistics. to appear.

Post, M. and Vilar, D. (2018). Fast lexically constrained decoding with dynamic beam allocation for neural machine translation. In *Proceedings of the 2018 Conference of the North American Chapter of the Association for Computational Linguistics: Human Language Technologies, Volume 1 (Long Papers)*, pages 1314–1324, New Orleans, Louisiana. Association for Computational Linguistics.

Song, K., Zhang, Y., Yu, H., Luo, W., Wang, K., and Zhang, M. (2019). Code-switching for enhancing NMT with pre-specified translation. In *Proceedings of the 2019 Conference of the North American Chapter of the Association for Computational Linguistics: Human Language Technologies, Volume 1 (Long and Short Papers)*, pages 449–459, Minneapolis, Minnesota. Association for Computational Linguistics.

Tiedemann, J. (2020). The Tatoeba translation challenge – realistic data sets for low resource and multilingual MT. In *Proceedings of the Fifth Conference on Machine Translation*, pages 1174–1182. Association for Computational Linguistics.

Corpus Creation and Evaluation for Speech-to-Text and Speech Translation

Corey Miller corey.a.miller@nvtc.gov
Evelyne Tzoukermann evelyne.tzoukermann@nvtc.gov
Jennifer Doyon jennifer.doyon@nvtc.gov
Elisabeth Mallard elisabeth.d.mallard@nvtc.gov
National Virtual Translation Center, Washington, DC, USA

Abstract

The National Virtual Translation Center (NVTC) seeks to acquire human language technology (HLT) tools that will facilitate its mission to provide verbatim English translations of foreign language audio and video files. In the text domain, NVTC has been using translation memory (TM) for some time and has reported on the incorporation of machine translation (MT) into that workflow (Miller et al., 2020). While we have explored the use of speech-to-text (STT) and speech translation (ST) in the past (Tzoukermann and Miller, 2018), we have now invested in the creation of a substantial human-made corpus to thoroughly evaluate alternatives. Results from our analysis of this corpus and the performance of HLT tools point the way to the most promising ones to deploy in our workflow.

1. Introduction

Among other offerings, NVTC provides verbatim human translations of both text and audio/video (AV) materials from foreign languages into English. NVTC places a great emphasis on identifying efficient workflows employing the latest HLT tools in the spirit of Augmented Translation (AT), a more encompassing form of Computer-Assisted Translation (CAT) (Miller et al. 2020). This paper focuses on AT in support of translation of AV. Miller and Tzoukermann (2018) showed efficiency advantages through the incorporation of both STT, ST and MT into human audio/video translation workflows. This paper describes the beginning stages of a more comprehensive exploration of that space, focused initially on the creation of a corpus and the running and scoring of several STT and ST engines using it. Subsequent work will focus on an analysis of MT vs. ST and the relative efficiency of such workflows.

2. Corpus

In order to identify relevant tools and processes for its data, NVTC sought to develop a corpus based on data that would be representative of the kinds of AV materials it typically receives for verbatim human translation. Criteria included typical languages, presence of multiple speakers, conversational/colloquial language, and pertinence to domains such as technological/scientific, cultural and political. Table 1 provides a summary of the languages sampled and the quantity of material in hours. All of the material was originally in video format and was converted to audio format so that both could be used as will be described below.

Language	Hours	Number of files
Arabic (Saudis speaking Modern Standard Arabic [MSA])	1	1
French (France)	2	1
Russian	6	4
Persian (Iran)	4	4

Table 1. Languages and quantity of associated data.

Once the source data had been identified, we developed a protocol for what kinds of human-produced output we wished to develop and how to instruct the participants to produce it. While NVTC's human translators (known as "linguists") typically only provide an English verbatim translation of foreign language source material, we sought to also include a foreign language transcription task since the most common speech analytics available today render a transcription in the same language as the AV input.

Accordingly, the first human-produced output we specified was a verbatim source-language transcription. Since verbatim translations (and transcriptions) often require timepoints and indications of who is speaking, we sought to identify a tool to facilitate linguists' annotation of this information. ELAN (2021) was deemed to be the most modern, flexible and well-supported of such tools.

Both the video and audio pertaining to a given file were loaded into an ELAN project. The video was included since it supplies useful information about who is speaking and provides extralinguistic context that facilitates transcription. Audio was provided in the form of a waveform in order to provide an easy way for linguists to demarcate the section being transcribed.

Linguists were asked to put the transcription of each speaker's utterances on a separate tier. They were asked to transcribe a single interpausal unit (IPU, Hosaka et al., 1994) at a time by selecting a portion of the waveform pertaining to the IPU and providing the source language orthographic transcription (to be described in more detail below) on an annotation tier identified with the speaker's name. This method obviated the linguist needing to explicitly annotate the start and end times of each IPU (a process subject to error), since they could be exported automatically from ELAN as will be described below.

Since people often do not speak in well-formed sentences, the IPU represents a convenient segmentation. In addition, its limited size lends itself to STT word error rate (WER) scoring (Jonathan Fiscus, personal communication) and serves as a spoken analogue of the translation unit (TU) (Hosaka et al., 1994), which is a normally a sentence in textual materials. Figure 1 shows the ELAN interface including French video, audio waveform, individual speaker tiers, and source language transcription of two IPUs by two speakers.

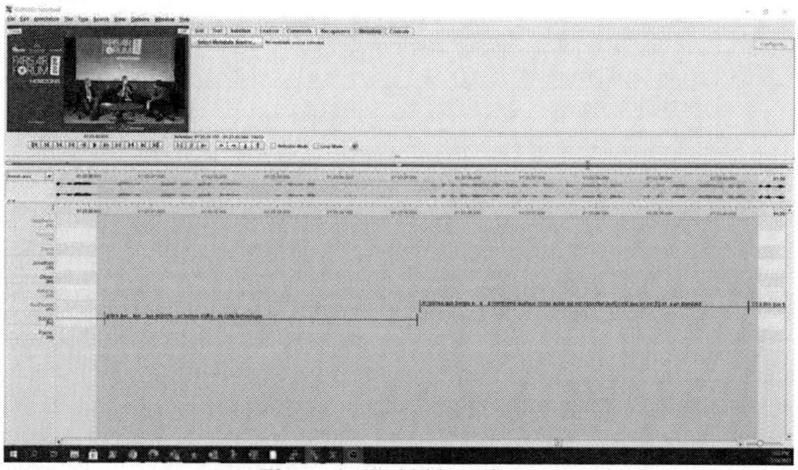

Figure 1. ELAN interface.

Once the transcription of a file was complete, its contents could be exported from ELAN as a tab-delimited text file containing the start time, end time, tier/speaker name and transcription of each IPU. This file could be loaded into an Excel spreadsheet, as shown in Figure 2, and then loaded into a CAT tool to be translated into English. Each transcribed IPU would serve as a source TU that would then be rendered as a target TU and serve toward the construction of a speech-oriented TM. Once the translation was completed, it could be output as an Excel spreadsheet, as shown in Figure 3.

Sergio [3]	4997.66	5000.375	mais il faudra un peu de temps pour l'implémenter
Sergio [3]	5000.375	5005.325	et ilf faudra une progressivité - je pense que on apprendra à utiliser la technologie-
Sergio [3]	5005.335	5010.279	de plus en plus, en fonction de [euh] de cas qui seront découverts
Sergio [3]	5010.279	5015.223	grâce aux... aux... aux apports - en termes d'offre - de cette technologie
Guillaume [2]	5015.266	5020.4	et j'pense que Sergio a... a... a mentionné quelque chose aussi qui est essentiel [euh] c'est que on est [f-] on a un standard.
Guillaume [2]	5020.412	5024.802	C't à dire que tous les aéroports [souffle] [euh] peuvent déployer ce... ce standard [souffle]

Figure 2. Sample Transcription File.

Sergio [3]	4997.66	5000.375	but it will take some time to implement
Sergio [3]	5000.375	5005.325	and it will need to be done gradually - I think we'll learn to use the technology...
Sergio [3]	5005.335	5010.279	more and more as new use cases are discovered
Sergio [3]	5010.279	5015.223	thanks to the benefits brought - in terms of offer - by this technology
Guillaume [2]	5015.266	5020.4	and I think Sergio also mentioned something that is essential, which is the fact that we do have a standard.
Guillaume [2]	5020.412	5024.802	It means that all airports can deploy this ... this standard

Figure 3. Sample Translation File.

In order to facilitate transcription and translation, linguists were instructed to follow their normal style guide. Traditionally, transcription for the purpose of STT evaluation has advised certain normalizations, such as lowercasing, avoiding punctuation and transcription of numbers as words rather than numerals[1]. However, given that we planned to evaluate several STT and ST systems, some of which transcribe numbers and punctuation in sophisticated ways, we felt it best to allow the linguists to transcribe things the way their final products were intended to be presented, e.g., including casing, punctuation and context-dependent representation of numbers as either numerals or words. That would give us an opportunity to evaluate these more sophisticated features should speech analytics attempt them. We also felt that normalization/simplification of standard forms, if necessary, would be easier than trying to infer the more sophisticated forms from simpler ones.

The style guide advises linguists to use standard orthography. We anticipated this might be a problem in Persian where there is typically a wide "diglossic" divergence between the written (standard) and spoken (colloquial) registers (Miller and Saeli, 2016; Saeli and Miller, 2018). However, we were surprised to see that French transcribers introduced a number of colloquial spellings as well, to be described below.

Finally, the style guide permits linguists to provide "exegetical remarks" in square brackets. In our case, these provided a useful way to isolate fillers/disfluencies such as *um* and *uh*, non-speech (e.g., music, coughs) and cut-off words (such as *hel-* or *-lo* for *hello*).

3. Speech Analytics and Scoring

Since our linguists most often translate foreign language source AV into English, our earlier work (Tzoukermann and Miller, 2018) led us to believe that ST would ultimately provide the best accuracy and efficiency outcomes with respect to enhancing translation workflows with HLT. Since ST goes from source language audio directly to target language text, it has access to rich audio information, such as stress/focus and emotion that would be lost in typical text STT output that the alternative of an STT + MT pipeline would provide. Salesky et al. (2021) offer a promising methodology for comparing STT+MT pipelines vs. ST that we hope to follow in our next stage of research.

Until then, we sought to obtain a baseline assessment of STT performance. The traditional metric is WER, but it should be noted there are several additional metrics we would like to explore as we proceed, including diarization error rate (DER), punctuation error rate (PER), and other advanced features considered in NIST's Rich Transcription Evaluation series[2].

WER calculations require an evaluation tool, reference transcriptions and hypothesis transcriptions for a given set of files. We used two evaluation tools, NIST's *sclite*[3] and a government off the shelf (GOTS) tool called *compute-wer*. Both tools take reference transcriptions in stm format and hypothesis transcriptions in ctm format. Figure 4 provides an example portion of an stm file corresponding to the transcription file shown above; they are both segmented at the IPU level. Note that it has been lowercased and most punctuation has been removed. In addition, square brackets have been converted to parentheses, so that this material can be ignored for the purposes of WER calculation (per *sclite's* -D or *compute-wer's* --sclite-parse options). Note also the presence of speaker names which allows speaker-specific WER calculation. This was helpful in identifying issues such as codeswitching as will be described below.

[1] Examples include https://docs.microsoft.com/en-us/azure/cognitive-services/speech-service/how-to-custom-speech-human-labeled-transcriptions and https://aws.amazon.com/blogs/machine-learning/evaluating-an-automatic-speech-recognition-service/.
[2] https://www.nist.gov/itl/iad/mig/rich-transcription-evaluation
[3] https://github.com/usnistgov/SCTK

Figure 5 provides an example of a hypothesis ctm file from one of the STT systems we evaluated. Note that it is segmented at the word level. Most of the STT engines we evaluated provide their output in json format. We are surprised that there does not seem to be any W3C guidance or standard for the presentation of STT output. Nevertheless, we were able to straightforwardly convert the various output formats to ctm via Python script.

```
french A Sergio 5000.37 5005.32 et ilf faudra une progressivité - je pense que on apprendra à utiliser la technologie-
french A Sergio 5005.33 5010.27 de plus en plus  en fonction de (euh) de cas qui seront découverts
french A Sergio 5010.27 5015.22 grâce aux    aux    aux apports - en termes d'offre - de cette technologie
french A Guillaume 5015.26 5020.40 et j'pense que Sergio a    a    a mentionné quelque chose aussi qui est essentiel (euh) c'est que on est (f-) on  a un standard
french A Guillaume 5020.41 5024.80  C't à dire que tous les aéroports (souffle) (euh) peuvent déployer ce    ce standard (souffle)
```

Figure 4. Sample portion of a reference stm file.

```
french A 5010.27 0.7599999999993088 grâce 0.993
french A 5011.04 0.6400000000003274 aux 0.983
french A 5011.69 0.2000000000007276 aux 0.974
french A 5011.89 0.7799999999997453 apports 0.96
french A 5012.82 0.2600000000002183 en 1.0
french A 5013.08 0.3599999999996726 termes 0.519
french A 5013.44 0.5300000000006548 d'offre 0.661
french A 5013.98 0.17000000000007276 de 1.0
french A 5014.15 0.18000000000029104 cette 0.993
french A 5014.33 0.569999999999709 technologie 0.992
french A 5015.12 0.32999999999992724 Et 1.0
french A 5015.45 0.07999999999992724 je 1.0
french A 5015.53 0.17000000000007276 pense 1.0
french A 5015.7 0.1199999999989086 que 1.0
french A 5015.82 0.11000000000058208 c'est 1.0
french A 5015.93 0.0999999999994543 un 1.0
french A 5016.03 0.13000000000010914 jeu 0.998
```

Figure 5. Sample portion of hypothesis ctm file.

Once the stm and ctm files were prepared, we were able to calculate WER for each file, language and speaker for each speech engine that featured the language. Table 2 shows the engines that we evaluated, in anonymized form. We considered four commercial off the shelf (COTS) and three GOTS engines. Each engine has a different set of languages available, and some engines provide more than one locale per language. We used the most relevant locales when available. Even though our French file was from France, COTS 2 only had Canadian French (CA), so we also tested Canadian French in addition to European French (FR) with COTS 1, which had both. Only one engine provided ST output; however, that engine also provided STT output, so that is what was used in the evaluation described here.

STT	ST	Languages
COTS 1		Arabic (SA[4], AE[5]), French (FR, CA), Persian, Russian
COTS 2		Arabic (EG[6]), French (CA), Persian, Russian
COTS 3		French (FR), Russian
COTS 4	✓	Arabic (SA, AE), French (FR), Russian
GOTS 1		Arabic, Russian
GOTS 2		Arabic, Russian
GOTS 3		Russian, Persian

Table 2. Speech Engines Evaluated.

4. STT Results

We present WER results per language, distinguishing between files when there is more than one. For French, we additionally provide per-speaker results. Since WER is an error rate, lower is better, so we order the engines in increasing order, with the better performing ones on top.

4.1. French

French STT results are shown in Table 3 where five STT engines were available. As discussed above, where possible, both Canadian and European French were tested, and when only Canadian French was available, that was used. As shown in Table 3, European French and Canadian French STT were very close in results for COTS 1, which had both locales.

Engine	WER
COTS 4	18.4
COTS 1-European French	20.3
COTS 1-Canadian French	20.8
COTS 3	24.4
COTS 2-Canadian French	49.1

Table 3. French STT Results.

Table 4 below breaks the results down by speaker; number of words are provided in order to indicate the relative quantity of speech per speaker. Note that the speaker who uttered the largest number of words, Guillaume, was generally better recognized than Stéphane who uttered less than half as many words. This shows that the WER is not a function of the amount of uttered speech, but rather a function of the quality of the uttered speech. Indeed, Guillaume was the facilitator of the debate, and he may well have been trained to speak very clearly. Sergio, who spoke the second-highest number of words, was the best recognized of all speakers across all the engines. His speech rate was slightly slower than the other speakers which we speculate accounts for the better performance on his speech.

[4] Saudi Arabia

[5] United Arab Emirates

[6] Egypt

		COTS 1 CA	COTS 1 FR	COTS 4	COTS 2	COTS 3
Speaker	**# Words**	**WER**	**WER**	**WER**	**WER**	**WER**
Antoine	1904	20.4	22	17.6	56.6	27.5
David	2008	24.2	24.4	22.3	53.9	24.4
Guillaume	5127	20.9	20.4	19.2	46.1	25.7
Jonathan	1681	24.2	21.1	18.2	57.4	24
Nicolas	2296	18.3	18.1	16.9	55.4	20.7
Olivier	1965	23.3	22	21.8	50.1	26.9
Pierre	1785	19.6	19	16	47.5	25.8
Sergio	3964	15.7	15.1	14.3	36.8	18.7
Stéphane	1216	30.2	29.7	24.2	60.4	33.6
Sum/Avg	**21946**	**20.8**	**20.3**	**18.4**	**49.1**	**24.4**

Table 4. French STT Results by Speaker.

The error analysis showed discrepancies between colloquial French and more formal French. Colloquial examples supplied in the reference include *y'a* for *il y a* 'there is', *p'tit* for *petit* 'small', *c'qui* for *ce qui* 'which'. These appear to be efforts by the transcribers (in contrast to the instructions in their style guide) to reflect the conversational nature of the speech by trying to capture a fast speech pronunciation rule, schwa deletion (Barnes and Kavitskaya, 2002), in a colloquial orthography. This would be akin to representing a word such as English *running* as *runnin'* to indicate the speaker had not articulated the standard /ŋ/. While it is possible such colloquial spellings might be welcome in some contexts, they are a source of errors unless an STT engine happens to use these at the same time as a transcriber. This introduces interesting questions about how register should be accommodated and controlled in STT, a topic we discussed earlier with respect to MT and CAT (Miller et al., 2018).

Additionally, word boundaries were the cause of multiple errors, particularly for French hyphenated words, where reference hyphenated multiword units such as *est-ce* 'is this', *c'est-à-dire* 'that is to say', *peut-être* 'perhaps', and *quand-même* 'still', were rendered differently by some STT engines, resulting in errors. One of the complexities of a multi-engine evaluation such as ours is that transcription normalization for the purpose of achieving "comparable" WERs would need to be engine-specific. Our philosophy at this stage is to get a general idea of performance without substantial investment in normalization, under the assumption that different engines will both benefit and suffer from the reference transcriptions as they are, and intensive normalization would not be likely to cause the engines to stratify particularly differently in terms of performance. Another consideration is that if we take the reference transcriptions as indeed what the target should look like, then altering them to achieve a "more realistic" WER would be counter-productive since any edit distance between the reference and the STT would have to be "corrected" by a linguist.

4.2. Russian

The Russian data consisted of four separate files and seven STT engines were available to test. Results for each system are provided in Table 5. Russian 2 and Russian 3 had some speakers speaking English, which appears to have worsened results compared to Russian 1. At present, we have run only Russian STT on these files, but we hope to experiment with language diarization so that English STT can be run when English segments are detected.

	Russian 1	Russian 2	Russian 3	Russian4
Engine	**Word Error Rate**			
GOTS 2	19.9	27.4	30.3	32.8
GOTS 1	28.4	35.7	36.8	35.3
COTS 4	27.5	36.1	43.2	35.4
COTS 1	34.8	44.8	45.6	44.4
COTS 2	37.8	46.8	50.2	49.9
GOTS 3	40.1	46.4	49.6	48.4
COTS 3	53.2	53.7	56.5	58.8

Table 5. Russian STT Results by Engine and File.

We focused on content words, rather than function words since content words are more semantically meaningful. When possible, we sought to determine which words in the reference transcriptions did not appear in the STT engine's lexicon: the out-of-vocabulary (OOV) words. We also examined the reference words that did not appear in an engine's hypotheses; these consisted of both OOV and in-vocabulary (IV) words. For the IV words, we suppose that an engine's failure to recognize them had to do either with the engine's pronunciation or language models or with the pronunciation or audio conditions of words as uttered.

Another class of errors consists of words that are not recognized for multiple reasons including text normalization, realization of numbers, word segmentation, and morphology. One example of text normalization is letter ё 'yo', which is often realized by transcribers and STT engines as е 'ye'. The interesting part is that all these classes overlap, thus the number of OOV words combined with morphology largely increases the number of problematic tokens. For example, the single adjective аддитивный meaning '3-d', as in '3-d printing', generates 186 morphologically inflected tokens covering a dozen inflected types.

For Russian, we particularly studied the results of GOTS 1, where 30% of the reference words did not appear in the hypotheses. Among these, 35% were OOVs and 65% were IVs but were presumably not recognized due to accent, position of the word in the sentence, ambient noise, etc. The following list samples recognition errors of various types of words:

- **OOV:** technical words and compounds, such as аддитивный '3-d', физическо-химических 'physico-chemical', экосистемы 'eco-systems'.
- **Mixed Russian and English Borrowings:** бизнес-задача 'business task', бизнес-модели 'business models', бизнес-секции 'business sections', интернет-площадке 'internet site'.
- **Borrowings:** слайд 'slide', принт 'print', лидер 'leader'
- **Morphology:** Russian has three genders (feminine, masculine and neuter) and 6 inflectional cases; this means that when one word is not recognized, all its inflected and derived forms will also likely be unrecognized. Morphological errors of IV items also occur such as технологий → технологии 'technology', которые → который 'which', развиваются → развивается 'are/is developing'.
- **Word segmentation:** какой-то / то 'some', вице-президент / президент 'vice-president / president', пост-обработка / постобработка 'post-processing / postprocessing'.

- **Numerals**
  - Normalization: 30 / тридцать '30 / thirty'
  - Normalization and morphology: 30-му / тридцатом '30 (dative) / thirty (prepositional)'

4.3. Persian

Our Persian data consisted of seven files, four of which have been analyzed so far. Results are presented in Table 6.

	Persian 1	Persian 3	Persian 4	Persian 6
Engine	**WER**			
COTS 1	45.8	32.9	52.2	38.3
GOTS 3	62	48	86.6	60.7
COTS 2	89.2	84.6	92.5	83.6

Table 6. Persian STT Results by File.

Typical errors were similar to those noted above under the colloquial rubric for French but often in reverse. For example, transcribers often used standard representations such as می کنند 'they do' and ندارد 'doesn't have' in cases where the best performing STT output colloquial forms such as می کنن and نداره. As in French and Russian, word segmentation issues also arose; for example, a transcriber might write میتونه where STT output می تونه 'is able'. Finally, we did make a concession to normalization by accounting for encoding issues, as different engines (and transcribers) sometimes used different Unicode codepoints for the letters ک 'kāf' and ی 'ye'.

4.4. Arabic

Arabic results are shown in Table 7. It turns out that Arabic, despite the perception that it is a complex language to recognize, demonstrates the best STT results. Top confusions evinced similar normalization issues to those discussed above, such as variable placement of *hamza* in reference and hypothesis.

Engine	WER
GOTS 2	12
COTS 2	19.8
GOTS 1	22
COTS 4 SA	22.2
COTS 4 AE	22.3
COTS 1 AE	27.8
COTS 1 SA	33.4

Table 7. Arabic STT results.

5. Conclusions

Since our main goal is to identify worthwhile insertions of HLT into the AV translation workflow, the work described here is really just the beginning. We are collecting additional details from linguists, such as time on task, which we are hoping to factor into our analysis. In addition, since completed translations also contain indications of who is speaking, we hope to incorporate an analysis of speaker diarization and potentially, speaker recognition. As has been made evident in the WER analyses of all the languages discussed here, getting to the bottom of how exactly certain classes of words should be represented in final transcriptions and translations, including register issues, will be important in order to assess to what extent speech analytics are contributing toward those objectives. We hope to look more carefully at the representation of numerals and punctuation, since if these are required in the end product, speech analytics that accurately represent them will be potentially more useful than those that omit or misrepresent them. Finally, we are keen to determine whether ST offers promise over STT and MT pipelines; if so, perhaps many of the source language transcription issues we have been discussing will cease to be important, since the focus will be on the translated English output.

References

Barnes, J. and Kavitskaya, D. (2002). Phonetic Analogy and Schwa Deletion in French. In *Berkeley Linguistics Society*, pages 39-50.

ELAN (Version 6.2) [Computer software]. (2021). Nijmegen: Max Planck Institute for Psycholinguistics, The Language Archive. Retrieved from https://archive.mpi.nl/tla/elan.

Hosaka, J., Seligman, M., and Singer, H. (1994). Pause as a Phrase Demarcator for Speech and Language Processing. In Proceedings of the 15th Conference on Computational Linguistics, vol. 2, pages 987-991, Kyoto.

Miller, C., Higgins, C., Havens, P., Van Guilder, S., Morris, R., and Silverman, D. (2020). Plugging into Trados: Augmenting Translation in the Enclave. In *Proceedings of the 14th Conference of the Association for Machine Translation in the Americas,* pages 469-477.

Miller, C. and Saeli, H. (2016). Second-level pluricentricity in the Persian of Tehran. In *Pluricentric Languages and Non-Dominant Varieties Worldwide*, R. Muhr (ed.), pages 191-204. Frankfurt.

Miller, C., Silverman, D., Jurica, V., Richerson, E., Morris, R. and Mallard, E. (2018). Embedding Register-Aware MT into the CAT Workflow. In *Proceedings of the 13th Conference of the Association for Machine Translation in the Americas*, vol. 2, pages 275-282.

Saeli, H. and Miller, C. (2018). Some linguistic indicators of sociocultural formality in Persian. In *Trends in Iranian and Persian Linguistics*, A. Korangy and C. Miller (eds.), pages 163-182. Berlin.

Salesky, E., Wiesner, M., Bremerman, J., Cattoni, R., Negri, M., Turchi, M., Oard, D. and Post, M. (2021). The Multilingual TEDx Corpus for Speech Recognition and Translation. In *Proceedings of Interspeech 2021*. Brno.

Tzoukermann, E. and Miller, C. (2018). Evaluating Automatic Speech Recognition in Translation. In *Proceedings of AMTA 2018*, vol. 2, pages 294-302, Boston.

From Research to Production: Fine-Grained Analysis of Terminology Integration

Toms Bergmanis*, Mārcis Pinnis*, Paula Reichenberg**

* Tilde, Vienības gatve 75A, Riga, Latvia, LV-1004

** Hieronymus, Stauffacherstrasse 100 CH-8004 Zürich, Switzerland

TILDE

HIERONYMUS
Translations by Lawyers for Lawyers

Thesis

Terminology integration is a **cascade** of

1. terminology management
2. terminology identification
3. terminology translation

thus it is **prone** to problems due to **error propagation**.

Photo credit: https://www.watergardeningdirect.com/acatalog/Neptune-Blue-Ceramic-Solar-Cascade-Water-Feature.html

Outline

1. Three aspects of Terminology Integration:
    - Terminology Management
    - Terminology Identification
    - Terminology Translation
2. Main takeaways

Terminology Management

- Terminology for humans is not the same as terminology for machines
- Humans can:
  - Disambiguate based on external/world knowledge and experience
  - Work with corrupted/noisy data
- How do we get to terminology that is useful for machines?

Terminology Management

Common issues:

- Specificity
  - ✗ sport, prize, China
    (Source: IATE, Dinu et.al 2019)
  - ✗ deaths, transmission, close contact, face mask
    (Source: WMT 2021 Terminology task)
  - ✓ angular ball bearing, ball peen hammer, companion flange
    (Source: Bergmanis and Pinnis 2021)

Solution: use Inverse Document Frequency based filtering of your glossary!

Terminology Management

Common issues:

- Specificity
- Ambiguity
  - ×sense ambiguity: *organ*

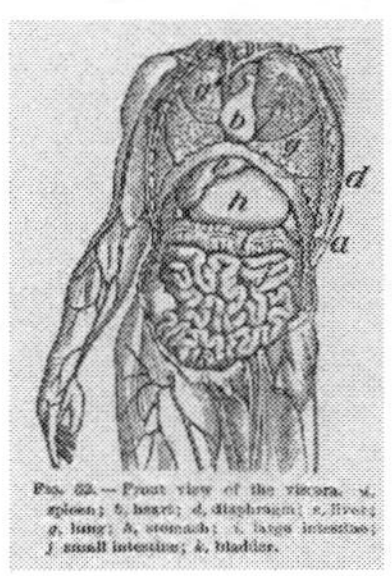

×1-to-many term entries:

- *disease outbreak* (EN) → apparition de maladie (FR); épidémie (FR)
- *rakovina* (CS, *cancer*) → Krebs(DE); Krebserkrankung (DE)

(Source: WMT 2021 Terminology task)

Solution: filter ambiguous terms and commit to just one translation per collection!

Terminology Management

Common issues:

- Specificity
- Ambiguity
- Needless wordiness:
  - × adopt the powers laid down in the Emergency Powers Act
    =
    valmiuslaissa säädettyjen toimivaltuuksien käyttöönotto

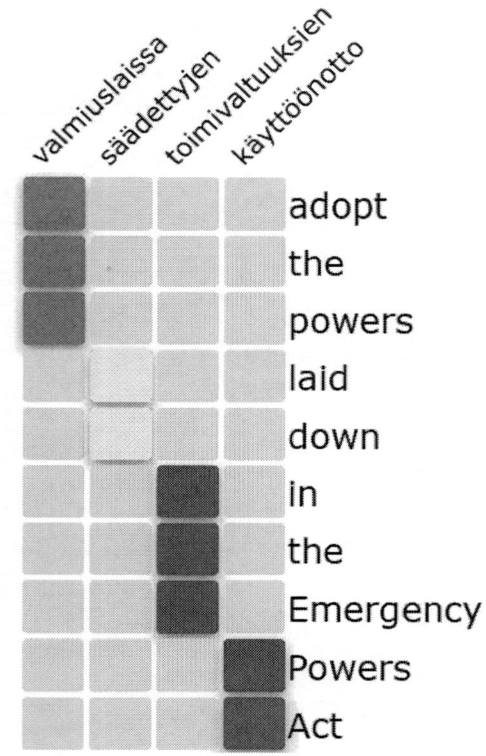

https://nlg.isi.edu/demos/picaro/

Solution: decompose long multiword expressions when possible!

Terminology Management: Type of terminological data

- **The minimalist's point of view** - a collection of bilingual term pairs for every domain
- **The maximalist's point of view** - a collection of bilingual term pairs with all the necessary meta-data:
  - Morphological information
  - Syntactic information
  - Domain information
- *The overwhelming majority of term collections used in practice are minimalist's term collections*

Terminology Identification

Common challenges:

- Morphological complexity
- Part-of-speech ambiguity*
- Term sense ambiguity*

* if unresolved using Terminology Management

Terminology Identification: Morphological Complexity

	Sing	Plural
NOM	vācietis	vācieši
GEN	vācieša	vāciešu
DAT	vācietim	vāciešiem
ACC	vācieti	vāciešus
INST	ar vācieti	ar vāciešiem
LOC	vācietī	vāciešos
VOC	vācieti!	vācieši!

Latvian: vācietis (English: *a German*)

- In morphologically complex languages terms can take many forms which hinder term identification
- Solution: use stemmer (fast, lower precision)
- Solution: use lemmatizer (slower, higher precision)

Terminology Identification: Part-of-speech ambiguity

Use the control. Control the execution.

A noun or a verb?

Dry clothes

A noun or an adjective?

This is clearly too ambiguous to tell

- Solution (partial): use morpho-syntactic taggers
- What if the term collection does not provide any morphological metadata?
  - Try enriching term collections automatically
  - Filter out terms that cannot be reliably supported

Terminology identification: Summary

- A practical solution:
  - Filter term collections to not include:
    - General language
    - Ambiguous terms that cannot be reliably supported by your method
  - Then, if term collections are minimalistic:
    - depending on language and tools that are available, identify terms using either:
      - Lemmatization, or
      - stemming
  - *If term collections are meta-data-rich, let us know – we would like to see that with our own eyes*.

Terminology Translation

- When we have a term collection and we can identify terms in the source text, what are our integration options?
  - Constrained Decoding (Post and Vilar, 2018)
  - Exact Target Annotations (Dinu et al., 2019)
  - Target Lemma Annotations (TLA) (Bergmanis and Pinnis, 2021)

Terminology Translation

- We use Target Lemma Annotations since they allow achieving the highest overall translation quality and term translation accuracy for morphologically rich languages
- For languages with simple nominal morphology, other methods (Post and Vilar, 2018; Dinu et al. 2019) are also viable

*Results from Bergmanis and Pinnis, 2021

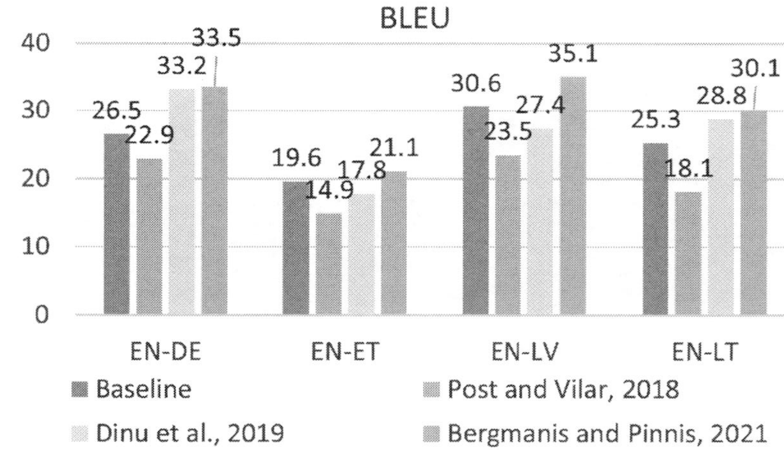

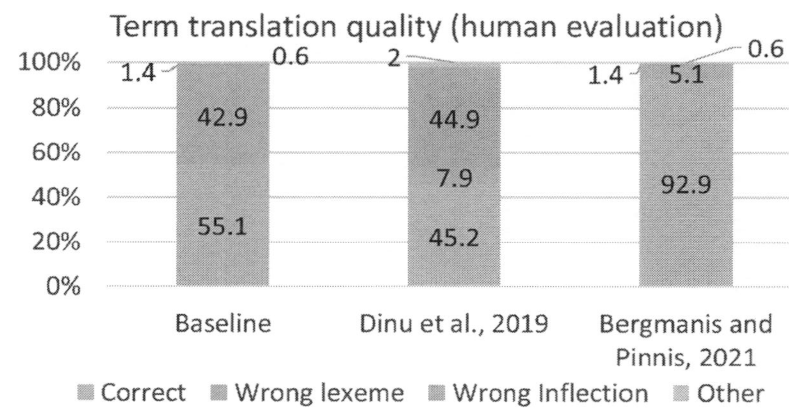

Terminology Translation: Target Lemma Annotation

Latvian (Target): *Rīks , kas der uzgriežņa galvai .*

Latvian Lemmas: *Rīks , kas derēt uzgrieznis galva .*

Word Alignments: *0-1 2-2 3-3 4-8 5-5 6-9*

English (Source): *A tool that fits the head of the nut .*

English with TLA: A tool that <fits|derēt> the head of the <nut|uzgrieznis>

We use linguistic input features (Sennrich and Haddow 2016) to facilitate annotation on the source side

* Example from Bergmanis and Pinnis, 2021

Terminology Translation: From Research to Production

- The goal of research – to publish
- The goal of production – to deliver a reliable product

- The main question that arose when deploying terminology integration in production:
  - How to prepare training data such that the trained systems will be capable of handling terms used by customers?

Terminology Translation: From Research to Production

- Challenge - Term length

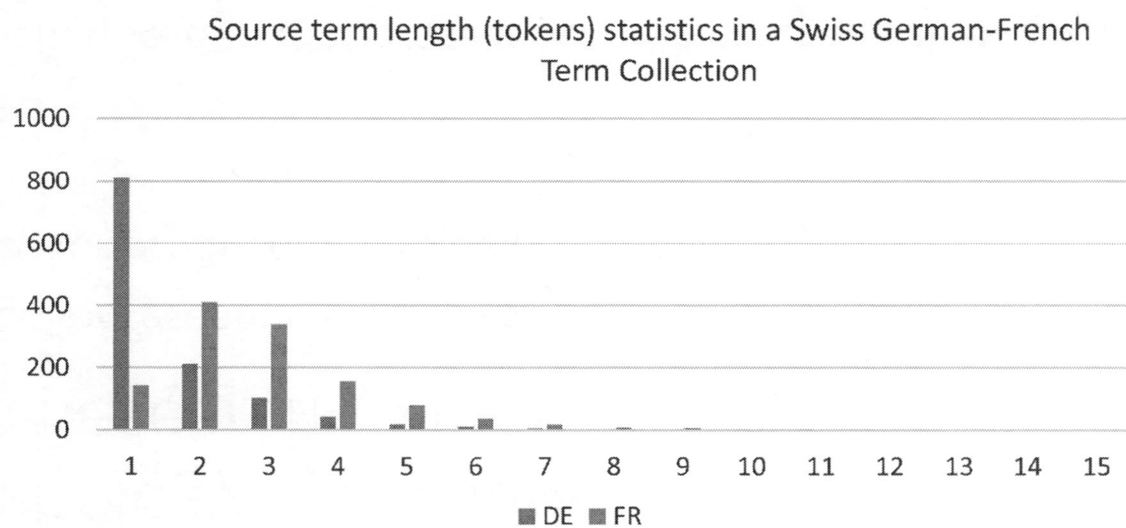

Terminology Translation: From Research to Production

- Challenge - Term length
- Solution – **annotate multi-word phrases with TLA**

Term translation quality for different lengths of terms (Swiss German->French)

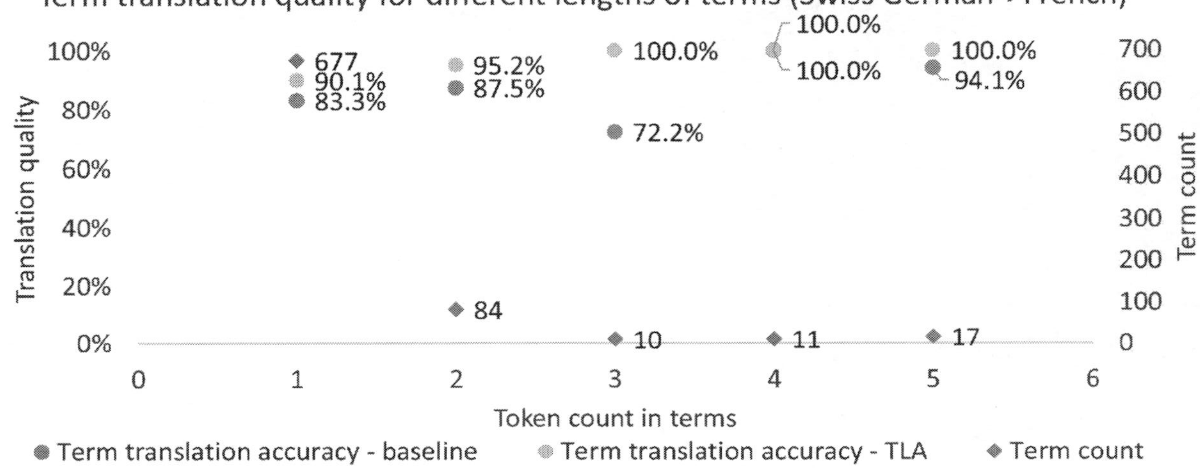

Terminology Translation: From Research to Production

- Challenge – multiword terms have complex syntactic structure

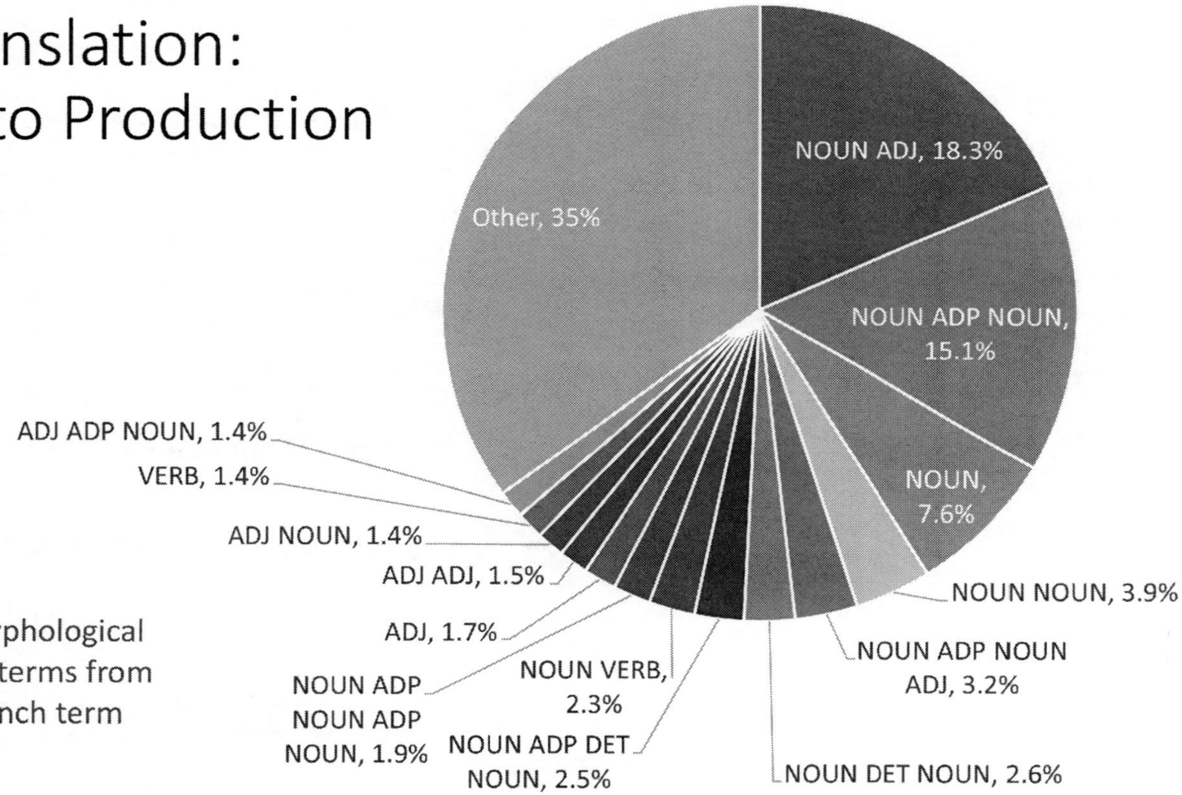

Statistics of the morphological structure of French terms from a Swiss German-French term collection

** Note that the part of speech tags were acquired using an automatic part-of-speech tagger and may be noisy!*

Terminology Translation: From Research to Production

- Challenge – multiword terms have complex syntactic structure
- Solution – make sure that you annotate phrases with syntactic structures representing terms

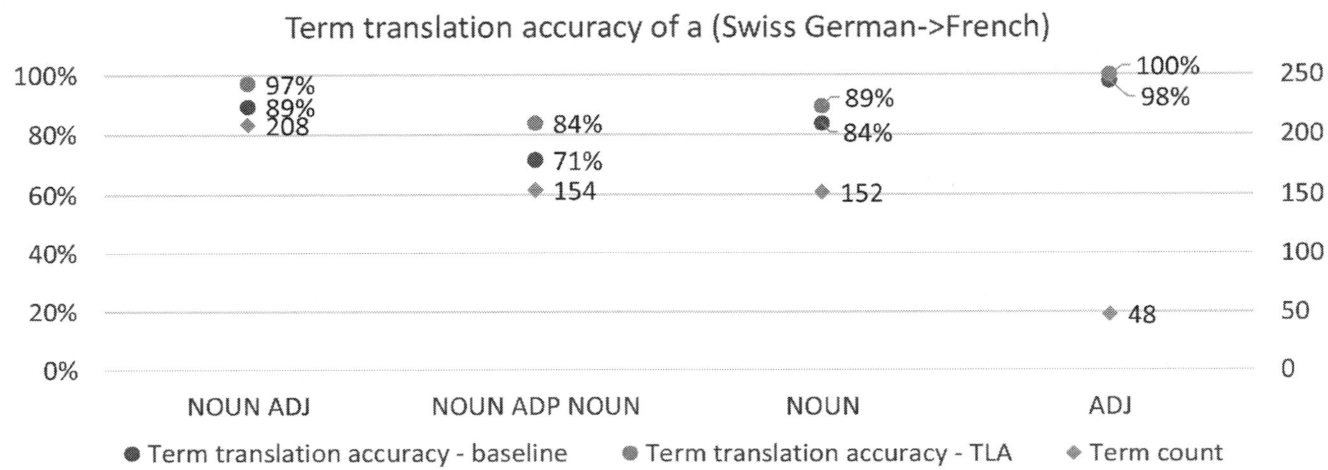

Terminology Translation: From Research to Production

- Challenge – some terms consist of rare BPE parts and are translated poorly
- Solution 1 – make sure that training data TLA contain BPE parts relevant to terms used at the test time
- Solution 2 – filter term collections such that out-of-vocabulary terms are ignored
- Solution 3 – use character representations of TLA (Niehues, 2021)

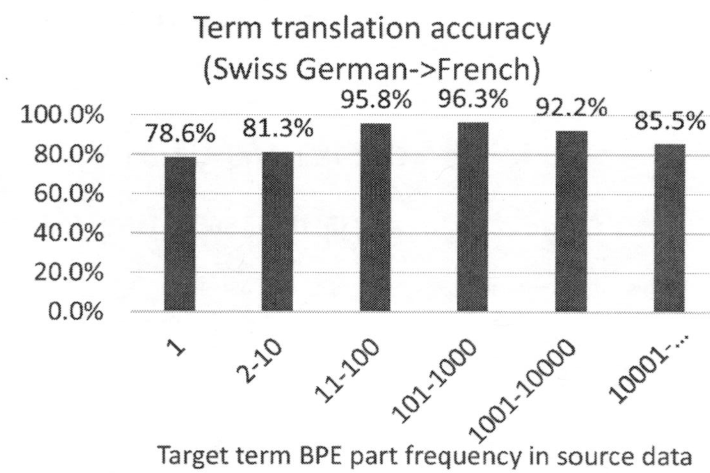

Main Takeaway

- Terminology integration is a **cascade** of terminology creation, curation, identification and only then translation using MT.
- Terminology creation and curation is and should be done by **professional translators and domain experts**.
- **Poor terminology management choices will be propagated in downstream processes** – terminology identification and terminology translation, and will impede the final translation quality.

Main Takeaway

To mitigate error propagation, pay attention to how terminology is managed and prepared for MT such that it is MT-ready

- Make sure that terminology is consistent
- Make sure that terminology is domain-specific
- Do not overexaggerate with needless wordiness
  - Online/dynamic learning, and translation memories may be better suited for such data
- Provide enough metadata such that your term identification method is able to function properly

References

Sennrich, Rico, and Barry Haddow. "Linguistic Input Features Improve Neural Machine Translation." *Proceedings of the First Conference on Machine Translation: Volume 1, Research Papers*. 2016.

Post, Matt, and David Vilar. "Fast Lexically Constrained Decoding with Dynamic Beam Allocation for Neural Machine Translation." *Proceedings of the 2018 Conference of the North American Chapter of the Association for Computational Linguistics: Human Language Technologies, Volume 1 (Long Papers)*. 2018.

Dinu, Georgiana, et al. "Training Neural Machine Translation to Apply Terminology Constraints." *Proceedings of the 57th Annual Meeting of the Association for Computational Linguistics*. 2019.

Bergmanis, Toms, and Mārcis Pinnis. "Facilitating Terminology Translation with Target Lemma Annotations." *Proceedings of the 16th Conference of the European Chapter of the Association for Computational Linguistics: Main Volume*. 2021.

Niehues, Jan. "Continuous Learning in Neural Machine Translation using Bilingual Dictionaries." *Proceedings of the 16th Conference of the European Chapter of the Association for Computational Linguistics: Main Volume*. 2021.

Glossary functionality in commercial machine translation: does it help? A first step to identify best practices for a language service provider

Randy Scansani rscansani@acolad.com
Loïc Dugast ldugast@acolad.com
NLP team, Acolad

Abstract

Recently, a number of commercial Machine Translation (MT) providers have started to offer glossary features allowing users to enforce terminology into the output of a generic model. However, to the best of our knowledge it is not clear how such features would impact terminology accuracy and the overall quality of the output. The present contribution aims at providing a first insight into the performance of the glossary-enhanced generic models offered by four providers. Our tests involve two different domains and language pairs, i.e. Sportswear En–Fr and Industrial Equipment De–En. The output of each generic model and of the glossary-enhanced one will be evaluated relying on Translation Error Rate (TER) to take into account the overall output quality and on accuracy to assess the compliance with the glossary. This is followed by a manual evaluation. The present contribution mainly focuses on understanding how these glossary features can be fruitfully exploited by language service providers (LSPs), especially in a scenario in which a customer glossary is already available and is added to the generic model as is.

1 Introduction

Correctly translating terminology is one of the main challenges in translation, and this is also true for Machine Translation (MT). A first approach to achieve this goal lies in data preparation and possibly appropriate training algorithms. However, there are cases in which data is not available or training a model is not an option.

A number of research works have explored ways to combine a bilingual glossary with an MT model at run-time, enforcing specific terminology in the output, e.g. Arthur et al. (2016); Chatterjee et al. (2017); Farajian et al. (2018); Hasler et al. (2018); Dinu et al. (2019); Exel et al. (2020); Bergmanis and Pinnis (2021). The proposed approaches range from simple post-translation replacement, to constrained decoding, down to methods that allow for soft constraints and are able to generate inflected forms of glossary terms – Dinu et al. (2019) improved by Bergmanis and Pinnis (2021). Such recent breakthroughs might not have made it yet to commercial implementation.

Nevertheless, a number of commercial MT providers have started to offer features allowing users to enhance a generic MT model by leveraging a bilingual glossary.[1] While language

[1]Some examples of MT providers offering a glossary feature: DeepL (`https://bit.ly/2UbHDyh`), Google Translate (`https://bit.ly/3rcUqwv`), Microsoft (`https://bit.ly/2U5os9v`), Amazon Translate (`https://amzn.to/3hC7WGO`), Systran (Michon et al., 2020).

service providers (LSPs) have to rely on those solutions, "the commercial providers usually leave us in the dark about the technology that is used for the implementation of that feature" (Exel et al., 2020).

Users may expect the addition of a domain-specific glossary to a generic MT model to bring improvements both in terminology translation and, as a result, in the overall output quality. The present contribution aims at understanding if the glossary features offered by some of the main MT providers are meeting such expectations. More specifically, being a relevant scenario for LSPs, we aim at understanding if a glossary extracted from a customer termbase can be leveraged as is, i.e. all experiments will be carried out using the glossaries without any preliminary cleaning up. We will further refer to this use case as *naive use of glossary*. Four different MT providers will be tested in the sportswear (En–Fr) and in the industrial equipment (De–En) domains, comparing their performance when the glossary feature is switched on and when it is not.

More in detail, the impact of the glossary feature on terminology translation will be assessed by checking the extent to which the MT output complies with the glossary entries. A first evaluation will follow strict parameters, i.e. glossary term matching is case-sensitive and happens on a token level. We will refer to this evaluation as *exact match*. In a second evaluation (henceforth *loose match*), we aim at finding any terminology improvement by matching terms on a lemma level and without considering differences in casing. The effect of the glossary on the overall output quality will be measured with Translation Error Rate (TER) (Snover et al., 2006). Based on term matching and on TER, we will then categorize each sentence based on the terminological and/or qualitative improvements (if any). To conclude, a manual evaluation will provide a more detailed overview on the glossary impact on the sentence.

The aim of the contribution is to start addressing the needs for best practices across the translation industry for the use of glossaries to improve MT output. Given the availability of glossary features, how can we leverage pre-existing glossaries?

The remainder of the present contribution is structured as follows. In Sect. 2, a description of the experimental setup will be provided, including descriptions of the MT providers, the data sets, the metrics and the evaluation methods. The following Section (Sect. 3) will present the results obtained with the *naive use of glossary* approach. First we will focus on each provider's behavior on the whole data sets (Sect. 3.1), then a sentence level analysis is carried out (Sect. 3.2), and finally we will present the results of a manual annotation (3.3). This is followed by a discussion of the results obtained (Sect. 4).

2 Experimental setup

2.1 Machine translation providers

In the present contribution, 4 providers were tested, comparing the performance of their generic model against the same model enhanced with the glossary functionality. We are not providing the name of the 4 engines since this paper does not claim to present an exhaustive benchmarking, but rather aims at investigating how to make the best out of such glossary functionalities in a scenario relevant to the language industry.

All MT providers disclose only a limited number of details on how the terms are matched and enforced into the output. The glossary feature of Provider 2 and 4 is described as a simple replacement of the target term(s) generated by the model with the one(s) included in the glossary, whenever a glossary item is matched in the source text. Provider 2 further specifies that the rest of the sentence is not adjusted after the term enforcement. To the best of our knowledge, Provider 1 and 3 have not published any technical specifications on their glossary feature.

Regarding the recommendations available, Provider 1, 2 and 4 indicate that the glossary feature is especially useful to enforce the preferred translation for product names and/or non-context dependent source terms for which we want to enforce a unique domain-specific translation. Provider 2 and 4 further indicate that the glossary functionality is case-sensitive, so the glossary term must match the casing used in the text.

Providers 1, 3 and 4 allow to specify a glossary at translation time, which will be enforced during translation. Provider 2 offers two different options. With the first one – henceforth referred to as Provider 2-preprocess – the source text can be preprocessed to tag glossary terms so that they can be identified by the model at translation time. With the second one – henceforth referred to as Provider 2-pretrained – a training is launched using a glossary as unique training data set. Even though there is a training step involved, the provider specifies that this option simply replaces the terms in the output with those included in the glossary.

In order to have better insight into how the different providers match terms in the source and enforce their translation in the target, we run some preliminary tests. The information retrieved from the tests and from the specifications mentioned above are summed up in Table 1. It is worth noting that for Provider 2-preprocess, its case-sensitivity on the source side does not depend on the provider specifications, but rather on the preprocessing method implemented by the user. In our case, the preprocessing procedure that tags source terms in the text is case-insensitive.

Provider	Source matching		Target insertion
	Case-sensitive	Matches lemmas	Sent. adjusted
Prov. 1	✓	✗	✗
Prov. 2-pretr.	✓	✗	✗
Prov. 2-preproc.	✗	✗	✗
Prov. 3	✗	✓	✓
Prov. 4	✓	✗	✗

Table 1: The *Source matching* columns describe how the matching happens in the source text for each provider. The *Target insertion* column specifies which providers adjust the target sentence after enforcing a glossary term.

2.2 Data sets

Two data sets in two different language pairs and domains were extracted for this task, i.e. De–En Industrial Equipment and En–Fr Sportswear. This allows to test the usefulness of the glossary features for two different types of contents. Also, we are interested in the possible differences between one language pair where the source language has more inflections than the target one (De–En), and a language pair where more inflections occurs on the target side (En–Fr).

After extracting a test set from the bilingual corpora of each customer, we select subsets by keeping only sentence pairs containing at least one source-target match from the glossary. A description of the matching method is provided in Sect. 2.3. The test set and glossary size are shown in Table 2. In this *naive use of glossary* approach (see Sect. 1) we are not preprocessing the two glossaries. However, one of the providers used does not allow multiple entries with the same source term. For this reason, we chose to randomly pick one of the target terms and discard the other ones. 51 entries were removed from the En–Fr glossary, while the De–En one did not contain any source duplicates.

2.3 Metrics

The different analyses carried out in this paper are focused on assessing the extent to which the outputs comply with the glossary terminology and on evaluating the overall output quality.

Domain	Source	Target	Term pairs	Sent. pairs
Industrial equipment	DE	EN	345	1063
Sportswear	EN	FR	1708	1673

Table 2: Domain, source and target language, number of term pairs and sentence pairs available for each data set used.

For the latter, we use (case-sensitive) TER (Snover et al., 2006), while the former assessment is performed by a specific script described in Algorithm 1.

Optional: Lemmatize terms in glossary and sentences in test set ;
Optional: Lowercase terms in glossary and sentences in test set ;
Find all occurrences of source terms;
Disambiguate overlapping source terms (choose longest entries first);
Count matches in the target language sentences;
Result: Match accuracy

Algorithm 1: Compute term matches within candidate translation

2.4 Automatic analyses method

In the first analysis, whose results are described in Sect. 3.1, the number of source and target terms matched by the algorithm is used to compute accuracy as in Alam et al. (2021), i.e. the proportion between the number of source terms whose target is matched in the target text and the total number of matched source terms.

While the first analysis provides insight into the performance of each provider on the whole data set, it does not allow for a more granular understanding of the glossary impact on a sentence level. To this aim, we perform a second analysis where we compare the generic output of each provider to the glossary-enhanced one on a sentence level. Each sentence is assigned to one of the six categories below, according to the accuracy and TER changes observed after the addition of the glossary. These six categories are similar to those suggested in Alam et al. (2021) for the classification of MT systems based on their ability to correctly handle terminology.

	TER (↓)	Acc. (↑)
Accuracy or both regressed	↑ or =	↓
TER only regressed	↑	=
Unchanged	=	=
TER only improved	↓	= or ↓
Accuracy only improved	= or ↑	↑
Both improved	↓	↑

Table 3: Description of the six categories used in the sentence-level analysis (results in Sect. 3.2). Any change in the TER or accuracy values is measured comparing the translation of each source sentence by the generic model and by the glossary-enhanced one.

2.5 Manual evaluation method

In order to better assess the effect of the glossary feature, we look into the target sentences to spot any difference between the output of the glossary-enhanced model and that of the generic model. In particular, we want to understand if terminology is inserted in the correct context, and how the rest of the sentence changes. For each category in Table 3, we pick a random set of 10 segments to be manually annotated by one annotator for each language pair. Sentences belonging to the *Unchanged* category are not annotated.

Differences between the two sentences in each pair are annotated with the following labels, distinguishing between regressions and improvements: `Casing`, `Inflection`, `Word order`, Part-Of-Speech (`POS`), `Terminology`, `Lexical choice`, `Other`. Please note that `Terminology` refers to changes impacting a matched source term and its translation, whereas `Lexical choice` includes any other lexical change.

3 Experimental results

3.1 Accuracy and TER on the whole data sets

Provider	De–En (%)			En–Fr (%)		
	Exact match Acc. ↑	Loose match Acc. ↑	TER ↓	Exact match Acc. ↑	Loose match Acc. ↑	TER ↓
Prov. 1	63.7	85.1	31.6	42.1	45.1	61.3
Prov. 1 + gloss.	99.6	95.8	33.0	95.2	77.7	60.5 †
Prov. 2	57.9	80.9	33.2	33.9	38.2	65.6
Prov. 2-pretr.	99.9*	95.5	34.4	98.6*	78.4	65.4 †
Prov. 2-preproc.	99.9*	97.0	34.1	95.2	87.8*	64.6 †
Prov. 3	45.5	68.9	32.3	43.2	46.0	61.0
Prov. 3 + gloss.	78.1	98.4*	29.9 †	78.6	79.5	59.2 †
Prov. 4	54.7	77.3	34.3	43.0	46.6	63.0
Prov. 4 + gloss.	88.7	93.4	33.9 †	90.9	75.1	61.3 †

Table 4: Accuracy and TER results for each provider with and without glossaries, and for each of the use cases (De–En industrial equipment, En–Fr Sportswear). TER is provided only once since the test set for the two evaluations is the same. † identifies a TER decrease when the glossary is added. * identifies the providers with the best accuracy.

Exact match In this evaluation, terms are matched on a token level (no lemmatization) and only when the casing in the output is the same as the one in the glossary. Results in Table 4 (*Exact match* and *TER* columns) show that Provider 1 and Provider 2 achieve the highest accuracy scores (99.9%) for both use cases (De–En Industrial Equipments and En–Fr Sportswear). However, the glossary impact on the overall quality is not on par. For De–En the use of the glossary decreases TER for Provider 3 and 4 only. For En–Fr TER always decreases when a glossary is added to the generic model, although some of these drops are rather limited, ranging from -0.18% (Provider 2-pretrained) to -1% (Provider 2-preprocess). Exact match accuracy for Provider 3 and 4 enhanced with glossary is lower than Provider 1 and 2 with glossary. This is expected since Provider 3 glossary feature is able to generate a different target inflection, which is not recognized in the exact matching. The quality increase is however larger. For example, we observe a -2.4% TER when a glossary is added to Provider 3 for De–En, and a 1.8% TER drop for the same provider on En–Fr.

Loose match In this evaluation, terms are matched on a lemma level and regardless of their casing. With respect to the first evaluation, this brings a higher accuracy for the generic models without glossary (see Table 4), which means that the generic models are often using the correct lemma. Provider 3 achieves the best accuracy for De–En (98.4%) and the 2nd best accuracy for En–Fr (79.5%), narrowing the gap with the best-performing model (Provider 2-preprocess, 87.8%) wrt the exact match results. Provider 2-preprocess accuracy drop from the exact match to the loose match evaluation is less evident than the accuracy drop of Provider 2-pretrained (which is case-sensitive) for both De–En and En–Fr. For En–Fr we observe a large accuracy drop wrt the previous evaluation for all Providers except Provider 3, due to its ability to match different inflections of a source term. Provider 1, 2 and 4 match source terms on a token level (see Table 1). To conclude, in this evaluation we see that Provider 3 has the best TER scores in both language pairs. As seen above, while TER always decreases when a glossary is added to the En–Fr models, for De–En the same happens only for Provider 3 and 4.

3.2 Sentence-level analysis

In this analysis we are comparing, for each provider, the output of the generic model to the output of the glossary-enhanced one. Sentences are assigned to one of the categories described in 2.4.

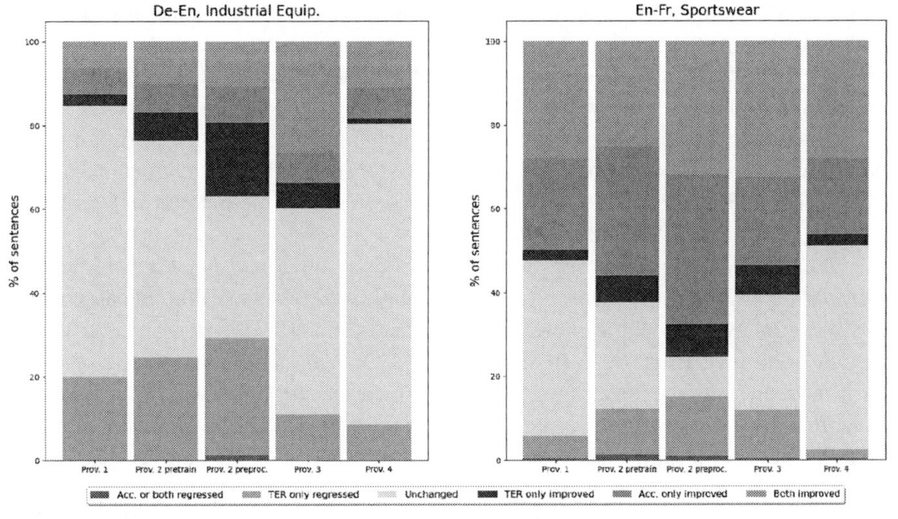

Figure 1: For each use case (De–En Industrial Equipment and En–Fr Sportswear) we report on the percentage of sentences produced by each provider that were assigned to one of the six categories described in Table 3. The six categories refer to the comparison between the generic model of a provider and its glossary-enhanced version.

As can be seen in Fig. 1, there are large differences between the two language pairs, the most evident being perhaps the higher quantity of Unchanged sentences for De–En. This could be motivated by the differences in the size of the two glossaries (see Table 2), but also by the differences between the two language pairs. Given the morphological complexity of German, matching the correct form of the term in the source text is more difficult than for English.

The percentage of sentences where only accuracy improved is higher for En–Fr than for De–En. This seems to suggest that using the glossary introduces more side effects if the target language has more inflections and concordances, thus TER does not improve.

Comparing the providers, Provider 2-preprocess seems to have the highest number of side effects, since the percentage of sentences where TER only improves or TER only regresses is the highest in both language pairs. Provider 3 (De–En) shows the highest percentage of sentences where both TER and accuracy improved, and the highest amount of sentences where the use of the glossary was beneficial (i.e. sentences assigned to *TER only improved*, *Accuracy only improved* or *Both improved*). For En–Fr Provider 2-preprocess shows the highest number of sentences where the use of a glossary had a positive impact, although the percentage of sentences belonging to *Both improved* is the same as that of Provider 3.

Provider 1 and 4 show similar performances when it comes to the sentences where the glossary-enhanced model is beneficial to either accuracy, or TER or both of them in both use cases. However, Provider 4 is the Provider with the lowest portion of sentences where TER only regresses. To conclude, the differences between Provider 2-pretrained and Provider 2-preprocess show that the latter approach is more effective.

3.3 Manual annotation

We chose to limit the annotation to Provider 2-preprocess and Provider 3, due to the good performance shown by both in the previous analyses (see Sect. 3.1 and 3.2), while their specifications differ. Since Provider 3 is able to handle morphology inflections, its impact on the output sentence might differ from that of the other providers. Also, we wanted to have a better understanding of Provider 2-preprocess performance given the apparently high number of unexpected behaviors of such provider, i.e. the high number of sentences where TER only regressed or TER only improved seen in Fig. 1.

Looking at Table 5, one of the most evident results is that most of the improvements for both providers in both language pairs are due to terminology. This confirms the results seen in Sect. 3.1 and 3.2, i.e. the glossary features does increase the amount of correct terms in the output.

As expected, we see a high number of both positive and negative side effects for both providers. For Provider 2-preprocess we see many side effects in different categories, especially in En–Fr, many of which are negative (see for example the `Inflection`, `POS` and `Word order` columns). Example A in Table 6 shows a casing issue and a wrong concordance. The term "noyeau" was specified in the glossary as the translation for *core* (both lowercased). It has to be reminded that `casing` issues are also due to our choice to tag terms in the source text regardless of their casings (see Sect. 2.1). This has increased the number of glossary matches, but it might have increased the number of casing issues in the target as well.

However, some `casing` issues are not due to the glossary. In En–Fr, Example B (Table 6) sees the MT lowercasing the whole sentence. The glossary contains a single entry for *outdoor*, which is lowercased and where the source English term is copied to the target side.

Some glossary entries were actually not valid terms, and their enforcement in the output might have harmed the translation quality/correctness in some cases. Indeed, we see a number of `terminology` regressions for both providers. In example C, Provider 3 produced a wrong translation because of a glossary entry that included a preposition, i.e. "NEXT" as the translation of "Vor".

Differences in terms of lexicon between the generic output and the glossary-enhanced one were annotated as `lexical choice` improvements or regressions, provided that such differences were not caused by the use of the glossary. As can be seen in Table 5, this class has many examples across all sentence categories and providers. In Example D (Table 6), although small, the translation of "Betriebsart" as *Operating mode* can be considered an improvement since the target term matches the source one exactly, while *mode* is a correct translation but not as accurate. These words were not included in the glossary. In Example E the translation for the German conjunction "weswegen" is missing, so the meaning of the sentence is not correctly conveyed.

Differences between the two language pairs can also be observed. For example, for De–En we see a higher number of `casing` regressions and improvements, probably due to the mismatch between the German and the English casing (see Example B, discussed above). Even more evident are the differences between the amount of `inflection` issues (and some im-

Provider, Lang. pair	Sent. Category	Casing	Infl.	Word ord.	POS	Term.	Lex.	Oth.
2 preproc., De–En	Acc. or both regressed	+++ - - -				- -	+++ - -	
	TER only regressed	+ - -		+ -	-		+ - - -	
	TER only improved	+ -		+++			+++ - - -	+
	Acc. Only improved	+ - - -		-		+++++ -	+ - -	
	Both improved	++ -		+ -		+++++ -	+++ -	
3, De–En	Acc. or both regressed							
	TER only regressed	++ -	+	+ - -	+	-	- - -	
	TER only improved	++		+			+++ - - -	
	Acc. Only improved	-				++++ - -	++ - - -	
	Both improved			+		+++++	-	

Provider, Lang. pair	Sent. Category	Casing	Infl.	Word ord.	POS	Term.	Lex.	Oth.
2 preproc., En–Fr	Acc. or both regressed	+ - -	- - -		- -	+	++ -	
	TER only regressed	- -	- -		- -	+	++ -	
	TER only improved	+ -	+ -	- -	-	++	+++ -	
	Acc. Only improved	-	- -	- -		+++++ - -	+ -	
	Both improved		- -	+ - -		+++++ - -	++ - -	
3, En–Fr	Acc. or both regressed	-				- - - -	-	
	TER only regressed	- - -					+ - -	
	TER only improved	+ - -		+ -		+	+ + + - -	
	Acc. Only improved		+		-	++++ -		
	Both improved		-		-	+++++ -	+	

Table 5: Results of the manual annotation on De–En (above) and En–Fr sentences produced by Provider 2-preprocess and Provider 3. The amount of errors in each error class (columns) was normalized over the number of sentences in that category (row). The higher the number of + or -, the higher the number of, respectively, improvements or regressions.

provements) for En–Fr *vs.* De–En, which is obviously due to the higher number of inflections and concordances in the French language.

At the same time, for En–Fr we see that the number of `inflection` issues is reduced for Provider 3. The same can be observed, e.g., for the `word order` class. For Provider 2-preprocess (En–Fr) `word order` regressions were seen in three sentence categories (TER only improved, Accuracy only improved and Both improved). For Provider 3 we see `word order` regressions in one category only (TER only improved).

Looking at differences between sentence categories, when there are regressions we can see a different number of causes, e.g. `lexical choice` regressions, `casing` regressions or `inflection` regressions (especially for En–Fr). On the other hand, the three categories where the glossary-enhanced output is better (TER only improved, Accuracy only improved or Both Improved) are highly influenced by `terminology` improvements, as can be seen by the high number of + symbols in the `terminology` column. An example of sentence where both accuracy and TER improved is example F in Table 6. Here, the use of a glossary term caused the output to be more similar to the reference text, which caused a TER decrease.

Ex.	Prov.	Gloss.	Sentence
A	source		(...) ABOVE *THE CORE*
	2-preproc.	✗	(...) AU-DESSUS *DU NOYAU*
		✓	(...) AU-DESSUS *DE LA noyau*
B	source		OUTDOOR GEAR LAB - TOP PICK
	3	✗	OUTDOOR GEAR LAB - TOP PICK
		✓	outdoor gear lab - premier choix
C	source		*Vor* der erstmaligen Wartung (...)
	3	✗	*Before* the unit is serviced for the first time (...)
		✓	*NEXT*, when the device is serviced for the first time (...)
D	source		*Betriebsart Timer* nicht möglich (...)
	2-preproc.	✗	*Timer mode* not possible (...)
		✓	*Operating mode Timer* not possible (...)
E	source		(...), *weswegen* in den letzten Jahren viele Projekte zur Wassergewinnung geplant wurden, (...)
	2-preproc.	✗	(...), many water extraction projects have been planned, (...)
		✓	(...), *which is why* many water extraction projects have been planned, (...)
F	source		Die Einstellungen am *Gerät* sind (...)
	3	✗	The settings on the *unit* are (...)
		✓	The settings on the *device* are (...)

Table 6: Examples of sentences from the two data sets (En–Fr and De–En). Italics is used to highlight the parts of the sentences that are discussed in Sect. 3.3.

4 Conclusion and future work

The experiments described in the previous sections illustrate how the naive use of a glossary may not always provide the expected outcome, i.e. a better terminological compliance together with an overall improved output quality. Results depend on the implementation of the glossary feature by the MT provider (how entries are matched and enforced on the target side), on the language pair and on the glossary itself.

Regarding the differences between providers, those that are able to handle morphology

(Provider 3) have shown to produce more sentences where terminology improvements result in a better overall quality. Most implementations seem to induce a number of undesirable side-effects on casing, morphology, word order. Moreover, some limitations remain for all providers tested. For example, none of them (including Provider 3) is able to match glossary source terms when these occur in a compound term (e.g. matching the German term *Batterie* if the source text contains *Batterietyp*). This would impact all agglutinative languages.

Besides the specifications of the glossary features, we saw that some glossary entries brought a lower translation quality, which raises questions about the quality of the glossary itself (see example C in Table 6). For instance, a glossary might have been created by the customer without the support of any terminologist – e.g. to update and/or validate the entries – and then provided to the LSP. As a result, the termbase might contain more target options for the same source term, or it might include entries that are not relevant (e.g. function words), or entries not domain-specific, whose POS is ambiguous or whose translation is highly context-dependent, even within a well-defined domain.

Starting from the assumption that a customer glossary as is does not comply with some of the specifications set by the providers (see Sect. 2.1), and focusing on a scenario in which we already chose which provider to use, how could we turn a preexisting termbase into an MT-compatible glossary? A manual revision of the whole glossary may be time-consuming and might not solve all issues. As mentioned by Bergmanis and Pinnis (2021), we cannot expect the user to provide for each entry all casing forms, and even less so all inflected forms. Automatic POS tagging could help identifying non-inflective entries, but will be prone to errors.

On the one hand, in order to adapt to the currently available technology, LSPs may have to define best practices. In future work, we intend to run similar tests with subsets of the client glossaries containing only entries that are compliant with the MT providers specifications. Such tests would involve the assessment of different procedures and tools to clean up glossaries. Besides being able to discard entries that are not relevant, a further step would be that of enhancing the glossary by identifying new terms that, if added to the entries, would bring further benefits to the output quality.

On the other hand, the results of the recent research endeavours in the filed of terminology and MT are expected to build momentum for new implementations in commercial solutions, which should narrow the gap between what is currently offered by MT providers and what LSPs are expecting.

References

Alam, M. M. I., Anastasopoulos, A., Besacier, L., Cross, J., Gallé, M., Koehn, P., and Nikoulina, V. (2021). On the evaluation of machine translation for terminology consistency. *CoRR*, abs/2106.11891.

Arthur, P., Neubig, G., and Nakamura, S. (2016). Incorporating discrete translation lexicons into neural machine translation. In *Proceedings of the 2016 Conference on Empirical Methods in Natural Language Processing*, pages 1557–1567, Austin, Texas. Association for Computational Linguistics.

Bergmanis, T. and Pinnis, M. (2021). Facilitating terminology translation with target lemma annotations. In *Proceedings of the 16th Conference of the European Chapter of the Association for Computational Linguistics: Main Volume*, pages 3105–3111, Online. Association for Computational Linguistics.

Chatterjee, R., Negri, M., Turchi, M., Federico, M., Specia, L., and Blain, F. (2017). Guiding neural machine translation decoding with external knowledge. In *Proceedings of the Second Conference on Machine Translation*, pages 157–168, Copenhagen, Denmark. Association for Computational Linguistics.

Dinu, G., Mathur, P., Federico, M., and Al-Onaizan, Y. (2019). Training neural machine translation to apply terminology constraints. In *Proceedings of the 57th Annual Meeting of the Association for Computational Linguistics*, pages 3063–3068, Florence, Italy. Association for Computational Linguistics.

Exel, M., Buschbeck, B., Brandt, L., and Doneva, S. (2020). Terminology-constrained neural machine translation at SAP. In *Proceedings of the 22nd Annual Conference of the European Association for Machine Translation*, pages 271–280, Lisboa, Portugal. European Association for Machine Translation.

Farajian, M. A., Bertoldi, N., Negri, M., Turchi, M., and Federico, M. (2018). Evaluation of terminology translation in instance-based neural MT adaptation.

Hasler, E., de Gispert, A., Iglesias, G., and Byrne, B. (2018). Neural machine translation decoding with terminology constraints. In *Proceedings of the 2018 Conference of the North American Chapter of the Association for Computational Linguistics: Human Language Technologies, Volume 2 (Short Papers)*, pages 506–512, New Orleans, Louisiana. Association for Computational Linguistics.

Michon, E., Crego, J., and Senellart, J. (2020). Integrating domain terminology into neural machine translation. In *Proceedings of the 28th International Conference on Computational Linguistics*, pages 3925–3937, Barcelona, Spain (Online). International Committee on Computational Linguistics.

Snover, M., Dorr, B., Schwartz, R., Micciulla, L., and Makhoul, J. (2006). A study of translation edit rate with targeted human annotation. In *Proceedings of Association for Machine Translation in the Americas*, pages 223–231, Cambridge, Massachussets.

Selecting the Best Data Filtering Method for NMT Training

Frederick Bane fbane@transperfect.com
Anna Zaretskaya azaretskaya@transperfect.com
TransPerfect, Barcelona

Abstract

Performance of NMT systems has been proven to depend on the quality of the training data. In this paper we explore different open-source tools that can be used to score the quality of translation pairs, with the goal of obtaining clean corpora for training NMT models. We measure the performance of these tools by correlating their scores with human scores, as well as rank models trained on the resulting filtered datasets in terms of their performance on different test sets and MT performance metrics.

1 Introduction

More and more parallel corpora are available today for MT training (Tiedemann, 2012; Smith et al., 2013). However, when using data from public sources we can never be certain of the data quality, which is extremely important for an MT system's performance (Khayrallah and Koehn, 2018). In a commercial setting like ours, we typically face several data-related challenges. First, we want to be able to use publicly available parallel corpora which are already aligned, such as the OPUS corpus (Tiedemann, 2012). Second, we want to align our customers' translated documents on a sentence level and reliably filter out misaligned or poor quality sentence pairs. And finally, we want to use our customers' translation memories (TMs) and be able to automatically select only the sentences that are relevant for NMT training.

A large part of the data we use for MT training comes from TMs where human translations are stored and are already aligned on a sentence level, which means that our data are generally better in terms of alignment and translation quality than the typical data collected from the web. However, there are other challenges that this type of corpora present for MT engine training. One example of this is that TMs can contain expanded acronyms (the source segment contains an acronym and the target segment contains this acronym together with its expanded version), which can cause hallucinations. That is why in this experiment we focus on the task of cleaning specifically TM data.

We explored different open-source tools that can be used for bilingual data cleaning. Our goal was to choose the one that yields the best results when it comes to MT performance in order to incorporate it into our MT engine training pipeline. As a first step, we randomly selected 5 million sentence pairs from a corpus that contains all our potential training data in five different language directions:

- English-Chinese;
- English-German;
- English-Japanese;

- English-Russian;
- English-Spanish.

These sentences were then scored by four tools:

- Marian Scorer[1] - part of the MarianNMT toolkit, computes negative log likelihood;
- LASER[2] - creates sentence representations in an aligned multilingual vector space;
- MUSE[3] - creates sentence representations in an aligned multilingual vector space;
- XLM-R[4] - creates sentence representations in an aligned multilingual vector space.

As a next step, we selected approximately 100 sentence pairs from each language direction to be scored by professional linguists according to their translation quality. We then correlated the scores produced by each of the tools with the human scores. In addition, we used the human scores to establish a threshold for filtering the data for the MT training, and proceeded to create separate corpora for each language direction using only the sentences with scores above the threshold for that tool. Next, we trained an NMT model with each data set for each language and compared the model performance. Based on these results we make conclusions on whether they are in line with the results we achieved based on the correlation with human scores and which of the tools will be our preferred option for data cleaning.

The remainder of the paper is structured as follows. Section 2 includes an overview of previous related research, Section 3 describes the experimental setup, and in Sections 4 and 5 we discuss the results and the conclusions respectively.

2 Related Research

Collecting and filtering parallel data has been a major topic in MT research. Now it is more relevant than ever since neural MT performance is highly dependent on the size of the training data (Koehn and Knowles, 2017) as well as its quality (Khayrallah and Koehn, 2018).

Most works in this area focus on filtering noisy data collected from the web. One of the earlier methods used an outlier detection algorithm to filter a parallel corpus (Taghipour et al., 2011). The method proposed by Xu and Koehn (2017) is based on generating synthetic noisy data (inadequate and non-fluent translations) and using these data to train a classifier to identify good sentence pairs from a noisy corpus. Cui et al. (2013) propose an unsupervised method to clean bilingual data, which uses a graph-based random walk algorithm and extracts phrase-pair scores to weight the phrase translation probabilities to bias towards more trustworthy ones. The method is based on the observation that better sentence pairs often lead to better phrase extraction and vice versa. Another method proposed by Carpuat et al. (2017) aims to identify semantic differences in translation pairs using cross-lingual textual entailment and additional length-based features.

More recently, a number of new methods were proposed within the shared task on parallel corpus filtering and alignment, which has existed since 2016, although initially it aimed only at collecting parallel document pairs and did not cover the task of sentence alignment (Buck and Koehn, 2016a). In the 2018 edition, the winning system proposed to use neural MT in both directions to score sentence pairs with dual cross-entropy (Junczys-Dowmunt, 2018). One of the winning systems of the 2020 task (Koehn et al., 2020) also used dual cross entropy from

[1] https://marian-nmt.github.io/docs/cmd/marian-scorer/
[2] https://github.com/facebookresearch/LASER
[3] https://github.com/facebookresearch/MUSE
[4] https://arxiv.org/abs/1911.02116

neural MT models trained in both directions but combined it with a number of other features: a bilingual GPT-2 model trained on source-target language pairs as well as monolingual GPT-2 model for each of the languages, and statistical word translation model scores Lu et al. (2020). Another winner of the 2020 task uses an end-to-end classifier that learns to distinguish clean parallel data from misaligned sentence pairs. The model first uses a Transformer model to obtain sentence representations, followed either by a classifier (Siamese network) or additional layers that are fine-tuned (Açarçiçek et al., 2020). Several other recent works use multilingual language models similarly to Lu et al. (2020), such as the 2019 shared task winner LASER (Chaudhary et al., 2019), as well as Lo and Joanis (2020).

Our task of cleaning TM data is, however, different in nature from the task of cleaning noisy data collected from the web. The specific task of cleaning TMs was addressed in the Automatic Translation Memory Cleaning Shared Task organized in 2016 (Barbu et al., 2016). The methods used at the time mostly treated the task as a machine learning classification problem and differ mainly in the sets of features used by the classifier (Ataman et al., 2016; Buck and Koehn, 2016b; Mandorino, 2016; Nahata et al., 2016; Wolff, 2016; Zwahlen et al., 2016).

Our goal is to find out if using multilingual models, which are the basis of many tools used for cleaning noisy corpora, can successfully be applied to our use case of filtering corpora consisting mostly of TM content.

3 Experimental Setup

3.1 Phase 1

In the first phase, we selected five million sentence pairs at random from a large corpus of parallel sentences covering a range of domains for each of five language pairs. The resulting corpora were then scored using the various tools. For LASER, MUSE, and XLM-R, the publicly available models were used. For Marian-scorer, we used our company's existing marian models for the various language directions.

Due to the impracticality of employing human reviewers to score millions of sentence pairs, a smaller corpus of approximately 100 sentence pairs was created for each language, which contained a mix of sentences selected based on different properties (the longest and shortest sentences, the sentences with the most unusual source:target length ratios, and the best and worst scoring sentences as scored by each tool, etc.) and randomly selected sentence pairs.

Professional linguists then reviewed these corpora and assigned a quality score on a scale from 1 to 100 to each translation pair. As translation quality is a subjective concept, special instructions were provided to the linguists that were tailored to our purpose of MT training. For example, linguists were instructed not to penalize spelling mistakes in the source, but to penalize spelling mistakes in the target. Finally, the scores obtained from each tool were compared with the human-assigned scores for each language pair.

The scores obtained from each tool were evaluated in comparison to the "ground truth" human evaluations. For each tool and language pair we calculated the Pearson correlation and root mean squared error (RMSE) between the scores obtained through that tool and the human-assigned scores. We also performed linear regression using the two sequences and calculated the goodness of fit.

3.2 Phase 2

As the relative performance of the tools was mostly consistent across each of the languages (described in greater detail in the Results section), in the second phase we compared only two language pairs, English to German and English to Japanese. We obtained filtered data sets for each tool by removing all sentences with scores below a threshold, which was the equivalent for that tool of a score of 72.5 from the human reviewer, calculated by linear regression. These

Filtering Method	EN→DE	EN→JA
LASER	0.86	0.81
Marian	-1.12	-1.20
MUSE	0.75	0.69
XLM-R	0.86	0.85

Table 1: Score thresholds equivalent to a human-assigned score of 72.5.

Filtering Method	EN→DE	EN→JA
LASER	2707000	2424216
Marian	3425803	3300907
MUSE	3666427	1641008
XLM-R	3168430	2907271
Random	3666427	3300907

Table 2: Number of sentence pairs in each dataset after score-based filtering.

threshold values are shown in Table 1. The value of 72.5 was determined empirically as representing a fair trade-off between the quality of the data and the size of the resulting training set. We also trained models using the full dataset of five million sentence pairs (no filtration), as well as a randomly selected dataset with the same number of segments as the maximum number selected by any of the tools. The number of segments in each dataset is provided in Table 2.

Instead of setting a score threshold, we also considered using the top n sentence pairs as scored by each tool. While this would provide a better direct comparison between the performance of the different models (by removing doubt that performance differences may be attributed to differences in the sizes of the training sets), for our purposes as a translation company, a score threshold made more sense, as this is what would be used in our training process. In future work we plan to experiment with a fixed data set size.

The engines trained on each different dataset were used to translate two test sets of withheld sentence pairs, one in-domain and the other out-of-domain. The in-domain test sets were comprised of 2000 sentences in each language pair drawn from the same distribution as the original five million sentence corpus. The out-of-domain test sets were the 2020 WMT News test sets. The translations were evaluated using the sacreBLEU python package,[5] with default tokenization for the English-German language pair and the mecab tokenizer for the English-Japanese language pair.

These data sets were then used to train a base transformer model for each tool. A baseline engine was also trained for each language pair using all five million sentence pairs (i.e. no data filtering was performed). To isolate the effects of data selection on the performance of the resulting engine, all configurations and hyperparameters were held fixed across all training runs.

4 Results

4.1 Phase 1

The results of of the Pearson correlation and the RMSE calculation are shown in Tables 3 and 4, respectively. Due to differences in the scoring methods, the scores were normalized in the following way prior to calculating the RMSE: 1 – (x/min(x)) for tools using negative log likelihood (where all scores are negative and a score closer to zero is better) and x/max(x) for

[5] https://pypi.org/project/sacrebleu/

Method	ENDE	ENES	ENJA	ENRU	ENZH	Combined
LASER	0.43	0.50	0.52	0.45	0.58	0.52
Marian	0.53	**0.71**	**0.56**	**0.58**	**0.61**	**0.63**
MUSE	**0.61**	0.60	0.48	0.53	0.60	**0.63**
XLM-R	0.47	0.60	0.52	0.50	0.56	0.60

Table 3: Pearson correlation of each method.

Method	ENDE	ENES	ENJA	ENRU	ENZH	Combined
LASER	0.39	0.36	0.34	0.32	0.36	0.35
Marian	0.37	**0.29**	**0.34**	0.33	0.36	0.35
MUSE	**0.32**	**0.29**	0.35	**0.28**	**0.33**	**0.31**
XLM-R	0.38	0.33	0.35	0.32	0.36	0.34

Table 4: RMSE of each method.

others (where all scores are positive and a higher score is better). We also performed linear regression using the two sequences and calculated the goodness of fit. The results of these calculations are shown in Table 5.

The results of the first phase of our experiment show that Marian-scorer and MUSE were the best predictors of the human-assigned scores. In terms of Pearson correlation with human-assigned scores, Marian-scorer was the best in all but the English-German language pair. When examined in terms of the root mean squared error, MUSE was the the best in all but the English-Japanese language pair. After performing linear regression and calculating the goodness of fit for each tool and the human-assigned scores, Marian-scorer was the best in the English-Spanish, English-Japanese, and English-Russian language pairs, and MUSE was best in the English-German and English-Chinese language pairs.

4.2 Phase 2

Of the models trained with a filtered dataset, the Marian-scorer tool showed the best validation scores and best performance on the in-domain test set. In the English-Japanese language pair, this model even out-performed the model trained on all 5 million sentence pairs, despite seeing only around two-thirds as much training data. In the English-German language pair, the model trained with the full dataset achieved the highest score. The validation BLEU and perplexity of each model during the training process are shown in Figures 1 and 2, respectively. The BLEU scores obtained by each model for the in-domain test set are provided in Table 6.

For the out-of-domain (WMT news) test set, the MUSE model performed best on the English-German language pair, while the model trained on the full dataset achieved the highest marks for the English-Japanese language pair. The BLEU scores obtained by each model for the out-of-domain test set are provided in Table 7.

Method	ENDE	ENES	ENJA	ENRU	ENZH	Combined
LASER	0.19	0.30	0.32	0.20	0.35	0.27
Marian	0.32	**0.53**	**0.44**	**0.40**	0.38	0.40
MUSE	**0.42**	0.49	0.31	0.35	**0.44**	**0.40**
XLM-R	0.25	0.43	0.43	0.30	0.37	0.36

Table 5: Goodness of fit of linear regression calculated with each method and human evaluation scores.

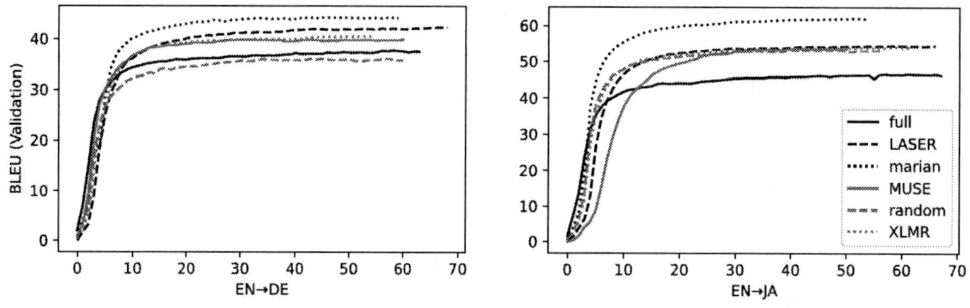

Figure 1: Validation BLEU scores for each model.

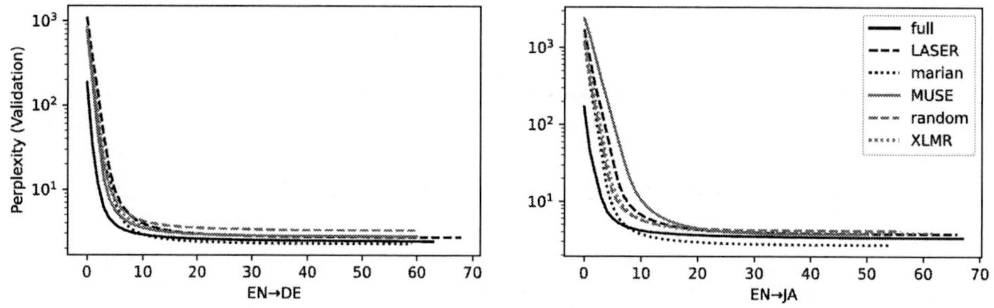

Figure 2: Validation perplexity scores for each model.

5 Conclusions and Future Work

The two phases of this study suggest that using the right method to filter training data can result in similar or improved engine performance despite reducing the total amount of data the engine is exposed to. While training on an unfiltered (larger) dataset typically produced better results in terms of automated metrics, in practice we have observed more hallucinations and unacceptable translations from models trained without any form of data filtering. This is particularly pronounced when there is noise in the target, such as [*sic*] tags or expanded acronyms that do not exist in the source. Among the data filtering methods we tested, our results show that marian-scorer and MUSE produce the best results. However, the limited scope and scale of the study mean that the results are far from generalizable. Future work is still required to confirm or deny the validity of the results on a larger scale.

Filtering Method	EN→DE	EN→JA
LASER	35.7	36.6
Marian	**36.3**	**37.5***
MUSE	36.0	32.3
XLM-R	35.6	36.3
Random	35.9	36.6
None (Full Dataset)	36.8	37.1

Table 6: SacreBLEU scores for different machine translation models on the in-domain test sets. Note: * indicates a result superior to the model trained on the full dataset.

Filtering Method	EN→DE News	EN→JA News
LASER	18.3	16.9
Marian	17.6	15.9
MUSE	**18.4***	13.6
XLM-R	17.9	**17.1**
Random	17.6	16.6
None (Full Dataset)	18.3	17.7

Table 7: SacreBLEU scores for different machine translation models on the out-of-domain test sets. Note: * indicates a result superior to the model trained on the full dataset.

For example, repeating the second phase of this experiment training three models per tool instead of one and taking the average score would help mitigate potential effects resulting from random weight initializations; human review of the model output would help ensure the automated evaluations in the second stage correspond with human judgment; and obtaining evaluations from more reviewers and calculating inter-rater reliability would help mitigate potential bias resulting from the use of a single reviewer on such a limited sample.

There are also additional practical considerations that call for further investigation. How can an appropriate score threshold be identified in an automated way? Do the appropriate threshold values vary across domains as well as languages? As the models trained on the full data set show some advantages over the models trained on filtered data, could using a two-step training process (training first on all available data, then fine-tuning on a subset of the cleanest data) produce superior models that demonstrate both robustness to input noise and high translation quality?

Beyond the topics enumerated above, our team plans to address several more analytical questions relevant to this line of inquiry in future research. Multiple factors contribute to translation quality, and several different types of errors affecting translation quality exist; are these tools more likely to identify certain error types than others? Do they identify problems with fluency equally as well as adequacy? Are the conclusions drawn in this paper as applicable to the life sciences domain as the leisure and hospitality domain? And what biases are introduced by filtering data in this way? Despite the limitations described here, we hope our work will provide a useful reference for other MT practitioners hoping to identify the best quality sentence pairs for use in their engine training.

References

Açarçiçek, H., Çolakoğlu, T., Aktan Hatipoğlu, P. E., Huang, C. H., and Peng, W. (2020). Filtering noisy parallel corpus using transformers with proxy task learning. In *Proceedings of the Fifth Conference on Machine Translation*, pages 940–946, Online. Association for Computational Linguistics.

Ataman, D., Sabet, M. J., Turchi, M., and Negri, M. (2016). FBK HLT-MT Participation in the 1st Translation Memory Cleaning Shared Task. Online.

Barbu, E., Parra Escartín, C., Bentivogli, L., Negri, M., Turchi, M., Orasan, C., and Federico, M. (2016). The first automatic translation memory cleaning shared task. *Machine Translation*, 30(3):145–166.

Buck, C. and Koehn, P. (2016a). Findings of the WMT 2016 bilingual document alignment shared task. In *Proceedings of the First Conference on Machine Translation: Volume 2,*

Shared Task Papers, pages 554–563, Berlin, Germany. Association for Computational Linguistics.

Buck, C. and Koehn, P. (2016b). UEdin participation in the 1st Translation Memory Cleaning Shared Task. Online.

Carpuat, M., Vyas, Y., and Niu, X. (2017). Detecting cross-lingual semantic divergence for neural machine translation. In *Proceedings of the First Workshop on Neural Machine Translation*, pages 69–79, Vancouver. Association for Computational Linguistics.

Chaudhary, V., Tang, Y., Guzmán, F., Schwenk, H., and Koehn, P. (2019). Low-resource corpus filtering using multilingual sentence embeddings. *CoRR*, abs/1906.08885.

Cui, L., Zhang, D., Liu, S., Li, M., and Zhou, M. (2013). Bilingual data cleaning for SMT using graph-based random walk. In *Proceedings of the 51st Annual Meeting of the Association for Computational Linguistics (Volume 2: Short Papers)*, pages 340–345, Sofia, Bulgaria. Association for Computational Linguistics.

Junczys-Dowmunt, M. (2018). Dual conditional cross-entropy filtering of noisy parallel corpora. In *Proceedings of the Third Conference on Machine Translation: Shared Task Papers*, pages 888–895, Belgium, Brussels. Association for Computational Linguistics.

Khayrallah, H. and Koehn, P. (2018). On the impact of various types of noise on neural machine translation. In *Proceedings of the 2nd Workshop on Neural Machine Translation and Generation*, pages 74–83, Melbourne, Australia. Association for Computational Linguistics.

Koehn, P., Chaudhary, V., El-Kishky, A., Goyal, N., Chen, P.-J., and Guzmán, F. (2020). Findings of the WMT 2020 shared task on parallel corpus filtering and alignment. In *Proceedings of the Fifth Conference on Machine Translation*, pages 726–742, Online. Association for Computational Linguistics.

Koehn, P. and Knowles, R. (2017). Six challenges for neural machine translation. In *Proceedings of the First Workshop on Neural Machine Translation*, pages 28–39, Vancouver. Association for Computational Linguistics.

Lo, C.-K. and Joanis, E. (2020). Improving parallel data identification using iteratively refined sentence alignments and bilingual mappings of pre-trained language models. In *Proceedings of the Fifth Conference on Machine Translation*, pages 972–978, Online. Association for Computational Linguistics.

Lu, J., Ge, X., Shi, Y., and Zhang, Y. (2020). Alibaba submission to the WMT20 parallel corpus filtering task. In *Proceedings of the Fifth Conference on Machine Translation*, pages 979–984, Online. Association for Computational Linguistics.

Mandorino, V. (2016). The Lingua Custodia Participation in the NLP4TM2016 TM Cleaning Shared Task. Online.

Nahata, N., Nayak, T., Pal, S., and Kumar Naskar, S. (2016). Rule Based Classifier for Translation Memory Cleaning. Online.

Smith, J. R., Saint-Amand, H., Plamada, M., Koehn, P., Callison-Burch, C., and Lopez, A. (2013). Dirt cheap web-scale parallel text from the Common Crawl. In *Proceedings of the 51st Annual Meeting of the Association for Computational Linguistics (Volume 1: Long Papers)*, pages 1374–1383, Sofia, Bulgaria. Association for Computational Linguistics.

Taghipour, K., Khadivi, S., and Xu, J. (2011). Parallel corpus refinement as an outlier detection algorithm. In *MT Summit XIII. Machine Translation Summit (MT Summit-11), 13., September 19-23, Xiamen, China*. NA.

Tiedemann, J. (2012). Parallel data, tools and interfaces in OPUS. In *Proceedings of the Eighth International Conference on Language Resources and Evaluation (LREC'12)*, pages 2214–2218, Istanbul, Turkey. European Language Resources Association (ELRA).

Wolff, F. (2016). Unisa system submission at NLP4TM 2016. Online.

Xu, H. and Koehn, P. (2017). Zipporah: a fast and scalable data cleaning system for noisy web-crawled parallel corpora. In *Proceedings of the 2017 Conference on Empirical Methods in Natural Language Processing*, pages 2945–2950, Copenhagen, Denmark. Association for Computational Linguistics.

Zwahlen, A., Carnal, O., and Läubli, S. (2016). Automatic TM Cleaning through MT and POS Tagging: Autodesk's Submission to the NLP4TM 2016 Shared Task. Online.

A Review for Large Volumes
of Post-edited Data
Silvio Picinini
ebay

Problem

- Review large volumes of data and have confidence in the quality
    - A frequent approach is a Sample Review: human error annotation with typology, and scoring (MQM)
    - For hundreds of thousands, or millions, of words, the sample has to be small, and leaves a lot of content unchecked

Wish List

➡ It would be welcome to have alternative ways to review and increase confidence!

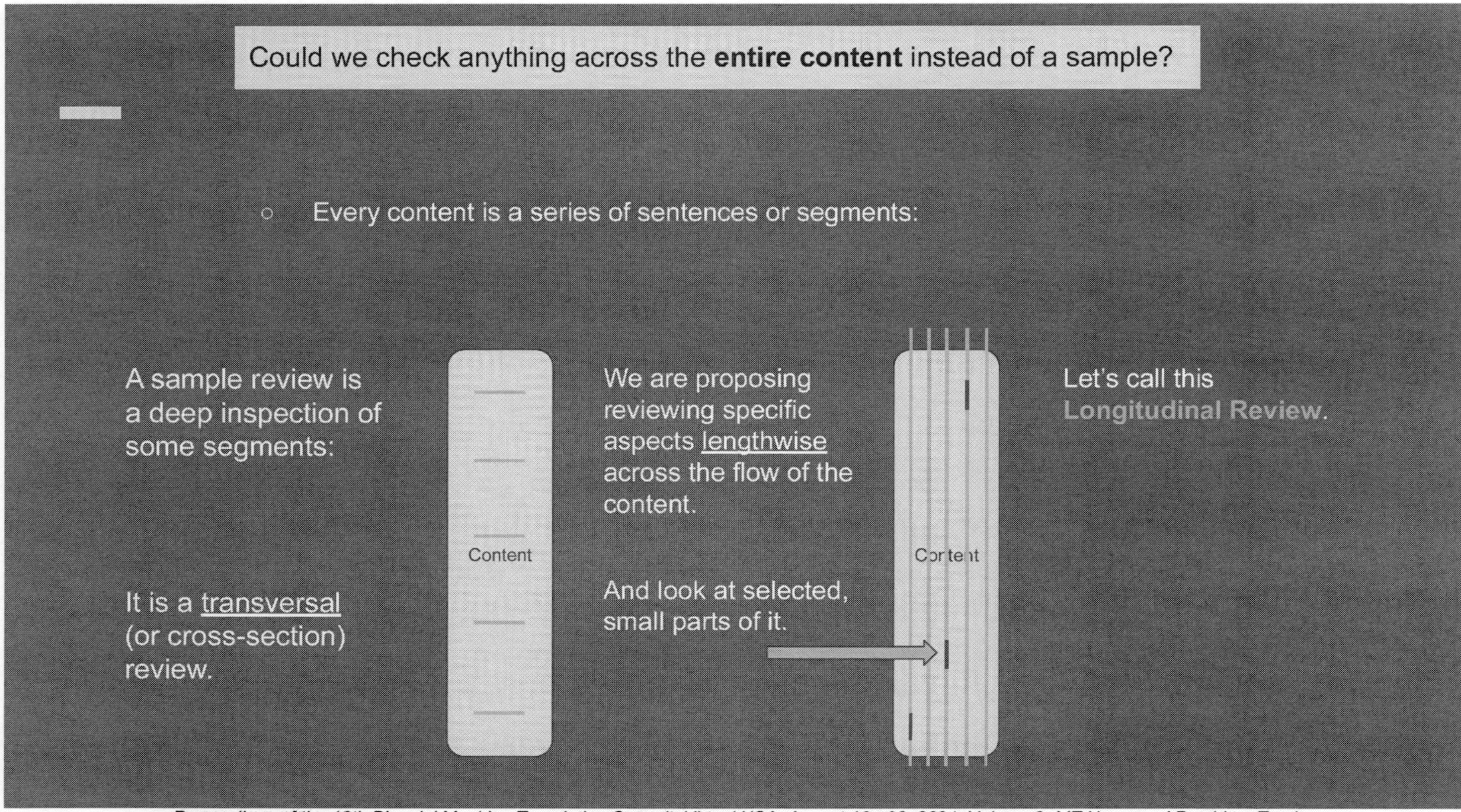
Could we check anything across the **entire content** instead of a sample?
Every content is a series of sentences or segments:
A sample review is a deep inspection of some segments:
It is a transversal (or cross-section) review.
Content
We are proposing reviewing specific aspects lengthwise across the flow of the content.
And look at selected, small parts of it.
Content
Let's call this Longitudinal Review.

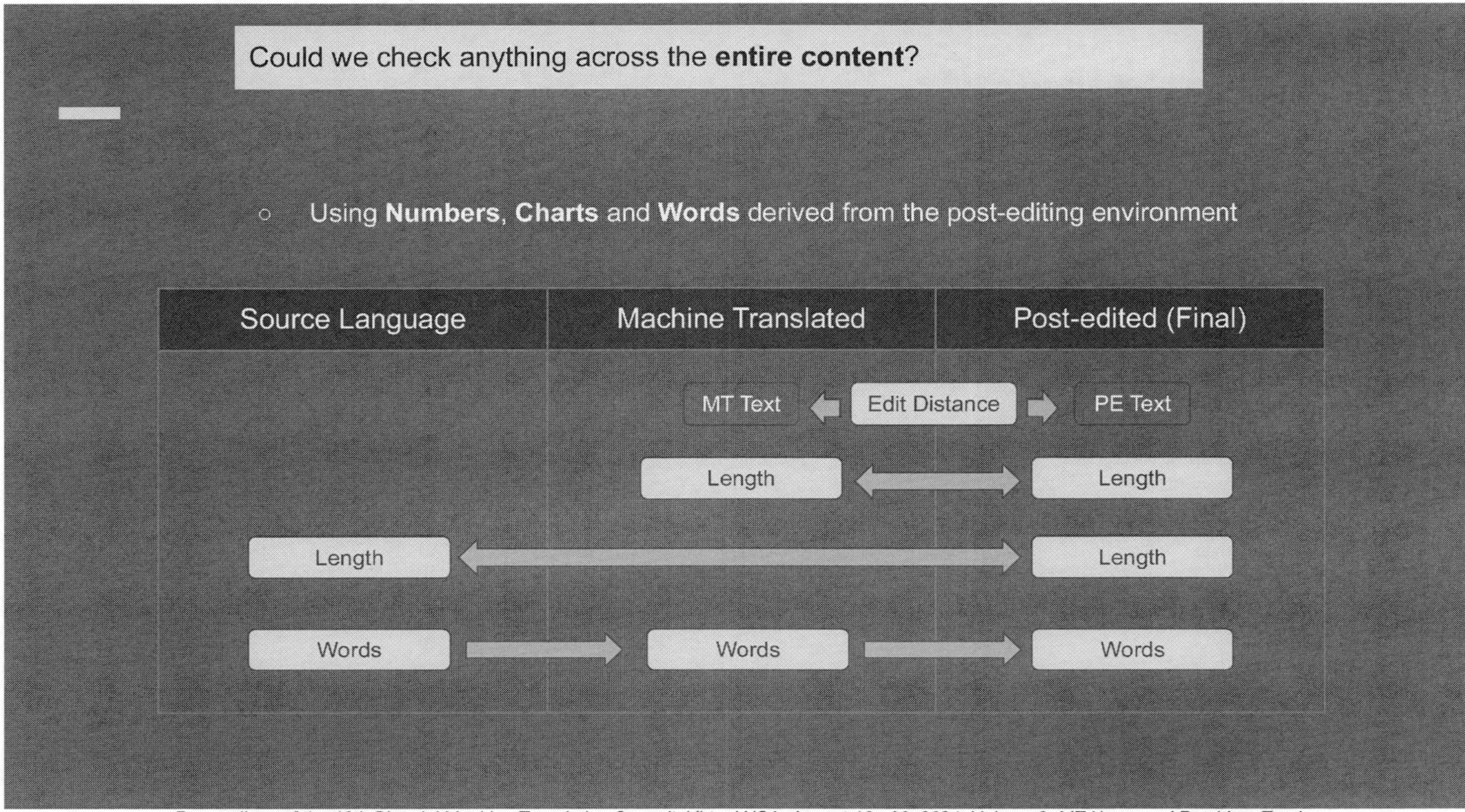
Could we check anything across the entire content?
Using Numbers, Charts and Words derived from the post-editing environment
Source Language
Machine Translated
Post-edited (Final)
MT Text
Edit Distance
PE Text
Length
Length
Length
Length
Words
Words
Words

Numbers

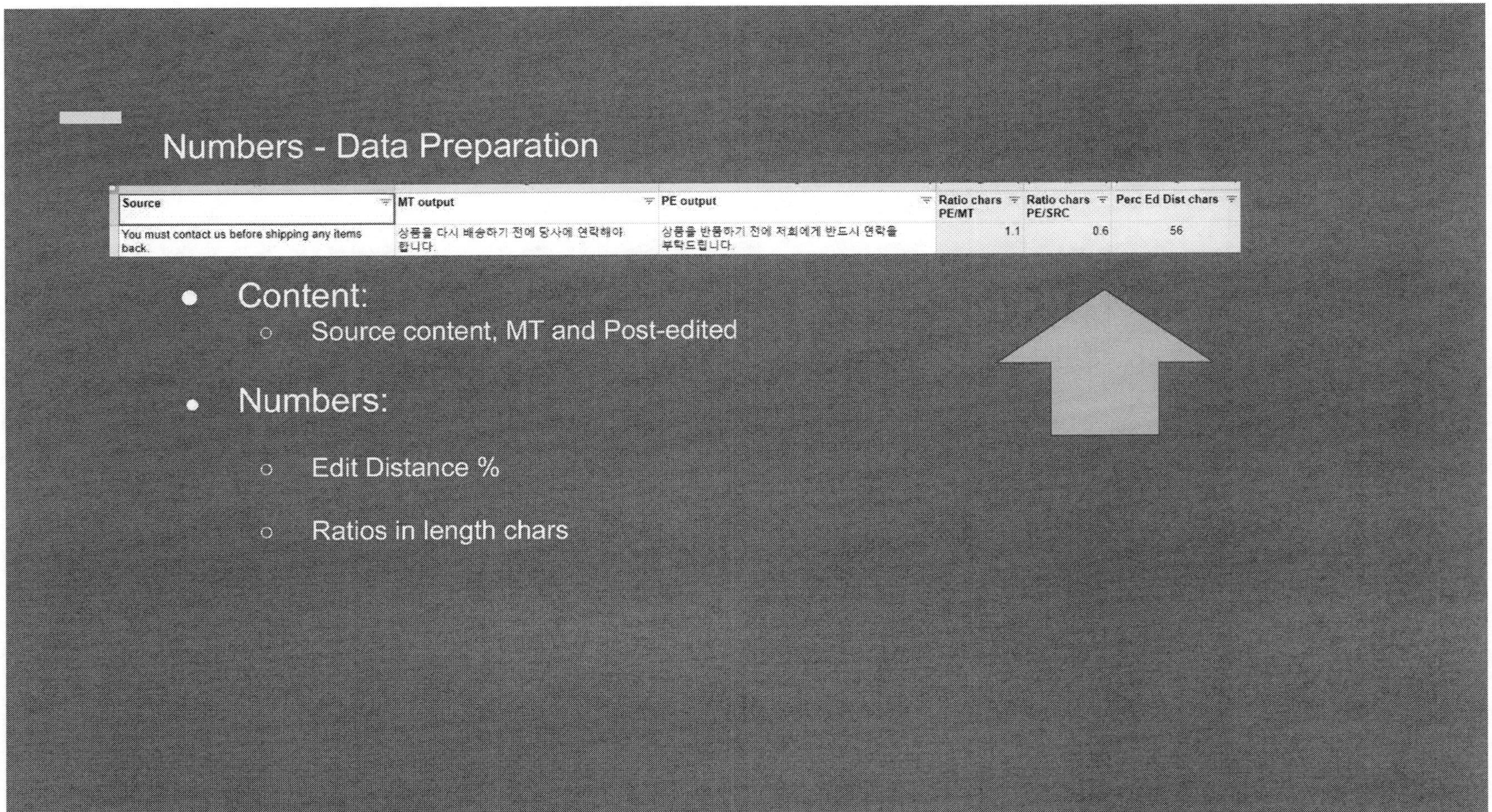
Numbers - Data Preparation
Source
MT output
PE output
Ratio chars PE/MT
Ratio chars PE/SRC
Perc Ed Dist chars
You must contact us before shipping any items back.
상품을 다시 배송하기 전에 당사에 연락해야 합니다.
상품을 반품하기 전에 저희에게 반드시 연락을 부탁드립니다.
1.1
0.6
56
Content:
Source content, MT and Post-edited
Numbers:
Edit Distance %
Ratios in length chars

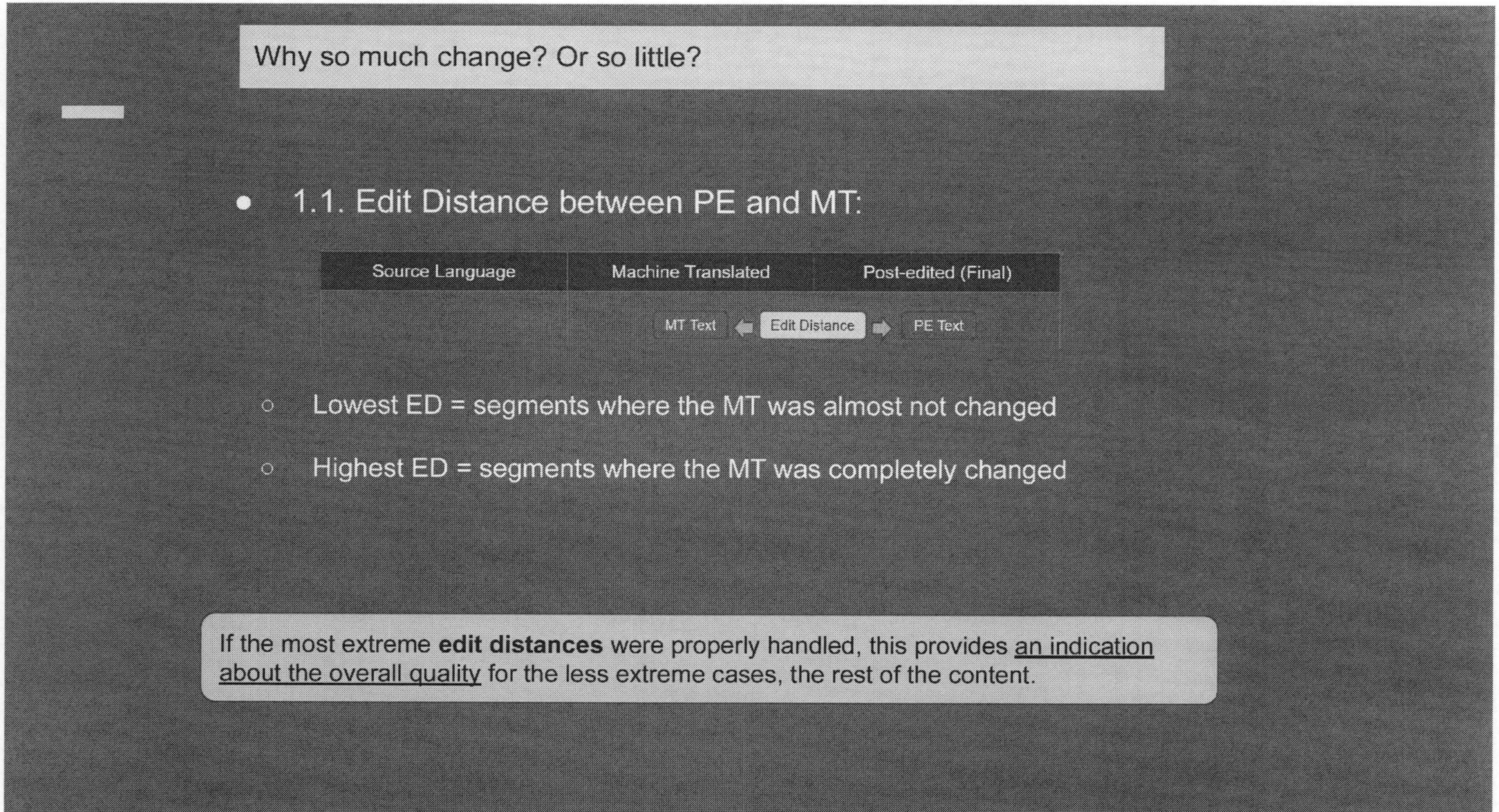
Why so much change? Or so little?
1.1. Edit Distance between PE and MT:
Source Language
Machine Translated
Post-edited (Final)
MT Text
Edit Distance
PE Text
Lowest ED = segments where the MT was almost not changed
Highest ED = segments where the MT was completely changed
If the most extreme edit distances were properly handled, this provides an indication about the overall quality for the less extreme cases, the rest of the content.

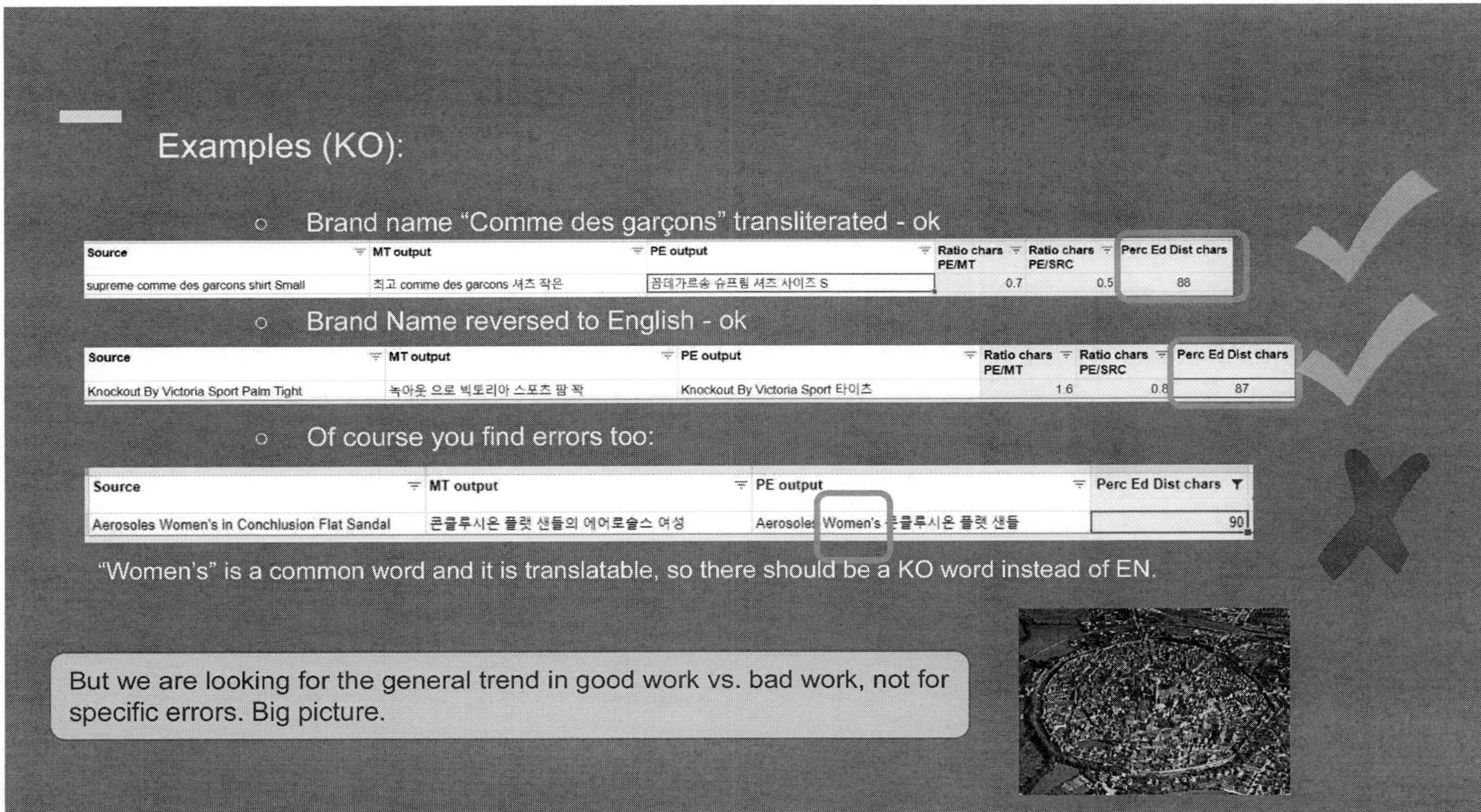
Examples (KO):
Brand name "Comme des garçons" transliterated - ok
Source | MT output | PE output | Ratio chars PE/MT | Ratio chars PE/SRC | Perc Ed Dist chars
supreme comme des garcons shirt Small | 최고 comme des garcons 셔츠 작은 | 꼼데가르송 슈프림 셔츠 사이즈 S | 0.7 | 0.5 | 88
Brand Name reversed to English - ok
Source | MT output | PE output | Ratio chars PE/MT | Ratio chars PE/SRC | Perc Ed Dist chars
Knockout By Victoria Sport Palm Tight | 녹아웃 으로 빅토리아 스포츠 팜 꽉 | Knockout By Victoria Sport 타이츠 | 1.6 | 0.8 | 87
Of course you find errors too:
Source | MT output | PE output | Perc Ed Dist chars
Aerosoles Women's in Conchlusion Flat Sandal | 콘클루시온 플랫 샌들의 에어로솔스 여성 | Aerosole Women's 클루시온 플랫 샌들 | 90
"Women's" is a common word and it is translatable, so there should be a KO word instead of EN.
But we are looking for the general trend in good work vs. bad work, not for specific errors. Big picture.

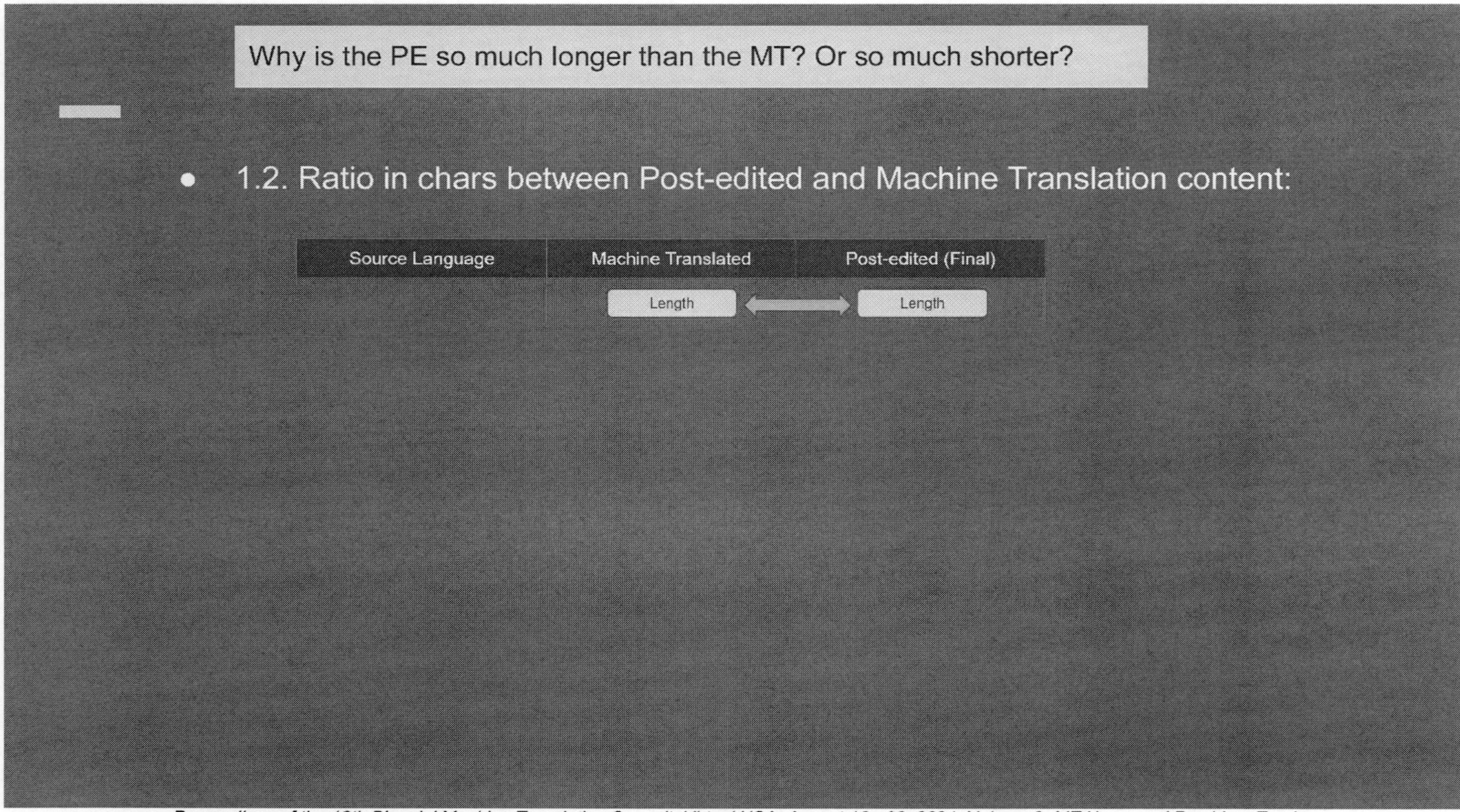
Why is the PE so much longer than the MT? Or so much shorter?
1.2. Ratio in chars between Post-edited and Machine Translation content:
Source Language
Machine Translated
Post-edited (Final)
Length
Length

Examples (KO):

MT was ok, but missing “outsole”. PE seems complete and richer:

Source	MT output	PE output	Ratio chars PE/MT
Rubber outsole for durable traction on any surface.	모든 표면에 내구성 견인고무.	모든 지면에 접지력을 발휘하는 뛰어난 내구성의 고무 아웃솔.	2.1
	Durable traction rubber on all surfaces.	Durable rubber outsole that provides grip on all grounds.	

MT was truncated, but the PE correctly did not miss that:

9.Height=_______ (from the top of head to floor without shoes)	9.Height=___	9. 높이=______(신발을 신지 않은 상태에서 머리부터 바닥까지)	3.2

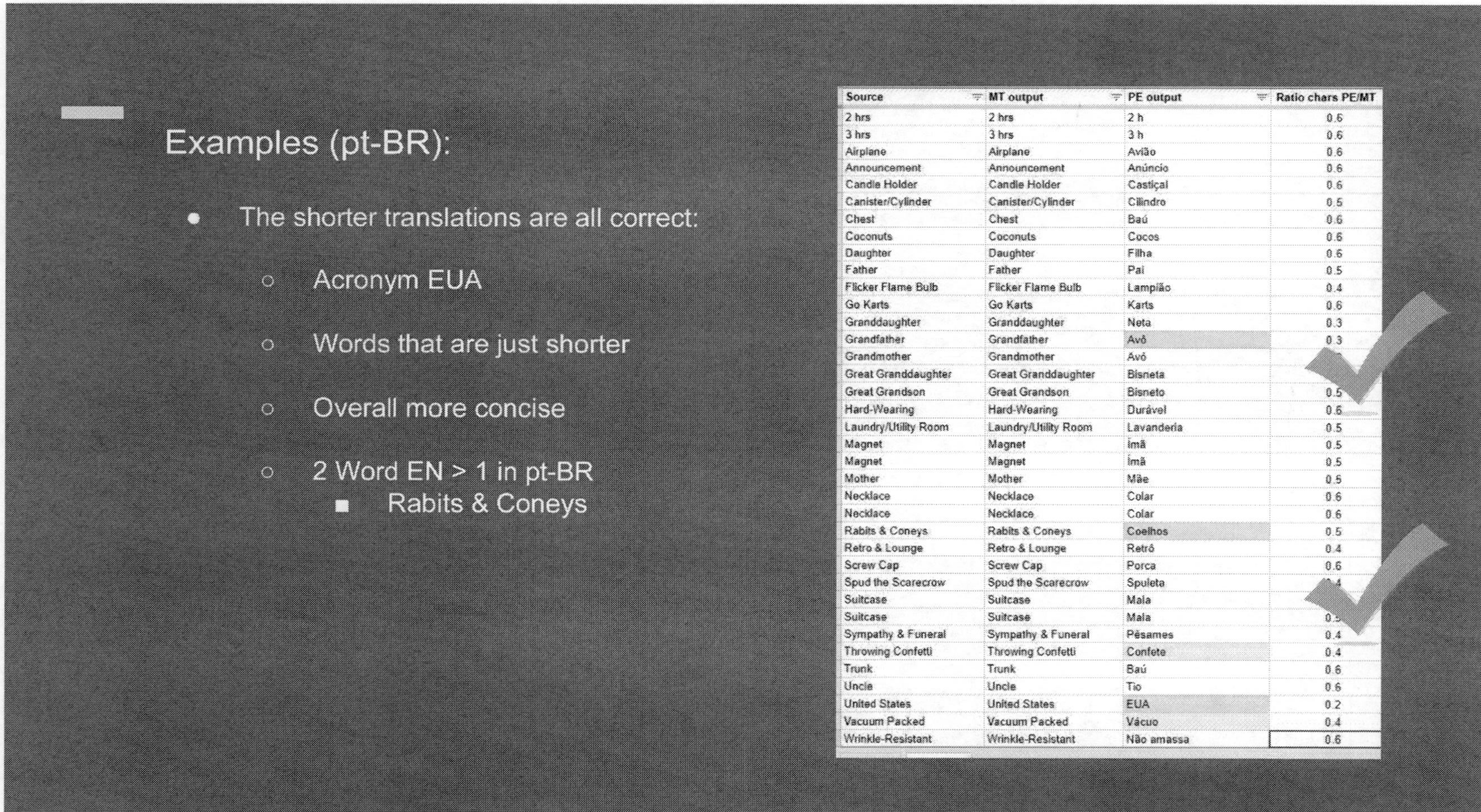

Source	MT output	PE output	Ratio chars PE/MT
2 hrs	2 hrs	2 h	0.6
3 hrs	3 hrs	3 h	0.6
Airplane	Airplane	Avião	0.6
Announcement	Announcement	Anúncio	0.6
Candle Holder	Candle Holder	Castiçal	0.6
Canister/Cylinder	Canister/Cylinder	Cilindro	0.5
Chest	Chest	Baú	0.6
Coconuts	Coconuts	Cocos	0.6
Daughter	Daughter	Filha	0.6
Father	Father	Pai	0.5
Flicker Flame Bulb	Flicker Flame Bulb	Lampião	0.4
Go Karts	Go Karts	Karts	0.6
Granddaughter	Granddaughter	Neta	0.3
Grandfather	Grandfather	Avô	0.3
Grandmother	Grandmother	Avó	[illegible]
Great Granddaughter	Great Granddaughter	Bisneta	[illegible]
Great Grandson	Great Grandson	Bisneto	0.5
Hard-Wearing	Hard-Wearing	Durável	0.6
Laundry/Utility Room	Laundry/Utility Room	Lavanderia	0.5
Magnet	Magnet	Ímã	0.5
Magnet	Magnet	Ímã	0.5
Mother	Mother	Mãe	0.5
Necklace	Necklace	Colar	0.6
Necklace	Necklace	Colar	0.6
Rabits & Coneys	Rabits & Coneys	Coelhos	0.5
Retro & Lounge	Retro & Lounge	Retrô	0.4
Screw Cap	Screw Cap	Porca	0.6
Spud the Scarecrow	Spud the Scarecrow	Spuleta	[illegible]
Suitcase	Suitcase	Mala	[illegible]
Suitcase	Suitcase	Mala	[illegible]
Sympathy & Funeral	Sympathy & Funeral	Pêsames	0.4
Throwing Confetti	Throwing Confetti	Confete	0.4
Trunk	Trunk	Baú	0.6
Uncle	Uncle	Tio	0.6
United States	United States	EUA	0.2
Vacuum Packed	Vacuum Packed	Vácuo	0.4
Wrinkle-Resistant	Wrinkle-Resistant	Não amassa	0.6

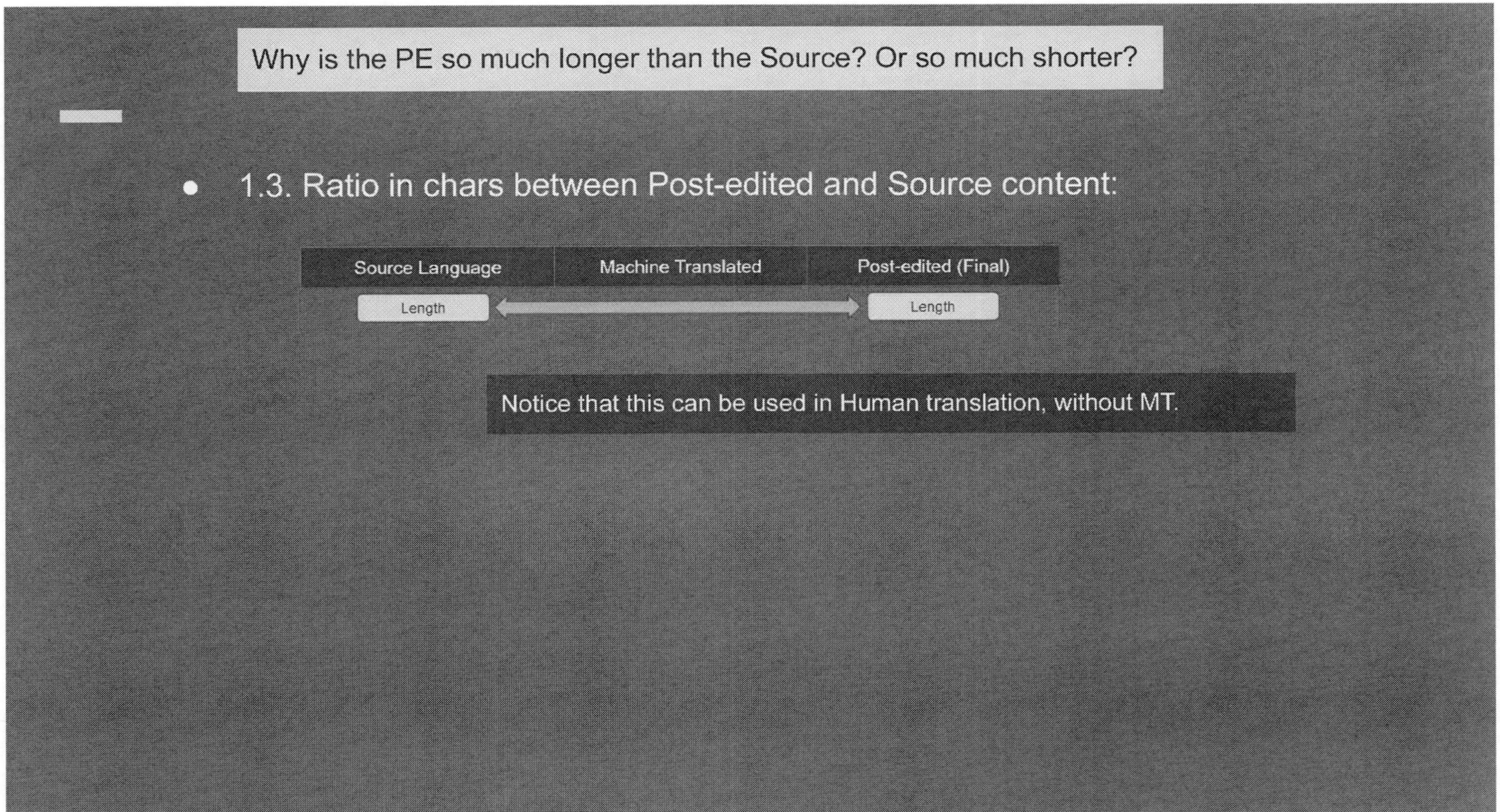
Why is the PE so much longer than the Source? Or so much shorter?
1.3. Ratio in chars between Post-edited and Source content:
Source Language
Machine Translated
Post-edited (Final)
Length
Length
Notice that this can be used in Human translation, without MT.

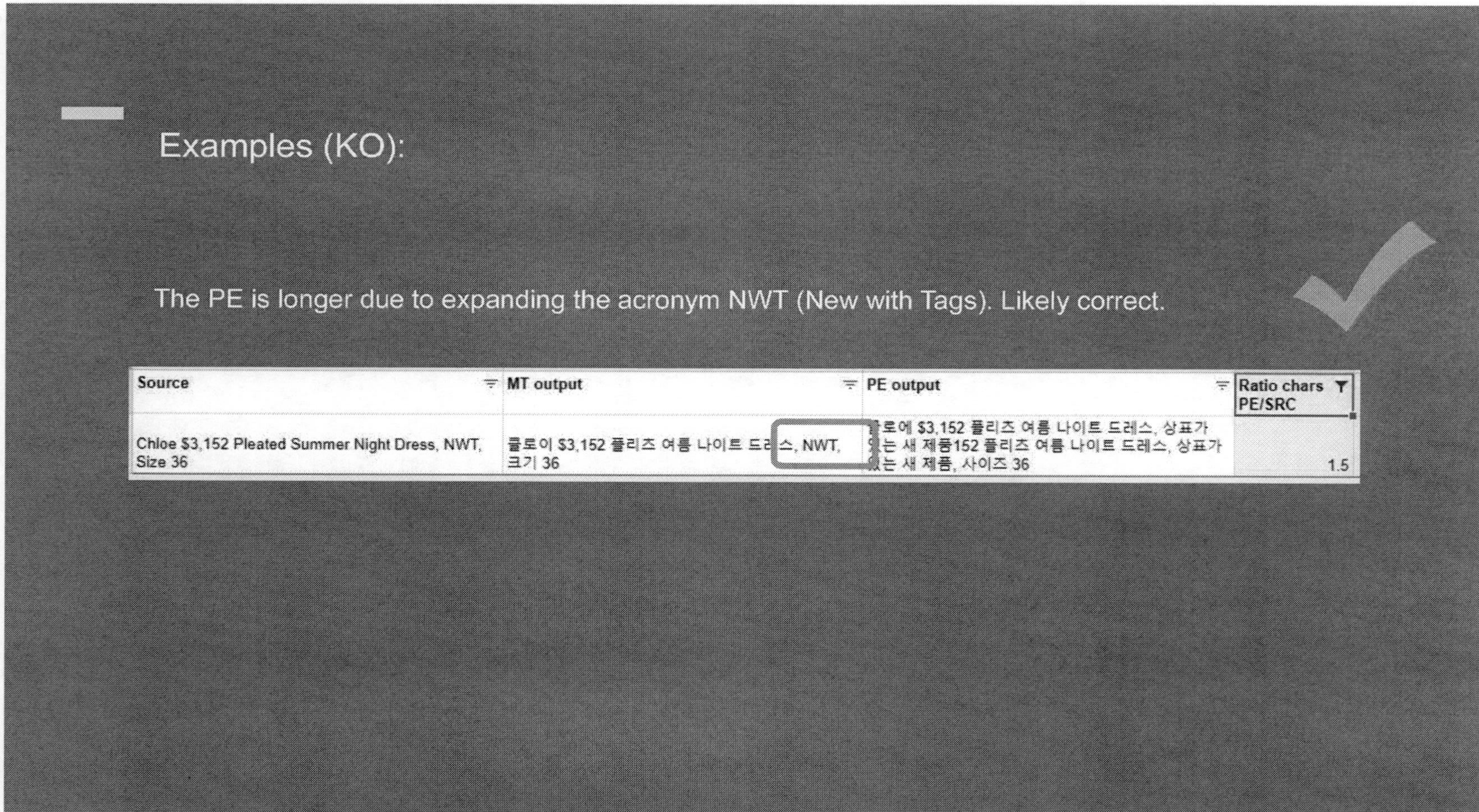

Source	MT output	PE output	Ratio chars PE/SRC
Chloe $3,152 Pleated Summer Night Dress, NWT, Size 36	클로이 $3,152 플리즈 여름 나이트 드레스, NWT, 크기 36	로에 $3,152 플리즈 여름 나이트 드레스, 상표가 는 새 제품152 플리즈 여름 나이트 드레스, 상표가 는 새 제품, 사이즈 36	1.5

Examples (KO):

The PE is longer due to transliteration into English, which uses more characters. Likely correct.

Source	MT output	PE output	Ratio chars PE/SRC
Healthy Cookbook for Two includes:	2인 건강한 요리책은 다음과 같습니다.	Healthy Cookbook for Two에는 다음이 포함됩니다.	1.1
Mind Over Mood will help you:	마음 위에 분위기는 당신을 도울 것입니다 :	Mind Over Mood는 다음과 같은 도움을 줍니다.	1.1
The Wisdom of the Enneagram includes:	에네나그램의 지혜에는 다음이 포함됩니다.	The Wisdom of the Enneagram에는 다음이 포함됩니다.	1.1
Google "Ameribuilt Steel Structures"	구글 "아메리에이제드 스틸 구조"	Ameribuilt Steel Structures를 구글에서 검색하십시오.	1.2

Examples (pt-BR):

- The longer translations are all correct:
  - Acronyms are expanded
    - EPP
  - Character names add the localized name in parenthesis
    - Dora (Dora, the Explorer)
  - 1 Word EN > 2 in pt-BR
    - Pillows
  - Translation "explains"
    - Lei
  - Gender
    - Nurse

Source	MT output	PE output	Ratio chars PE/SRC
Blower	Blower	Soprador, ventoinha	3.2
Brad	Brad	Brad (Preguinho)	4
Corn Bulb	Corn Bulb	Lâmpada no formato de espiga de milho	4.1
Cowhide	Pele curtida de animal	Pele curtida de animal	3.1
Dora	Dora	Dora (Dora, a Aventureira)	6.5
Elissabat	Elissabat	Elissabat (Veronica Von Vamp)	3.2
EPP Beads	EPP Beads	Esferas de polietileno expandido (EPP)	4.2
EPS Beads	EPS Beads	Esferas de poliestireno expandido	3.7
Iron Hot	Iron Hot	Passar com temperatura alta	3.4
Iron Man	Iron Man	Iron Man (Homem de Ferro)	3.1
Lei	Lei	Colar havaiano de flores	8
Li Shang	Li Shang	Li Shang (Capitão Li Shang)	3.4
Lotso	Lotso	Lotso (Lotso, o ursinho fofo)	5.8
Mailbox	Mailbox	Caixa de correspondência	[illegible]
Nurse	Nurse	Enfermeiro, enfermeira	[illegible]
Olimar	Olimar	Olimar (Capitão Olimar)	3.8
Open Storage	Open Storage	Caixa/compartimento de armazenagem aberto	3.4
Party Cone	Party Cone	Chapéu de festa em forma de cone	3.2
Pillows	Pillows	Travesseiros e almofadas	3.4
Pillows	Pillows	Travesseiros e almofadas	3.4
Prank Box	Prank Box	Caixa com acessórios para pegadinhas	4
Serveware	Serveware	Peças e utensílios para serviço de mesa	4.3
Sign	Sign	Placas/letreiros	4
Sign	Sign	Placas/letreiros	4
Sky Lanterns	Sky Lanterns	Balões de soltar (ex.: balão de São João)	3.4
Snaps	Snaps	Fechos de pressão	3.4
Steven	Steven	Steven (Steven Universo)	[illegible]
Table Runner	Table Runner	Toalha de mesa decorativa, caminho de mesa	[illegible]
Table Runner	Table Runner	Toalha de mesa decorativa, caminho de mesa	3.5
Tableware	Tableware	Louças, talheres e copos/taças de mesa	4.2
Tableware Set	Tableware Set	Jogo de mesa (louças, talheres, copos/taças)	3.4
Tableware Set	Tableware Set	Jogo de mesa (louças, talheres, copos/taças)	3.4
Toilet Mug	Toilet Mug	Caneca em forma de vaso sanitário	3.3
Veneer	Veneer	Revestimento de folha de madeira/laminado	6.8
Wall Trunk	Wall Trunk	Baú com tampa de abertura totalmente vertical	4.5
Zarina	Zarina	Zarina (A Fada Pirata)	3.7

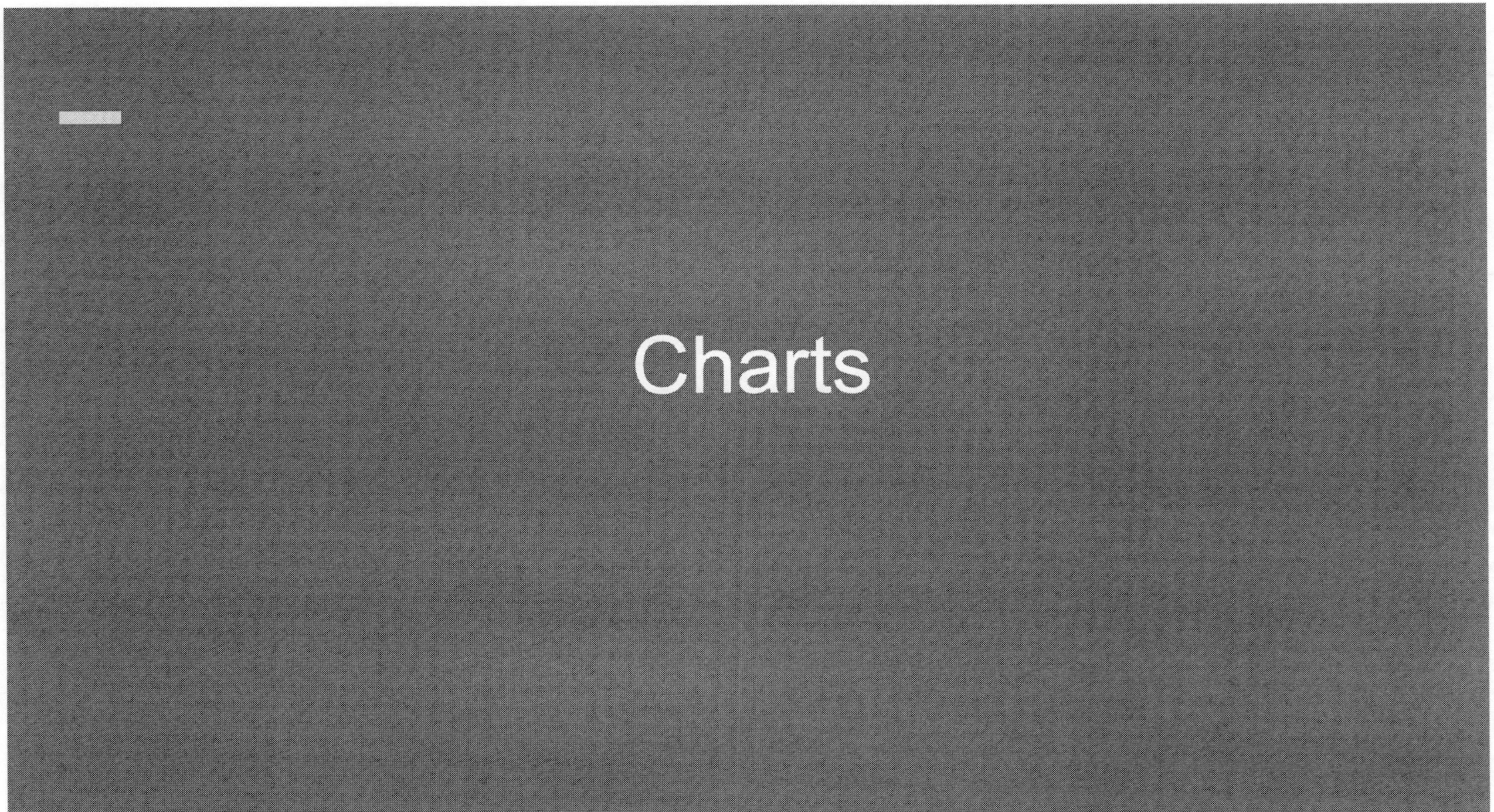
Charts

How did change progressed through the PE?

- 2. Chart for Edit Distance through the content:
    - Plotting the edit distance though the content may reveal patterns of behavior during PE.
        - A consistent post-editing will provide a consistent chart, even if there are variations in the edit distance for each segment:

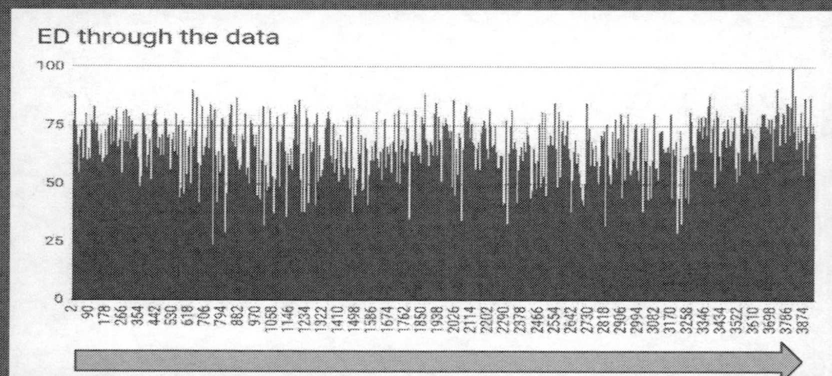

How did change happened through the PE?

- Chart for Edit Distance through the content:
  - However, one part of the content showed this behavior below.
  - Whatever the reason, there were large blocks of segments that were not post-edited.

- The gaps in PE that appeared on the chart were not detected with a sample review.
- Half of the file was done, masking the evaluation of a sample.

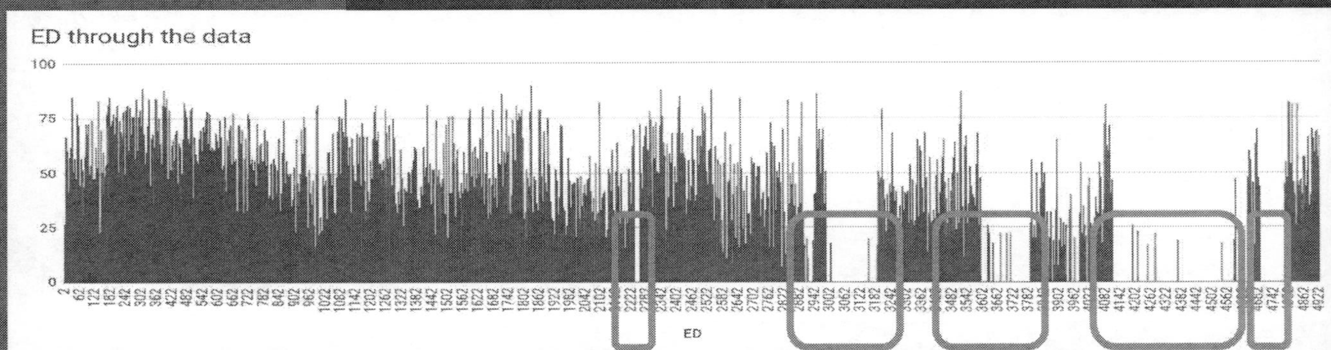

Please notice how a non-speaker of the target language will be able to have some insight into the quality. For example, a project manager (or you, right now).

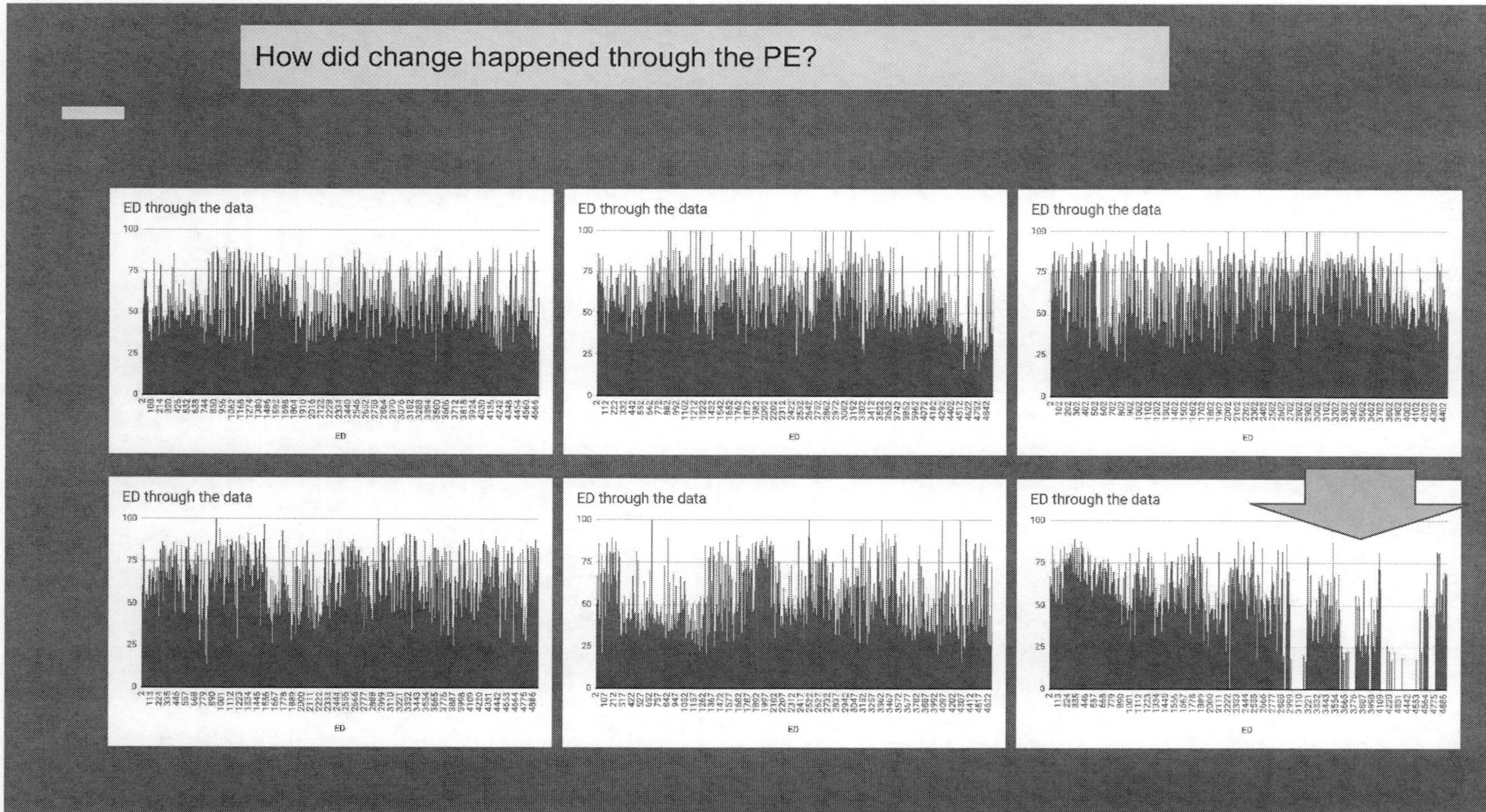
How did change happened through the PE?
ED through the data
ED through the data
ED through the data
ED through the data
ED through the data
ED through the data

Words

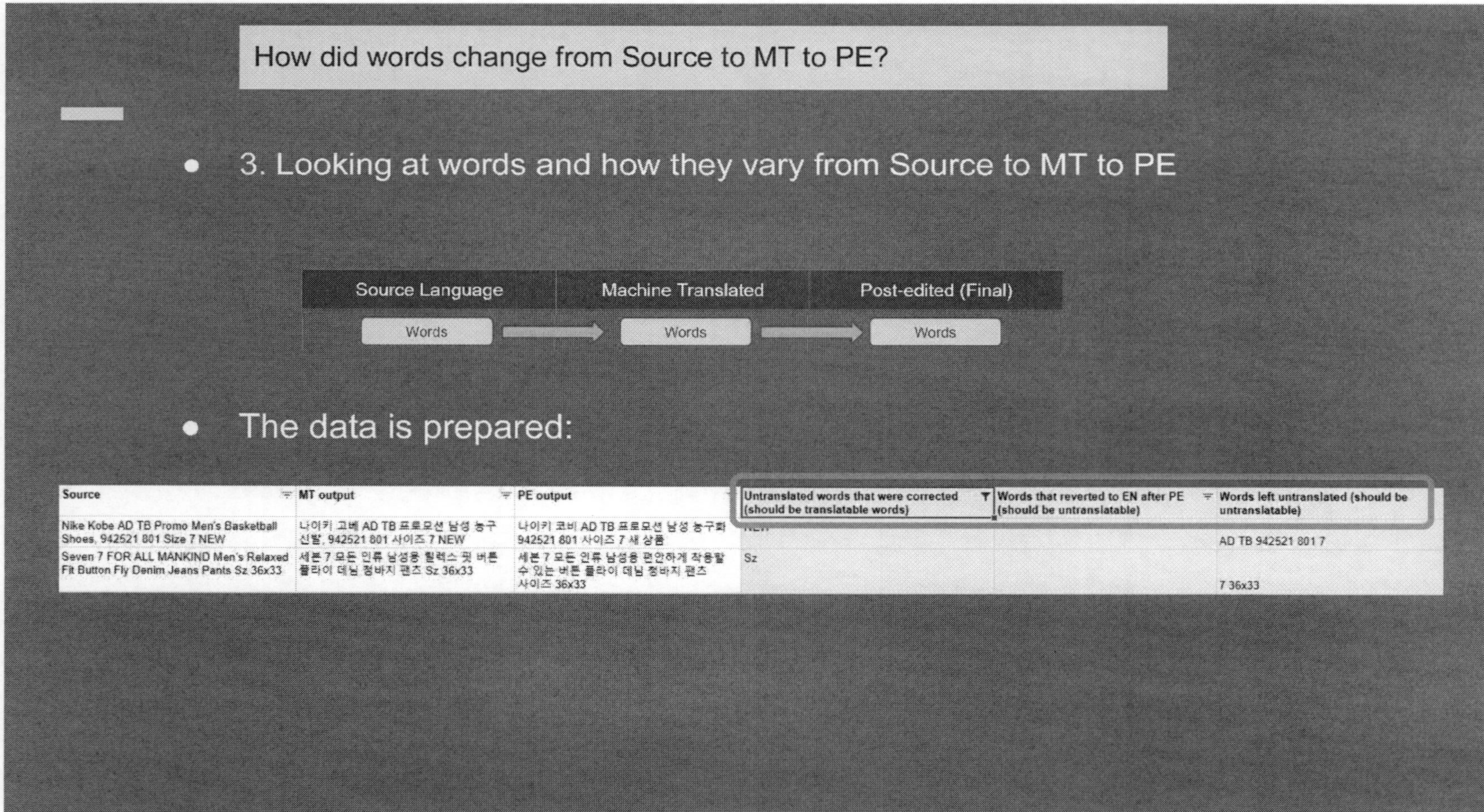

Source	MT output	PE output	Untranslated words that were corrected (should be translatable words)	Words that reverted to EN after PE (should be untranslatable)	Words left untranslated (should be untranslatable)
Nike Kobe AD TB Promo Men's Basketball Shoes, 942521 801 Size 7 NEW	나이키 고베 AD TB 프로모션 남성 농구 신발, 942521 801 사이즈 7 NEW	나이키 코비 AD TB 프로모션 남성 농구화 942521 801 사이즈 7 새 상품	NEW		AD TB 942521 801 7
Seven 7 FOR ALL MANKIND Men's Relaxed Fit Button Fly Denim Jeans Pants Sz 36x33	세븐 7 모든 인류 남성용 릴렉스 핏 버튼 플라이 데님 청바지 팬츠 Sz 36x33	세븐 7 모든 인류 남성용 편안하게 착용할 수 있는 버튼 플라이 데님 청바지 팬츠 사이즈 36x33	Sz		7 36x33

How did words change from Source to MT to PE?

- 3.1. Untranslated words that were corrected

Source	MT output	PE output	Untranslated words that were corrected
Nike Kobe AD TB Promo Men's Basketball Shoes, 942521 801 Size 7 NEW	나이키 고베 AD TB 프로모션 남성 농구 신발, 942521 801 사이즈 7 NEW	나이키 코비 AD TB 프로모션 남성 농구화 942521 801 사이즈 7 새 상품	NEW

- "New" is a <u>common word</u>, and is translatable. The MT left it in EN, instead of translating into KO. So this is an MT error.
- The post-edited content does not have the word in EN anymore.
- So, an <u>error</u> was probably <u>corrected</u>.

- And that is what we wanted to know.

Please notice how a non-speaker of the target language will be able to have some insight into the quality. For example, a project manager.

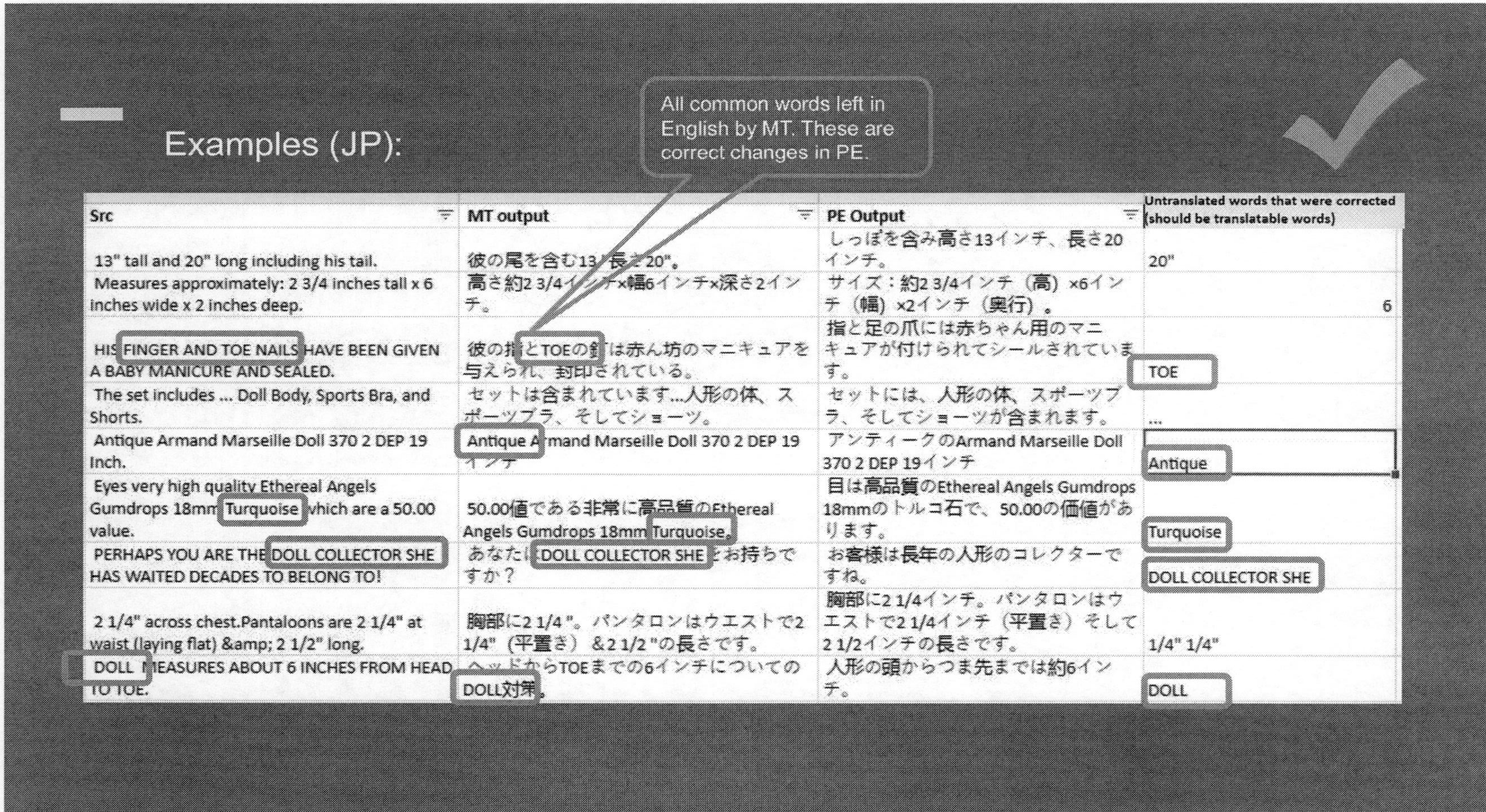
Examples (JP):
All common words left in English by MT. These are correct changes in PE.
Src | MT output | PE Output | Untranslated words that were corrected (should be translatable words)
13" tall and 20" long including his tail. | 彼の尾を含む13 長さ20"。 | しっぽを含み高さ13インチ、長さ20インチ。 | 20"
Measures approximately: 2 3/4 inches tall x 6 inches wide x 2 inches deep. | 高さ約2 3/4インチ×幅6インチ×深さ2インチ。 | サイズ：約2 3/4インチ（高）×6インチ（幅）×2インチ（奥行）。 | 6
HIS FINGER AND TOE NAILS HAVE BEEN GIVEN A BABY MANICURE AND SEALED. | 彼の指とTOEの は赤ん坊のマニキュアを与えられ、封印されている。 | 指と足の爪には赤ちゃん用のマニキュアが付けられてシールされています。 | TOE
The set includes ... Doll Body, Sports Bra, and Shorts. | セットは含まれています...人形の体、スポーツブラ、そしてショーツ。 | セットには、人形の体、スポーツブラ、そしてショーツが含まれます。 | ...
Antique Armand Marseille Doll 370 2 DEP 19 Inch. | Antique Armand Marseille Doll 370 2 DEP 19インチ | アンティークのArmand Marseille Doll 370 2 DEP 19インチ | Antique
Eyes very high quality Ethereal Angels Gumdrops 18mm Turquoise which are a 50.00 value. | 50.00値である非常に高品質のEthereal Angels Gumdrops 18mm Turquoise. | 目は高品質のEthereal Angels Gumdrops 18mmのトルコ石で、50.00の価値があります。 | Turquoise
PERHAPS YOU ARE THE DOLL COLLECTOR SHE HAS WAITED DECADES TO BELONG TO! | あなたはDOLL COLLECTOR SHEをお持ちですか？ | お客様は長年の人形のコレクターですね。 | DOLL COLLECTOR SHE
2 1/4" across chest.Pantaloons are 2 1/4" at waist (laying flat) & 2 1/2" long. | 胸部に2 1/4"。パンタロンはウエストで2 1/4"（平置き）&2 1/2"の長さです。 | 胸部に2 1/4インチ。パンタロンはウエストで2 1/4インチ（平置き）そして2 1/2インチの長さです。 | 1/4" 1/4"
DOLL MEASURES ABOUT 6 INCHES FROM HEAD TO TOE. | ヘッドからTOEまでの6インチについてのDOLL対策。 | 人形の頭からつま先までは約6インチ。 | DOLL

Examples (KO)

Source	MT output	PE output	Untranslated words that were corrected
HERMES HER BAG PM 2 in 1 2way Hand Bag Beige Black Toile H Officier G03570g	헤르메스 그녀의 가방 오후 2 에 1 2 way 핸드 백 베이지 블랙 토일 H Officier G03570g	에르메스 에르백 PM 투인원 손잡이 2개 핸드백 베이지 블랙 트왈 H 오피시어 G03570g	1 Officier
GUCCI Bamboo 2way Hand Tote Bag Brown Leather Italy Vintage Authentic AK31686e	구찌 대나무 2way 핸드 토트 백 브라운 레더 이탈리아 빈티지 정품 AK31686e	구찌 대나무 투웨이 핸드 토트백 브라운 레더 이탈리아 빈티지 정품 AK31686e	2way
EILEEN FISHER NWT $258 Silk Cotton Jersey Soft Tiered Maxi Skirt Size Large	아일린 피셔 NWT $258 실크 코튼 저지 소프트 티어 맥시 스커트 크기 큰	아일린 피셔 상표가 있는 새 상품 $258 실크 코튼 저지 소프트 티어드 맥시 스커트 사이즈 라지	NWT
Hanes Her Way 100% Cotton Briefs 6 Pair Value Pack Sz 9 High Waisted 1999 NOS	하네스 그녀의 방법 100% 면 브리프 6 페어 밸류 팩 Sz 9 하이 웨이스트 1999 NOS	Hanes Her Way 100% 면 브리프 6개 밸류 팩 사이즈 9 하이 웨이스트 1999 팔리지 않은 재고 상품	Sz NOS
issey miyake PLEATS PLEASE pleats tops women JPN size 3 MINT	이세이 미야케 플리즈 플리즈 탑 여성 JPN 사이즈 3 민트	이세이 미야케 플리즈 여성용 상의 일본 사이즈 3 상태 좋음	JPN
Versace Jeans Couture Womens Button Up Collar Blazer Jacket Red Wool Size EUR 44	베르사체 청바지 꾸뛰르 여성 버튼 업 칼라 블레이저 재킷 레드 울 사이즈 EUR 44	베르사체 진 꾸뛰르 여성 버튼 업 칼라 블레이저 재킷 빨간색 울 사이즈 유럽 44	EUR
Peace Love World Comfy Knit Jogger Pants Black M NEW A296572	평화 사랑 세계 편안한 니트 조거 팬츠 블랙 M NEW A296572	Peace Love World 편안한 니트 조거 팬츠 블랙 M 새 상품 A296572	NEW
Free People We The Free Main Squeeze Hacci Top Nectar Medium M NWT OB1013578	무료 사람들 우리는 무료 주요 짜기 Hacci 최고 넥타 중간 M NWT OB1013578	Free People We The Free 메인 스퀴즈 Hacci 상의 넥타르 미디엄 M 상표가 있는 새 상품 OB1013578	NWT
NIKE DRI-FIT SPORTS BRA WOMENS SIZE M RETAIL $60.00 SALE $35.00	나이키 DRI-FIT 스포츠 브래지어 여성 용 사이즈 M 소매 $60.00 판매 $35.00	나이키 드라이 핏 스포츠 브래지어 여성용 사이즈 M 소매 $60.00 세일 가격 $35.00	DRI-FIT
Lisa Rinna Collection Women's Top Sz XL Mesh Panel Knit Ivory A277013	리사 린나 컬렉션 여성 탑 Sz XL 메쉬 패널 니트 아이보리 A277013	Lisa Rinna Collection 여성 상의 사이즈 XL 메쉬 패널 니트 아이보리 A277013	Sz
Rag & Bone Jean Womens Skinny Pants Olive Green Size 26	걸레 & 본 진 여성 스키니 팬츠 올리브 그린 사이즈 26	랙앤본 진 여성 스키니 바지 올리브 그린 사이즈 26	&
Andrew Marc Women's Black Faux Suede Pull On Pants Size XL NWT ������	앤드류 마크 여성의 블랙 인조 스웨이드 풀 에 바지 크기 XL NWT	앤드류 마크 여성용 블랙 인조 스웨이드 풀온 팬츠 크기 XL 상표가 있는 새 상품	NWT
1794 Express Mid Rise Stretch Skinny Legging Jeans Sz 8 Short Black	1794 익스프레스 미드 라이즈 스트레치 스키니 레깅스 진 Sz 8 쇼트 블랙	1794 익스프레스 미드 라이즈 스판 스키니 레깅스 진 8 쇼트 블랙	Sz
TALBOTS Woman 100% cotton blouse 1/2 button 2x	TALBOTS 우먼 100% 코튼 블라우스 1/2 버튼 2x	탈보츠 여성용 100% 코튼 블라우스 1/2 버튼 2x	TALBOTS
AMERICAN EAGLE BRAND JEANS SZ 6 REG JEGGING SUPER STRETCH EUC !	아메리칸 이글 브랜드 청바지 SZ 6 REG 제깅 슈퍼 스트레치 EUC!	아메리칸 이글 브랜드 청바지 사이즈 6 레귤러 제깅스 슈퍼 스트레치 상태 좋음!	SZ REG
IMAN Global Chic Luxury Resort 3/4-Slv Draped Tunic Jet Black M # 597-689	IMAN 글로벌 시크 럭셔리 리조트 3/4-Slv 드레이프 튜닉 제트 블랙 M # 597-689	IMAN Global 시크 럭셔리 리조트 3/4-소매 드레이프드 튜닉 제트 블랙 M # 597-689	3/4-Slv
Jimmy Choo blue multi L6.5 R6 ankle strap platform sandal shoe NEW $995 MISMATCH	지미 추 블루 멀티 L6.5 R6 발목 스트랩 플랫폼 샌들 신발 NEW $995 미스매치	지미 추 블루 멀티 L6.5 R6 발목 스트랩 플랫폼 샌들 신발 신상 $995 미스매치	NEW
APT 9 Women's Lace Pullover Top Short Sleeve Stretch 3 Colors Size L NWT	APT 9 여성 레이스 풀오버 탑 반소매 스트레치 3 색 사이즈 L NWT	APT 9 여성 레이스 풀오버 상의 반소매 스트레치 3 색 사이즈 L 상표 있는 새 상품	NWT
AMERICAN EAGLE Skinny Super Stretch Denim Jeans, Women's Size 6, EUC!!	아메리칸 이글 스키니 슈퍼 스트레치 데님 청바지, 여성 사이즈 6, EUC!!	아메리칸 이글 스키니 슈퍼 스트레치 데님 청바지, 여성 사이즈 6, 상태 좋음!!	EUC!!

Examples (pt-BR):

- Translatable words were correctly translated

Source	MT output	PE output	Untranslated words that were corrected (should be translatable words)
Photo Albums	Photo Albums	Álbuns de fotografia	Photo Albums
Photo Booth	Photo Booth	Cabine de fotografia	Photo Booth
Photo Booth Props	Photo Booth Props	Adereços para cabine de fotografia	Photo Booth Props
Photo Card	Photo Card	Cartão com foto	Photo Card
Photo Favors	Photo Favors	Fotos para lembrancinha	Photo Favors
Photo Favors	Photo Favors	Fotos para lembrancinha	Photo Favors
Photo Gift	Photo Gift	Fotografia para presente	Photo Gift
Picnic Set	Picnic Set	Conjunto para piquenique	Picnic Set
Pictures/Phrases	Pictures/Phrases	Imagens/Frases	Pictures/Phrases
Pillow Top	Pillow Top	Almofada	Pillow Top
Pillows	Pillows	Travesseiros e almofadas	Pillows

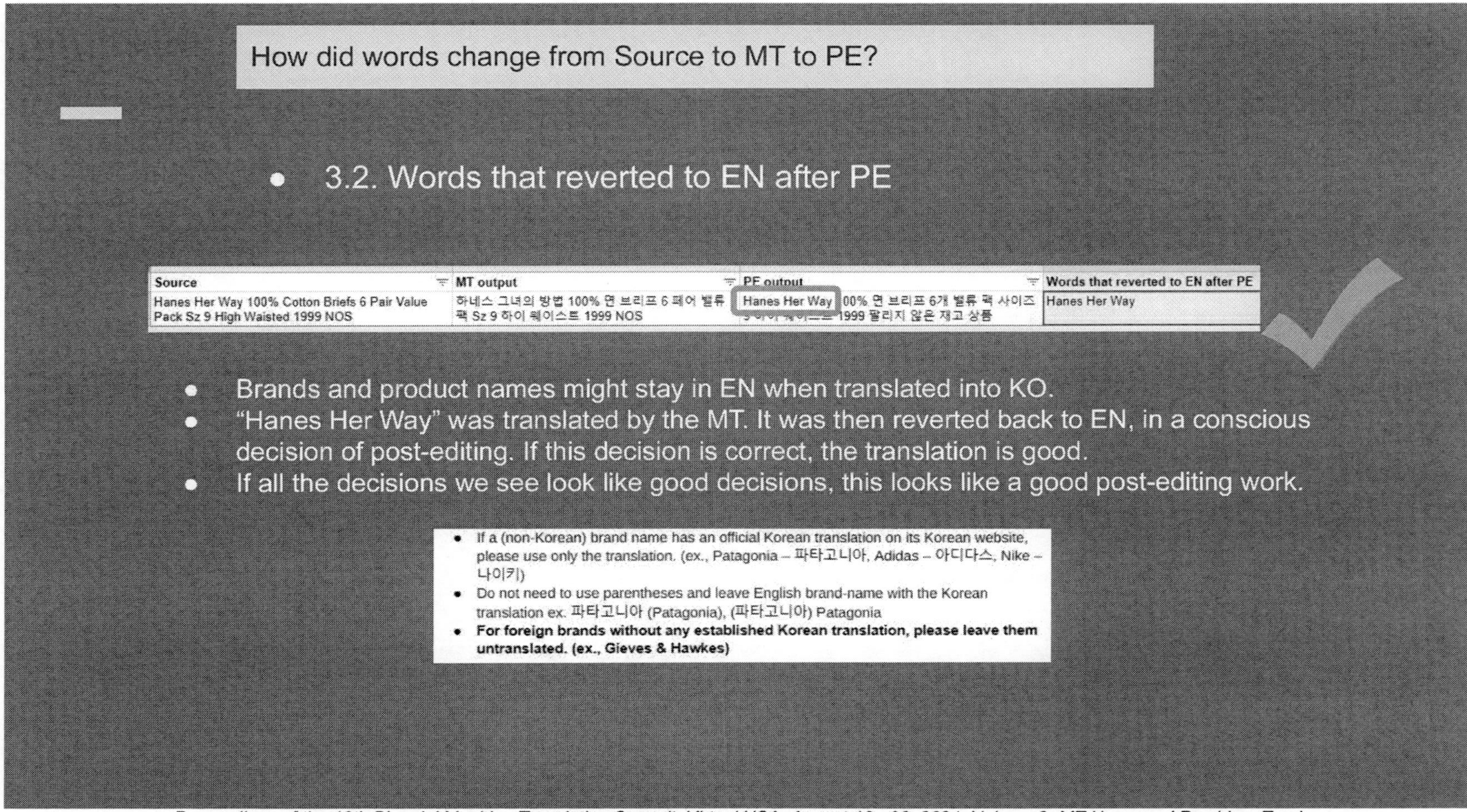
How did words change from Source to MT to PE?
3.2. Words that reverted to EN after PE
Source
Hanes Her Way 100% Cotton Briefs 6 Pair Value Pack Sz 9 High Waisted 1999 NOS
MT output
하네스 그녀의 방법 100% 면 브리프 6 페어 밸류 팩 Sz 9 하이 웨이스트 1999 NOS
PE output
Hanes Her Way 00% 면 브리프 6개 밸류 팩 사이즈 1999 팔리지 않은 재고 상품
Words that reverted to EN after PE
Hanes Her Way
Brands and product names might stay in EN when translated into KO.
"Hanes Her Way" was translated by the MT. It was then reverted back to EN, in a conscious decision of post-editing. If this decision is correct, the translation is good.
If all the decisions we see look like good decisions, this looks like a good post-editing work.
If a (non-Korean) brand name has an official Korean translation on its Korean website, please use only the translation. (ex., Patagonia – 파타고니아, Adidas – 아디다스, Nike – 나이키)
Do not need to use parentheses and leave English brand-name with the Korean translation ex. 파타고니아 (Patagonia), (파타고니아) Patagonia
For foreign brands without any established Korean translation, please leave them untranslated. (ex., Gieves & Hawkes)

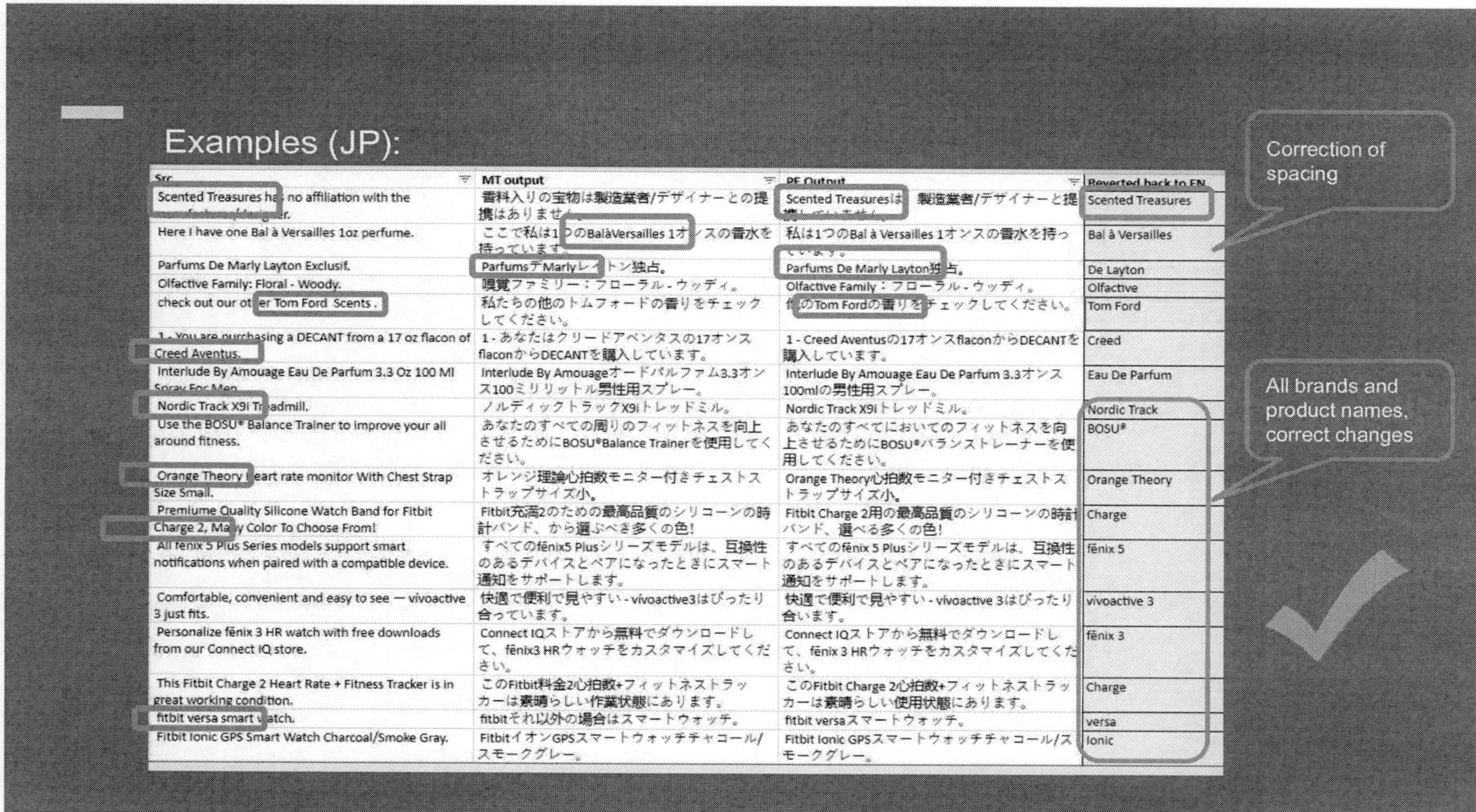

Src	MT output	PE Output	Reverted back to EN
Scented Treasures has no affiliation with the manufacturer/designer.	香料入りの宝物は製造業者/デザイナーとの提携はありません。	Scented Treasuresは　製造業者/デザイナーと提携していません。	Scented Treasures
Here I have one Bal à Versailles 1oz perfume.	ここで私は1つのBalàVersailles 1オンスの香水を持っています。	私は1つのBal à Versailles 1オンスの香水を持っています。	Bal à Versailles
Parfums De Marly Layton Exclusif.	Parfumsデ Marlyレイトン独占。	Parfums De Marly Layton独占。	De Layton
Olfactive Family: Floral - Woody.	嗅覚ファミリー：フローラル - ウッディ。	Olfactive Family：フローラル - ウッディ。	Olfactive
check out our other Tom Ford Scents .	私たちの他のトムフォードの香りをチェックしてください。	他のTom Fordの香りをチェックしてください。	Tom Ford
1 - You are purchasing a DECANT from a 17 oz flacon of Creed Aventus.	1 - あなたはクリードアベンタスの17オンスflaconからDECANTを購入しています。	1 - Creed Aventusの17オンスflaconからDECANTを購入しています。	Creed
Interlude By Amouage Eau De Parfum 3.3 Oz 100 Ml Spray For Men.	Interlude By Amouageオードパルファム3.3オンス100ミリリットル男性用スプレー。	Interlude By Amouage Eau De Parfum 3.3オンス100mlの男性用スプレー。	Eau De Parfum
Nordic Track X9i Treadmill.	ノルディックトラックX9iトレッドミル。	Nordic Track X9iトレッドミル。	Nordic Track
Use the BOSU® Balance Trainer to improve your all around fitness.	あなたのすべての周りのフィットネスを向上させるためにBOSU®Balance Trainerを使用してください。	あなたのすべてにおいてのフィットネスを向上させるためにBOSU®バランストレーナーを使用してください。	BOSU®
Orange Theory Heart rate monitor With Chest Strap Size Small.	オレンジ理論心拍数モニター付きチェストストラップサイズ小。	Orange Theory心拍数モニター付きチェストストラップサイズ小。	Orange Theory
Premiume Quality Silicone Watch Band for Fitbit Charge 2, Many Color To Choose From!	Fitbit充满2のための最高品質のシリコーンの時計バンド、から選ぶべき多くの色!	Fitbit Charge 2用の最高品質のシリコーンの時計バンド、選べる多くの色!	Charge
All fēnix 5 Plus Series models support smart notifications when paired with a compatible device.	すべてのfēnix5 Plusシリーズモデルは、互換性のあるデバイスとペアになったときにスマート通知をサポートします。	すべてのfēnix 5 Plusシリーズモデルは、互換性のあるデバイスとペアになったときにスマート通知をサポートします。	fēnix 5
Comfortable, convenient and easy to see — vivoactive 3 just fits.	快適で便利で見やすい - vivoactive3はぴったり合っています。	快適で便利で見やすい - vivoactive 3はぴったり合います。	vivoactive 3
Personalize fēnix 3 HR watch with free downloads from our Connect IQ store.	Connect IQストアから無料でダウンロードして、fēnix3 HRウォッチをカスタマイズしてください。	Connect IQストアから無料でダウンロードして、fēnix 3 HRウォッチをカスタマイズしてください。	fēnix 3
This Fitbit Charge 2 Heart Rate + Fitness Tracker is in great working condition.	このFitbit料金2心拍数+フィットネストラッカーは素晴らしい作業状態にあります。	このFitbit Charge 2心拍数+フィットネストラッカーは素晴らしい使用状態にあります。	Charge
fitbit versa smart watch.	fitbitそれ以外の場合はスマートウォッチ。	fitbit versaスマートウォッチ。	versa
Fitbit Ionic GPS Smart Watch Charcoal/Smoke Gray.	Fitbitイオン GPSスマートウォッチチャコール/スモークグレー。	Fitbit Ionic GPSスマートウォッチチャコール/スモークグレー。	Ionic

How did words change from Source to MT to PE?

- 3.3. Words that were untranslated and left untranslated

Source	MT output	PE output	Words left untranslated (should be untranslatable)
Nike Kobe AD TB Promo Men's Basketball Shoes, 942521 801 Size 7 NEW	나이키 고베 AD TB 프로모션 남성 농구 신발, 942521 801 사이즈 7 NEW	나이키 코비 AD TB 프로모션 남성 농구화 942521 801 사이즈 7 새 상품	AD TB 942521 801 7
Seven 7 FOR ALL MANKIND Men's Relaxed Fit Button Fly Denim Jeans Pants Sz 36x33	세븐 7 모든 인류 남성용 릴렉스 핏 버튼 플라이 데님 청바지 팬츠 Sz 36x33	세븐 7 모든 인류 남성용 편안하게 착용할 수 있는 버튼 플라이 데님 청바지 팬츠 사이즈 36x33	7 36x33
Rare 2001 Tomb Raider Lara Croft Movie Promo t-shirt mens 2XL Made USA Vintage	희귀 2001 톰 레이더 라라 크로프트 영화 프로모션 티셔츠 남성 2XL 만든 미국 빈티지	희귀한 2001 톰 레이더 라라 크로프트 영화 프로모션 티셔츠 남성 2XL 원산지 미국 빈티지	2001 2XL

- Codes, year and sizes might stay in EN when translated into KO.

Examples (pt-BR)

Aspect	Category	Source	MT output	PE output	Words left untranslated (should be untranslatable)
Type	Party. Celebration & Occasion Supply	Banner	Banner	Banner	Banner
Type	Party, Celebration & Occasion Supply	Banner	Banner	Banner	Banner

Source	MT output	PE output	Untranslated words that were corrected (should be translatable words)	Words that reverted to EN after PE (should be untranslatable)	Words left untranslated (should be untranslatable)
ACME Christa	ACME Christa	ACME Christa			ACME Christa
ACME Christella	ACME Christella	ACME Christella			ACME Christella
ACME Colt	ACME Colt	ACME Colt			ACME Colt
ACME Commerce	ACME Commerce	ACME Commerce			ACME Commerce
ACME Cyrille	ACME Cyrille	ACME Cyrille			ACME Cyrille
ACME Danville	ACME Danville	ACME Danville			ACME Danville

Final Thoughts

Does the Longitudinal Review align with the Sample Review results?

- Not always. For one data set:
  - The gaps in PE were not detected with a sample revi
- However:
  - 14 passes on Longitudinal matched 14 passes on Sample.
- So, Longitudinal got:
  - aligned in 14 cases
  - better detection in 1 case

Takeaways

- These checks cover the entire content in a systematic way.
- They can spot issues that a sample review would not spot.
- They can give insights to non-speakers.
- They might <u>not</u> be a definitive statement of final quality.
- But they do enhance the confidence on the quality evaluation.

Thank you!

MT Summit 2021

James Phillips
Director

PCT Translation Division, WIPO

August 2021

WIPO
WORLD
INTELLECTUAL PROPERTY
ORGANIZATION

Outline: Main Topics

- (A)MTQE
- Neural Machine Translation Evaluation

WIPO
WORLD
INTELLECTUAL PROPERTY
ORGANIZATION

PCT Translation Division

- Translation of patent abstracts and patentability reports
- From: AR, DE, EN, ES, FR, JA, KO, PT, RU, ZH (10 languages)
- Into: EN, FR
- 680,000 translations / 183 million translated words in 2020
- In-house translators + outsourcing (91%)
- CAT tools

WIPO FOR OFFICIAL USE ONLY

WIPO

WIPO translation technology stack

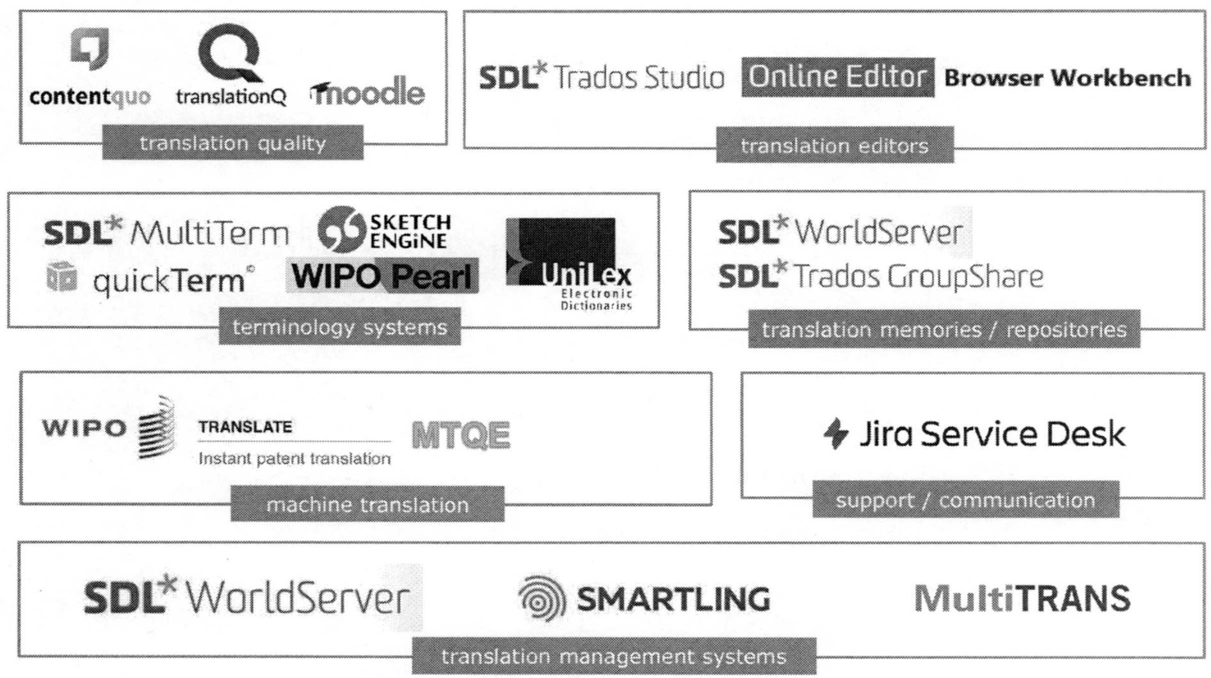

WIPO FOR OFFICIAL USE ONLY

WIPO

WorldServer high-level architeture

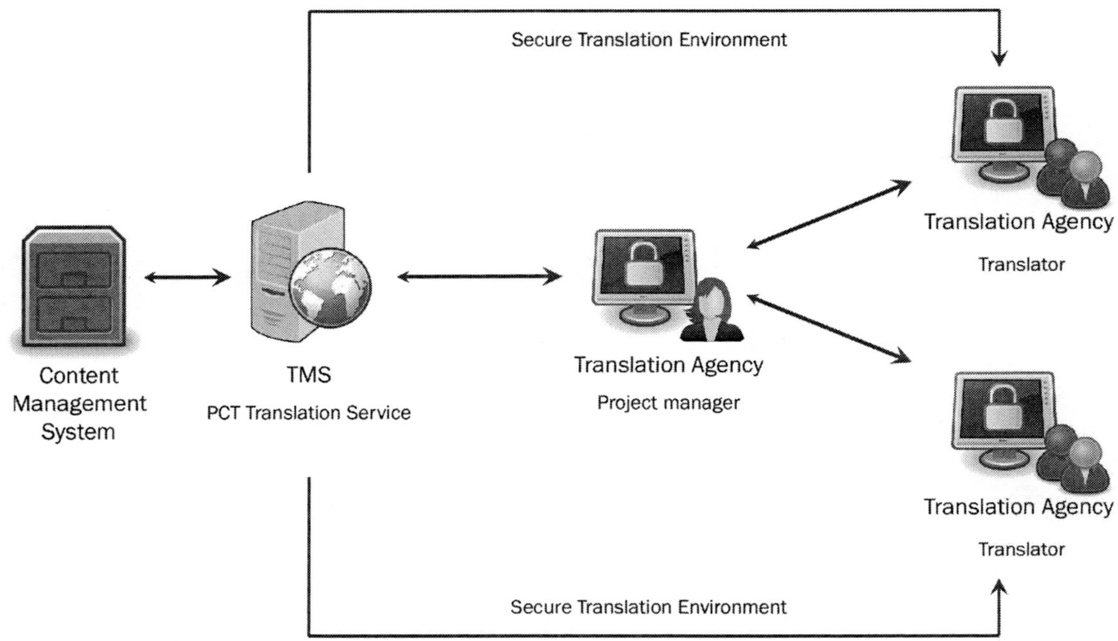

WorldServer high-level architeture

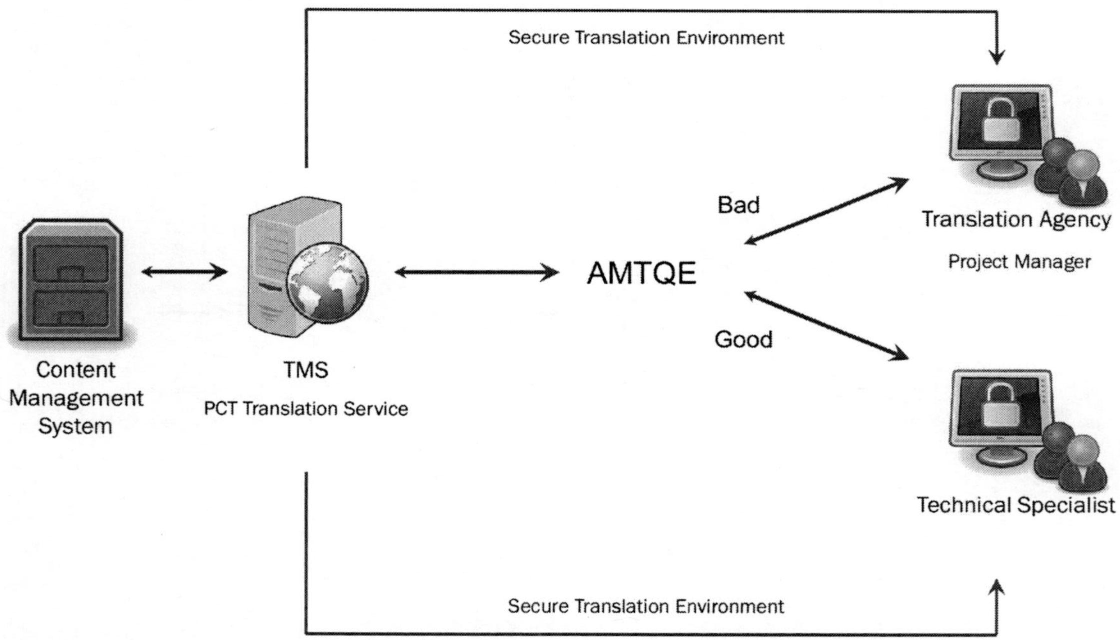

WIPO FOR OFFICIAL USE ONLY

WIPO

Post-editing at WIPO-PCT

Could visually observe that some of the machine translations were good and decided to try to identify them.

Started collecting triplets (source, NMT output, final agency translation) in 2016. Took six months to build-up sufficient triplets.

Initially difficult to confirm quality threshold at which post-editing becomes feasible. This evaluation process has now been refined.

Decided to attempt AMTQE (Automatic Machine Translation Quality Estimation) using the QuEst framework by Lucia Specia.

AMTQE score distribution & human evaluation

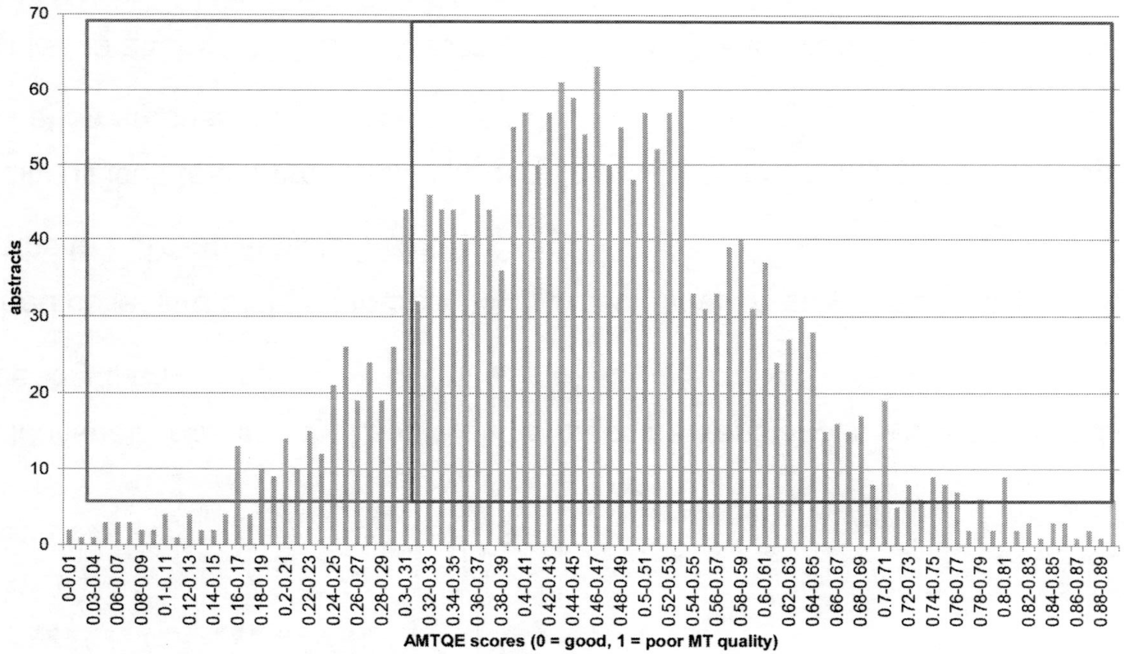

WIPO FOR OFFICIAL USE ONLY

WIPO

AMTQE

- 3 human evaluation rounds conducted to determine reliability of AMTQE score.
- Evaluators asked to think in number of necessary post-edits.

- Threshold of 0.3 identified
  - AMTQE scores of < 0.3 effectively correlate well with translators' perception of good MT quality for documents of up to 50 words in length.
  - Strong correlation between document length and good AMTQE score.

Post-editing at WIPO-PCT

Project 1: Post-editing by Technical Specialists

- Technical specialists (not translators) only given documents in their field.
- Combination of Automatic Machine Translation Quality Estimation score and IPC routing could potentially mean we could adopt post-editing without a dip in quality.

Recruiting challenges

- Recruitment and testing procedures were gradually refined.
- Providing training without imparting bias critical.
- Incorporating translation guidelines into WorldServer glossary extremely helpful.

Post-editors : Impact of MTQE on QC results (2018-2020)

Post-editor	Start date	MTQE introduction date	QC volume Q1-Q2 2018			QC sores Q1-Q2 2018		QC volumes Q3-Q4 2018			QC scores Q3-Q4 2018		Difference Q1-Q2 2018 vs. Q3-Q4 2018
			Vol	A	NA	A	NA	Vol	A	NA	A	NA	
PE1	Q1 2018	Q3 2018	59	37	22	63%	**37%**	22	12	10	55%	**45%**	-8%
PE2	Q1 2018	Q3 2018	70	44	26	63%	**37%**	39	21	18	54%	**46%**	-9%
PE3	Q1 2018	Q3 2018	86	62	24	72%	**28%**	59	49	10	83%	**17%**	11%
PE4	Q1 2018	Q3 2018	93	66	27	71%	**29%**	65	58	7	89%	**11%**	18%
PE5	Q1 2018	Q3 2018	53	39	14	74%	**26%**	58	49	9	84%	**16%**	11%
PE6	Q1 2018	Q3 2018	65	46	19	71%	**29%**	45	43	2	96%	**4%**	25%
PE7	Q1 2018	Q3 2018	108	84	24	78%	**22%**	66	59	7	89%	**11%**	12%
Post-editor	**Start date**	**MTQE introduction date**	**QC volume Q1 2020**			**QC sores Q1 2020**		**QC volume Q2-Q3-Q4 2020**			**QC scores Q2-Q3-Q4 2020**		**Difference Q1 vs. Q2-Q3-Q4 2020**
			Vol	A	NA	A	NA	Vol	A	NA	A	NA	
PE8	Q1 2020	Q1 2020	46	34	12	74%	**26%**	107	89	18	83%	**17%**	9%
PE9	Q1 2020	Q1 2020	53	26	27	49%	**51%**	24	9	15	38%	**63%**	-12%
PE10	Q2 2020	Q1 2020	53	48	5	91%	**9%**	107	98	9	92%	**9%**	1%
PE11	Q1 2020	Q1 2020	38	16	22	42%	**58%**	29	20	9	69%	**45%**	27%
PE12	Q1 2020	Q1 2020	46	34	12	74%	**26%**	107	102	5	95%	**5%**	21%
PE13	Q1 2020	Q2 2020	22	11	11	50%	**50%**	68	50	18	74%	**36%**	24%

WIPO FOR OFFICIAL USE ONLY

WIPO

Post-editing at WIPO-PCT

Project 2 : Light post-editing

Instigated from the bottom-up as a result of observations by the translators

Use internal resources

5 to 6 days of work/week

Preselection of abstracts

Only abstracts with good MT are (lightly) post-edited

500 abstracts translations per week under project 1

WIPO FOR OFFICIAL USE ONLY

WIPO

NMT Evaluation

Evaluate multiple engines and translator profiles

Minimum Team: Senior Translator, Junior translator, external translator, multiple engines, minimum two revisers (must be different people)

Penalty scoring system: 4 point deduction for major error, 0.5 points for minor error

Recently published documents only (two weeks)

Ten documents minimum (same field)

Error Categories

	Error Categories (Major/Minor Errors Applied)		Document or sentence level?	
1	Meaning	Over-translation: more specific. Under-translation: less specific. Verity: contradictions that are not pivotal language. Mistranslations	Sent.	
2	Terminology		Sent.	Doc.
3	English usage	Poor/incorrect English usage	Sent.	
4	Omission/Addition	Addition Omission	Sent.	
5	Consistency		Sent.	Doc.
6	Proof-reading/Spelling	Numbers, citations, reference signs, spelling errors, currency, dates, names, etc.	Sent.	Doc.
7	Clarity	Penalty if difficult to understand, misleading, or ambiguous.	Sent.	
8	Fluency	Penalty if not fluent. How smoothly does it read? To be restricted to being a minor error only when the sentence does not read smoothly at all. It could, for example, be grammatically correct, accurate, and clear, but quite painful to read, which would incur a fluency penalty.	Sent.	
9	Pivotal Language (Reports Only)	Contradictions that are pivotal to the document. i.e. calling something novel when the document says not novel. To be classed as a critical error.		

WIPO FOR OFFICIAL USE ONLY

WIPO

ABS-FR-EN-NMT-eval Google
4.5 / 10
evisions > 01ELEC0920 > ABS-FR-EN-NMT-eval Google
1
DISPOSITIF D'AFFICHAGE, APPAREIL DE TÉLÉVISION OU MONITEUR D'ORDINATEUR UTILISANT UN TEL DISPOSITIF D'AFFICHAGE
DISPLAY DEVICE, TELEVISION DEVICE, OR COMPUTER MONITOR USING SUCH DISPLAY DEVICE
2
Dispositif d'affichage (1) comprenant depuis une face avant (1av) et vers une face arrière (1ar), une dalle (2), un plan de masse (3), et une unité de traitement (4) reliée à la dalle et comprenant une antenne de réception et/ou émission d'une onde pour une connexion à un réseau sans fil.
Display device (1) comprising from a front face (1av) and towards a rear face (1ar), a panel (2), a ground plane (3), and a processing unit (4) connected to the panel and comprising an antenna for receiving and / or transmitting a wave for connection to a wireless network.
3
Le dispositif d'affichage comprend en outre une pluralité d'éléments réglables (6) reliés à l'unité de traitement, chaque élément réglable ayant une impédance qui peut être modifiée par l'unité de traitement pour modifier la manière dont l'onde
The display device further comprises a plurality of adjustable elements (6) connected to the processing unit, each adjustable element having an impedance which can be changed by the processing unit to change the way the wave is
ITEMS
FEEDBACK
SCORE
#
Item
Correction
Category
Score
1
DISPLAY DEVICE, TELEVISION
DISPLAY DEVICE, AND TELEVISION
7 - Clarity
-0.5
Yes
No
1
TELEVISION DEVICE
TELEVISION SET
2 - Terminology
0
Yes
No
1
DISPLAY DEVICE, TELEVISION DEVICE,
DISPLAY DEVICE, AND TELEVISION SET OR
7 - Clarity
-0.5
Yes
No

	Average	Abs. 1	Abs. 2	Abs. 3	Abs. 4	Abs. 5	Abs. 6	Abs. 7	Abs. 8	Abs. 9	Abs.10
Difficulty		E	D	E	E	M	D	M	M	M	D
Senior Translator	9.75	10	10	10	10	9.5	8.5	10	10	9.5	10
Junior Translator	9.45	10	8	9	10	10	8	10	10	9.5	10
Agency Translator	8.55	8.5	8.5	8.5	9.5	8.5	7	8	9	9.5	8.5
Engine 1	-2.85	4.5	-13	-1.5	9	1	-20	4.5	-0.5	0	-12.5
Engine 2	-3.9	8	-7.5	-2	7.5	-1.5	-23	8	-10	3	-21.5
Engine 3	-5.55	-3.5	-8	2	-2	5	-16.5	0.5	-3.5	0	-29.5
Engine 4	-6.5	0	-8.5	-2.5	-6	-3.5	-20.5	3.5	-17	-1.5	-9
Engine 5	-15.85	3	-11.5	-11	-8.5	-5.5	-39.5	-14.5	-18	-17	-36

WIPO FOR OFFICIAL USE ONLY

WIPO

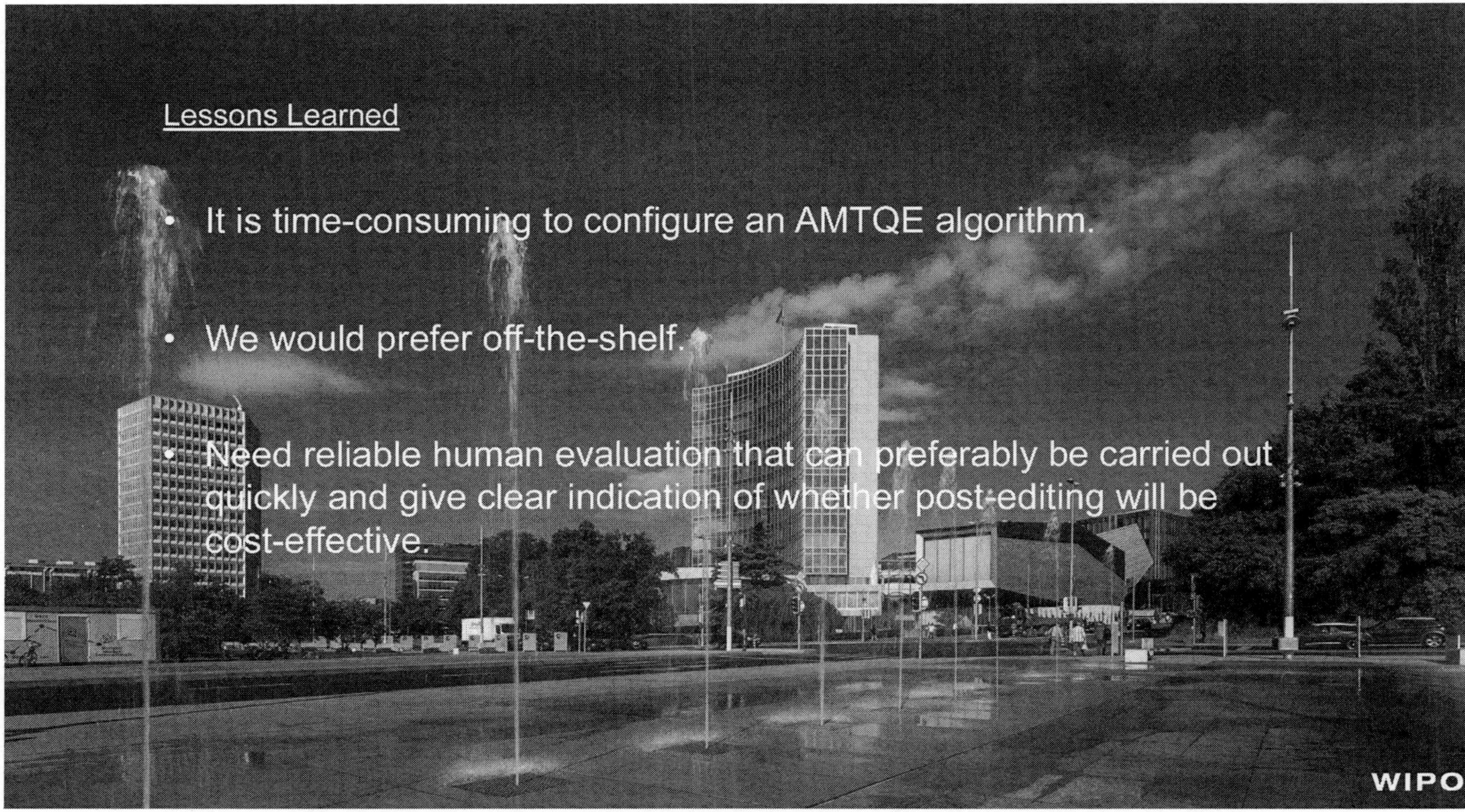
Lessons Learned
• It is time-consuming to configure an AMTQE algorithm.
• We would prefer off-the-shelf.
• Need reliable human evaluation that can preferably be carried out quickly and give clear indication of whether post-editing will be cost-effective.
WIPO

Thank you!

james.phillips@wipo.int

laurent.gottardo@wipo.int

Photo credits:

MT Human Evaluation
Insights & Approaches
Paula Manzur
vistatec

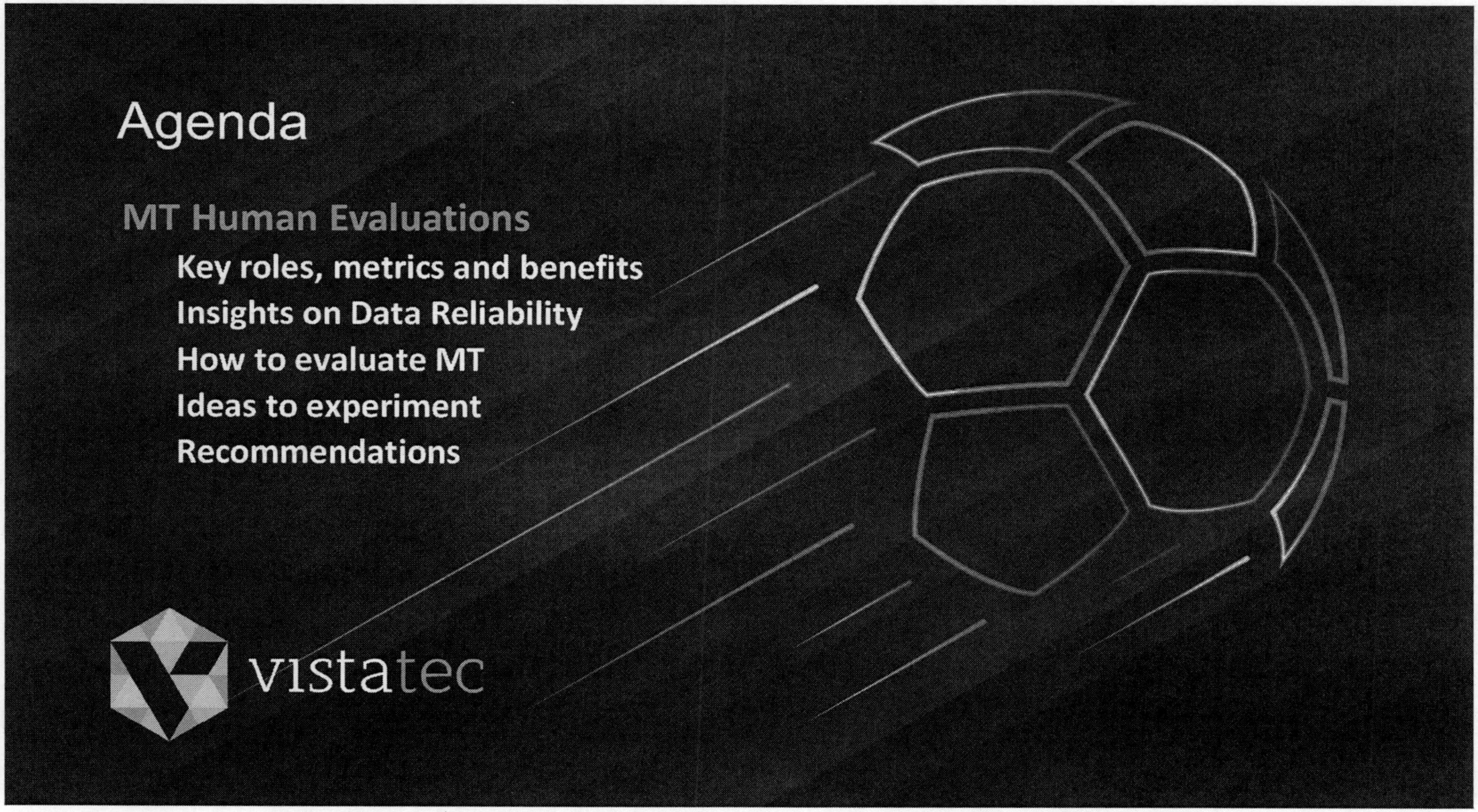
Agenda
MT Human Evaluations
Key roles, metrics and benefits
Insights on Data Reliability
How to evaluate MT
Ideas to experiment
Recommendations
vistatec

MT Human Evaluations

vistatec

Key roles

MT quality assessment of one or more engines for future implementation in localization workflow and for MT engine improvement. Collaborate with Customer on Quality Expectations

---

Use data to negotiate buy/sell MTPE rates (which need to be aligned with MT quality output) with Customers and Translators – even for baseline engines

MT Human Evaluations

vistatec

Key metrics	Automatic Metrics (e.g. BLEU, METEOR, TER)	Human Assessment (by error annotation, classification, corrections to the target text)
Key benefits	Allow translators (who will become post-editors) to get involved in the validation of the MT system	Allow Customers to make an informed decision on MT implementation with reliable data

Think Global

MT Human Evaluations
Insights on Data Reliability

vistatec

MT Automatic Metrics

Objective

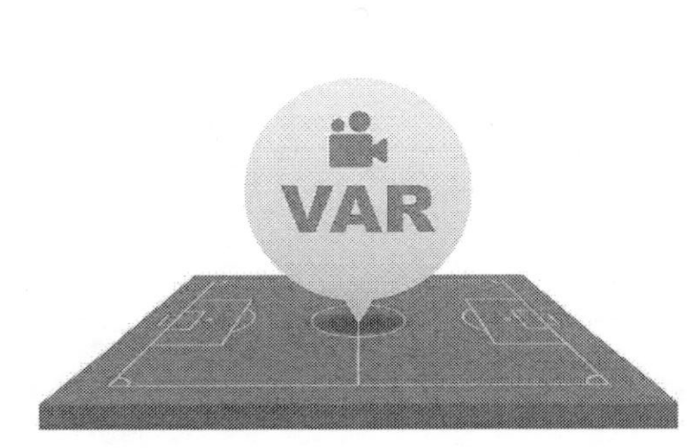

Human Assessment

Subjective

MT Human Evaluations
Insights on Data Reliability

vistatec

- Automatic metrics need a reference, a "golden" human translation – *only one "correct" translation is possible otherwise the score will go down.*
- Human assessment can be done without a golden reference – *more than one "correct" translation possible?*
- What makes a translation to be "the correct one" if there are different ways to translate the same sentence? – *there might be other options that are "good enough" for the use case.*

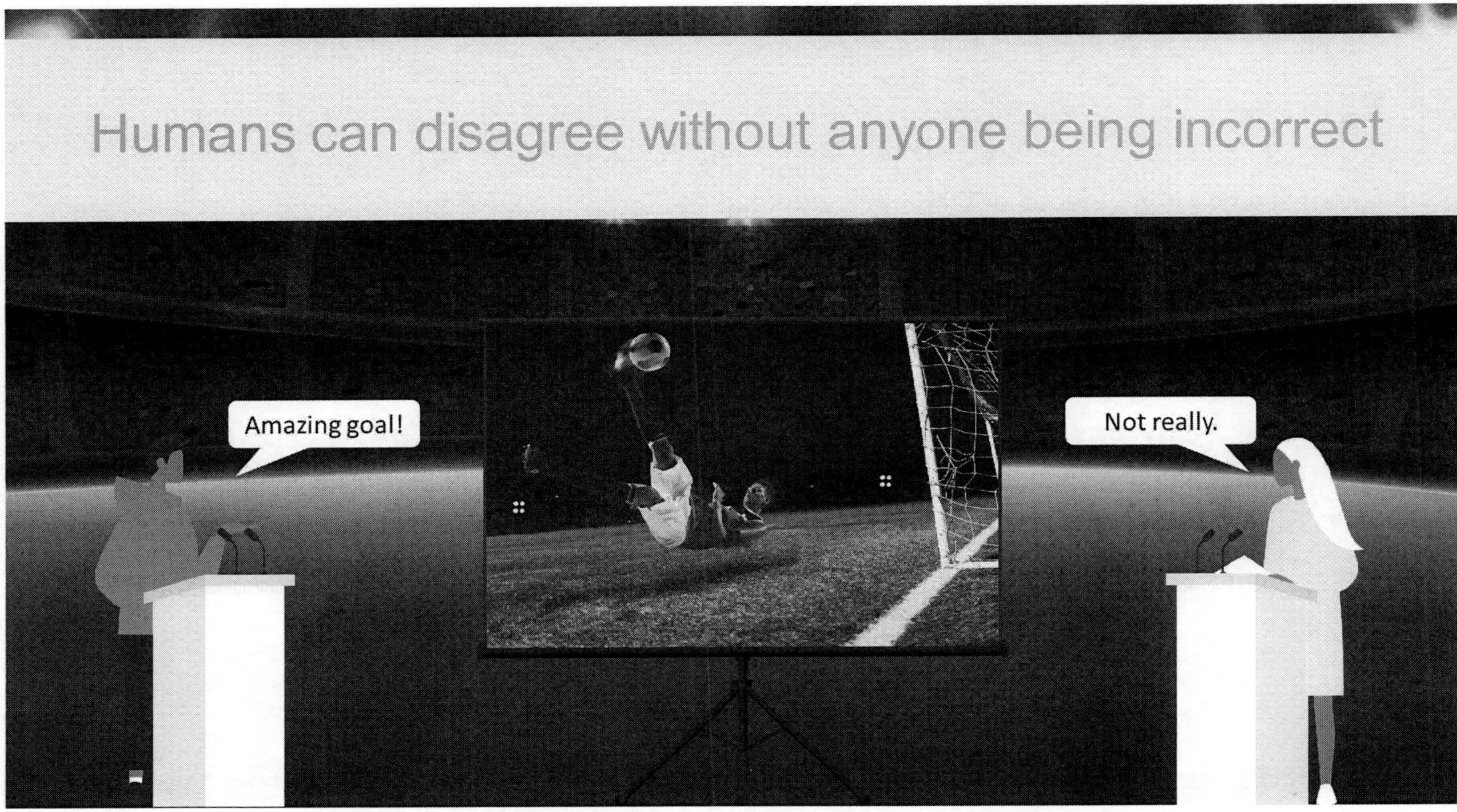
Humans can disagree without anyone being incorrect
Amazing goal!
Not really.

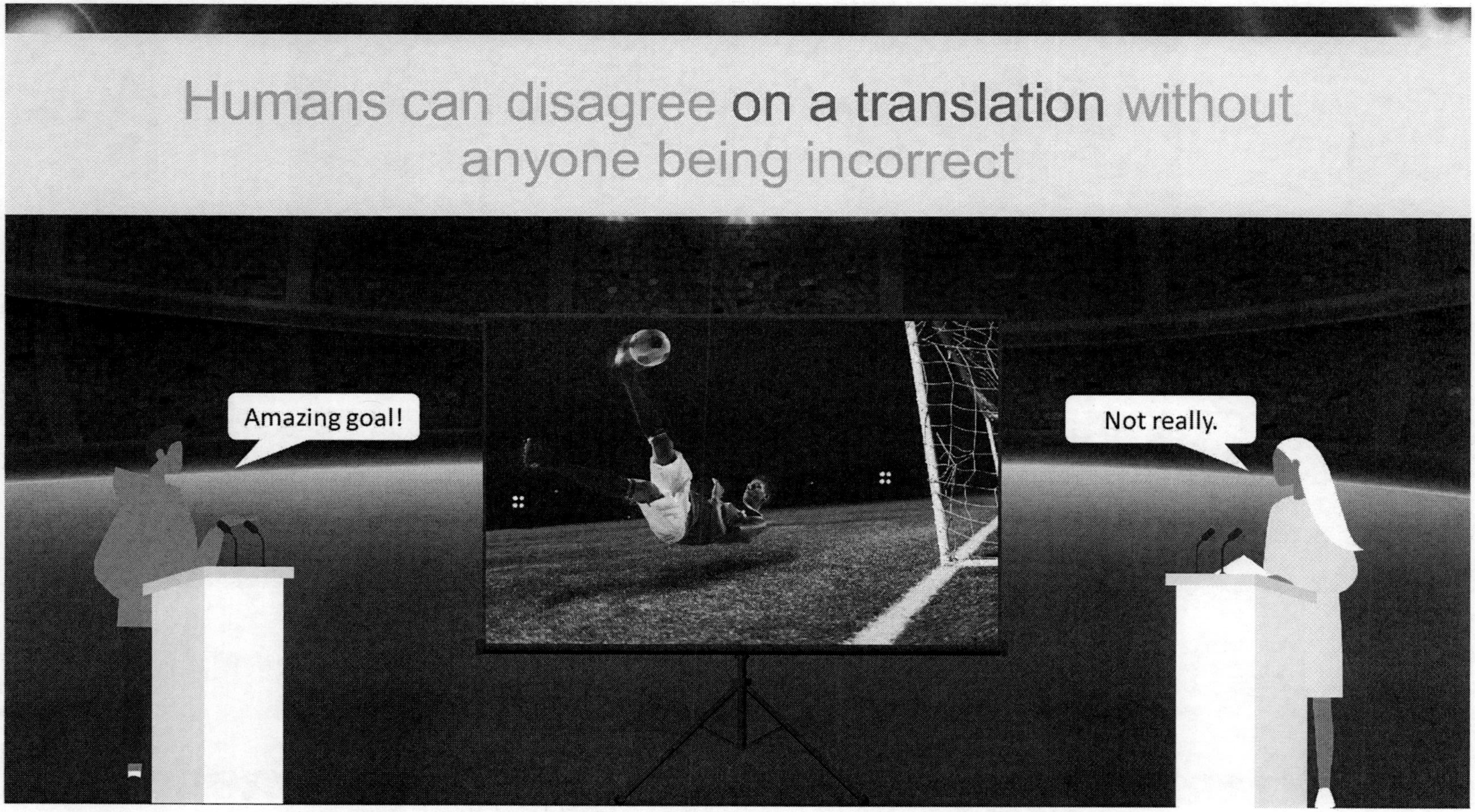
Humans can disagree on a translation without anyone being incorrect
Amazing goal!
Not really.

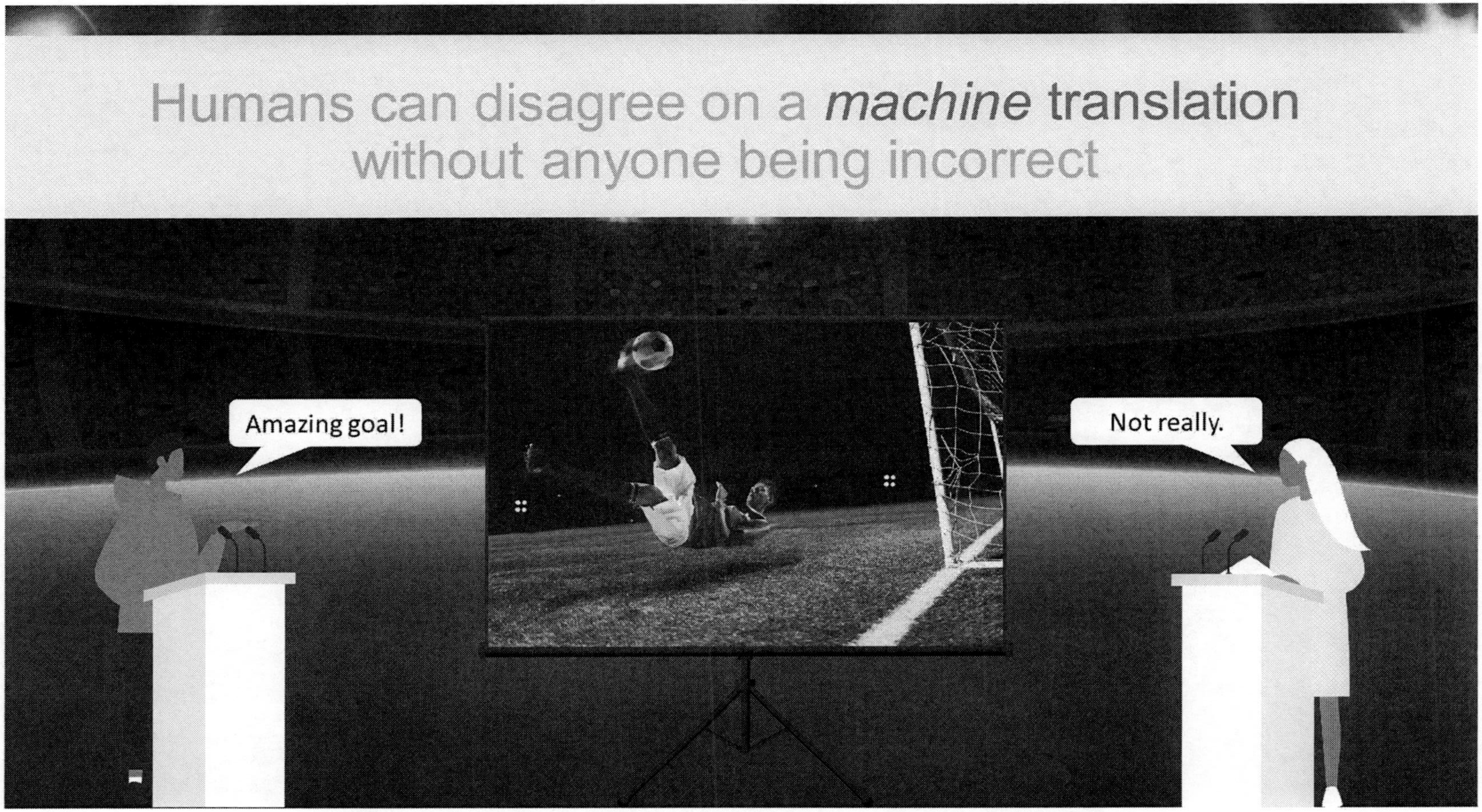
Humans can disagree on a *machine* translation
without anyone being incorrect
Amazing goal!
Not really.

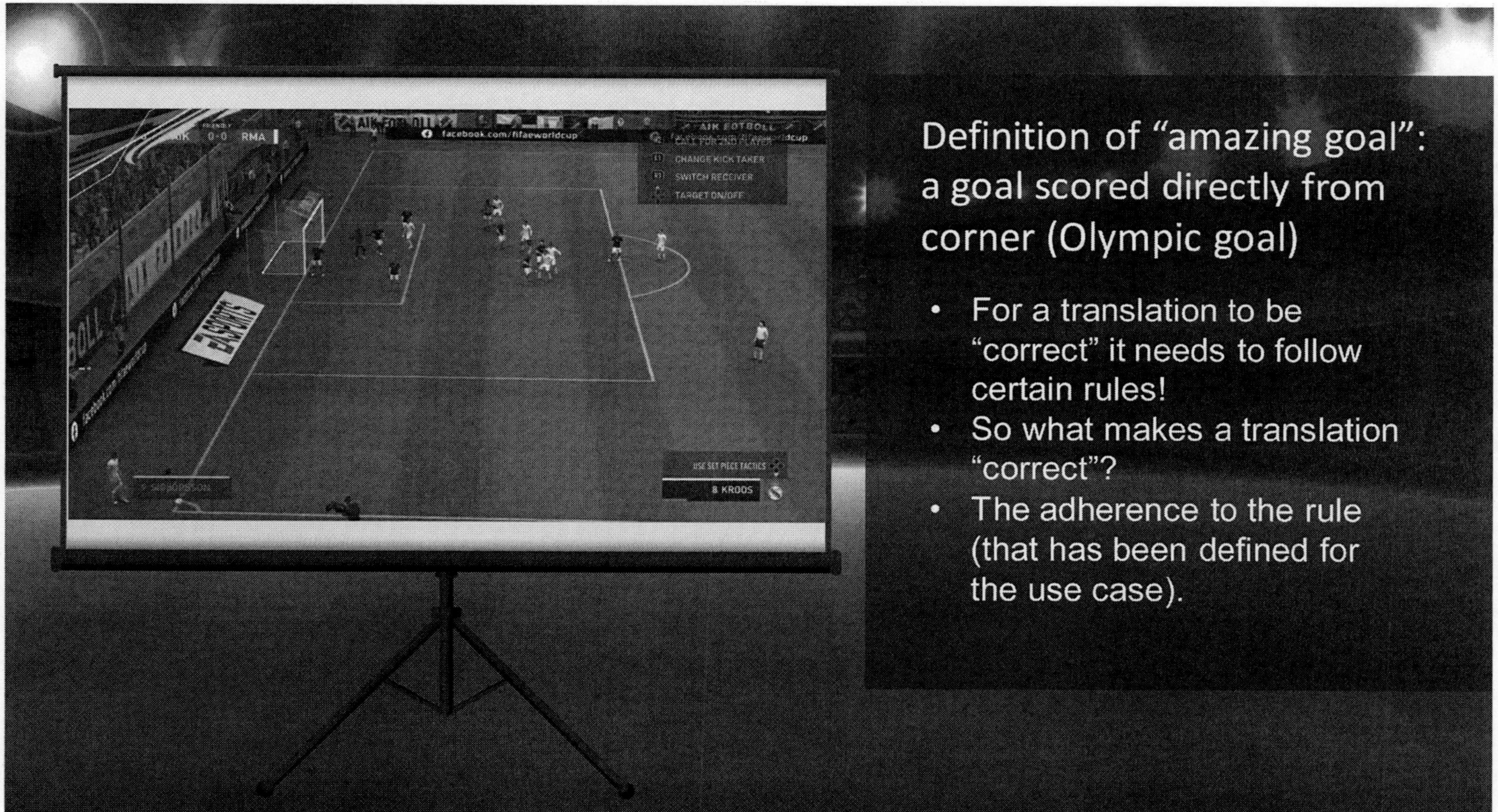
Definition of “amazing goal”: a goal scored directly from corner (Olympic goal)
• For a translation to be “correct” it needs to follow certain rules!
• So what makes a translation “correct”?
• The adherence to the rule (that has been defined for the use case).

When MT is involved, why and where do we (humans) apply rules?
Un gol olímpico es lo más espectacular visto en el fútbol.
An Olympic goal is the most spectacular sight in football.
An Olympic goal is the most amazing sight in soccer.
An Olympic goal is the most amazing thing seen in football.
Olympic goals are the most fantastic sight in soccer.

How to evaluate MT then? Again, with rules!

vistatec

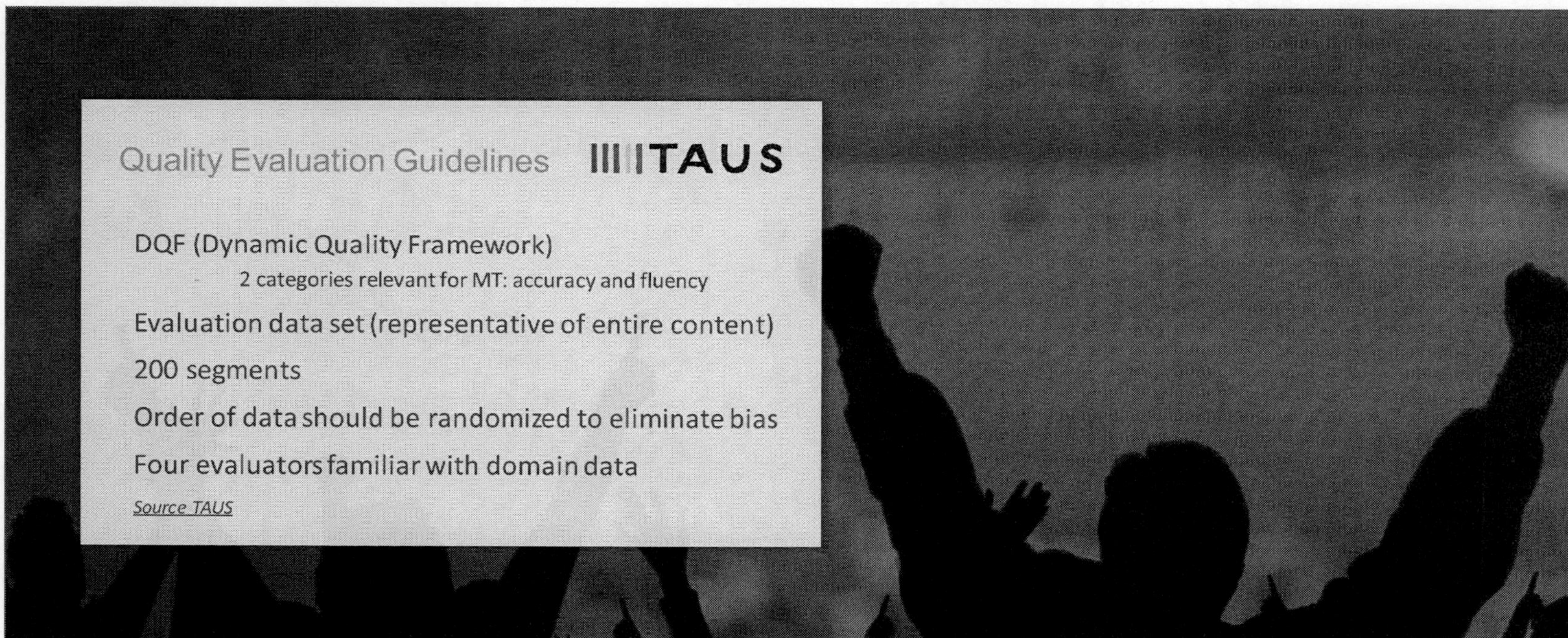

How much of these guidelines can we follow in practice?

vistatec

Quality Evaluation Guidelines

TAUS

DQF (Dynamic Quality Framework)

- 2 categories relevant for MT: accuracy and fluency

Evaluation data set (representative of entire content)

200 segments

Order of data should be randomized to eliminate bias

Four evaluators familiar with domain data

Source TAUS

- Other categories might be relevant for the use case, such as Compliance and style.
- Is there a "perfect" evaluation data set? Why not a pilot project with Post-Editing in CAT?
- Budget and time might be a constraint. Usually 1 hour as allocated time for error annotation.
- If you randomize data, translators might ask for context. But can include a mix of sentences as long as they're from the same domain.
- Budget and time constraints again. Usually 2 evaluators is possible, a 3rd could be a Language Specialist on Customer's side.

Some Ideas to Experiment

vistatec

A common error from MT is related to Gender Bias:

Source	**Target – Raw MT**	**Target – Post Edited**
Marie Curie was born in Warsaw. The distinguished scientist received the nobel prize in 1903 and 1911.	Marie Curie nació en Varsovia. El distinguido científico recibió el premio Nobel en 1903 y 1911.	Marie Curie nació en Varsovia. La distinguida científica recibió el premio Nobel en 1903 y 1911.

Diff. between the versions

Marie Curie nació en Varsovia.
La distinguida científica ~~El distinguido científico~~
recibió el premio Nobel en 1903 y 1911.

In this example, MT is still comprehensible, and mostly usable up to a certain point – general idea can be understood but is not grammatically correct

Some Ideas to Experiment

vistatec

During Human Evaluation all is left is to choose an Error Category and Scoring:

Diff. between the versions

Marie Curie nació en Varsovia.
La distinguida científica ~~El distinguido científico~~
recibió el premio Nobel en 1903 y 1911.

Primary Issue	Scoring
Language - Grammar, syntax	3-Mostly comprehensible and fluent, 1-2 minor issues; mostly usable

Evaluators see the errors they fixed and annotate the type of error

This data allow us to assess the level of MT usability to identify efficiency gains

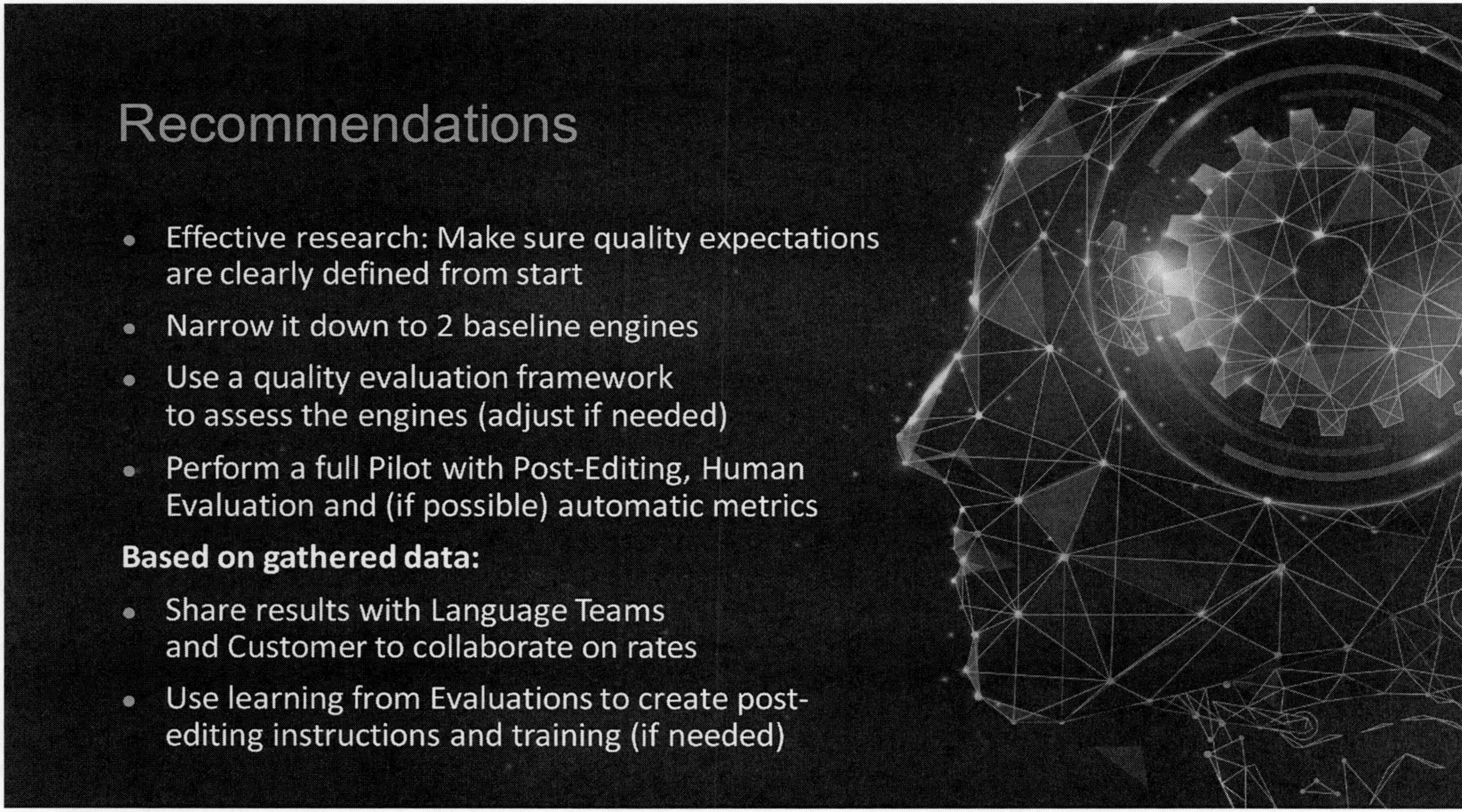
Recommendations
Effective research: Make sure quality expectations are clearly defined from start
Narrow it down to 2 baseline engines
Use a quality evaluation framework to assess the engines (adjust if needed)
Perform a full Pilot with Post-Editing, Human Evaluation and (if possible) automatic metrics
Based on gathered data:
Share results with Language Teams and Customer to collaborate on rates
Use learning from Evaluations to create post-editing instructions and training (if needed)

Thank You
Paula Manzur
Paula.Manzur@vistatec.com
Vistatec Machine Translation Team
VistatecMT@vistatec.com
vistatec

A Rising Tide Lifts All Boats?

Quality Correlation between Human Translation (HT) and Machine Assisted Translation (MAT)

EVELYN YANG GARLAND, CT

RONY GAO, CT

Introduction

- Does the human who produces the best translation without MT also produce the best translation with the assistance of MT?
- Are translation and post-editing completely different skills?
- Is “human + machine” always better than machine alone in terms of quality?

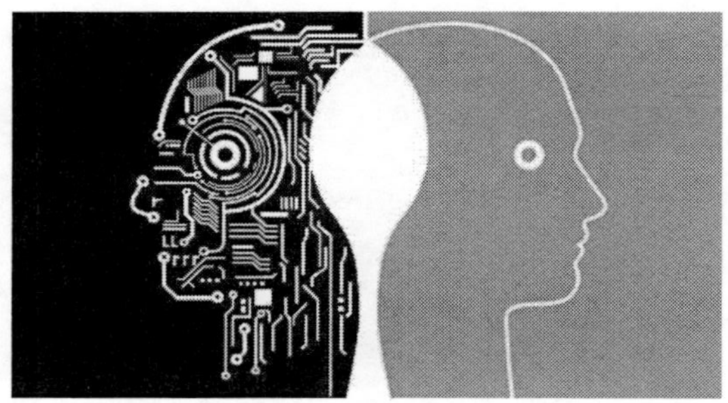

Methodology

- Main hypothesis: positive correlation between HT quality and MAT quality
- Subjects: 8 volunteers (English-to-Chinese translation practice group)
- Source Texts: two 250-word passages in English similar in style and difficulty level
  - Passage A. Human Translation (HT): MT tools NOT allowed
  - Passage B. Machine-Assisted Translation (MAT): one MT version provided as reference; all other MT tools allowed
- Quality Evaluation: ATA grading framework

Results 1: Correlation between HT and MAT?

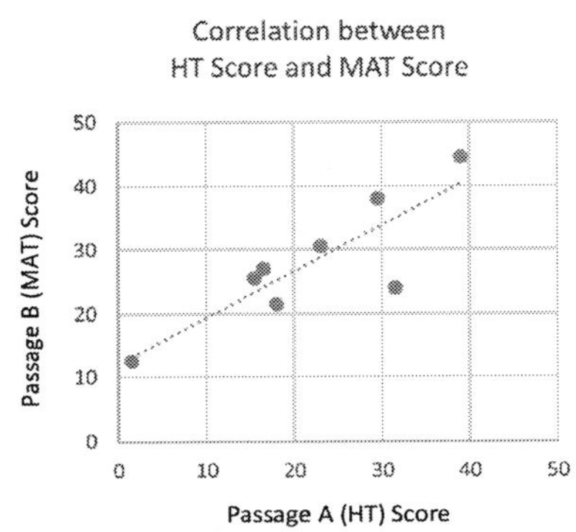

Descriptive Statistics			
	Passage A (HT)	Passage B (MAT)	p-value
Mean	21.8	27.9	0.025
Median	20.5	26.3	
Range	37.5	32.0	
Standard Deviation	10.9	9.2	
N	8	8	

Correlation			
		t-stat	p-value
Pearson	0.85	3.99	0.007

Results 2: How do MAT and raw MT compare?

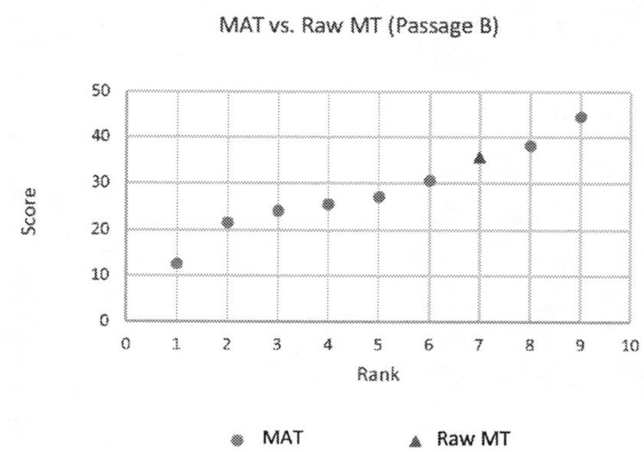

Discussion 1

- Does the human who produces the best translation without MT also produce the best translation with the assistance of MT?
- Are translation and post-editing completely different skills?
- Is "human + machine" always better than machine alone in terms of quality?

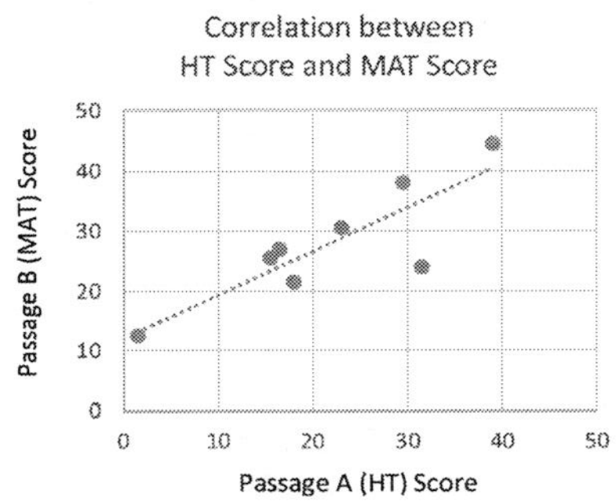

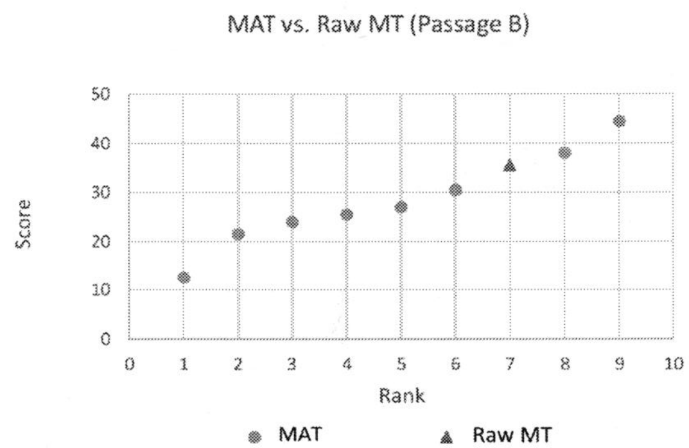

Discussion 2

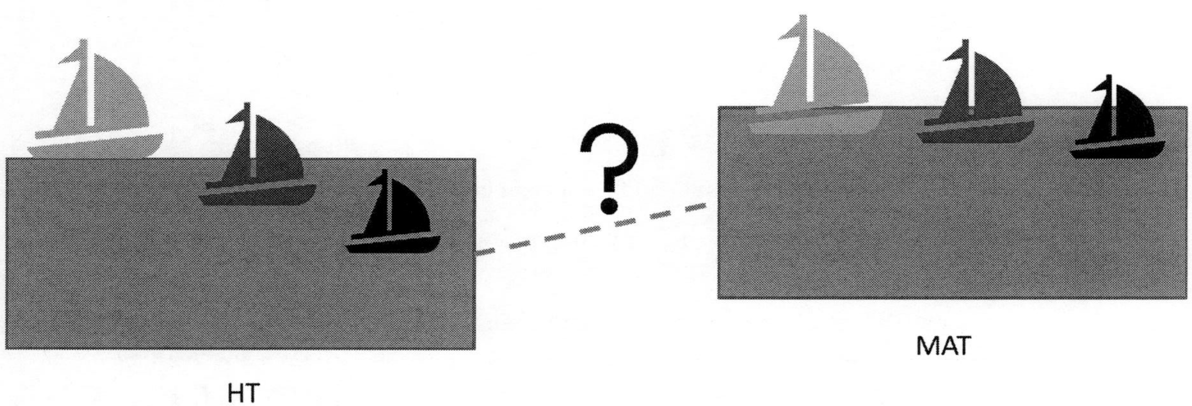

Limitations

- Small sample size
  - Uncontrolled before-and-after study
  - No personal or professional information collected
- Lack of empirical data to confirm the difficulty levels of the two passages
- Only one evaluation criterion: quality score under the ATA grading framework
  - Time, productivity, or cost not measured

Acknowledgement

- American Translators Association (ATA)
- Chinese Language Division of ATA
- Jessie Lu, Tianlu Redmon, Larry Bogoslaw & Geoffrey Koby
- *Most importantly, translators and evaluators who most generously donated their time and expertise*

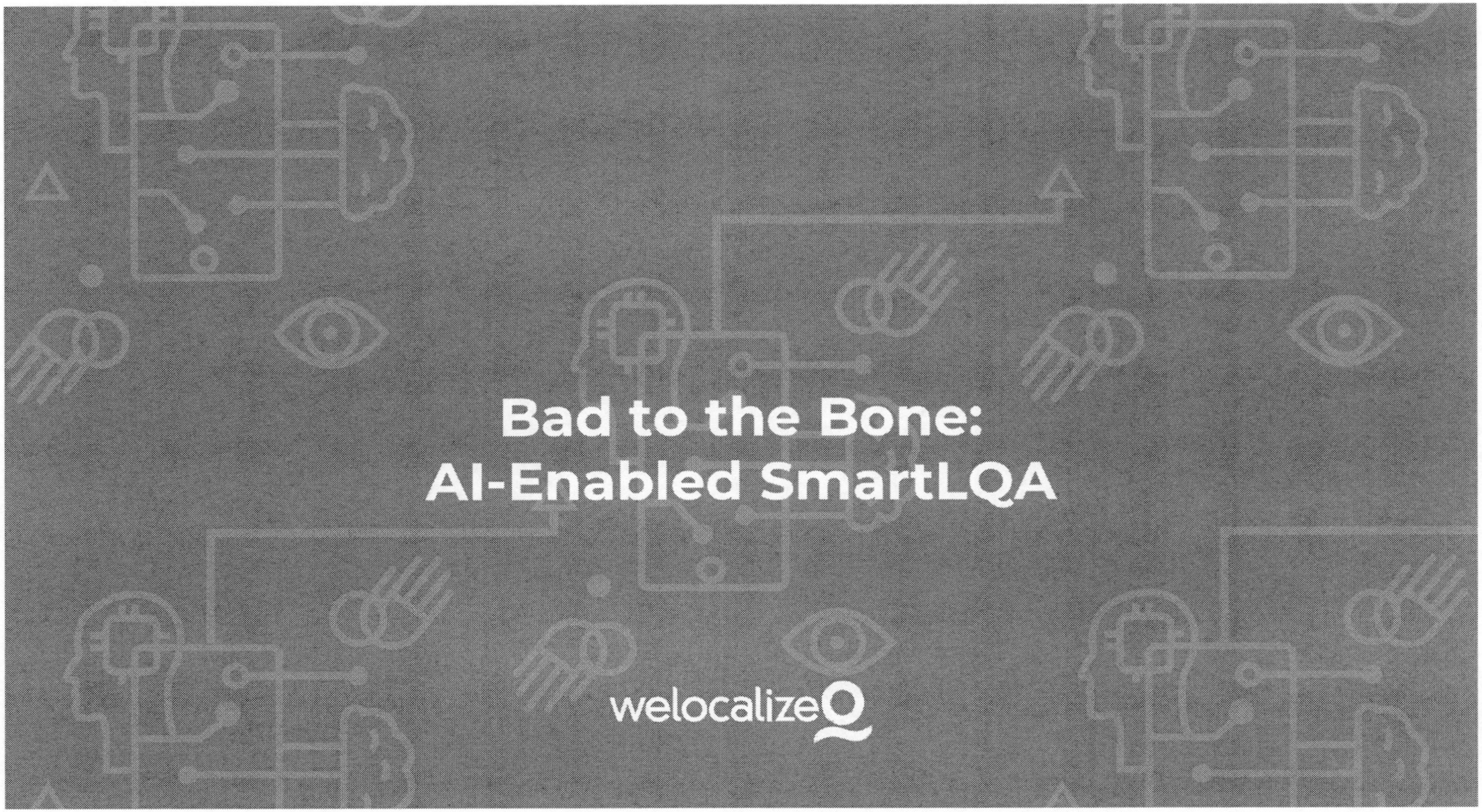

Bad to the Bone:
AI-Enabled SmartLQA
welocalize

Alex Yanishevsky

Director,
AI Deployments
Welocalize

SmartLQA Agenda

- WHAT IS IT?
- WHEN IS IT USED?
- HOW IS IT USED?
- WHAT'S NEXT?

What is it?

Methodology to inform strategic global content business decisions through AI

- SOURCE SUITABILITY
- PREDICT AT-RISK CONTENT
- "SPENDING SMART" VIA TARGETED LQA
- MTQE CORRELATION
- PE DISTANCE CORRELATION

What is it?

AI-Driven Quality Management

Inform data-driven content decisions through AI

1.

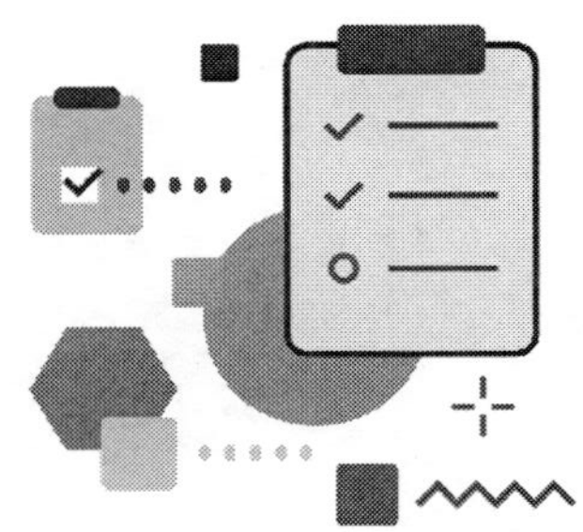

SOURCE SUITABILITY

AI can **identify** errors in poor source content and **predict** 'at-risk' content:

- Content written by non-native authors
- Content created by technical specialists for a non-technical audience
- Dated content not adhering to brand tone and voice

Does the source content need to be re-written <u>before</u> translation?

What is it?

AI-Driven Quality Management

Inform data-driven content decisions through AI

2.

TARGET SUITABILITY

- Does the translation deviate from previous style?
- Does the translation introduce unnecessary complexity?

Does the target need go through LQA for data-driven checks and corrections?

What is it?

AI-Driven Quality Management

Inform data-driven content decisions through AI

3.

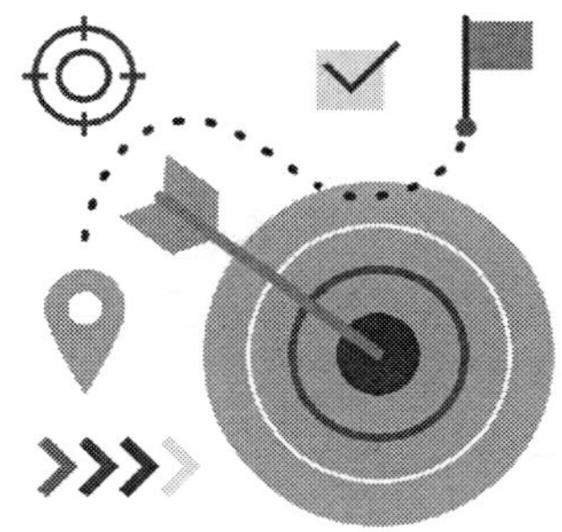

AI-DRIVEN LQA + MT RETRAINING

- Targeted "SmartLQA" focuses on problematic files and segments within them
- Data can be used to **retrain engines (dynamically)**

When Is It Used?
Where this fits into the Content Lifecycle

1.

How is it Used? Configuring Thresholds

THRESHOLDS

- Based on average plus standard deviation(s)
- Relative measure
- Captures outliers for that specific domain/product

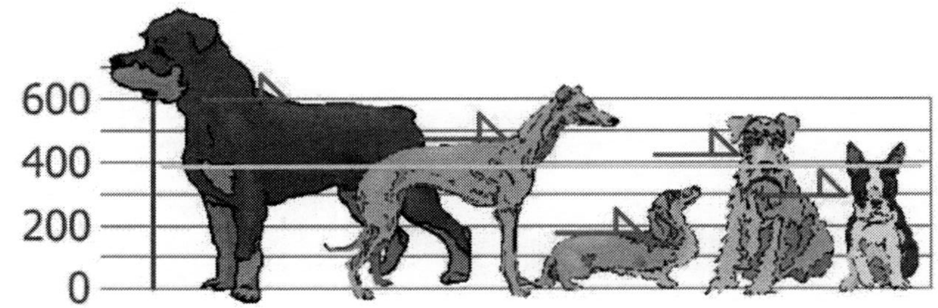

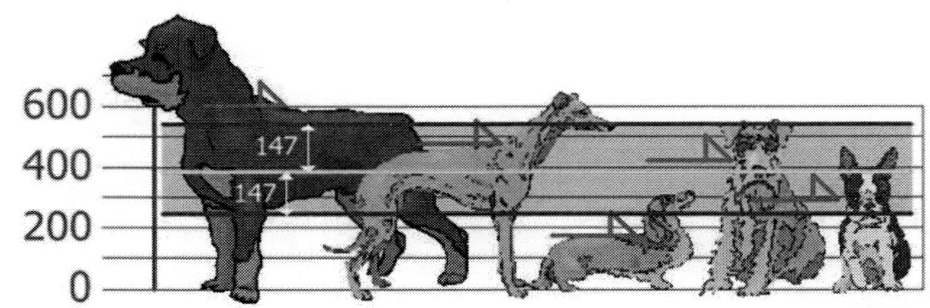

How is it Used? Configuring Thresholds

2.

THRESHOLDS

- Based on average plus standard deviation(s)
- Relative measure
- Captures outliers for that specific domain/product

Content Type	Avg. ADJ Count	Avg. NOUN Count	Avg. PROPN Count	Avg. Word Count	Avg. Long Word Count	Avg. Complex Word Count	Avg. FleschReadingEase
Legal	3.89	18.55	0.49	57.13	17.60	11.84	66.38
Legal	4.66	18.77	0.46	54.43	17.91	12.44	51.97
Legal	3.60	14.61	0.27	48.10	14.88	9.71	68.19
Legal	3.25	18.42	0.11	46.48	15.15	8.89	63.59
Legal	2.76	14.23	0.25	45.24	12.51	7.35	82.17
Legal	5.05	20.30	0.40	67.33	19.90	13.33	60.53
Repair insructions	0.36	2.71	0.68	9.05	1.80	0.81	49.87
Repair insructions	0.36	2.71	0.68	9.05	1.80	0.81	49.87
Life Sciences	0.00	4.00	0.00	6.00	3.00	1.00	31.55
Life Sciences	1.00	4.00	0.00	16.00	7.00	6.00	31.97
Life Sciences	1.00	4.00	4.00	22.00	5.00	4.00	87.86
Life Sciences	1.08	2.67	0.42	12.08	4.50	2.75	64.97
Transactional 1	1.05	5.27	0.17	15.39	4.36	2.89	48.77
Transactional 2	1.14	6.12	0.06	19.45	5.22	3.25	37.26
Transactional 3	1.94	6.54	0.18	19.90	5.76	3.60	41.68
Transactional 4	1.24	6.52	0.02	20.85	5.65	3.72	35.98
Transactional 5	1.36	5.98	0.60	20.23	5.43	3.38	35.69
Transactional 6	1.23	5.65	0.10	16.12	5.00	3.05	30.40
Transactional 7	1.61	5.80	0.43	18.52	5.56	4.09	31.82
Marketing	0.75	3.36	0.25	13.89	1.93	1.18	87.45
Marketing	0.67	3.00	0.27	12.17	1.77	1.17	86.95
Marketing	0.77	3.50	0.77	17.09	3.73	2.23	80.60
Marketing	0.80	3.00	0.65	16.20	3.15	1.45	78.34
Marketing	0.68	3.96	1.42	16.99	3.79	1.99	85.50
Marketing	0.88	3.42	0.54	13.71	3.38	1.54	97.83
Marketing	0.92	4.58	0.21	16.96	3.04	0.88	89.07
Average score	**1.62**	**7.37**	**0.52**	**24.24**	**6.88**	**4.36**	**60.63**

How is it Used? Identifying Salient Features

1.

FEATURES

- Parts of speech such as adjectives, nouns, proper nouns, numbers
- Adjective/noun density
- Long words, complex words, short and long sentences
- Stylistic similarity/dissimilarity
- Readability and complexity metrics
- Correlations to PE Distance and MT

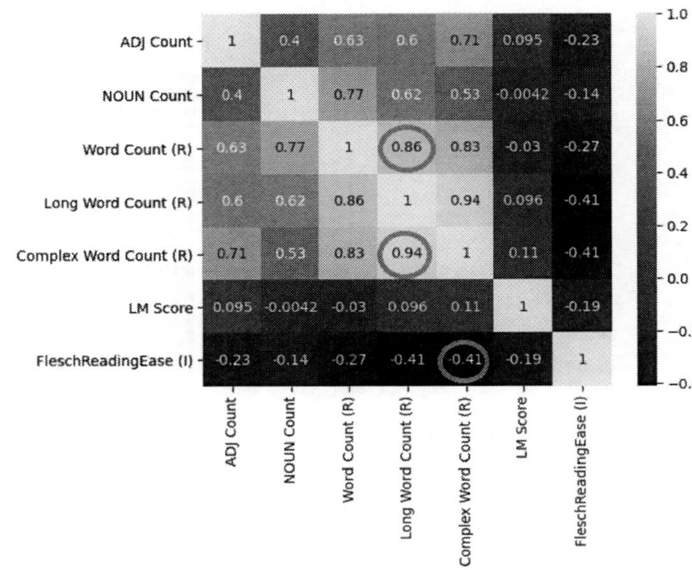

How is it Used?
Identifying Salient Features

2.

FEATURES

- Parts of speech such as adjectives, nouns, proper nouns, numbers
- Adjective/noun density
- Long words, complex words, short and long sentences
- Stylistic similarity/dissimilarity
- Readability and complexity metrics
- Correlations to PE Distance and MT Quality Estimation metrics

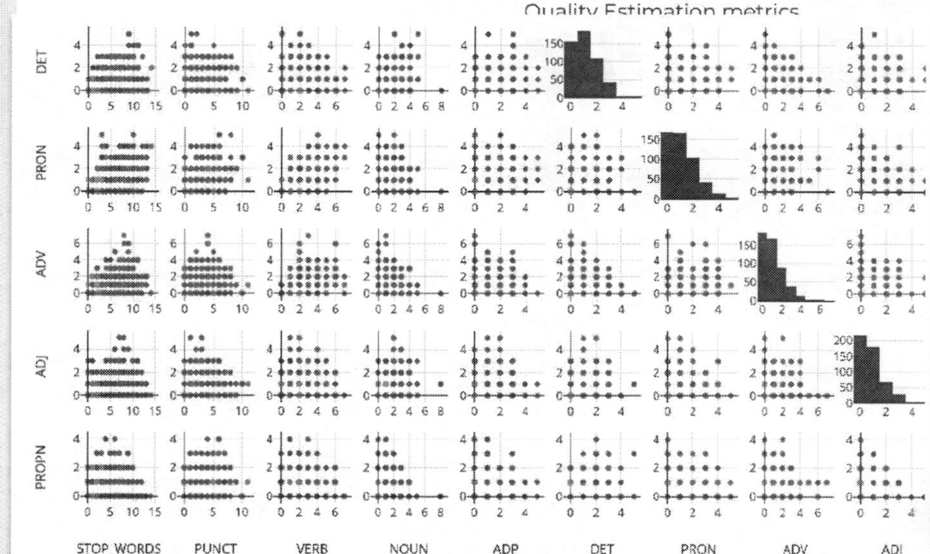

How is it Used? Source Suitability

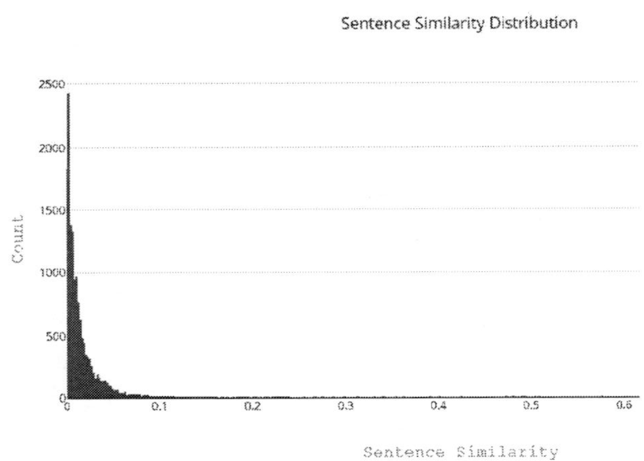

POSSIBLE REMEDIES

- Don't run the project till source is improved
- Route to transcreation, human translation, different MT engines
- Alert of higher LQA risk to all production people (PM, linguists, LQA)

How is it Used? Source Query Analysis

PROCESS

- Analyzed over historical 600 segments for potential DNT
- Analyzed almost historical 400 segments for source ambiguity and meaning (almost 200 for each category)
- Identified thresholds for each category
- Ran thresholds for all categories and identified over 400 potential queries
- Savings of 6K

Text		NOUN Count	PROPN	PROPN Count	ADJ/NOUN Density	Long Word Count (R)	Word Count (R)	FleschReadin
Boomi Molecule	0	0	Boomi | Molecule	2		1	2	-6.695
Delete incomplete target configuration failed, suspect permission or driver issue.	0	5		0	'NOUN 2', 'NOUN 2'	4	10	-6.355
Drive error recovery FW improvements and enhancements	0	5		0	'NOUN 4'	3	7	-5.727142857
In addition, on November 11th, Sheltered Harbor announced that Powe	0	8	November | Sheltered | Harbor | PowerProtect | Cyber | Recovery | Sheltered |	11	'NOUN 4'	15	31	-2.017096774
Identity query failed user=1000 to name status=STATUS_ACCESS_DENIED.	0	5		0	'NOUN 2', 'NOUN 2'	2	9	0.3
IR Camera (User-Facing fixed focus) with low light + TNR + capability +IPU6 + Proximi	0	27	ExpressSign	1	'NOUN 2', 'NOUN 2', 'NOUN 2'	8	41	4.273658537
Standardized earned MDF expiration timelines aligned to fiscal quarter end dates	0	7		0	'NOUN 3', 'NOUN 3'	7	16	5.5325
Disable Lock Terminal	0	2		0	'NOUN 2'	2	3	6.39

Quick calculation: 405 queries save 15 mins per query = 6075 minutes = 101 hours at $60/hr (if not more) = **$6075** saved

How is it Used? Target Suitability - "Spending Smart"

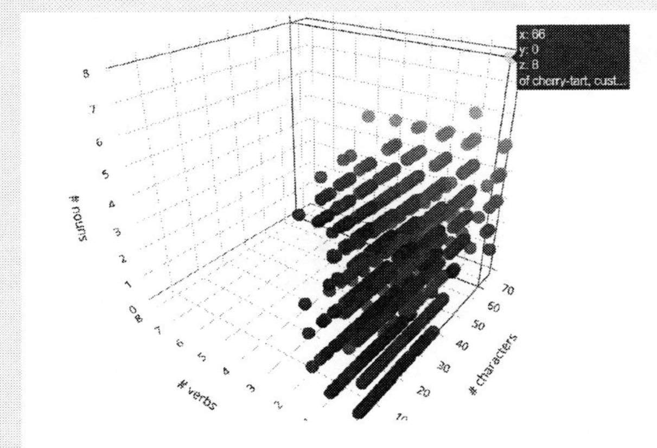

POSSIBLE REMEDIES

- Go back to linguist for more editing
- Alert of higher LQA risk
- Use information to retrain MT engine (dynamic?)
- Map to client LQA methodology
- Spend LQA $$ where it counts
- Confirm MTQE
- Confirm PE Distance and/or TER
- Confirm productivity metrics

How is it Used?

Summary View

- How many features failed?
- Pass/Fail/Review per segment
- Aggregated to pass/fail per file

1.

Text	ADJ Count Pass	Noun Count Pass	PROPN Count Pass	Long Word Count Pass	Complex Word Count Pass	Nominalization Count Pass	Word Count Pass	LM Pass	FleschReadingEase (l) Pass	Segment Pass/Fail/Review	Segment comment
In addition to the game's deep	TRUE	FALSE	FALSE	TRUE	FALSE	TRUE	FALSE	TRUE	TRUE	Fail	
With twelve maps, five modes, and	TRUE	TRUE	TRUE	TRUE	FALSE	TRUE	FALSE	TRUE	TRUE	Review	
As easy it is to drop into MP and pick it up, Nathan	TRUE	TRUE	TRUE	TRUE	TRUE	FALSE	TRUE	TRUE	TRUE	Pass	

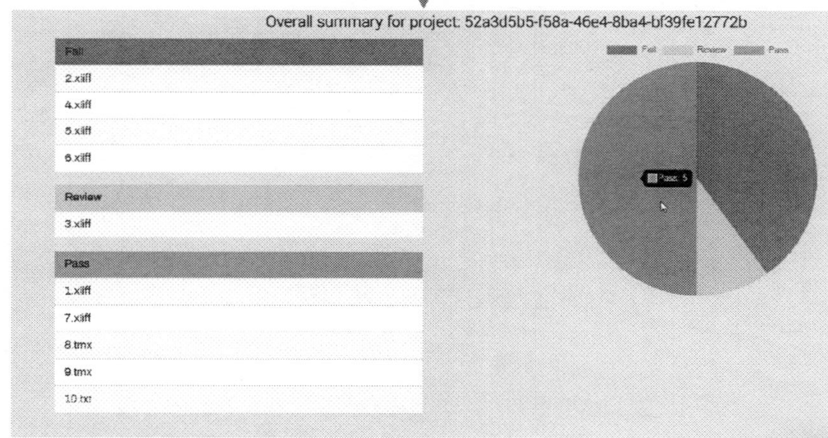

How is it Used?

Summary View

- Passes/fails per domain
- Passes/fails per locale pair

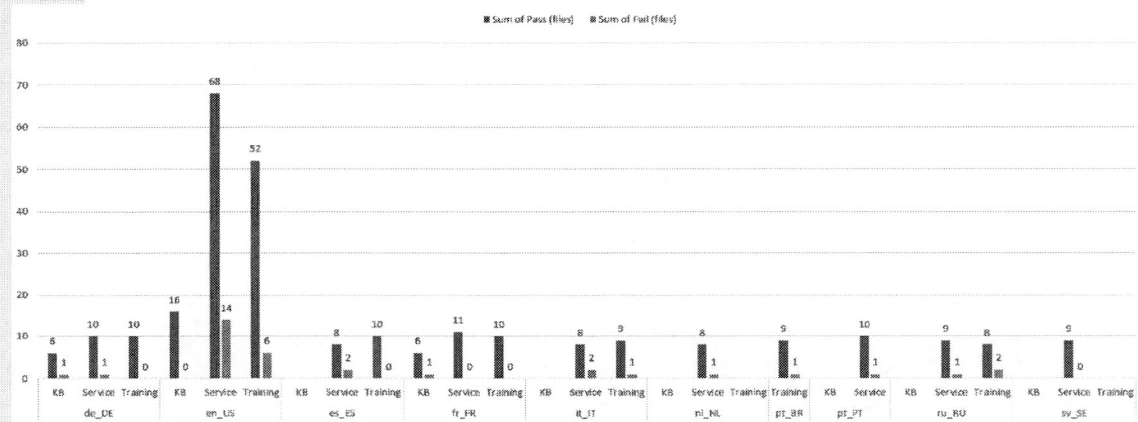

2.

How is it Used?
Garbage In, Garbage Out

- TRACING SOURCE TO TARGET CORRELATIONS
- POOR SOURCE LEADS TO POOR TARGET

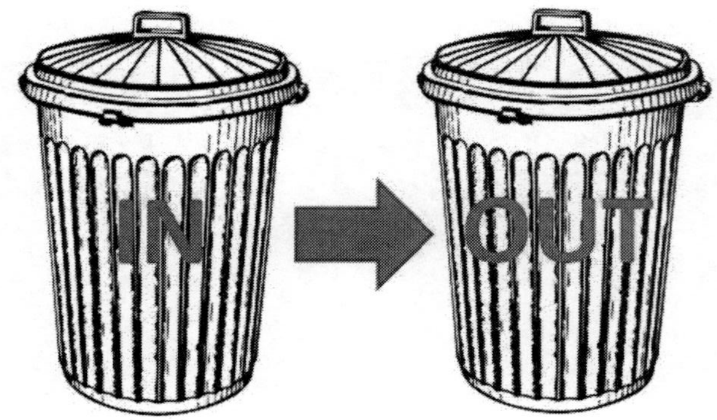

	EN									DE								
File name	ADJ Count	NOUN Count	PROPN Count	Word Count	Long Word Count	Complex Word Count	Nominalization Count	LM Score	FleschReadingEase	ADJ Count	NOUN Count	PROPN Count	Word Count	Long Word Count	Complex Word Count	Nominalization Count	LM Score	LIX
TASK10196529	0.666667	3.333333	1.311111	9.266667	3.555556	0.577778	0.355555556	648.734	53.9952	0.888889	2.333333	1.977778	9.088889	3.844444	0.911111	0.266666667	569.1765	55.52887
TASK10196533	0.954545	4.318182	0.681818	12.45455	5.363636	3.181818	0.454545455	257.5985	36.08856	1.727273	3.363636	1.363636	12.04545	6.136364	2.272727	0.272727273	372.648	59.00989
TASK10196537	0.766667	3.266667	1.366667	9.866667	3.633333	1.633333	0.3	411.9258	55.52377	1.121212	2.272727	2.30303	9.242424	3.878788	0.969697	0.212121212	2095.755	50.82482
TASK10276202	1.338983	3.966102	0.711864	14	4.525424	2.694915	0.355932203	445.9728	52.33312	1.542373	3.932203	0.881356	15.45763	5.745763	1.474576	0.440677966	607.4004	55.07588
TASK10294494	1.142857	3.97619	0.619048	12.42857	4.380952	2.238095	0.428571429	1075.118	50.6495	1.452381	3.214286	1.309524	12.28571	4.785714	1.047619	0.357142857	1761.157	58.67438
TASK10294496	2.433333	8.266667	1	23.83333	9.266667	6.166667	0.833333333	227.824	29.01318	2.266667	7.333333	1.366667	22.93333	10.56667	2.866667	0.366666667	456.5975	66.27447
TASK10354283	0.608696	2.717391	0.73913	6.902174	2.706522	1.141304	0.293478261	2668.863	42.92559	0.684783	2.26087	1.336957	7.141304	3.108696	0.652174	0.217391304	1856.129	58.27621

How is it Used? How Bad is the File?

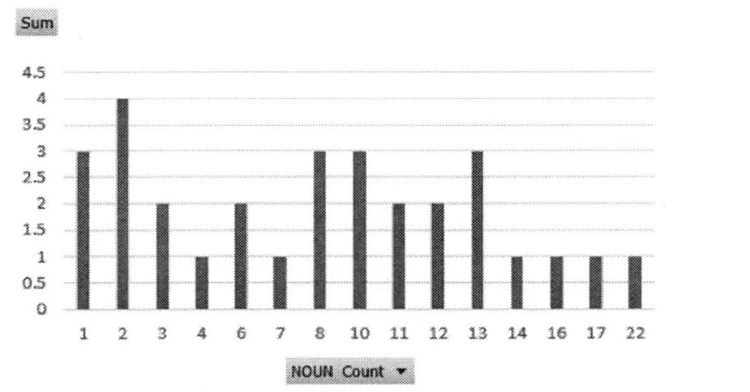

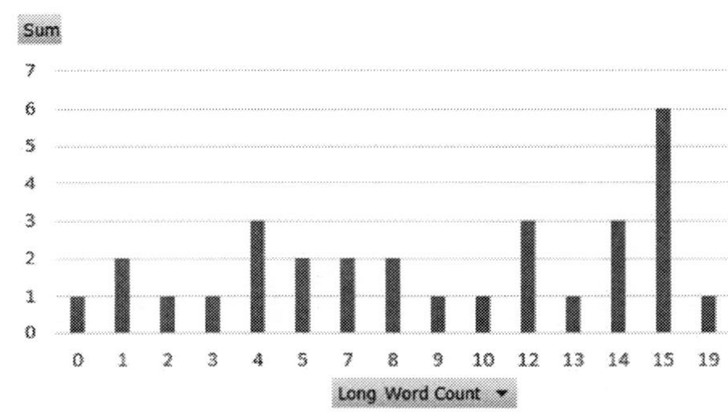

More than half of the file has 6 or more nouns

Half of the file has 8 long words or more

How is it Used? A Telling Example

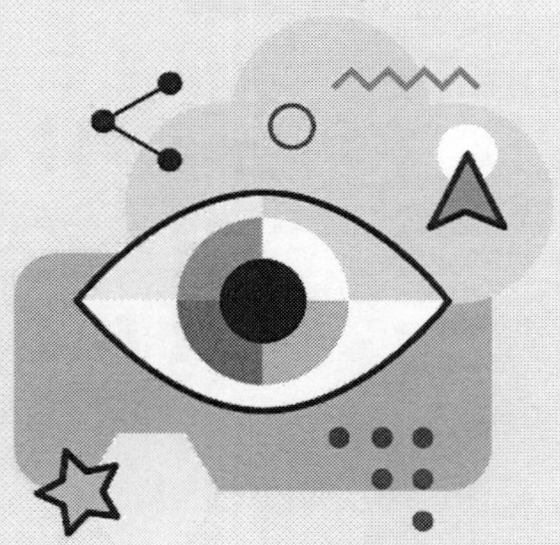

Today's machines enable industrial workers to carry out complex Computer Aided Design, Manufacturing and Engineering (CAD, CAM, CAE) operations, model Computational Fluid Dynamics (CFD), accomplish thermal, stress and fatigue analysis, or visualise and test designs and models using immersive Virtual Reality (VR).

And now the statistics

- **42 words**
- **22 nouns**
- **19 long words**
- **9 complex words**

List of nouns

Today | machines | workers | Computer | Design | Manufacturing | Engineering | CAD | CAM | CAE | operations | model | Computational | Fluid | Dynamics | CFD | thermal | stress | fatigue | analysis | designs | models

10

How is it Used? Under the Hood

NLP frameworks
Human validation
Predictive modeling

NLP

- Language Models
- Tokenization & PoS tagging (NLP frameworks)
- Readability features (FleschKincaid, complex words, long words, nominalization)

Human Input

Definition of features, review and calibration of features, fine-tuning, data analysis

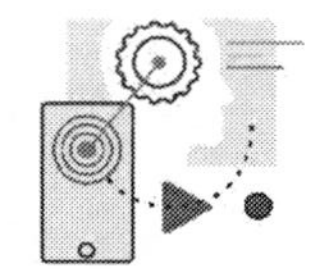

Predictive Modeling

Long-term vision
if sufficient data available

How is it Used?
Process Optimization

Reducing time to market and costs while improving linguist acquisition and retention

15-20%
LQA Time Saved

20%
LQA Pass Rate Improvement

10%
LQA Spend Reduction

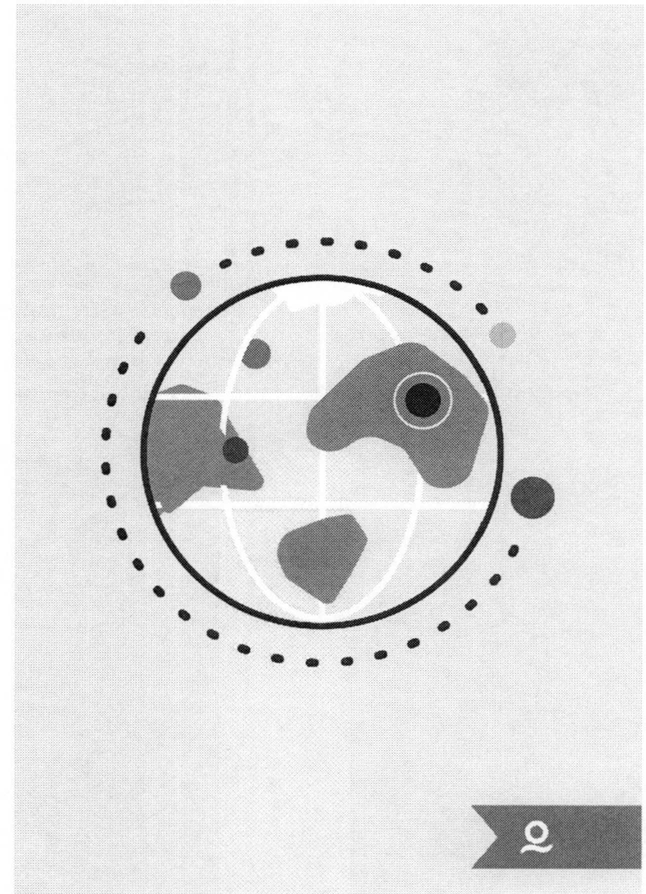

What's Next?

- Continued human validation
- Build predictive models using machine learning (ML) algorithms

- Human validation comment

"I think this is a very interesting tool that has a **lot of potential**. The output statistics provide some **interesting insights about the nature and style of the source**, and more importantly, also **the target text**. With the help of these figures, a source text can be analyzed for its complexity, while **a translation can be characterized and possibly rated** with regard to certain stylistic guidelines."

Questions?

Thank you
welocalize

Machine Translation Post-Editing (MTPE) from the Perspective of Translation Trainees: Implications for Translation Pedagogy

Abstract

This paper introduces data on translation trainees' perceptions of the MTPE process and implications on training in this field. This study aims to analyse trainees' performance of three MTPE tasks the English-Polish language pair and post-tasks interviews to determine the need to promote machine translation post-editing skills in educating translation students. Since very little information concerning MTPE training is available, this study may be found advantageous.

Keywords: MTPE training, translation pedagogy, translation technology, post-editing, machine translation.

1. Introduction

Although initial attempts at machine translation (MT) were taken already in the first half of the twentieth century, greater interest in this field may have been observed for just over a decade. Therefore, it is conceivable that data on the subject is still scarce. Nevertheless, intensive technological development is fuelling MT research and helping to fill the knowledge gap. The field, firstly distrusted by the translation community, is now attracting interest not only of academics, but also a growing number of private companies implementing MT systems to improve the flow of information within the company. Both studies conducted by the companies and researchers point to post-editing (PE) as an essential element of success in the translation industry and a bridge between machine solutions and skills that so far can only be demonstrated by humans. Hence, this paper has been motivated by the growing importance of post-editing and the technologically induced changing image of the translation industry and the translator's work. Furthermore, the literary background was another impetus for research into the perspective of MTPE trainees and possible future implications for translation pedagogy.

A definite precursor of awareness of education in the field is O'Brien (2002), who created a proposal for course content on teaching PE. Later, Belam (2003) presented a workshop on PE guidelines in a machine-assisted translation course. Another scholar, Kliffer (2008), has introduced PE teaching as a component of the MT programme for the pre-professional level. Further, Depraetere (2010) analysed a corpus of texts post-edited by ten translation trainees and concluded a distinct need to raise the students' awareness of typical MT errors. Other contributions to MTPE training have been made by Pym (2013). He presented a list of ten skills arranged in three categories: "learning to learn, learning to trust and mistrust data, and learning to revise with enhanced attention to detail" as an implication to technology adapted translation pedagogy. Flanagan & Christensen (2014) proposed training measures to address competency gaps that may cause difficulties in interpreting PE guidelines and introduced new post-editing guidelines. Doherty & Kenny's (2014) study was another step towards adapting translation technology in translation studies. They designed and evaluated an SMT curriculum for postgraduate students in translation studies at Dublin City University in 2012. The most recent and in line with the subject of this paper is the research of Guerberof Arenas & Moorkens (2019). They presented a course description of machine translation and post-editing together with an MT project management module. As can be seen from the above, the knowledge of MTPE training is limited, and students' perspective for education in this direction remains neglected. Furthermore, a common feature of the presented research findings is an attempt to adapt to the ever-changing conditions of translation technology without evaluating the results in an educational setting.

The influence of technological development on the translator's work and translation students' education has not escaped Polish researchers' attention. Świątek (2015) addressed the potential and limitation of statistical machine translation. Her conclusions suggested that a computer is not an opponent, but a tool in the translator's hands and that automation of the translation will develop positively. These outcomes were also confirmed by Witczak (2016), assuring that the automation of translation could not exist without a significant agent of the process — a translator. In the same year, Witczak conducted a study focusing on the attitude of translation students to the introduction of a post-editing component into a computer-assisted translation course. The data collected indicated that while MT of technical texts brought 'positive surprise', it was described as 'some disillusionment' in the journalistic texts. Nevertheless, Witczak emphasised the need to give translation education a direction consistent with technological development. These conclusions correspond with the studies by Nikishina (2018) and Tomaszkiewicz (2019), both of whom pointed to the lack of consistency and precise guidelines in the education of future translators. The latter additionally stressed the need for pedagogy in line with EMTs' assumptions. Among these, knowledge and the ability to use tools supporting the work of translators were introduced as one of the necessary competencies in this profession. Brożyna-Reczko (2020) also discussed digital tools in translation didactics, concluding that technological tools for verification, glossaries and corpora, which translation students can use to improve the translation process, facilitate the translator's work and deserve a place in education. The sources above indicate that the Polish translation community is unanimous in calling for research into standardising translation curricula in line with available technologies. As Jan Rybicki, Professor of English Studies at Jagiellonian University, underscored at the CALT conference (2021), programmes that not long ago distinguished between human-performed and machine-performed translations are now almost helpless in the light of the ongoing development of neural machine translation.

Therefore, the author of the paper attempted to investigate the demand for education in line with the contemporary translation market, namely machine translation post-editing, from the perspective of students of English Philology with Translation Studies at the Faculty of Philology of the University of Białystok. For this purpose, the studies were divided into two stages — the first one based on task completion, where participants received a set of 3 post-editing activities. The tasks concerned the English-Polish language pair. The follow-up phase of the study was an interview conducted with each participant individually. The study results aimed to determine the students' attitudes towards MTPE, the demand for the inclusion of a course on MTPE in their curricula and their awareness of MTPE tools. The research results were also to serve as a basis for the elaboration of a proposal for a unified post-editing machine translation course.

2. Methodology

The study aims, among others, to examine the opinions of translation students on teaching the MTPE process. In accordance with González Davies (2004:4) remark that 'new paths should be explored instead of keeping to one approach to translation or to its teaching,' the author hypothesized that there is a need to promote machine translation post-editing skills, and these abilities should be improved in the process of educating translation trainees. In particular, this study examines three main research questions analysed with the secondary level side questions:

1. What is the participants' (English Philology and Translation students) attitude towards MTPE?
   a. How do participants evaluate given tasks?
   b. What is the participants' view on the idea of including MTPE in an educational programme for future translators?
2. What are the implications for teaching the MTPE process?
   a. What kind of errors do participants make in given tasks?
   b. What problems do participants encounter during performance of tasks?
3. What is the state of the participants' knowledge about MTPE?
   a. What kind of translation digital tools are research participants' familiar with?

Procedure

Due to the outbreak of the global coronavirus pandemic, the whole study was carried out online using digital tools. The studies performed to obtain data for analysis were divided into two stages. The first one based on tasks completion. Participants received a set of 3 post-editing activities by e-mail. Each task was accompanied by written instructions, and tasks number two and three by attachments. On account of the level of complexity of the third assignment and the limited possibility of conducting the study to a remote working environment, an instructional video was attached to Task 3, recorded purposely to facilitate the task. The subjects were informed of the procedure and how they could contact the researcher in case of any inquires. After tasks completion, all nine subjects sent their answers back via e-mail. The follow-up phase of the study was an interview conducted with each participant individually via a platform designed for online meetings – Zoom.us. Proceeding the interviews subjects received an e-mail with a link to the meeting and available on YouTube instructional video explaining how to enter the Zoom. The subjects were informed in advance about the issues that was to be discussed during the interview. The data was recorded on a digital audio recorder provided by Zoom.us, transcribed using an online programme Gglot.com and then corrected manually by the researcher. The obtained audio files are between 4:44 and 10:07 minutes long. The participants signed an agreement to record and use the data collected with their help to carry out the research for the paper.

Techniques and tools

As mentioned above, the micro-level research procedure was divided into two phases. Each of them was based on a different methodology. Although both represent a qualitative approach, the first stage was process-oriented and consisted of a set of exercises that explored various competences. The tasks were constructed on particular activities conducted during MT Summit Workshop on Post-Editing Technology and Practice launched by O'Brien. Task 1 (Appendix 1) aimed to familiarize participants with different MT versions, draw their attention into diversity in MT and problems that can emerge during the post-editing process. The subjects were given three outputs of MT: Yandex Free, Google Translate and DeepL. They read three versions and then decided which one is, in their opinion, the best and why. The second assignment (Appendix 2) was designed to introduce the concept of pre-editing as well as the rules that should be applied in the process of pre-and post-editing - English Controlled Language rules (Appendix 3). The participants were provided with an original text in English. They chose from three to five most problematic sentences and tried to rewrite them using English Controlled Language rules. Then, they translated the rewritten versions of the sentences into Polish using the tool they chose in the previous assignment. The third task (Appendix 4) provided for combining skills learned from two previous exercises and introduced students to the CAT tool. It also intended to show students how to combine different tools in the post-editing process. The subjects first watched instructional video prepared for the purpose of this exercise. Then they were given a task to create a project on smartcat.ai. The students used the previously made glossary (Appendix 5) and implemented it into their projects. Finally, they translated the text (Appendix 6) in created projects on smartcat.ai platform. After tasks completion, subjects sent their answers back via e-mail.

Contrary to the first one, the second stage of research was based on a participant-oriented method – a semi-structured interview conducted in Polish to allow the research participants to express themselves freely. It consisted of a set of six open questions designed to correspond with the research questions stated in the paper. The interview questions were as follows:

1. Have you ever used machine translation tools like Goggle Translate? If so, which ones?
2. In the first task, you were asked to choose, in your opinion, the best machine translation and to justify your choice. Were you surprised that the versions of these translations can differ? Were you surprised by the quality of the translations?
3. In the second task, you were asked to translate selected problematic sentences into English using the English Controlled Language rules (ECL) and then translate chosen units employing a preferred tool. In your opinion, was the final version better due to this procedure (ECL rules) or was it not significantly different? Do you find practising these rules necessary? Would that be useful in your work as a translator?
4. In the third task, you were asked to translate an extract from an article using a CAT (computer-assisted translation) programme, in this case, available on the SmartCat.com platform. Have you ever employed such a programme? Which one? Did you find the programme helpful? In this exercise, you also used the prepared earlier glossary. Did you find the glossary helpful? Do you think it is worth preparing for translation and post-editing in this way?
5. What is your overall attitude towards the performed tasks? Do you think that you have learned something by completing them?
6. Would you like the post-editing exercises to be included in your educational programme at university?

The interview was conducted with each participant individually via Zoom.us.

Participants

For the purpose of the research procedure and data collection, nine students of the University in Białystok were recruited. The subjects were selected on the basis of their level of English proficiency, specialization and field of study. The participants were between 23 and 25 years old. All subjects received a Bachelor's degree in English Philology. They were during their first year of their Master's degree in English Philology with Translation Studies with a specialization in linguistics. At the time of the research procedure the participants completed the following classes:

- 15h of Assessment of Translation Equivalence in Translation,
- 30h of General Translation Practice,
- 30h of Journalistic Translation,
- 15h of Polish Language in Translation
- and one lecture:
- 30h of Introduction to the Theory of Translation.

It is necessary to mention that the research author and participants are acquainted and have been studying together in the same group. This fact will be regarded as one of the limitations to the study.

Limitations of the study

Limitations of the study may be classified as externally and internally derived. The latter refers to the characteristics of the research methodology used, i.e. semi-structured interview. An interviewer is not free from personal attribute and unintentional expectancy effect. This threat can impact participants' answers; however, as Saldanha and O'Brien (2014: 29-30) explained it, it is likely to occur under particular conditions:

- when due to the ambiguity of the assignment or question, participants ask a researcher for advice on how to perform;
- when an interviewer affects respondents' answers by unconsciously revealing the type of results they expect.

Although threats above may relate to the research, especially since the author of the paper is personally acquainted with participants (as a co-student), it is vital to acknowledge that many commentators recognize this as an unavoidable consequence of the character of social research, which has to be dealt with through self-reflexivity (Saldanha, O'Brien 2014:29-30). Furthermore, the questions were designed in a way to limit the possibility of the author imposing her opinion. It is also worth noting that the less formal form of communication with participants may have encouraged them to ask questions if necessary. It is important given the exclusively internet-mediated form of contact during the various stages of the study.

Another (external) limitation was caused by the occurrence of coronavirus, which resulted in lockdown. Initially, the procedure was designed to be conducted in the form of a regular class. However, due to the outbreak of the pandemic and the associated restrictions, the nature of the research was changed. The contact with the participants of the study was narrowed to online tools such as emails, instant messaging, video and online meetings. It induced multiple issues:

- the participants were limited to online tools of contact in case of encountering concerns while solving the tasks;
- during interviews, there was a minor disruption due to a poor internet connection
- one of the participants could not use the Zoom platform.

All mentioned above threats were overcome and the research data was collected.

3. Data analysis

In the process of data analysis of qualitative research, an inductive approach was implemented with research tasks and questions acting as a prism through which to view the information and choose relevant items. Both the first and second phase of the study were to be examined accordingly to the following stages:

- Code units were selected from the acquired data.
- Units were encoded by their content.
- Units were grouped into categories accordingly to the stages of research.
- The themes were identified.
- The representative extracts of the transcribed interviews were selected in order to exemplify the categories and themes.

Mentioned above procedure describes 'thematic' analysis, which according to Matthews and Ross (2010:373), describes as "[a] process of working with raw data to identify and interpret key ideas or themes".

The preliminary stage of research– task completion is to be studied in terms of the difficulties that may have occurred in the process of performing the activities, errors appearing in individual stages of post-editing, the level of understanding of the instructions and the effectiveness of the assignments. While all of the aspects mentioned above will be reviewed in each task, the last one measuring the effectiveness of the activities will be most visible in the third exercise, which aimed to use the skills acquired in the previous tasks. Furthermore, the difficulty and level of understanding of the instructions will be evident from the analysis of the questions asked by the participants through online communication. To sum up, this part of the research provides data for implications for MTPE pedagogy and forms the foundation of MTPE course.

The second stage of the study conducted with the application of a semi-structured interview will be analysed to offer answers to the two remaining research questions. The examination will be provided in the order presented in section Techniques and tools. Inquiries number one, two and four of the interview will attempt to answer the third research question providing insight on participants experience with digital translation tools and their general state of knowledge on MTPE. Consequently, question number five is to determine participants' attitude towards post-editing. Interrogatives number two, three and four evaluate provided exercises. Finally, the participants' view on the idea of including MTPE in the educational programme for future translators might be revealed by analysing answers to the last interview question.

Tasks evaluation

The first study phase concerns the evaluation of research assignments. As already described, Task 1 aimed to familiarise participants with different MT versions, highlight diversity in MT and the problems that can emerge during the post-editing process.

	S1	S2	S3	S4	S5	S6	S7	S8	S9
Stylistics	1	1							
Readability	1	1		1		1	1		
Consistency/accuracy			1				1		
Grammar							1	1	
Errors		1			1	1			1
Vocabulary				1					

Table 1 Answers from Task 1.

All nine participants completed the task correctly. Each participant provided an explanation of their choice. Of the nine subjects, two pointed out statistical correctness, five participants emphasized that the text they preferred is easy to read and understand, one person remarked that the text selected was consistent and also one that it was precise. Grammar correctness was noted twice. Of nine participants, four commented on errors in the texts. Only one person emphasized vocabulary as an essential factor in evaluating the quality of translations. The data provide a preliminary suggestion that such a translation evaluation form could be useful in that kind of activity or as a part of introductory exercises. Instead of a form, the instruction could include a set of translation quality indicators to be noted.

The second assignment (Task 2) was designed to introduce the concept of pre-editing as well as rules that should be applied in the process of pre-and post-editing.

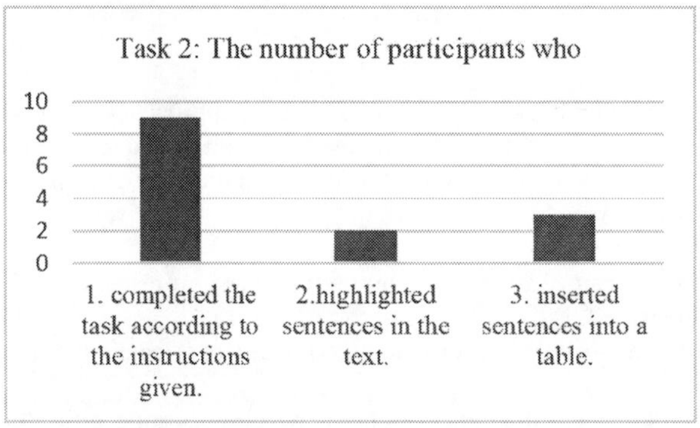

Figure 1 The evaluation of Task 2.

Although all participants completed the task as instructed, it is worth noting that five of them implemented additional elements to the exercise. Two subjects highlighted sentences selected for correction in the text, and three inserted these units into a table. Concluding, Task 2 lacked space in the table for a pre-edited version.

The assignment number three provided for combining skills learned from two previous exercises and introduced students to a CAT tool. It also intended to show students how to combine different tools in the post-editing process. The findings depict a repeated occurrence of one type of language error - inflectional – in two units

(17) firma SpaceX wystrzelił [orig: SpaceX launched]

(18) partię swoich satelity [orig: the first batch of its Starlink]

This error emerged in the responses of 7 out of 9 participants. Two participants (S4 and S9) performed this assignment flawlessly and as directed. The fact that they had asked questions about this task's procedure may help determine why such errors occurred in the rest of the cases. The enquires were as follows:

(1) S4: [So in general we don't show any creativity and we do exactly what we see on the video, yes?]

(2) S9: [Can I split sentences if I want to?]

Having been instructed that after creating a project on the SmartCat.com platform, the output text should be edited as much as they felt appropriate, the participants performed the task autonomously and correctly. Simultaneously, the rest of the participants who lacked this information were limited to following the video instruction and did not apply post-editing. These findings confirm that corrections to the instructions should be applied and that Task 3 should be split into separate activities to ensure that they are more precise and understandable.

Interview analysis

The final stage of the analysis discusses the results of the interview carried after all participants had completed the three MTPE tasks. The first interview question was to evaluate the level of interviewees" familiarity with MT tools.

	Number of participants familiar with enumerated machine translation tools
Google Translate	9
DeepL	4
SmartCat	1
PONS	1

Table 2. Summary of answers to the first interview question.

All nine subjects used Google Translate before, four of which declared that they did not employ other tools. Three participants were accustomed to DeepL. One person pointed out SmartCat.com and also one PONS text translation. The findings revealed that although all participants were accustomed to MT tools, their state of knowledge on the subject was not extensive.

The next question that was asked during the interview related to the subjects' reaction to MT outputs differentiation, also in terms of quality.

Interview Question 2		**S1**	**S2**	**S3**	**S4**	**S5**	**S6**	**S7**	**S8**	**S9**
Were you surprised that the versions of these translations can differ?	Yes					1	1			
	No	1	1	1	1			1	1	1
Were you surprised by the quality of the translations?	Yes	1		1	1	1	1			1
	No		1					1	1	

Table 3. Summary of answers to the second interview question.

Seven out of nine participants declared that they were not surprised that machine translations performed with various tools were different. Two of the subjects also wrote a paper on machine translation and used this argument to explain their lack of surprise. Two students expressed a reaction of surprise. First, Google Translate turned out to be of a higher standard than expected, and second, it was an interesting phenomenon. Considering the quality of MT, the situation was as follows. Six out of nine subjects claimed to be surprised by the quality of the translations, three of them – positively. One found the differences in the translations amusing. Two expressed disappointment of the level of quality in one of the outputs. Three interviewees were not surprised by the quality of the translations. The majority of participants were aware of the variety in MT outputs. Still, more than half of the group admitted that the quality of the translations was, to some degree, unexpected. These responses revealed that although the participants were aware of the existence of the different MT tools, they still showed little knowledge of the quality of the results of these tools.

The third interview question was based on the participants' experience after completion of Task 2 and was designed to establish their attitude towards the concept of pre-editing.

Interview Question 3		**S1**	**S2**	**S3**	**S4**	**S5**	**S6**	**S7**	**S8**	**S9**
In your opinion, was the final version better due to this procedure (ECL rules) or was it not significantly different?	It was better	1	1	1	1	1		1	1	
	It was not significantly different									
	Other						1			1
Do you find practising these rules necessary? Would that be useful in your work as a translator?	Yes	1	1	1	1	1	1	1	1	
	No									
	Other									1

Table 4 Summary of answers to the third interview question.

Asked about the usefulness of employing pre-editing tools in the MTPE process, 7 out of 9 interviewees reported that, to some extent, the final version was improved through the process. Two subjects emphasized the significance of Muegge's (2002) first CLOUT rule that sentences should be no longer than 25 words. One participant stated that she relied on her already acquired knowledge during the task, regardless of the attached guideline. The last subject pointed out that pre-editing improved lower quality fragments but that post-editing should also be used eventually. The second part of the third question provided similar findings. Eight subjects agreed that the application of ECL rules, which represent the pre-editing phase of the MT process, is assumed to support translator's work. One participant stated that following the ECL rules may support developing translation skills. Two subjects emphasized the necessity of simplifying sentences in the MTPE process. One interviewee noted that the rules do not exhaust the topic of pre-editing because they do not cover the issue of metaphors or other phraseological compounds in the text. Finally, one of the participants did not answer the question directly but pointed out an interesting correlation between the principles stated in Belczyk's book *Poradnik Tłumacza* [Translator's Guide], which, inter alia, discusses translation rules and the principles mentioned by Muegge (2002). Although the vast majority of the survey participants confirmed the validity of implementing the pre-editing phase in the MTPE process, their comments indicated that ECL rules could be enriched, such as rules covering idioms, metaphors and phrasal verbs.

The aim of the next question was to evaluate whether participants were familiar with CAT programme and tools associated with that software and their attitude towards CAT after completing Task 3.

Interview Question 4		**S1**	**S2**	**S3**	**S4**	**S5**	**S6**	**S7**	**S8**	**S9**
Have you ever employed such a programme? Which one?	Yes									1
	No	1	1	1	1	1	1	1	1	
Did you find the programme helpful?	Yes	1		1	1	1	1	1	1	1
	No									
	Other		1							
Did you find the glossary helpful? Do you think it is worth preparing for translation and post-editing in this way?	Yes	1	1	1	1	1	1	1	1	1
	No									

Table 5Summary of answers to the fourth interview question.

Only one participant had used this type of software (SmartCat) before the study. It is worth mentioning that the person who previously used this programme wrote his master's thesis on machine translation. For the rest of the group, it was their first encounter with a CAT tool. Two participants commented that CAT software seemed complicated in use. One subject said that the programme was not as difficult as it appeared at first. Moreover, S1 added that he had learnt something by completing the assignment. The second part of the same question showed almost unanimity in the survey participants' opinions on the advantage of CAT tools in translator's work. Apart from one person, who called the use of the software a 'challenge', all the rest agreed on its usefulness. Finally, respondents were asked about their attitudes towards implementing the MTPE pre-editing tool, namely, the glossary. All participants were in favour of this means. Furthermore, two trainees expressed approval for the glossary, confirming their opinion on the usefulness of CAT programmes. Three of nine subjects underlined that it may be helpful when dealing with a professional, specialist or problematic vocabulary. One person described the glossary as an improvement to the result of the work. Another participant described it as making the translator's work easier. Two interviewees stressed that receiving a glossary from a client is very important as it ensures that a translator sticks to the required vocabulary. Finally, one person remarked that the glossary helps with maintaining terminological consistency in the source text.

The fifth question from the research interview measured the participants' overall attitude towards the performed tasks. It also evaluated whether they considered the experience beneficial in acquiring new skills necessary for their work as translators.

Participants' attitude to and comments on the tasks performed		**Number of participants**
Beneficial experience		9
in terms of:	• familiarising themselves with CAT software	7
	• acquiring new skills	1
	• improving skills	1
Challenging experience		1

Experience that showed the importance of the translator's role in the MTPE process	1

Table 6 Summary of answers to the fifth interview question

All nine participants in the study agreed that the performance of the project tasks was beneficial in various ways. Some of them appreciated acquiring or improving translation skills. Others emphasized learning CAT software as a positive experience. Still, one person found it challenging, suggesting that this kind of activity is even more appropriate for translator trainees.

The final research interview question addressed the participants' position on including post-editing training in university educational programme.

Interview Question 6		**Number of participants**
Would you like the post-editing exercises to be included in your educational programme at university?	Yes	9
Other comments:	• it would help in career as a translator	5
	• it would be interesting	3
	• it would be an adaptation to today's technologically developed approach to translation	3
	• it would improve and simplify the translator's work	2
	• it is odd that there is no class concerning CAT tool	1

Table 7 Summary of answers to the sixth interview question

Not only would the research participants like to have MTPE training, but they also enumerated the advantages of such exercises. They suggested it would support, simplify and improve their future work as translators. Furthermore, they referred to introducing such activities as a positive adaptation in an educational system and accurate to today's technologically developed approach to translation. Finally, they described MTPE training as enjoyable, which implies that they would be actively engaged in learning new skills.

4. Conclusions and discussion

This study attempted to employ existing findings from the field of MTPE to research tasks with a view of investigating the translation trainees' perspective. Further, it intended to derive the implications for translation pedagogy. Based on the current state of the art, the author hypothesized that there is a need to promote machine translation post-editing skills, and these abilities should be improved in the process of educating translation trainees. To this end, the research analysis was divided into three stages: the review of the participants' questions concerning assignments, tasks evaluation and the analysis of the interview. The subjects of the study were nine first-year students of a Master's degree in English Philology with Translation Studies with a specialization in linguistics between 23 and 25 years old. In the process of data analysis of qualitative research, an inductive approach was implemented with research tasks and questions acting as a prism through which to view the information and choose relevant items.

The primary focus of the study was to assess the attitudes of translation trainees towards MTPE. The answers collected to the fifth and sixth interview questions indicate that participants view training in post-editing machine translation as positive. In Question 5, all nine participants acknowledged that they benefited in various ways from completing the tasks. As advantages, they enumerated acquiring or improving translation skills and learning CAT software. Yet, one person found it challenging, which may indicate a knowledge gap that should be filled. Question 6 provides information on participants' views on the inclusion of MTPE in the training programme for future translators. Not only would the research participants like to have MTPE training, but they also supported their opinion, suggesting that it would ease, simplify and improve their future work as translators. Furthermore, they referred to introducing such activities as a positive adaptation in an educational system and accurate to today's technologically developed approach to translation. Finally, they described MTPE training as enjoyable, which implies that they would actively learn new skills. Question 3 measured participants' approach to the concept of pre-editing using English Controlled Language rules (ECL). Most trainees (7 out of 9) reported that, to some extent, the final version was improved through post-editing and, in consequence, agreed that the application of ECL rules is assumed to support the translator's work. Similarly, answers to Question 4 showed almost unanimity in the survey participants' opinions on the advantage of computer-assisted and terminology management tools in the translator's work.

Implications for teaching the MTPE process were another concern of the study. In particular, attention was brought to the errors that the study participants made in the tasks. Two of the three tasks were completed flawlessly by all participants. Only the third task revealed one type of language error - inflectional - made by seven of the nine participants. It is worth noting that the two participants who did not make this error (they performed the task correctly) asked for additional information and received the answer that the machine translation output should be post-edited. Therefore, it can be concluded that the third task should be supplemented with precise information about the need to post-edit the output from the task. The fact that Task 3 was complex may have also contributed to this error. Most of the participants (8 out of 9) were exposed to CAT software and terminology management for the first time. In summary, the results indicate that changes should be made to both the instruction and the structure of Task 3, preferably breaking it into separate tasks. In addition to errors, the study also examined problems encountered by the participants during the performance of the tasks. Analysis of Task 2 explicated that participants (five out of nine) implemented additional elements to the exercise. Two subjects highlighted sentences selected for correction in the text, and three inserted these units into a table. These findings revealed that Task 2 lacked space in the table for a pre-edited version. Therefore, one might be tempted to conclude that tasks should be designed carefully considering each stage of the student's work, and even more so when it comes to a process as complex as the post-editing of machine translations. Other implications to translation pedagogy may be acquired from the participants' comments during the interviews. In Question 3, one interviewee noted that the ECL rules do not exhaust the topic of pre-editing because they do not cover the issue of metaphors or other phraseological compounds in the text. This comment leads to the conclusion that ECL rules could be enriched with the mentioned above points.

The final issue discussed in the study is the participants' knowledge of MTPE. The first interview question estimated that although all participants are accustomed to MT tools, their state of knowledge on the subject is not extended. Even though each participant declared familiarity with Google Translate, as many as four of them did not use any other tools and three only used DeepL. Other tools mentioned one time were SmartCat and PONS. Question 2 revealed that most participants (7 out of 9) were aware of the variety in MT outputs. Still, more than half of the group admitted that the quality of the translations was, to some degree, unexpected. These responses unveiled that although the participants anticipated the differentiation of MT outputs provided from various MT tools, they showed little knowledge of the quality of the results of these instruments. The analysis of the answers to Question 4 confirmed the inadequate expertise of translation support tools of translation trainees. Out of the 9, only one person, who wrote a dissertation on machine translation himself, was familiar with CAT software.

These conclusions point to the need to include a machine translation post-editing course in the educational programme of future translators. They also indicate that translation support tools, such as computer-assisted and terminology management tools and guidelines, including ECL, should be introduced in the process of developing MTPE skills. Nevertheless, it is worth highlighting that the components included in the course and the state of knowledge about them are constantly evolving, and therefore both the guidelines and the general approach to teaching in this field should remain open to change.

***

The results addressing the main research problem yielded some interesting findings. First, they tentatively support the claim that the participants positively evaluate machine translation post-editing, perceiving benefits such as acquiring or improving translation skills and learning CAT software. Second, they reveal the correlation between Zhechev's (2014) and Silva's (2014) findings that the effort to implement and adapt machine translation in the translation process induces positive results on many levels and students' perspective that the skills gained from the MTPE tasks are an opportunity to facilitate, simplify and improve their future work as translators. Finally, they emphasise the correlation between MTPE and a positive adaptation in an educational system, accurate to today's technologically developed approach to translation mentioned by Brożyna-Reczko (2020) and Witczak (2016).

Another research problem tackled in this study concerned the implications for teaching the MTPE process, focusing on possible errors made by the trainees. The general picture emerging from this part of the analysis is that when confronted with performing a translation using a CAT tool, MT and a glossary, trainees may forget to post-edit TT and thus make apparent errors. Another reason for the appearance of inflectional error may be an insufficiently specified instruction. However, such an explanation is not consistent with the conclusions of Čulo,

Gutermuth, Hansen-Schirra and Nitzke (2014), who assumed that the output of MT itself provokes errors. An additional reason is given by O'Brien (2002) and Depraetere (2010). They suggested that the critical solution to these problems is to train novice translators in post-editing and raise awareness of typical MT errors. Unfortunately, at present, it is not possible to identify one main factor contributing to such errors.

There are also two interesting side findings. First implies that practitioners intuitively aid their performance by adapting enhancements to the exercise structure. This situation occurred in the case of the inclusion of an additional column for a selected sentence from the ST in Task 2. Such practice may indicate the experience of confronting complex sentences in translation contexts. Future research will have to clarify whether the provided explanation is accurate. The second concerned the ECL rules. The results suggest that ECL does not exhaust the topic of pre-editing because they do not cover metaphors or other phraseological compounds in the text. This finding leads to the conclusion that ECL rules could be enriched with the above-mentioned points. Further research in this area is advised.

The results relating to the last issue addressed by the study – the participants' knowledge of MTPE - provided some surprising findings. They show that trainees do not use most of the translation support tools currently available, with most of them reporting experience solely with Google Translate. The situation may imply that after graduation, the trainees would not be prepared for their work as translators according to the assumptions of EMT, which list knowledge and the ability to use tools supporting the work of translators as one of the necessary competencies in this profession.

However, it is worth emphasising that these findings are not generalisable beyond the participants interviewed. In Poland, out of 13 institutions providing BA and MA studies, eight include CAT in their curricula, of which four introduce MT and two MTPE. Thus, students' experience (from institutions with at least CAT in their curricula) with MTPE and the tools in question is likely to be different. Although it can be assumed that the results of this study would provide similar outcomes at universities offering a translation specialisation without including an MTPE course (or CAT or MT), in order to be able to draw further conclusions and translate the results of this work to a broader scope, the study should be replicated. Additionally, it is also worth noting that as the research's main hypothesis is the need for integrating MTPE education into the university teaching system, where MTPE courses are already taught, such a study would not be justified.

Overall, this study confirms the validity of integrating MTPE into the educational programme for future translators. More broadly, this means adapting teaching to the pace of technological development. In order to provide the best possible education aligned with the needs of the translation market, while at the same time increasing the employability of translation graduates in the future, an MTPE course should be included. This summary is in line with the conclusions of Świątek (2015), who suggested that the computer is not an adversary, but a tool in the translator's hands and that translation automation will develop positively. Based on Jan Rybicki's (May 2021) words , the difference between human and machine translation is less and less conspicuous in light of the progressive development of neural machine translation. The changes that are taking place in the field of translation can no longer be ignored. On the contrary, such ignorance may lead to the opposite effect –translators will be less and less qualified, and the level of their work will decline.

Given the need expressed by Nikishina (2018) and Tomaszkiewicz (2019) for consistency and precise guidelines in the education of future translators, the research findings led the author to attempt to design an MTPE course. The set of 15 lessons of 1.5 hours each is considered to be an impulse to introduce this component in the university curriculum. The course is structured to include an introduction, the three stages of the MTPE process, time for exercises to consolidate and test the knowledge and skills acquired, as well as a discussion on the future of post-editing and students' evaluation of course. The tasks are arranged in such a way that trainees systematically learn and improve the MTPE process. Upon completing the course, the participants should be equipped with basic knowledge of the discussed field and skills that will enable them to work independently in processing machine translations within various fields. The author encourages the researchers to investigate whether the above assumptions are achievable and to suggest further adjustments.

The above MTPE course proposal includes using tools such as light and full post-editing guidelines and ECL rules. However, these measures do not differentiate and address the needs of the fields from which the texts originate. In other words, a different approach would be needed for literary, academic or journalistic texts and another for texts from the field of law or medicine. Therefore, the next step to improve the MTPE course and enrich the state of knowledge of working with machine translations should be to adapt (or construct) separate guidelines and rules for varied disciplines. Again, a suitably adapted tool could be a valuable contribution to the development of MTPE.

Acknowledgement

I would like to thank my supervisor Beata Piecychna, PhD for her guidance and support during this project.

References

Belam, J. (2003). Buying up to falling down: A deductive approach to teaching post-editing. In *MT Summit IX Workshop on Teaching Translation Technologies and Tools (T4 Third Workshop on Teaching Machine Translation),* pages 1–10. Citese.

Brożyna-Reczko, M. 2020. Narzędzia Cyfrowe w Dydaktyce Przekładu: Zasoby Leksykalne Oraz Narzędzia Korpusowe Do Edycji Tekstu. In *Roczniki Humanistyczne,* No. 68, 181-193.

Depraetere, I. (2010). What counts as useful advice in a university post-editing training context? In *EAMT 2010: Proceedings of the 14th annual conference of the European association for machine translation,* pages 1–9, Saint-Raphaël, France.

Doherty, S. and Kenny, D. (2014). The design and evaluation of a statistical machine translation syllabus for translation students. In *The Interpreter and Translator Trainer 8(2),* pages 295–315.

Flanagan, M. and Paulsen Christensen, T. (2014). Testing post-editing guidelines: how translation trainees interpret them and how to tailor them for translator training purposes, In *The Interpreter and Translator Trainer*, 8:2, pages 257-275.

Folaron, D. (2010). Translation tools. In *Gambier, Yves and Luc van Doorslaer (eds.) Handbook of Translation Studies:* vol. 1., pages 429–436, Amsterdam / Philadelphia: John Benjamins Publishing.

González Davies, M. (2004). *Multiple voices in the translation classroom: activities, tasks and projects. Vol. 54.* Amsterdam/Philadelphia: John Benjamins Publishing.

Guerberof Arenas, A. and Moorkens, J. (2019). Machine translation and post-editing training as part of a master's programme. In *The Journal of Specialized Translation Issue 31,* pages 217-238.

Kliffer, M. (2008). Post-Editing Machine Translation As an FSL Exercise. In *Porta Linguarum: revista internacional de didáctica de las lenguas extranjeras. Nº. 9,* pages 53-68.

Matthews, B. and Ross, L. (2010). *Research Methods: A Practical Guide for the Social Sciences,* Edinburgh: Pearson Education Ltd.

Nikishina, M. 2018. MT-assisted TM translation: the future of translation or just a fad? In *Applied Linguistics Papers* 25/4, University of Warsaw, 91–100.

O'Brien, S. (2002). Teaching post-editing: a proposal for course content. In *6th EAMT Workshop Teaching Machine Translation*, pages 99–106.

Pym, A. (2013). Translation Skill-Sets in a Machine-Translation Age. In *Meta: Translators' Journal*, vol. 58, n° 3, pages 487-503.

Rybicki, J. 2021. Stylometry 0, Machine Translation 1. Deep Learning Based MT Scores Important Away Win. In *Book of abstracts CALT 2021* https://docs.google.com/document/d/e/2PACX-1vRWAAgOpMCWqGniXJAULzCra1e4We2U7lQj53e7qbKNIgHvjLGmHrwlsqbqCJCQIwJ11tztjQVmXMu6/pub.

Świątek, J. 2015. The Potential and Limits of Statistical Machine Translation http://cejsh.icm.edu.pl/cejsh/element/bwmeta1.element.desklight-77fcb44a-60a8-4ace-87df-6b71106d3df2/c/art18.pdf.

Tomaszkiewicz, T. 2019. Ewolucja kształcenia tłumaczy zawodowych w kontekście wyzwań współczesnego przekładoznawstwa i wymogów rynku pracy. In *Między Oryginałem a Przekładem* 44, 199-216.

Witczak, O. 2016a. Tłumacze kontra maszyny, czyli o tłumaczeniu wspomaganym komputerowo. In *Tłumacz – praktyczne aspekty zawodu* Publisher: Wydawnictwo Naukowe UAM, 203-234.

--------------2016b. Incorporating post-editing into a computer-assisted translation course. A study of student attitudes. In *Journal of Translator Education and Translation Studies,* (1), 35-55.

Raw Machine Translation

A way to make essential information available for potential customers

Sabine Peng

Senior Localization Program Manager

August 2021

vmware

Agenda

- Why Raw MT
- What's the Strategy
- How to implement Raw MT
- Case Study
- Achievements
- Recap & What's Next
- Q&A

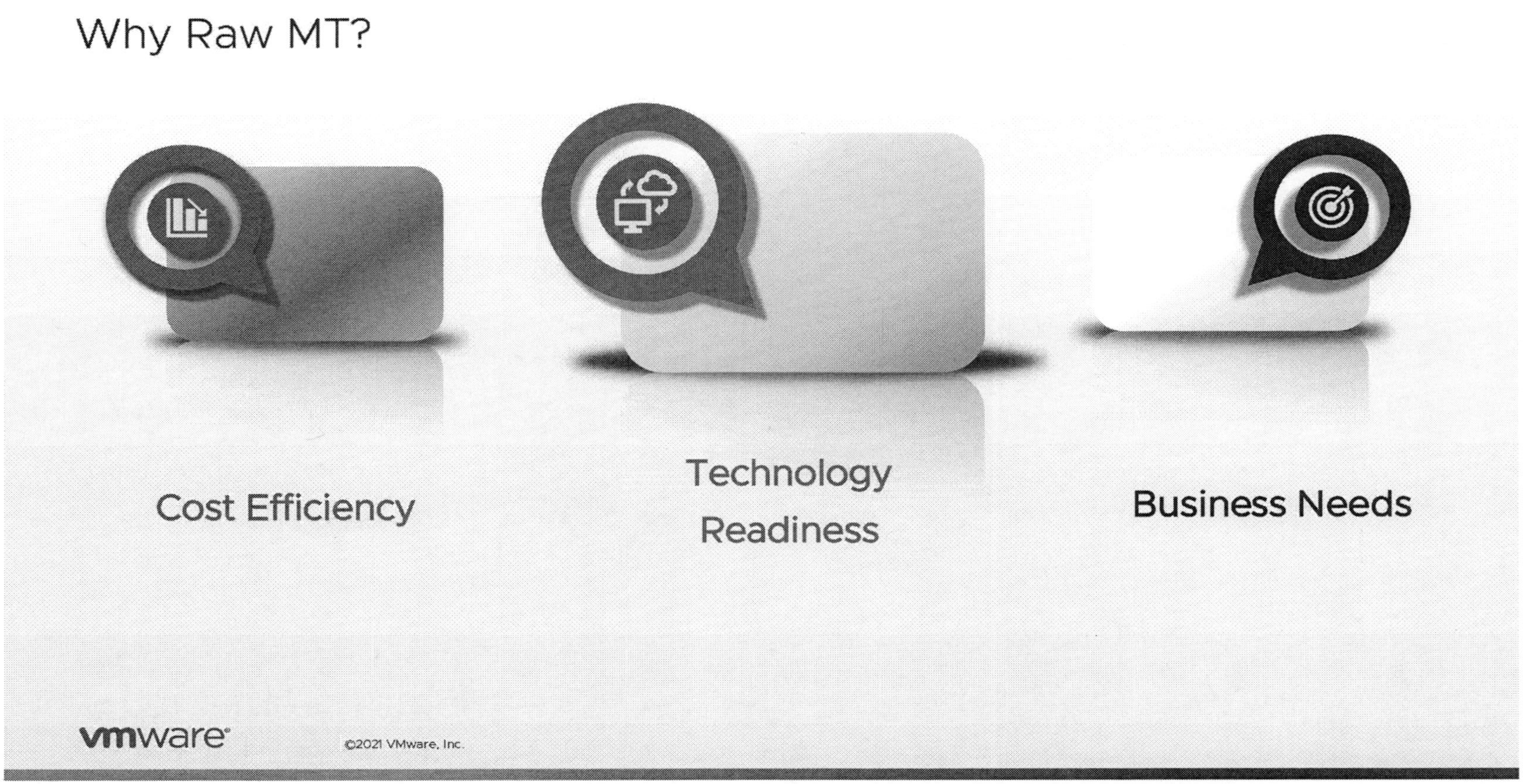
Why Raw MT?
Cost Efficiency
Technology Readiness
Business Needs
vmware
©2021 VMware, Inc.

What's the Strategy?

Part of Tiered Localization

Raw MT is part of Tiered Localization, the solution package with pre-defined and customized solutions for different scenarios.

Docs First

Raw MT is applied to Docs First considering that UI localization is more complex with higher risk.

Business Requirements

Raw MT is requested for some specific Business Requirements.

Specific for Some Locales/Products

Raw MT is used in Selected Languages and Products based on the data analysis.

vmware

Tiered Localization Introduction

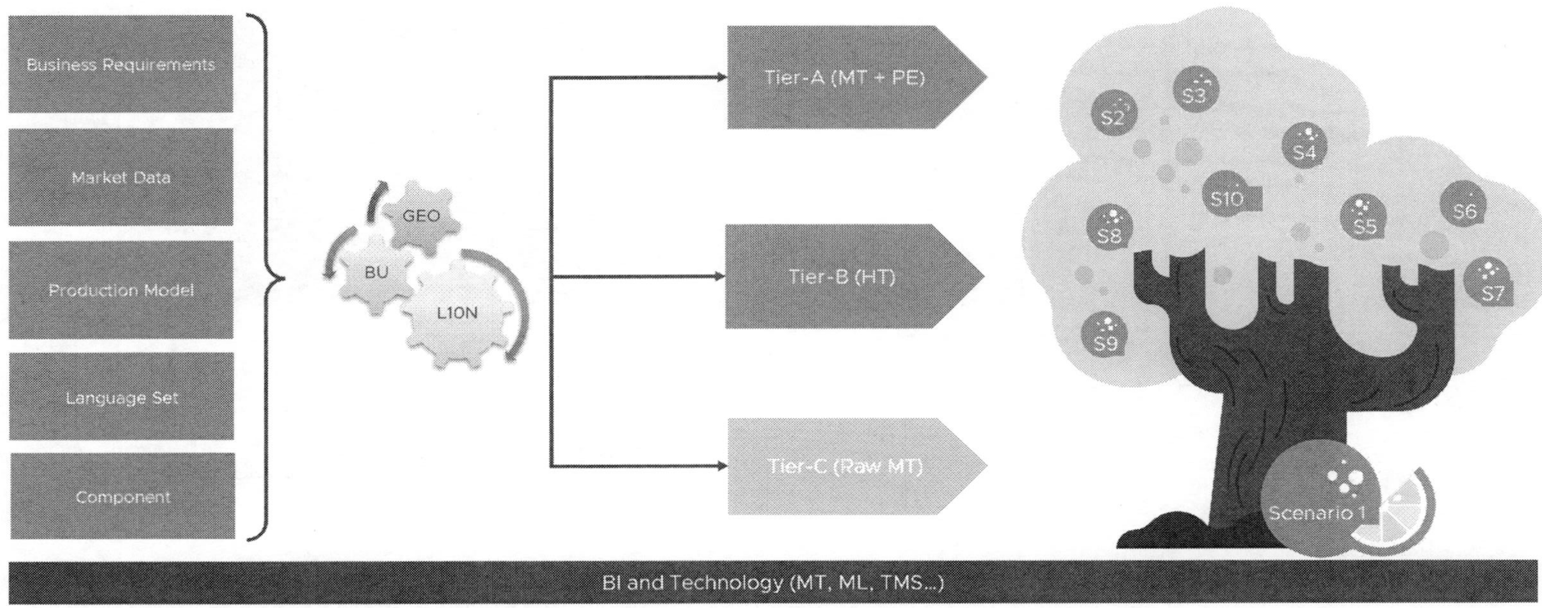

vmware®

Business Requirements

Product Documentation

As per customer survey, customers prefer using localized documentation, so Raw MT is implemented in some scenarios.

Hands-on-Lab

Raw MT is required for the updates of localized manuals, quick with no cost.

Knowledge Base

Raw MT is applied to some selected relatively high viewed articles in selected languages, while top viewed articles use MT + PE.

Internal Reference

Raw MT is used for internal document requests.

vmware

Selected Languages

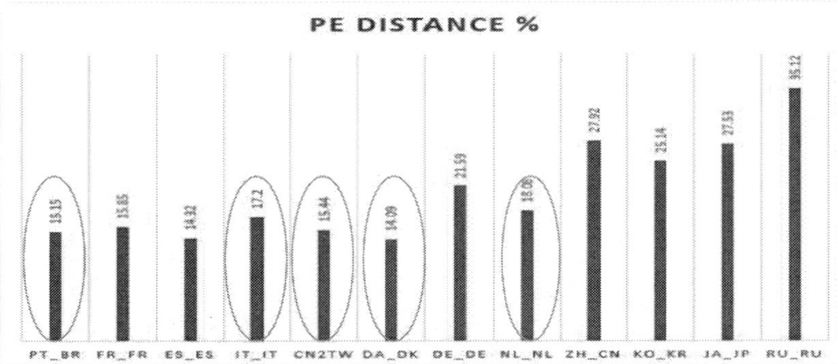

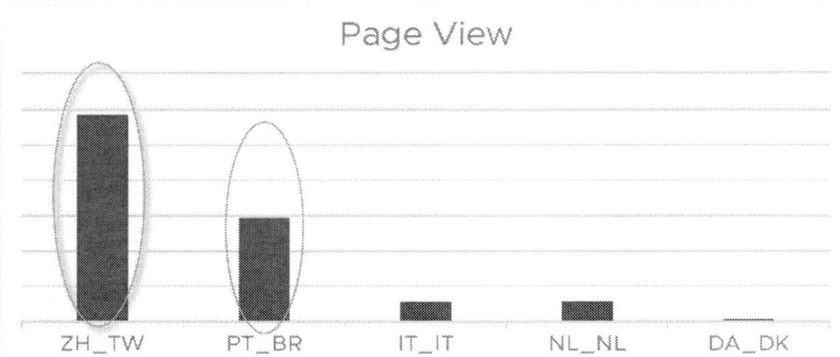

Language Candidates

- Brazilian Portuguese
- Italian
- Traditional Chinese
- Danish
- Dutch

Selected Languages

- Traditional Chinese
- Brazilian Portuguese

vmware

Selected Products

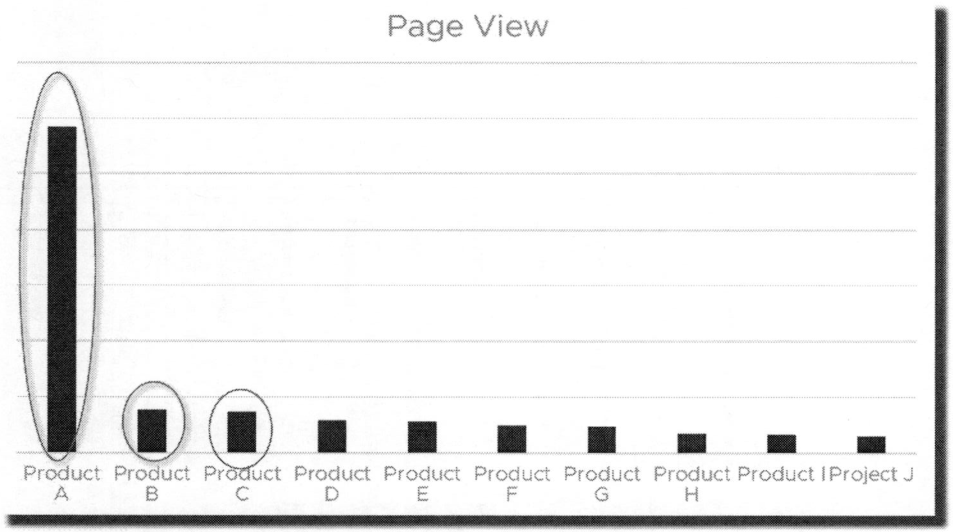

Top 3 Products Selected

- Product A
- Product B
- Product C

Workflow Readiness

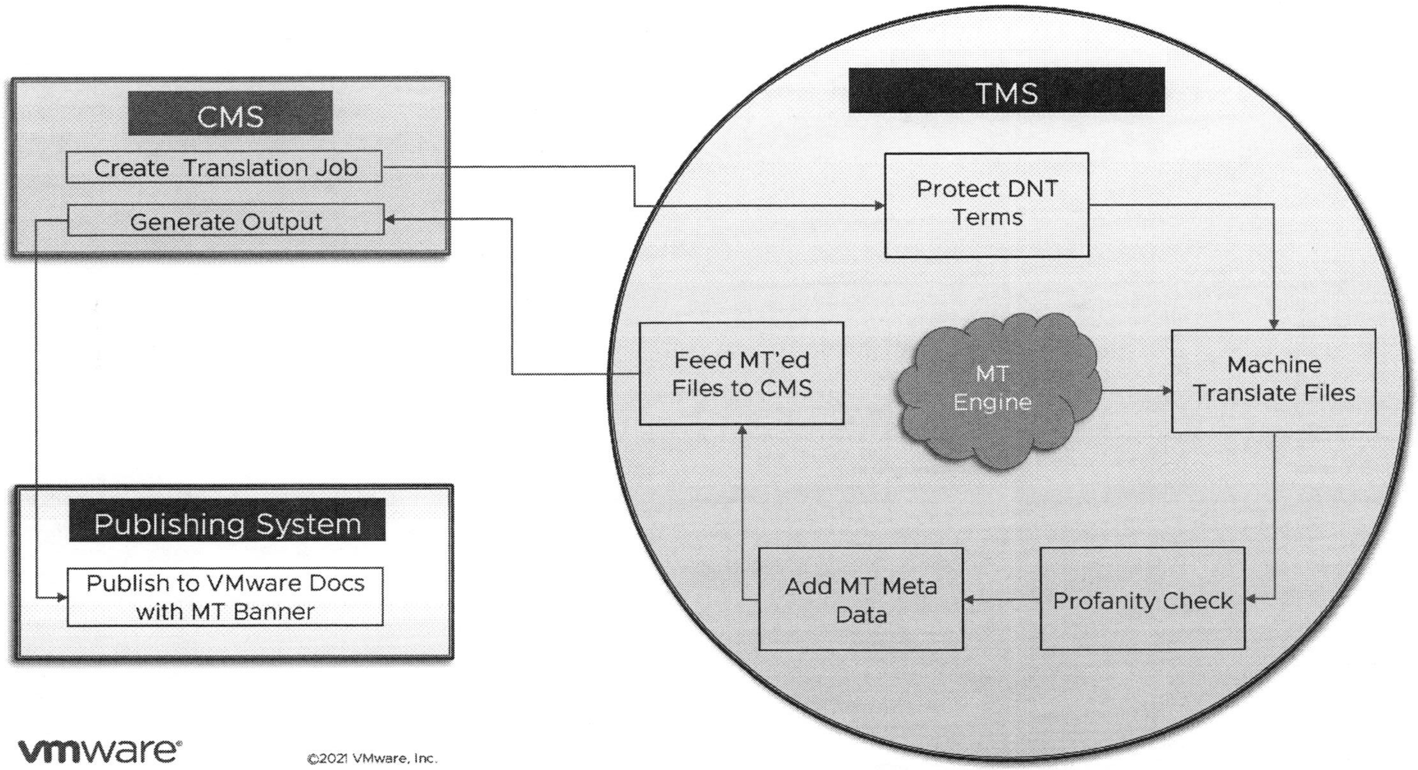

Raw MT Output Evaluation

Prediction Model in Place

Prerequisite - Prediction Model in Place
- Golden translation
- Normal translation – PED% ≤ 20%
- Bad translation – PED% >20%

Formula Ready & Validation

Formula:
- Overall score = Sum of Prediction Score for each Segment ÷ No. of Segments
- Validation Result - Pass

AA Ready in TMS Raw MT Workflow

Project Name	Locale	Workgroup	Project #	Creation Date	Description	Overall Quality Score
test score33333	de_DE_utf16	R&D G11n	72283	11/11/20, 10:30 PM		80
test score222	fr_FR_utf16	R&D G11n	72282	11/11/20, 10:26 PM		78
test score	pl_PL_utf16	R&D G11n	72281	11/11/20, 10:22 PM		50

vmware

Sample

vmware ©2021 VMware, Inc.

Case Study 1 – CN2TW

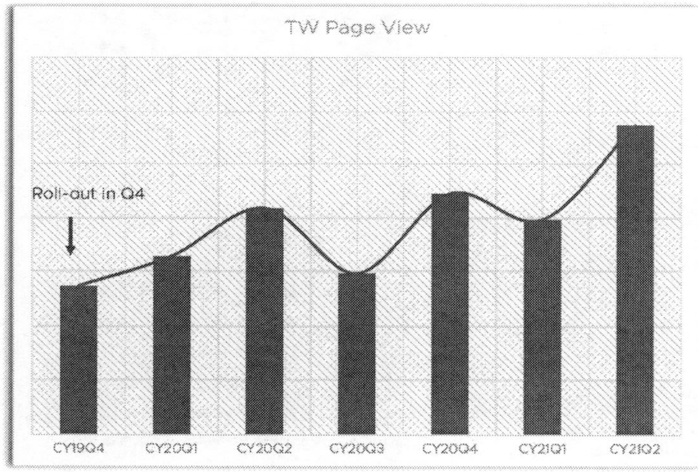

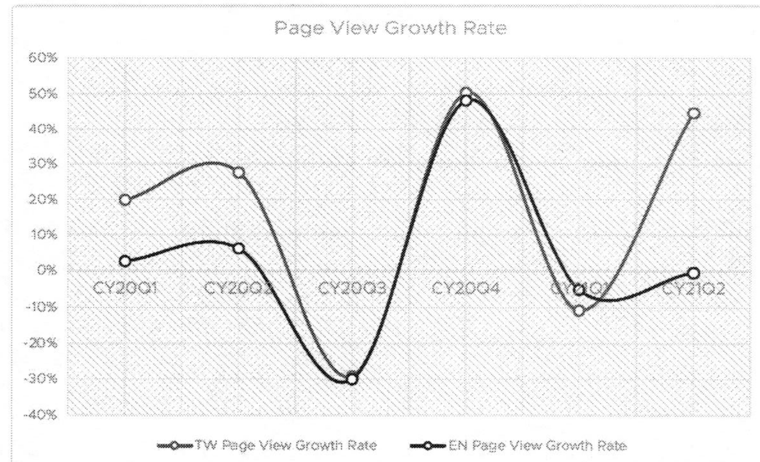

TW Page View Trend

The trend of TW page view is increasing after Raw MT roll-out.

Page View Growth Rate Trend

TW page view growth rate is almost equal to or higher than EN page view growth rate after Raw MT roll-out.

Q/Q Growth rate = (page view this month – page view last month) / page view last month

vmware

Case Study 2 – EN2BR

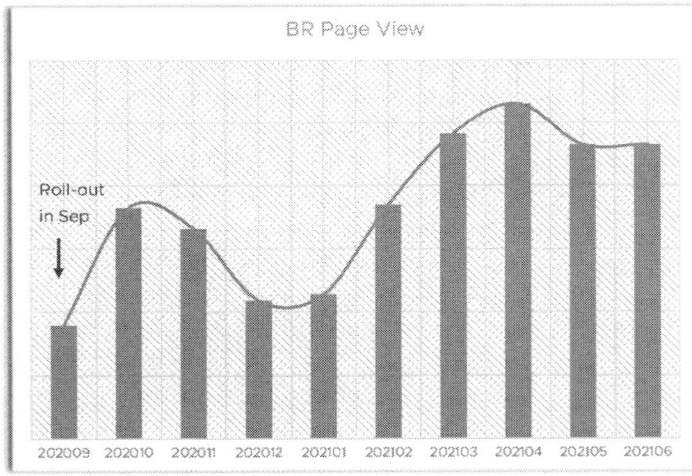

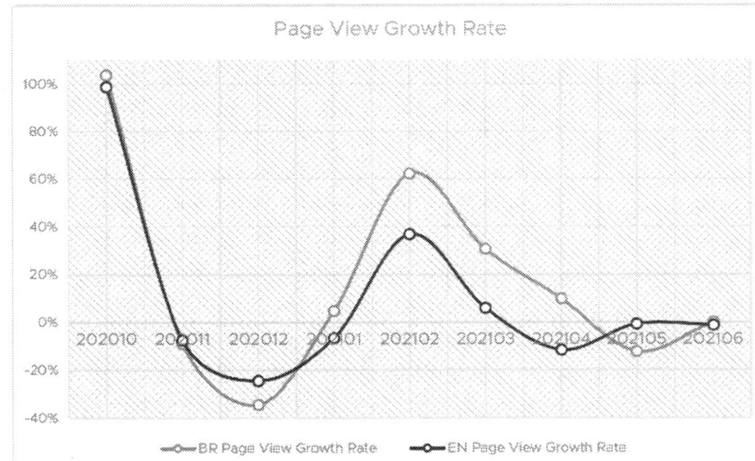

BR Page View Trend

The trend of BR page view is increasing after Raw MT roll-out.

Page View Growth Rate Trend

BR page view growth rate is higher than EN page view growth rate most of the time after Raw MT roll-out.

Q/Q Growth rate = (page view this month – page view last month) / page view last month

Achievements

BU Quotes

"Thanks for the update! Good to know this project is being used by our users."
"I'm looking forward to the page view data of MT translation 😉"

Cost Avoidance

Cost avoidance takes **~7%** of the total cost last fiscal year.

Page View Growth

Page view increases over **100%** after Raw MT roll-out.

vmware®

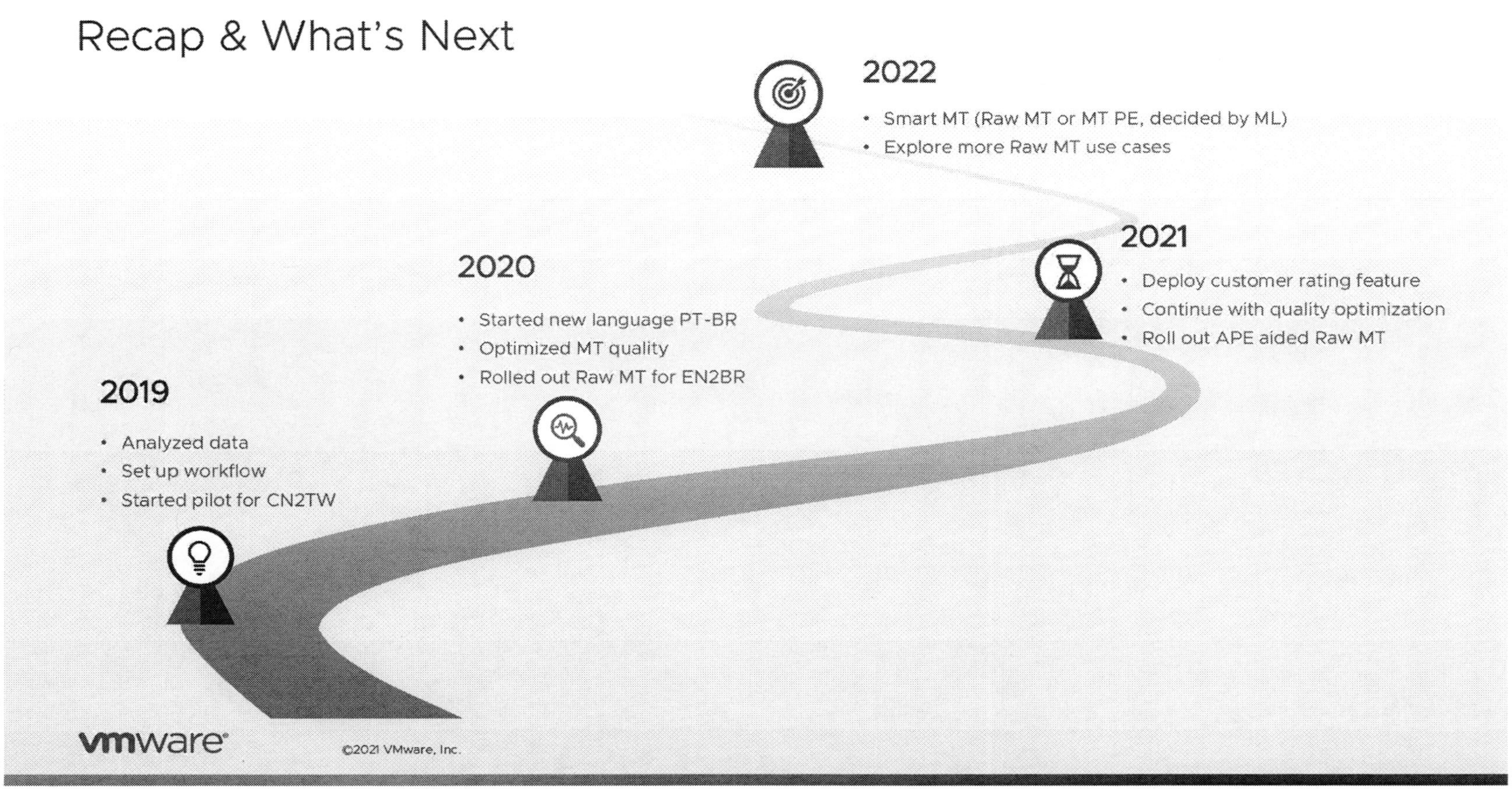
Recap & What's Next
2022
• Smart MT (Raw MT or MT PE, decided by ML)
• Explore more Raw MT use cases
2021
• Deploy customer rating feature
• Continue with quality optimization
• Roll out APE aided Raw MT
2020
• Started new language PT-BR
• Optimized MT quality
• Rolled out Raw MT for EN2BR
2019
• Analyzed data
• Set up workflow
• Started pilot for CN2TW
©2021 VMware, Inc.

Thank You

Field Experiments of Real-Time Foreign News Distribution Powered by MT

Keiji Yasuda ke-yasuda@mindword.jp
MINDWORD Inc., 7-19-11, Nishishinjuku, Shinjuku-ku, Tokyo 160-0023, Japan
Ichiro Yamada yamada.i-hy@nhk.or.jp
NHK Science and Technology Research Laboratories, 1-10-11, Kinuta, Setagaya-ku, Tokyo 157-8510, Japan
Naoaki Okazaki okazaki@c.titech.ac.jp
Tokyo Institute of Technology, 2-12-1, Ookayama, Meguro-ku, Tokyo 152-8550, Japan
Hideki Tanaka hideki.tanaka@nict.go.jp
NICT Universal Communication Research Institute, 3-5, Hikaridai, Seika-cho, Soraku-gun, Kyoto 619-0289, Japan
(was with NHK Engineering system when this work was done)
Hidehiro Asaka asaka@jiji.co.jp
Jiji Press Ltd., 5-15-8, Ginza, Chuo-ku, Tokyo 104-8178, Japan
Takeshi Anzai takeshi.anzai@toppan.co.jp
Toppan Printing Co., Ltd.,1-3-3, Suido, Bunkyo-ku, Tokyo 112-8531, Japan
Fumiaki Sugaya fsugaya@mindword.jp
MINDWORD Inc., 7-19-11, Nishishinjuku Shinjuku-ku, Tokyo 160-0023, Japan

Abstract

Field experiments on a foreign news distribution system using two key technologies are reported. The first technology is a summarization component, which is used for generating news headlines. This component is a transformer-based abstractive text summarization system which is trained to output headlines from the leading sentences of news articles. The second technology is machine translation (MT), which enables users to read foreign news articles in their mother language. Since the system uses MT, users can immediately access the latest foreign news. 139 Japanese LINE users participated in the field experiments for two weeks, viewing about 40,000 articles which had been translated from English to Japanese. We carried out surveys both during and after the experiments. According to the results, 79.3% of users evaluated the headlines as adequate, while 74.7% of users evaluated the automatically translated articles as intelligible. According to the post-experiment survey, 59.7% of users wished to continue using the system; 11.5% of users did not. We also report several statistics of the experiments.

1. Introduction

Due to economic globalization, quick distribution of foreign news is becoming increasingly important. There are two important aspects of foreign news. One is freshness, which can help readers make economic decisions; for example, overseas trends must be grasped quickly in order to make investment decisions. The other aspect is accuracy, since wrong information could cause readers to make wrong decisions. Regarding freshness, ICT technologies such as mobile networks, mobile devices and SNS enable users to access the latest news. However, it still takes time to distribute foreign news because the translation process is done manually. Meanwhile, machine translation (MT) has drastically improved in recent years. For translation between language in the same or close family, some systems show a comparable performance with human translators.

This paper introduces a real-time foreign news distribution system which incorporates MT, and shows the results of field experiments for the language pair of Japanese and English. Since these languages are of completely different families, even the latest MT systems produce translation errors. To help understand of the news correctly, the distribution system has a function to request post-editing by human translators.

Section 2 introduces the natural language technologies used for the proposed news distribution system. Section 3 shows the configuration of the system. Section 4 explains the field experiments and shows their results. Finally, section 5 provides some conclusions.

2. System components

The news distribution features two key technologies: MT which enables users to read foreign news articles in their mother language, and a text summarization function which generates news headline. These technologies are outlined below.

2.1. Machine Translation

The MT system (Mino, 2020) used for this research is a transformer-based encoder-decoder model (Vaswani, 2017). We constructed different types of parallel news corpora to develop our MT system. The primary corpus was built by manually translating Japanese news articles. The remaining corpora were respectively constructed by different approaches: an automatic sentence alignment method between Japanese and English news articles; post-editing of the aligned news articles manually; and a back-translation technique (Sennrich et al., 2016) to leverage monolingual news articles. To exploit multiple corpora with different features, we extend a domain-adaptation method by using multiple tags to train an NMT model effectively. This improves the translation quality of the MT system.

2.2. Headline Generation using Text Summarization Technology

2.2.1. Text Summarization Technology

The text summarization method used for our research is a transformer-based abstractive text summarization method (Matsumaru, 2020), which is trained to output headlines from the leading sentences of news articles. Using this method, the text summarization system for our news distribution system was trained on the corpus provided by Jiji Press Ltd.

2.2.2. Headline Generation in Target Language

News headlines are very important in news distribution, because most readers decide whether to read the full news articles or not based on their headlines.

As shown in Fig. 1, given a pair of a news headline and an article in the source language, there are several ways to generate a headline in the target language. The first way is to apply direct machine translation to the source-language headline. This method only requires MT, which was explained in the previous subsection. The second way applies text summarization to generate a headline in the source language, then MT to translate the generated headline to the target language. The third way is the reverse of the second way: it uses MT to translate the whole article first, then text summarization to generate the headline in the target language.

To compare these methods, we carried out evaluation experiments using BLEU score (Papineni, 2002) as an evaluation metric. Since news headlines normally contain only a few words, we adjusted the maximum n-gram length to 2 to calculate the BLEU score.

Figure 2 shows the evaluation results of the headline generation experiments. Here, the translation direction is English to Japanese. As shown in the figure, the third way gives the best results in terms of the BLEU score. Considering these results, our foreign news distribution system automatically translates articles first, then applies text summarization to generate headlines.

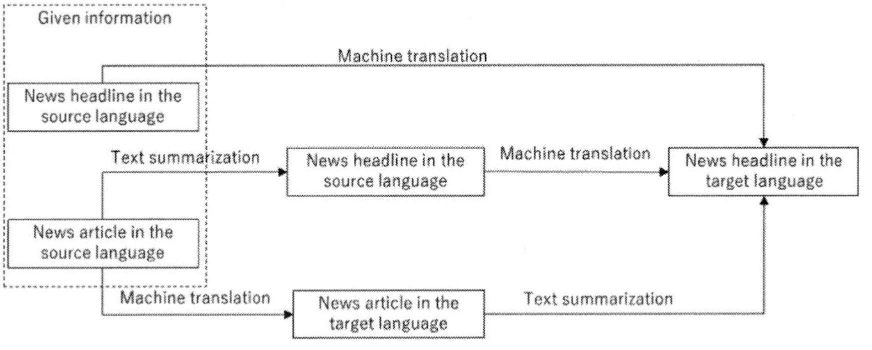

Figure 1. Method of generating headlines in the target language.

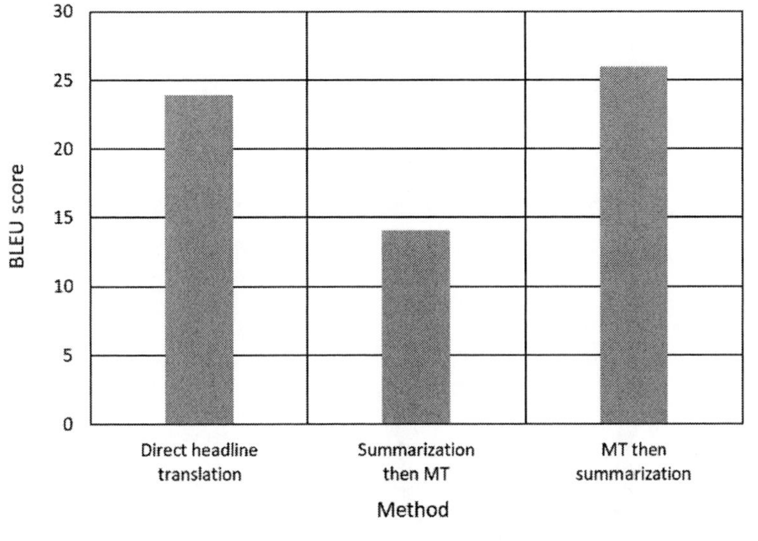

Figure 2. Evaluation results of headline generation methods.

3. Foreign News Distribution System

This section explains the foreign news distribution system which we developed. Figure 3 shows the system configuration. As shown in the figure, the system distributes news via the LINE[1] app, which has the highest market share in Japan among messaging apps. The original news information is provided in the format of XML files from a news article server operated by Jiji Press Ltd. The contents processing block in the figure includes news article extraction from XML files. Then, the news distribution server interacts with MT and headline generation servers to obtain headlines and articles in the target language.

The system distributes the translated headlines and links of machine translated articles as LINE messages. The users can set the distribution frequency (1 to 12 hours) and preferred news categories from 10 kinds including politics, economy and sports. Excluding breaking news, the news distribution server controls the distributed articles, timing and order according to users' preferences. For breaking news, the system distributes the news as soon as possible regardless of preferences. If users cannot understand the MT-generated news articles, they can request manual post-edit via the LINE app. Figure 4 shows screenshot of the news distribution system on the LINE app. By clicking on a headline sent as a LINE message, the user can read the translated article in full.

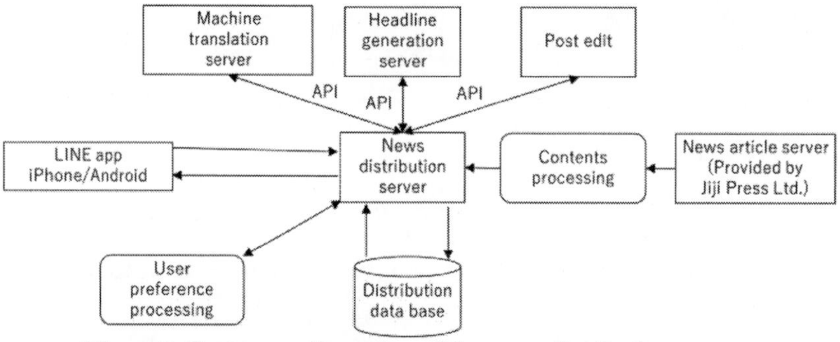

Figure 3. System configuration of the news distribution system.

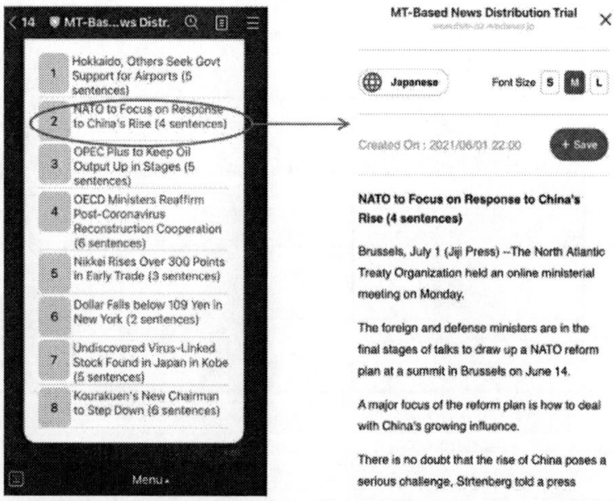

Figure 4. Screenshot of the news distribution system on LINE app.

[1] https://line.me/en/

4. Field Experiments

4.1. Experimental Settings

Field experiments were carried out on the developed system, with the participation of 139 Japanese LINE users during period of December 9 to 22, 2020. During this period, users viewed about 40,000 articles translated from English to Japanese. We carried out surveys both during and after the experiments.

4.2. Experimental Results

Table 1 shows the ratio of the distributed articles and post-edit requested articles aggregated by the 10 news categories. By comparing the distributed and post-edit requested ratio, the top three most frequently distributed categories tended to be requested the most. Especially, news in the politics category had a high ratio of post-edit requests. The average time to complete manual post-editing after user's request was 2 hours and 45 minutes. The survey showed that 88.9% of users felt the intelligibility of post-edited articles had been improved.

Figure 5 shows the results of the post-experiment survey on the quality of headline generation and article translation. According to the results, 79.3% of users evaluated headlines as adequate, while 74.7% of users evaluated automatically translated articles as intelligible. Another post-experiment survey revealed that 59.7% of users wished to continue using the foreign news distribution service, while 11.5% did not.

News category	Ratio of distributed articles	Ratio of post-edit requested articles
Politics	23.3%	**38.0%**
Economy	17.4%	**18.9%**
Sports	15.6%	**17.3%**
Health	14.5%	10.4%
Social	14.6%	10.0%
Culture	5.7%	2.4%
Dispute	5.8%	1.3%
Science	1.7%	1.1%
Local	1.2%	0.5%
Education	0.3%	0.1%

Table 1. Ratio of distributed news articles and post-edit requested articles.

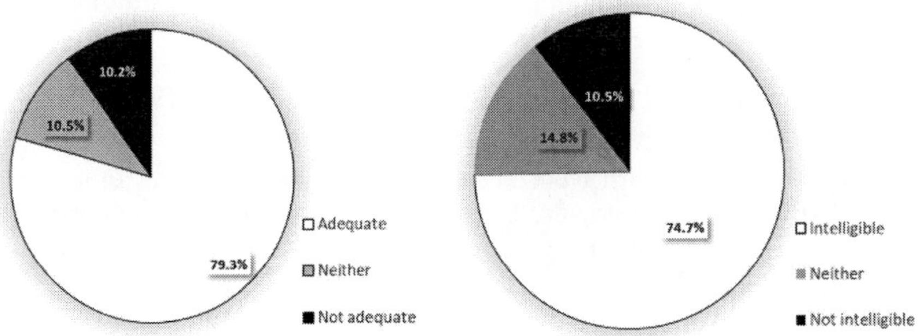

Figure 5. Results of survey on adequacy of headlines and intelligibility of translated articles.

5. Conclusions

We developed a foreign news distribution system that generates headlines and articles in the target language by using text summarization and MT technologies. The system handles English-to-Japanese translation of news articles, which are not easy to translate even for the s latest MT systems.

However, 74.7% of users evaluated the automatically translated articles as intelligible, while 79.3% of users evaluated the automatically generated headlines as adequate. The system also provides a function to request manual post-edit to resolve translation errors, which helps users to understand news articles correctly.

Acknowledgements

This research was commissioned by the National Institute of Information and Communications Technology (NICT, Grant Number 19701 and 21101), Japan.

References

Matsumaru, K., Takase, S., and Okazaki, N. (2020). Improving Truthfulness of Headline Generation., In *Proceedings of the 58th Annual Meeting of the Association for Computational Linguistics*, pages 1335–1346.

Mino, H., Tanaka H., Ito, H., Goto, I., Yamada, I., and Tokunaga T. (2020). Content-Equivalent Translated Parallel News Corpus and Extension of Domain Adaptation for Neural Machine Translation. In *Proceedings of the 12th Conference on Language Resources and Evaluation*, pages 3616–3622.

Papineni, K., Roukos, S., Ward, T., and Zhu, W.-J. (2002). Bleu: a method for automatic evaluation of machine translation. In *Proceedings of the 40th Annual Meeting of the Association for Computational Linguistics*, pages 311–318.

Sennrich, R., Haddow, B., and Birch, A. (2016). Improving neural machine translation models with monolingual data. In *Proceedings of the 54th Annual Meeting of the Association for Computational Linguistics*, pages 86–96.

Vaswani, A., Shazeer, N., Parmar, N., Uszkoreit, J., Jones, L., Gomez, A. N., Kaiser, L. U., and Polosukhin, I. (2017). Attention is all you need. In *Advances in Neural Information Processing Systems*, pages 5998–6008.

GALA
MTPE Training
Special Interest Group

A Common Machine Translation Post-Editing Training Protocol by GALA

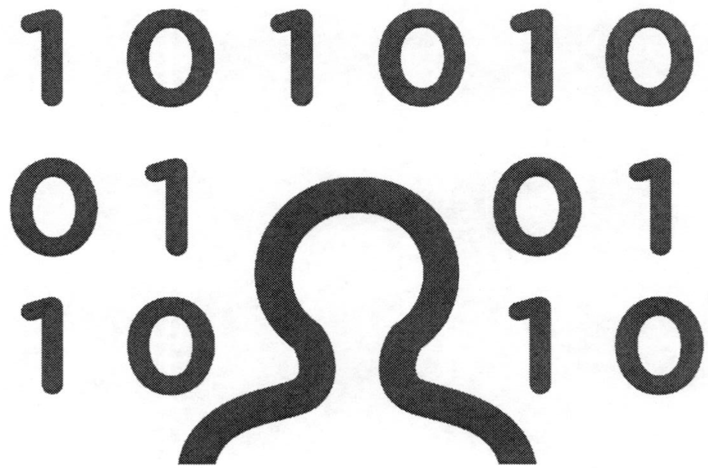

16th August 2021

GALA Globalization & Localization Association

MT SUMMIT 2021 VIRTUAL
The 18th Biennial Machine Translation Summit

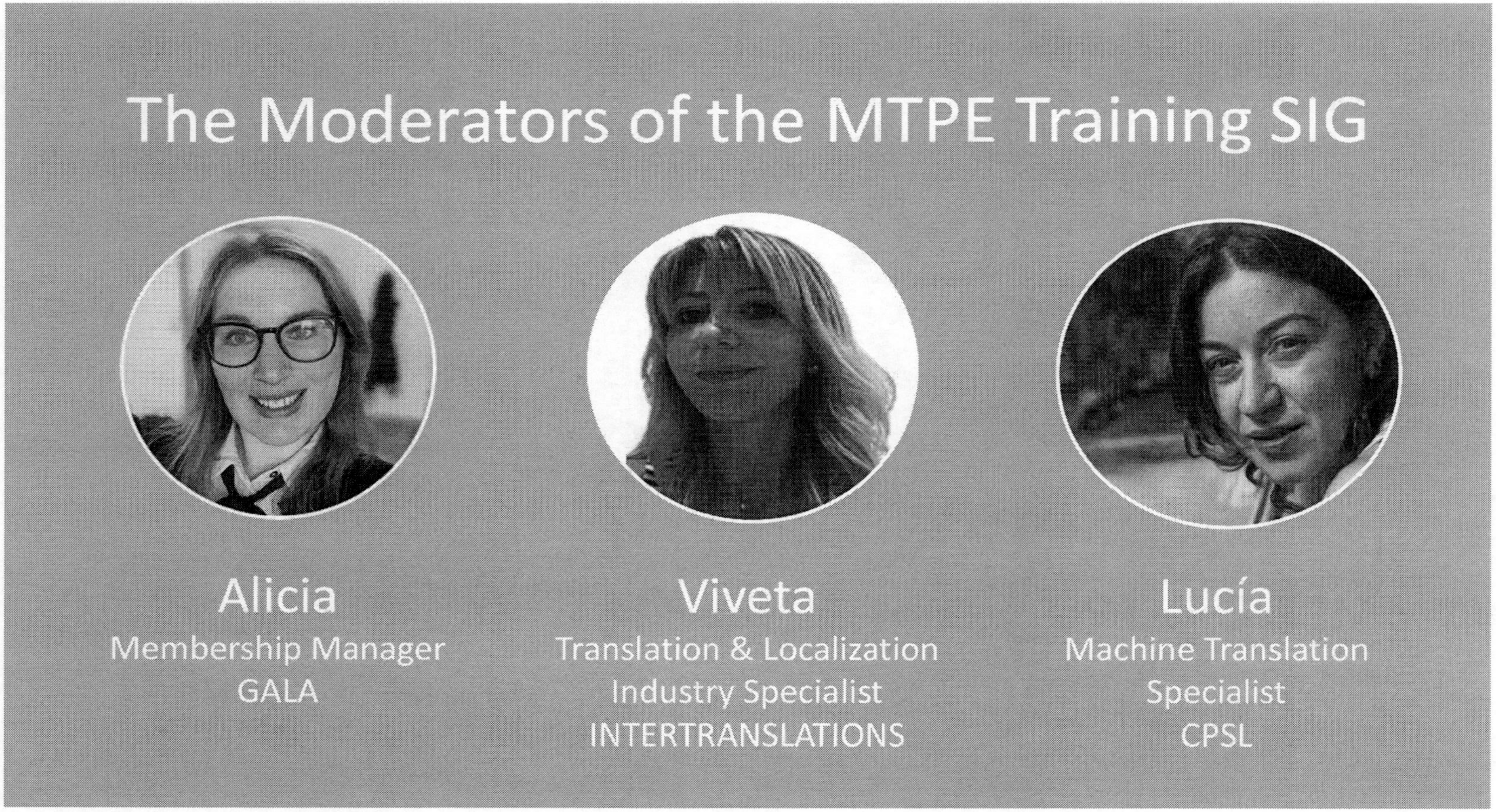
The Moderators of the MTPE Training SIG
Alicia
Membership Manager
GALA
Viveta
Translation & Localization
Industry Specialist
INTERTRANSLATIONS
Lucía
Machine Translation
Specialist
CPSL

A few Words about the Moderators

Viveta Gene, The Inspirator

Intertranslations

Viveta Gene is Translation & Localization Industry Specialist at **Intertranslations S.A.** With more than 15 years of experience as a linguist and vendor manager, she recently decided to combine her expertise and know-how to become a Language Solutions Specialist. Viveta has an MA in Translation and New Technologies from the Department of Foreign Languages and Interpreting from the Ionian University. Her main focus is to promote new trends in the industry, where translation skills meet MT technology. MT tools and Post-Editing techniques are amongst her key fields of interest. She is a PhD Candidate in Translation with main focus on Post-Editing Effort, Quality and Training. This year, she is leading as Moderator the GALA MTPE Training SIG in an attempt to create a common Post-Editing Training Protocol for LSPs, Clients and Universities. She has been recently a speaker at TC42 presenting The Role and Perspective of Post-Editor.

Lucía Guerrero, The Facilitator

CPSL

Lucía Guerrero is a Machine Translation Specialist at **CPSL** and part of the affiliated teaching staff at the Universitat Oberta de Catalunya. She holds a degree in Translation and Interpreting, and in Humanities. Having worked in the translation industry since 1998, she has also been a Senior Translation and Localization Project Manager specialized in international institutions, has managed localization projects for Apple Computer and has translated children's and art books. At CPSL she is currently in charge of the company's machine translation strategy. Some of her tasks include training and evaluation of MT systems, designing custom-tailored workflows and creating support materials for posteditors. She has been speaker at international conferences about language and technologies, such as AMTA or Asling, mainly focusing on the role of the posteditor and on the importance of adding qualitative feedback to raw MT output evaluation.

www.gala-global.org

Presentation of the MTPE Training SIG

AN INITIATIVE FOR A COMMON POST-EDITING TRAINING PROTOCOL FOR Academia, Clients, LSPs & Post-editors

- A Common Post-Editing Training Protocol to address the challenges we currently face and promote our cooperation

GALA Webinar: The Management & Training Challenges of Post-Editing (Part I & Part II)

Viveta Gene, Intertranslations S.A., May 2020

https://www.gala-global.org/events/events-calendar/management-and-training-challenges-post-editing-part-1

www.gala-global.org

The Vision of the MTPE Training SIG

The MTPE Training SIG is a collaborative, community-driven initiative to develop and evangelize best practices in the training and preparation of professionals handling the post-editing of machine translated content.

The goal of the group is to :

- Share experience in the field of training post-editors, common practices, and standards
- Identify the training needs for post-editors based on this common pool of experience from all parties, Academia, Clients, LSPs and Post-Editors
- Develop a common Post-Editing Training Protocol

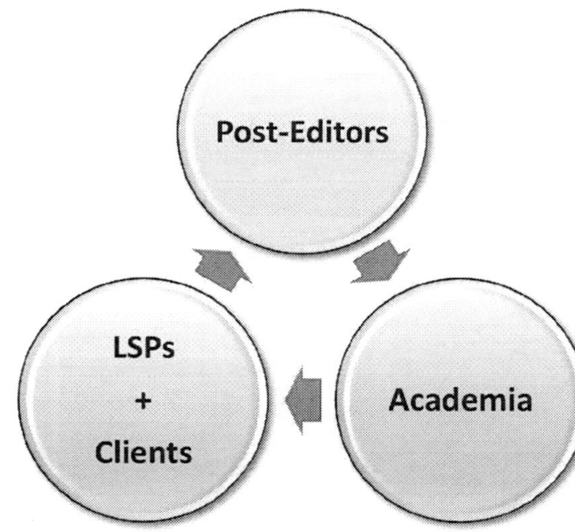

The deliverable of the MTPE Training SIG

a. a List of Actions for each community involved (Academia, Clients, LSPs, Post-Editors) to facilitate the training of professionals per community

b. a Common MTPE Training Protocol for all Parties Involved in the form of a handbook with guidelines on how to build a training model for professional post-editors

The Structure & Working Method of the MTPE Training SIG

- Moderators are responsible for the organization and content of all actions
- Each Group is coordinated by its representative
- Each Representative is the ambassador of the ideas of his/her group
- All Ideas/Actions/Documents are kept in Basecamp and updated by Representatives/Moderators
- Moderators compile all information to design the next actions and draft the sections of the handbook

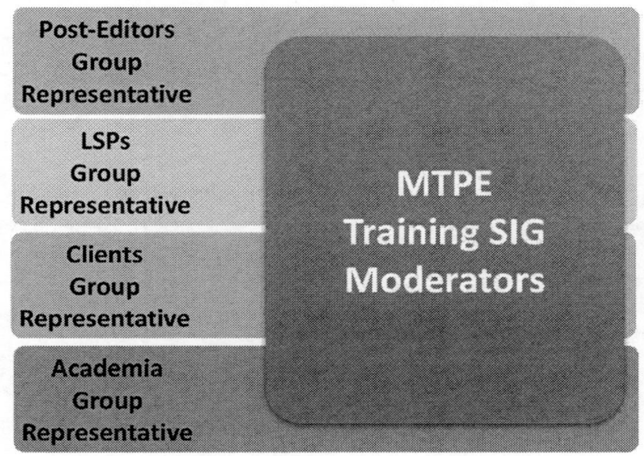

www.gala-global.org

Group Representatives
Clients Group Representative
LSPs Group Representative
Post-Editors Representative
Academia Group Representatives
Cristina
Machine Translation Lead
ELECTRONIC ARTS
Diego
Founder & CEO
CREATIVE WORDS
Jessica
Head of Translations Technology Implementation Specialist
BROMBERG & ASSOCIATES, LLC.
Pete
Chief Analytics Officer
Professor
UNIVERSITY OF TEXAS ARLINGTON
Sabrina
Doctoral Assistant
Faculty of Translation and Interpreting
UNIVERSITE DE GENEVE

Our Basecamp Platform for Continuous Interaction

- <u>What is Basecamp?</u>
- Group Documents,
  Minutes & Announcements
- Chatting Options

GALA's Basecamp enables SIG members to come together between monthly meetings, review the meeting slides and minutes and continue the conversation with other group members.

Around the World –

3 different weekly sessions to cover all time zones

A common space, a common hour for chatting **every Wednesday**

The MTPE Training Challenges for Academia, Clients, LSPs and Post-Editors

Academia:
1. Translators in their majority find that the syllabus offered by Universities is not adapted to the translation industry needs
2. LSPs and Universities seem to be isolated with no strong connection link between them
3. Lack of Trainers

Clients:
1. Quality Standards
2. Not clear quality expectation
3. Negatively biased
4. Classification of Translation/PE Tasks
5. Lack of Post-Editing Guidelines

LSPs:
1. Training in Post-Editing Recruitment, Workflow, Compensation Strategy, Productivity/Quality Evaluation
2. Mutual Collaboration: establish new relationships with translators through training
3. Move towards a translator-centered approach
4. Investment in training, time, effort, communication, research

Post-Editors:
1. Post-editing skills and competencies
2. Training opportunities in the MTPE Training Process
3. Transparent compensation strategies
4. Ambiguity of MTPE tasks
5. Ambiguity of metrics
6. Lack of mutual collaboration LSPs/Translators in terms of training

www.gala-global.org

Make our Plan Fun!

Q1 2021 Topic:
1. Set a golden standard for the skills of the Post-Editor to based upon the MTPE Training
2. Investigate what is the current situation, define the service of MTPE based on the reality and the standards.

Q2-Q3 2021 Topic:
1. Examine the "pains" of the Clients/LSPs/Universities/Post-Editors to check what should be included and solved with the creation of a MTPE Training.
2. Match the profile and skills of the Post-Editor with relevant training sessions to build a draft model of the content of the Training Protocol.

Q4-Q1 2022 Topic:
1. Build the final structure of the Training Protocol.
2. Divide the MTPE Training Protocol in Sections and finalize each section from one call to the other.

- Polls
- Short Interviews on MTPE with Members of the SIG
- Online Surveys
- Workshops

www.gala-global.org GALA

A ROADMAP FOR THE NEXT 12 CALLS

1. POST-EDITING SKILLS & COMPETENCIES: WHAT SHOULD BE INCLUDED IN A COMMON TRAINING PROTOCOL?
2. THE CURRENT STATE OF POST-EDITING TRAINING
3. THE CURRENT GAPS OF POST-EDITING TRAINING
4. SPECIFICATION OF THE EXPERTISE, CONTENT, CAT TOOLS, MT ENGINES AND TYPES OF POST-EDITING
5. **POST-EDITING EFFORT AND QUALITY EXPECTATIONS IN CORRELATION WITH TRAINING**
6. GUIDELINES FOR SETTING A BASIC POST-EDITING WORKFLOW
7. GUIDELINES FOR DEALING WITH COMPENSATION MODELS
8. GUIDELINES FOR MANAGING POST-EDITORS' ERGONOMICS
9. THE GOLD STANDARD FOR POST-EDITING TRAINING - FROM UNIVERSITY TO FINAL CLIENT
10. WHAT SHOULD BE INCLUDED IN THE GOLD STANDARD FOR POST-EDITING TRAINING PER GROUP?
11. THE ACTIONS NEEDED TO BUILD A SOLID POST-EDITING TRAINING PER GROUP
12. THE CODE OF CONDUCT OF POST-EDITING

www.gala-global.org GALA

Join our MTPE Training SIG!
Shape the MTPE Training with us!

Register here:

https://app.smartsheet.com/b/form/9d5cf819f50142fdb471a4b11fab8250

Viveta Gene
Translation & Localization Industry Specialist

INTERTRANSLATIONS S.A.
Greece / United Kingdom / France
4 El. Venizelou Ave., GR 176 76, Kallithea, Athens

T. +30 21 0922 5000
E. v.gene@intertranslations.com

Lucía Guerrero
Machine Translation Specialist

CPSL - Language Services
Spain / Germany / United Kingdom / USA
Gran Vía 8-10, 3º-4ª - 08902 Hospitalet de Llobregat - Barcelona - Spain
T (+34) 93 445 17 63 - ext. 212
E. lguerrero@cpsl.com

MT SUMMIT VIRTUAL 2021
aws
du
Preserving MT Quality for Content With Inline Tags
Grigory Sapunov,
* Konstantin Savenkov,
Pavel Stepachev
INTENTO
© Intento, Inc. / August 2021

AGENDA

Why tags and placeholders are important?

MT + tags = it's complicated

Intento Solution: **Smart Tag Handling**

Experimental setting

Experimental results

Current status and next steps

Intento

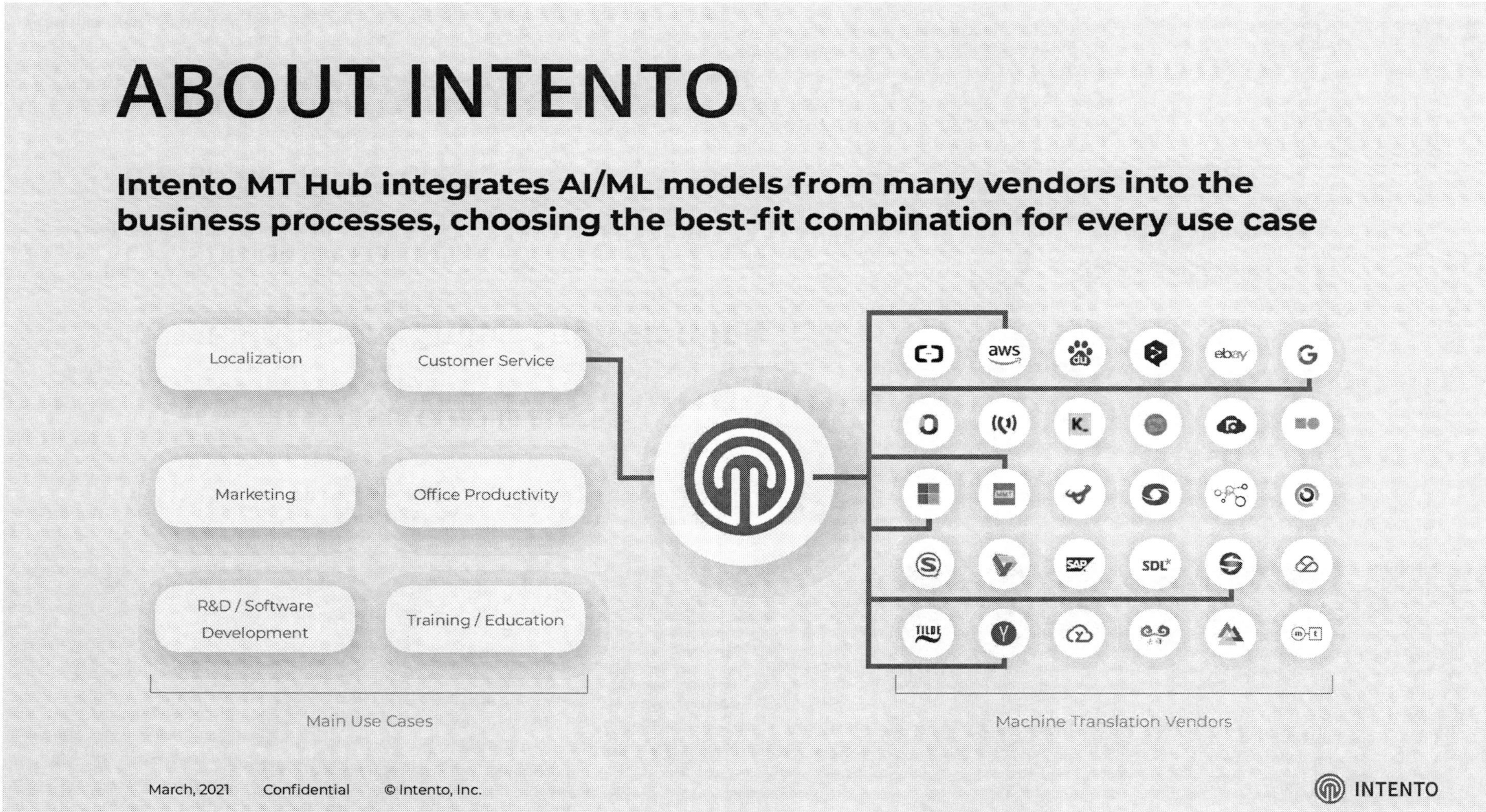
ABOUT INTENTO
Intento MT Hub integrates AI/ML models from many vendors into the business processes, choosing the best-fit combination for every use case
Localization
Customer Service
Marketing
Office Productivity
R&D / Software Development
Training / Education
Main Use Cases
aws
ebay
G
K
SAP
SDL
TILDE
Machine Translation Vendors
March, 2021
Confidential
© Intento, Inc.
INTENTO

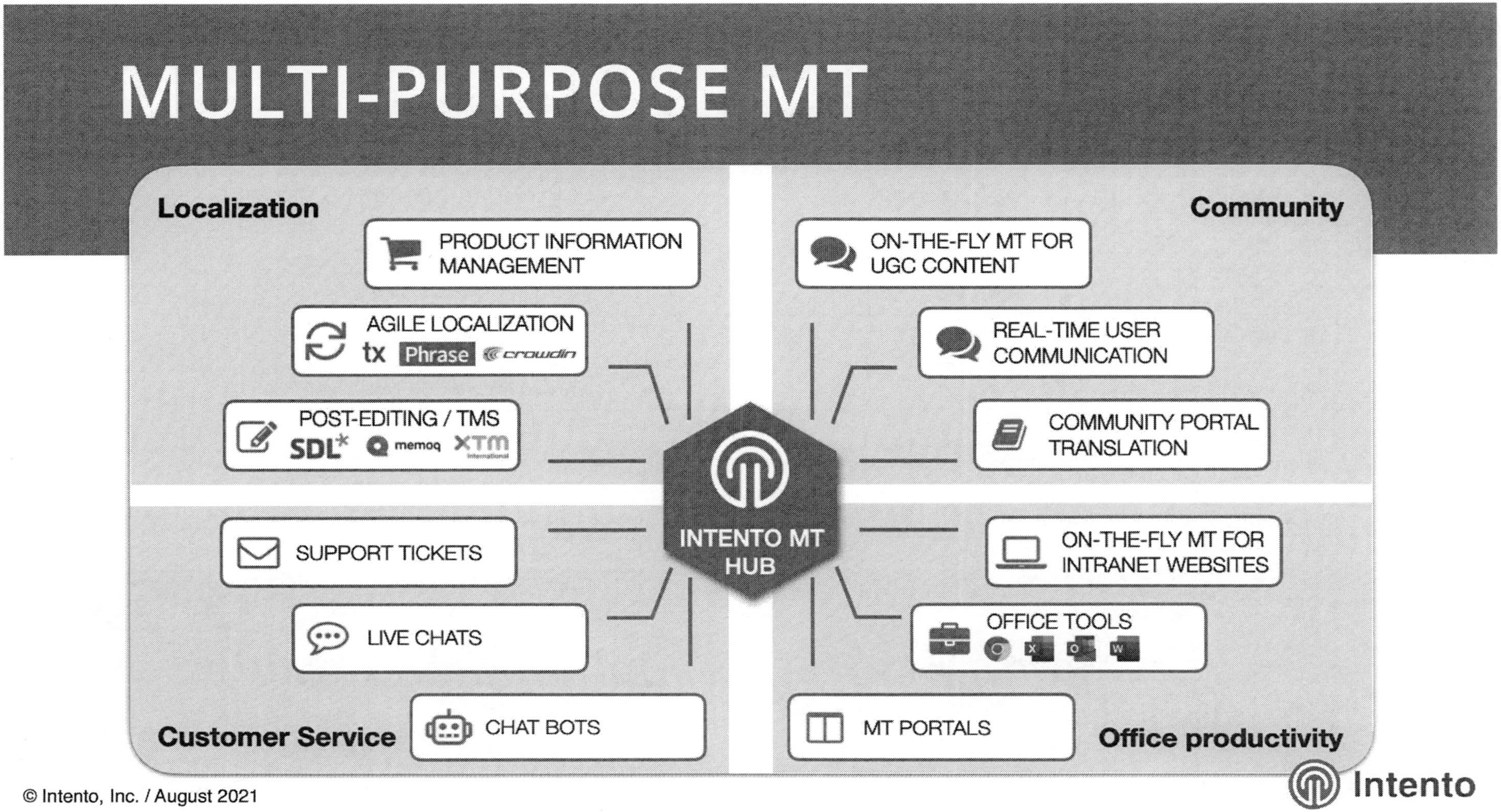
MULTI-PURPOSE MT
Localization
PRODUCT INFORMATION MANAGEMENT
AGILE LOCALIZATION
tx Phrase crowdin
POST-EDITING / TMS
SDL memoq XTM
Community
ON-THE-FLY MT FOR UGC CONTENT
REAL-TIME USER COMMUNICATION
COMMUNITY PORTAL TRANSLATION
INTENTO MT HUB
Customer Service
SUPPORT TICKETS
LIVE CHATS
CHAT BOTS
Office productivity
ON-THE-FLY MT FOR INTRANET WEBSITES
OFFICE TOOLS
MT PORTALS
© Intento, Inc. / August 2021
Intento

MT REQUIREMENTS MATRIX
EVERY CASE HAS ITS OWN NEEDS

	large text translation	batch translation	latency and jitter	tolerance to bad source	language detection	tag support	multilingual source	profanity control	metadata protection	entity protection	custom terminology	tone of voice control
Post-editing / TMS		●				●					●	
Support tickets	●				●		●	●	●	●	●	
Live chats			●	●	●			●		●	●	●
Subtitle translation			●	●	●	●		●		●	●	●
On-the-fly UGC		●	●	●	●	●	●	●		●		●
Real-time communication			●	●						●		●
Knowledge bases	●					●			●		●	

Intento

USE-CASE SPECIFIC MT FEATURES

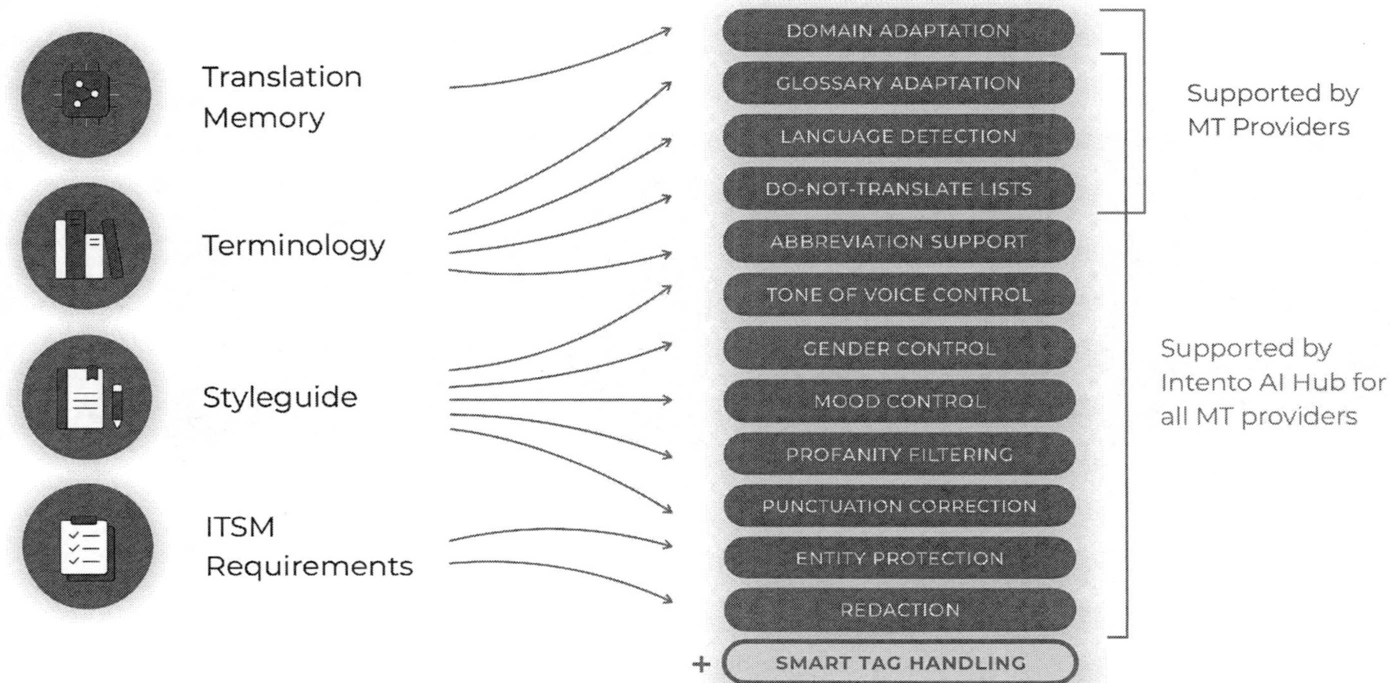

Intento

SMART TAG HANDLING

Intento

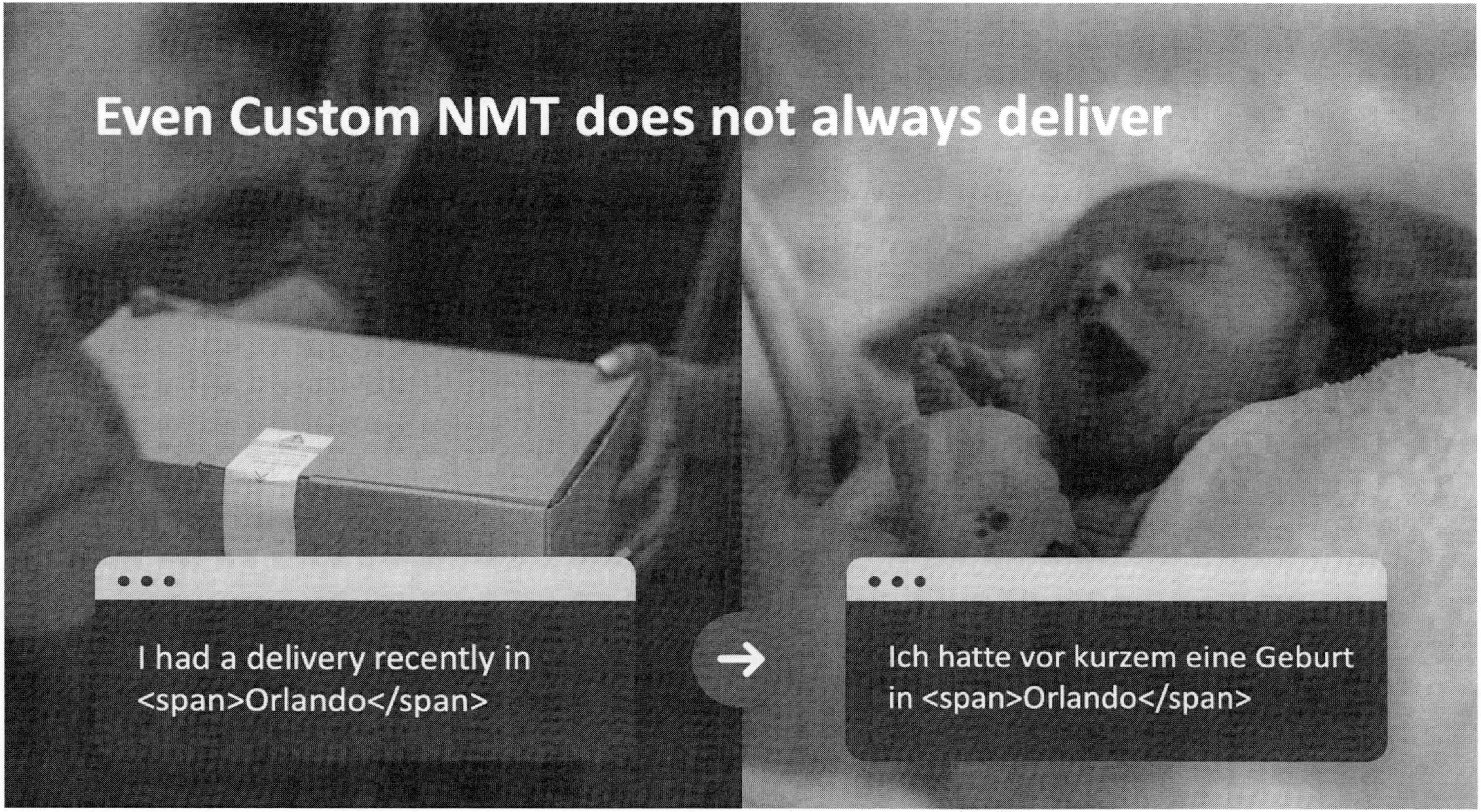
Even Custom NMT does not always deliver
I had a delivery recently in <span>Orlando</span>
Ich hatte vor kurzem eine Geburt in <span>Orlando</span>

NMT + TAGS
IT'S COMPLICATED

Inconsistent across MT providers and language pairs.

—

Customized models may fall back onto baseline because of tags.

—

Placeholders are impossible for MT to interpret.

—

Glossaries also break as they often rely on tags.

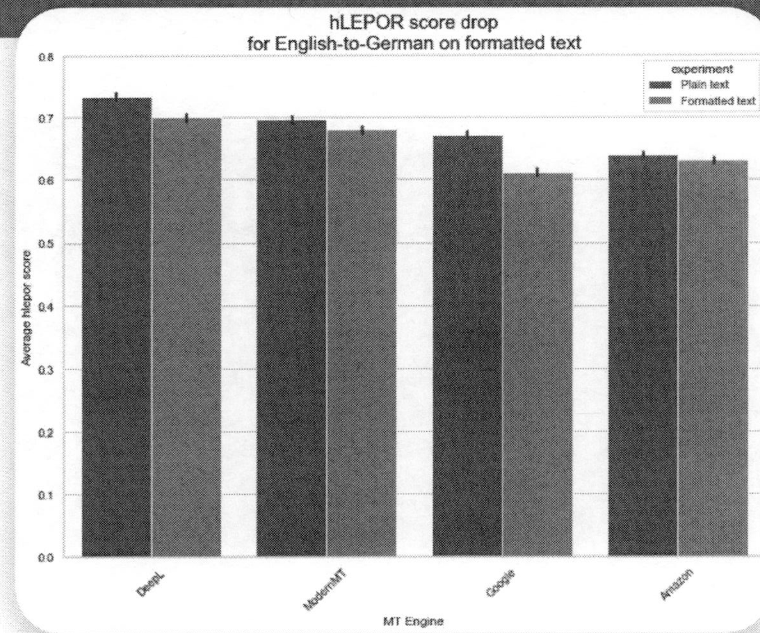

Intento

CURRENT SOLUTIONS

Raw MT: 🤷

—

MTPE: either spend post-editor time on editing broken language, or remove tags and spend post-editor time on putting them back.

—

Our primary use-case: **video translation** (mistreated tags are critical, editing them is complicated)

Intento

MOVING TAGS OUT OF THE EQUATION

```
I had a delivery recently
<timestamp class='timestamp'
   start='00:00:13,230'
   end='00:00:17,690'/>
in <ph/>
```


Intento

MOVING TAGS OUT OF THE EQUATION

(1) Removing inline tags

I had a delivery recently in <ph/>

↓

<timestamp
class='timestamp'
start='00:00:13,230'
end='00:00:17,690'/>

Intento

MOVING TAGS OUT OF THE EQUATION

(2) Filling placeholders with generative models

I had a delivery recently in New York

```
<timestamp
class='timestamp'
   start='00:00:13,230'
   end='00:00:17,690'/>
```

```
<ph/>
```


Intento

MOVING TAGS OUT OF THE EQUATION

(3) Translating plain text

I had a delivery recently in New York

↓

Ich hatte kürzlich eine Lieferung in New York

```
<timestamp
class='timestamp'
   start='00:00:13,230'
   end='00:00:17,690'/>
```

```
<ph/>
```


Intento

MOVING TAGS OUT OF THE EQUATION

(4) Performing word alignment

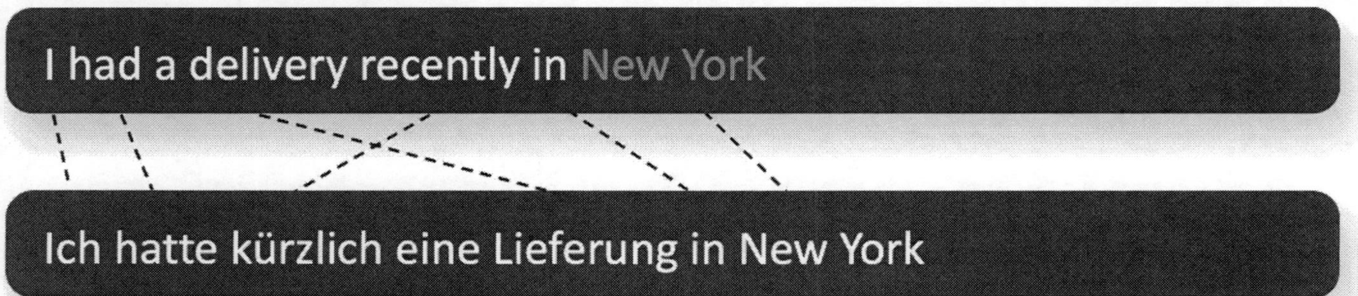

<timestamp
class=‘timestamp’
start=‘00:00:13,230’
end=‘00:00:17,690’/>

<ph/>

Intento

MOVING TAGS OUT OF THE EQUATION

(5) Putting tags back

I had a delivery recently in New York

Ich hatte kürzlich eine Lieferung<timestamp
class=‘timestamp’
start=‘00:00:13,230’
end=‘00:00:17,690’/>
in <ph/>

Intento

EXPERIMENTS

EXPERIMENTS
TWO EXPERIMENTS

A: HTML FORMATTING

How much MT quality suffers from simple HTML tags?

—

Using Smart Tag Handling to put tags back after MT

B: PLACEHOLDERS

How much MT quality suffers from words replaced by placeholders?

—

Does translating text w/o placeholders help?

—

Using Smart Tag Handling to put placeholders back after MT

—

Does expanding placeholders help?

Intento

EXPERIMENTS
ORIGINAL DATASET

EN-DE corpus from TAUS

—

Domain - Financial Services

—

1955 segments

—

> 5 tokens per segment

The investigation confirmed the complainant's legal claim that the C-57 Amendment to the Canadian Trade-Marks Act violates Articles 23.1 and 2 as well as Article 24.3 (the so-called standstill clause) of TRIPS and that such infringements cannot be justified on the basis of the exception under Article 24.6 of TRIPS.	Die Untersuchung bestätigte die rechtliche Behauptung des Antragstellers, das Gesetz C-57 zur Änderung des kanadischen Handelsmarkengesetzes verstoße gegen Artikel 23 Absätze 1 und 2 sowie Artikel 24 Absatz 3 (die so genannte Stillhalteklausel) des TRIPS, und dieser Verstoß könne nicht durch die Ausnahmeregelung des Artikels 24 Absatz 6 des TRIPS gerechtfertigt werden.

Intento

A - TAGGING

DATA PREPARATION A - TAGGING

1-3 tag entries per segment

—

tags: 1-place (img, br) or 2-place (span, i, em, a, b, strong, u, s)

—

nesting: 1-3 levels

The investigation confirmed the complainant's legal <b> claim that the C-57 Amendment to the Canadian Trade-Marks Act violates Articles 23.1 and <a href="https://example.com/index.html"> 2 as well as <s> Article 24.3 </s> (the so-called standstill clause) of TRIPS </a> and that such infringements cannot be justified on the basis of the exception </b> under Article 24.6 of <img src="https://example.com/image.png" alt="Some image"/> TRIPS.

Intento

A - TAGGING
SCORING

Calculate hLEPOR score for:

—

(1) Plain text NMT

(2) Tagged text NMT after tag removal

(3) Tagged text NMT+STH after tag removal

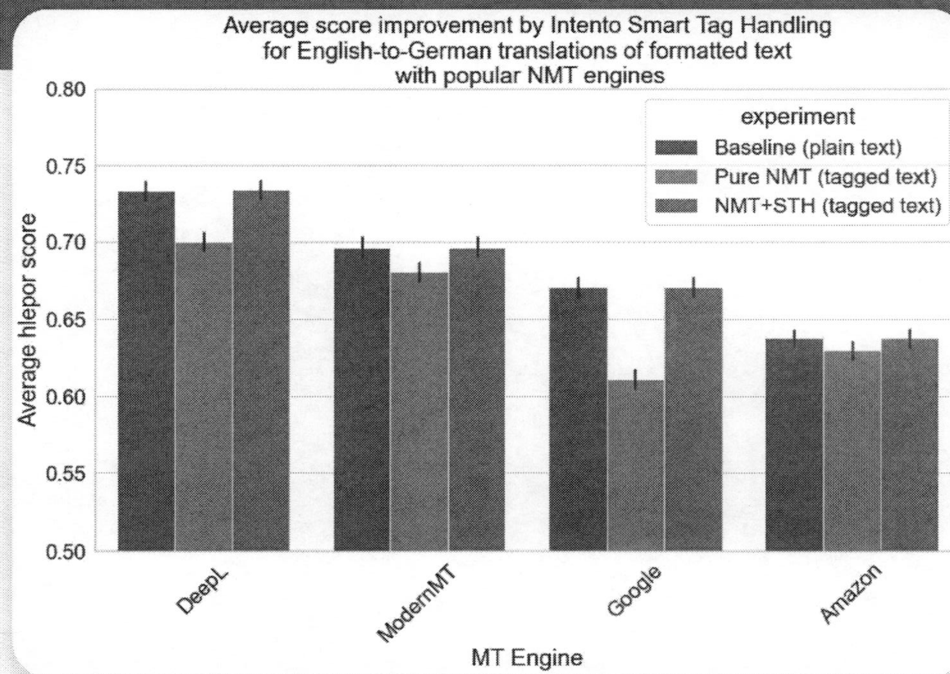

Intento

A - TAGGING
SEGMENT DEGRADATION DUE TO TAGS

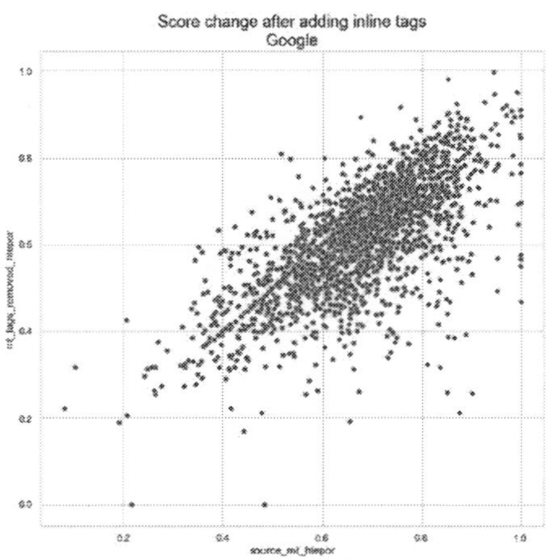

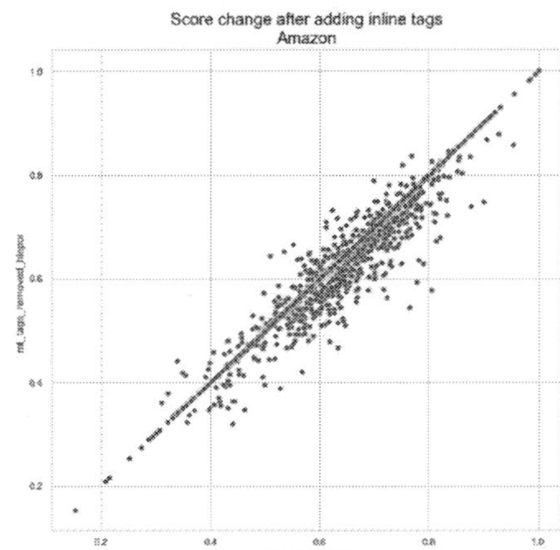

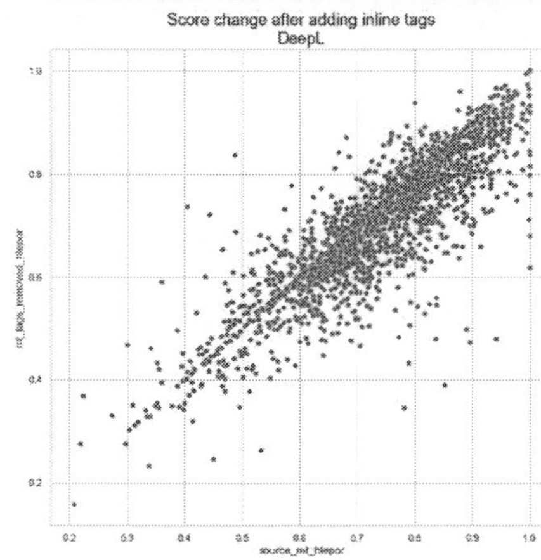

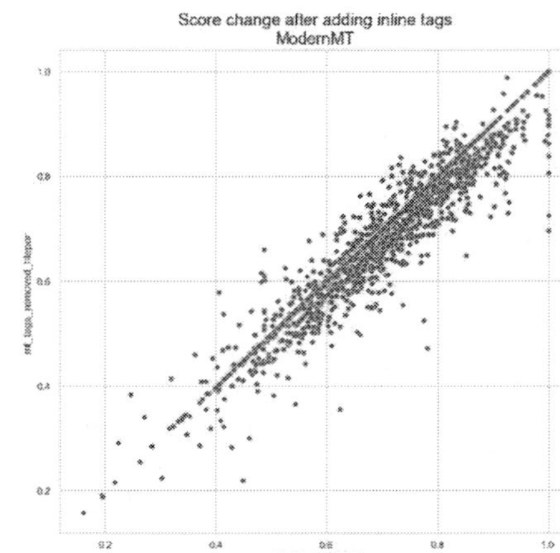

A - TAGGING
DISCUSSION

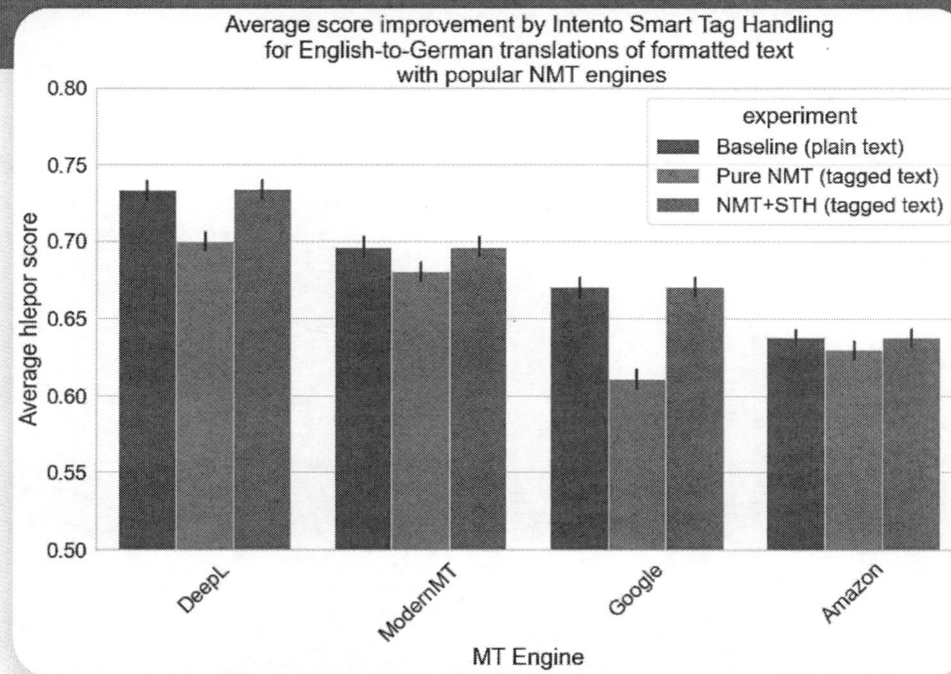

Even innocent HTML tags degrade NMT quality (as of today).

—

The way to improve the quality is to translate text with tags removed and insert them back after MT

—

Benefits: (1) same level of translation quality as plain text, (2) post-editor does not spend time to move tags, (3) natively integrated into the existing AVT workflow.

Intento

B - PLACEHOLDERS

DATA PREPARATION

Same dataset, 367 segments with DNT.

—

Non-translatables replaced with placeholder tags.

The investigation confirmed the complainant's legal claim that the <ph/> Amendment to the Canadian Trade-Marks Act violates Articles 23.1 and <ph/> as well as Article 24.3 (the so-called standstill clause) of <ph/> and that such infringements cannot be justified on the basis of the exception under Article 24.6 of <ph/ >.	Die Untersuchung bestätigte die rechtliche Behauptung des Antragstellers, das Gesetz <ph/> zur Änderung des kanadischen Handelsmarkengesetzes verstoße gegen Artikel 23 Absätze 1 und <ph/> sowie Artikel 24 Absatz 3 (die so genannte Stillhalteklausel) des <ph/>, und dieser Verstoß könne nicht durch die Ausnahmeregelung des Artikels 24 Absatz 6 des <ph/> gerechtfertigt werden.

Intento

B - PLACEHOLDERS
DATA PREPARATION

Same dataset, 367 segments with DNT.

—

Non-translatables replaced with placeholder tags.

—

Placeholder tags are expanded with dummy values using multilingual generative language model.

The investigation confirmed the complainant's legal claim that the <ph/> Amendment to the Canadian Trade-Marks Act violates Articles 23.1 and <ph/> as well as Article 24.3 (the so-called standstill clause) of <ph/> and that such infringements cannot be justified on the basis of the exception under Article 24.6 of <ph/>.	The investigation confirmed the complainant's legal claim that the <span>Second</span> Amendment to the Canadian Trade-Marks Act violates Articles 23.1 and <span>23.2</span> as well as Article 24.3 (the so-called standstill clause) of <span>NAFTA</span> and that such infringements cannot be justified on the basis of the exception under Article 24.6 of <span>NAFTA</span>.

Intento

B - PLACEHOLDERS
SCORING

Calculate hLEPOR score for:

—

(1) Plain text NMT with removed DNT vs reference translation with removed DNT (Baseline)

(2) Text with <ph/> vs reference (Raw NMT)

(3) Text with <ph/> vs reference (NMT+STH)

(4) Text with expanded <ph/> vs reference

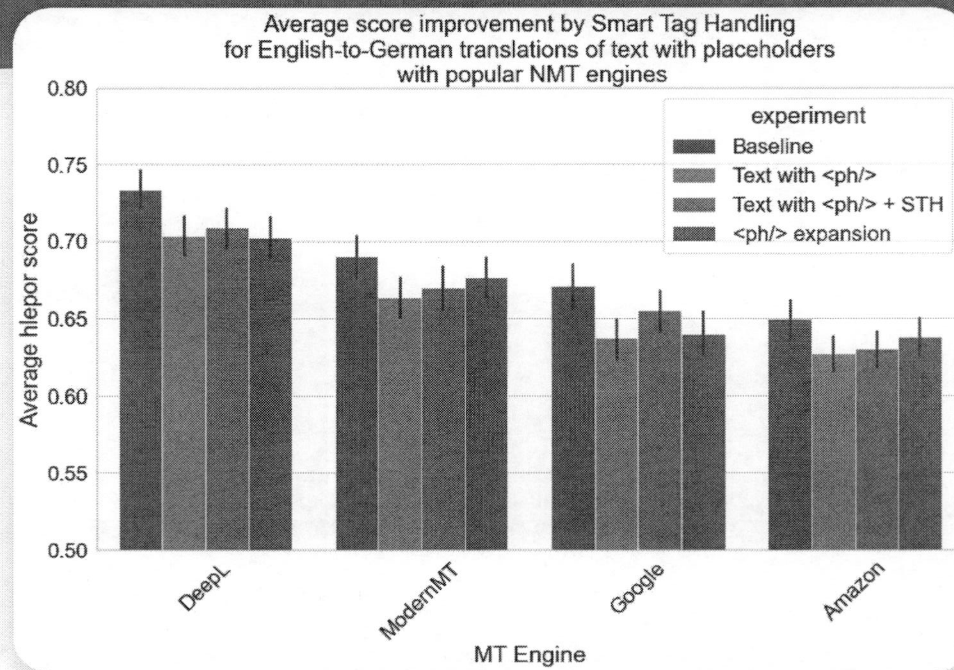

B - PLACEHOLDERS
DISCUSSION

Adding placeholders significantly decreases MT quality for all MT engines.

—

Using STH for <ph/> improves MT quality. Level of improvement depends on how well MT engine deals with incomplete sentences vs. sentences with <ph/> tags.

—

Expanding placeholders further helps for some engines (ModernMT and Amazon), should not be used for others (Google and DeepL).

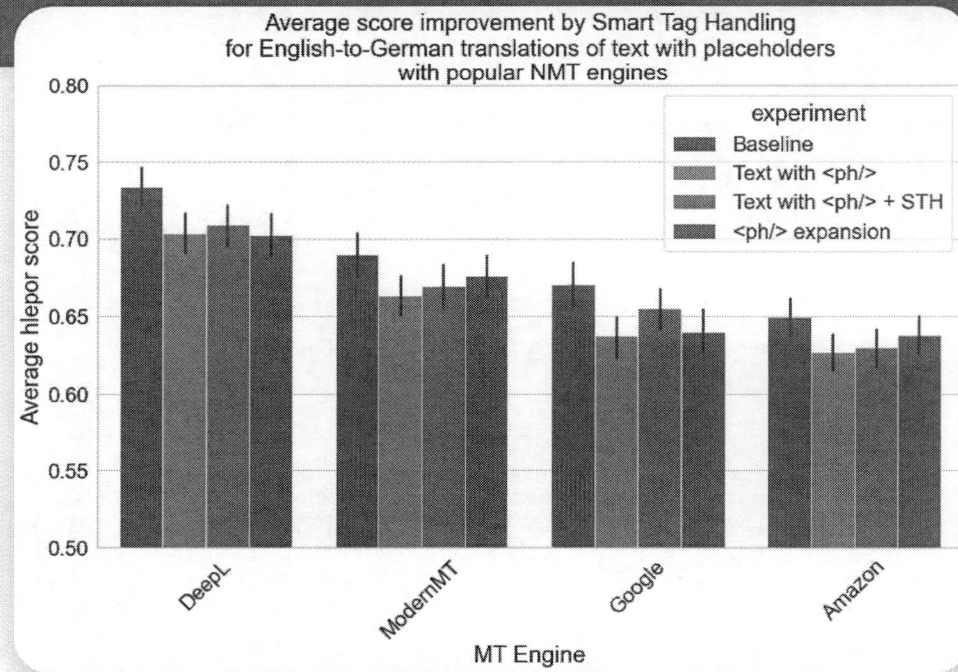

CONCLUSIONS

Even innocent HTML tags degrade NMT quality (as of today). Placeholders too.

—

The way to improve the quality is to translate text with tags removed and insert them back after MT.

—

Also, this is a must for MT engines that are best for certain languages, but lack tag support (Tencent, Baidu, Naver, etc)

—

For placeholders, removing placeholders from translation altogether also improves the MT quality.

—

Placeholder expansion helps for some MT engines, for others it needs improvement.

Intento

CURRENT STATUS

Available as an automated post-editing via API for selected customers.

—

The main use-case so far - subtitle translation in TMS, to reduce time spent on both text editing and timestamp re-placement.

—

We are planning to evaluate ROI (cost and TAT decrease) for AVT with one of our customers, we'll keep you posted :-)

Intento

REMAINING ISSUES AND NEXT STEPS

Our tag placement algorithm works decently for single-position tags (timestamps, img, br).

—

Putting back deeply nested HTML structures requires further improvement.

—

Placeholder expansion requires improvement to avoid using tags to track the position of the expanded <ph/>.

Intento

MT SUMMIT 2021 VIRTUAL
Using MT for inline tags?
Let us know!
ks@inten.to
INTENTO
https://inten.to
Konstantin Savenkov, CEO
ks@inten.to
2261 Market Street, #4273
San Francisco, CA 94114

UP14
Early-stage development of the SignON Application & open Framework - Challenges & Opportunities
Dimitar Shterionov, Tilburg University
John J O'Flaherty, Edward Keane, Connor O'Reilly, MAC
Marcello Paolo Scipioni, Marco Giovanelli, Matteo Villa, FINCONS
This project has received funding from the European Union's Horizon 2020 research and innovation programme under grant agreement No 101017255
MT SUMMIT 20 21 VIRTUAL
SIGNON
MTSummit2021, UP14, 18/08/2021, https://signon-project.eu

SignON - Sign Language Translation Mobile Application & Open Communications Framework

SignON is an EU Horizon 2020 Research & Innovation project, that is developing

- a **smartphone Application** & an **open Framework** to facilitate **translation between different European Sign, Spoken & Text languages.**
- The Framework will incorporate state of the art sign language recognition & presentation, speech processing technologies & multi-modal, cross-language machine translation.
- The Framework, dedicated to the computationally heavy MT tasks & distributed on the cloud powers the Application -- a lightweight app running on a standard mobile device.
- The Application & Framework are being researched, designed & developed through a co-creation user-centric approach with the European deaf & hard of hearing communities.

This project has received funding from the European Union's Horizon 2020 research and innovation programme under grant agreement No 101017255

MTSummit2021, UP14, 18/08/2021, https://signon-project.eu

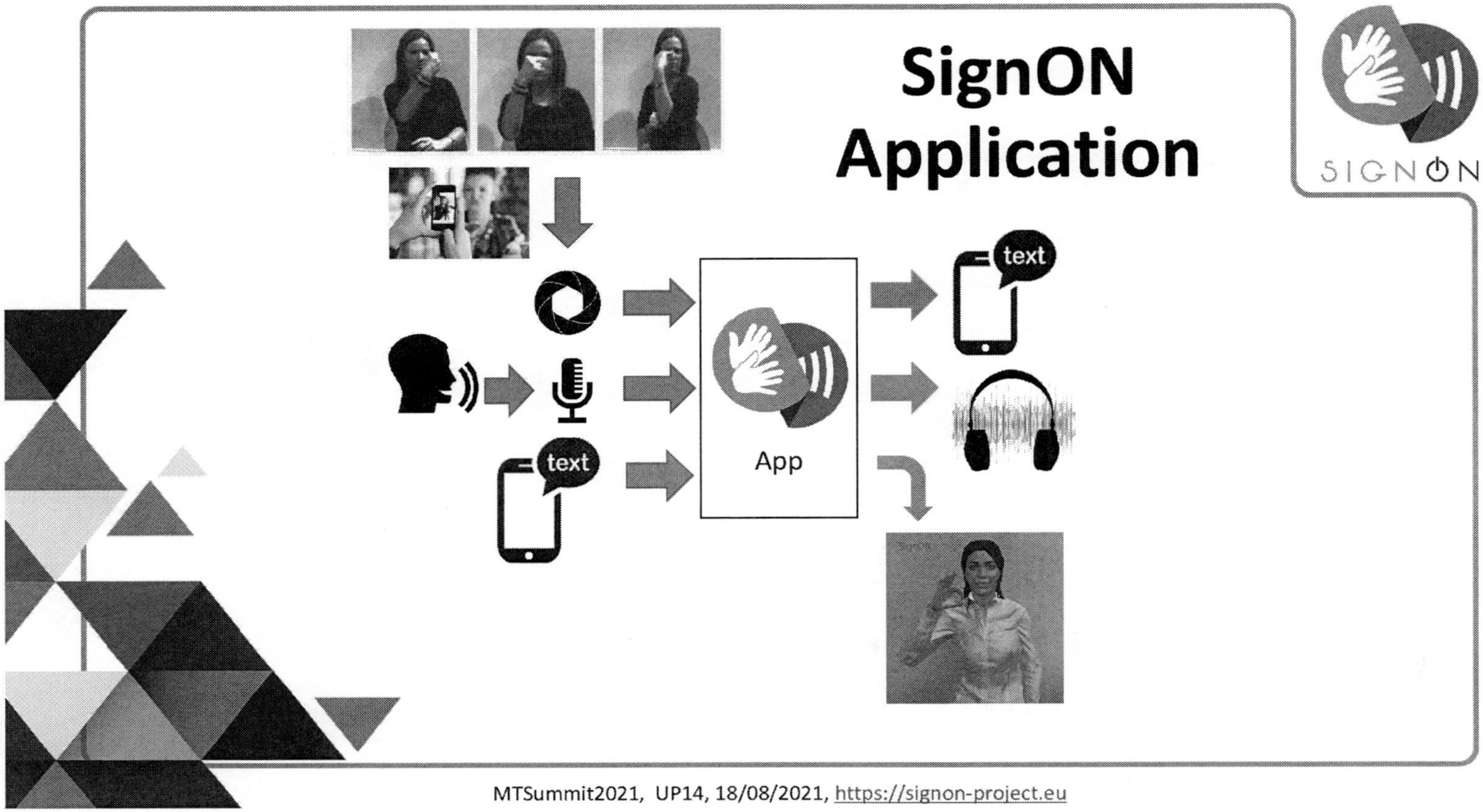
SignON
Application
SIGNON
text
text
App
MTSummit2021, UP14, 18/08/2021, https://signon-project.eu

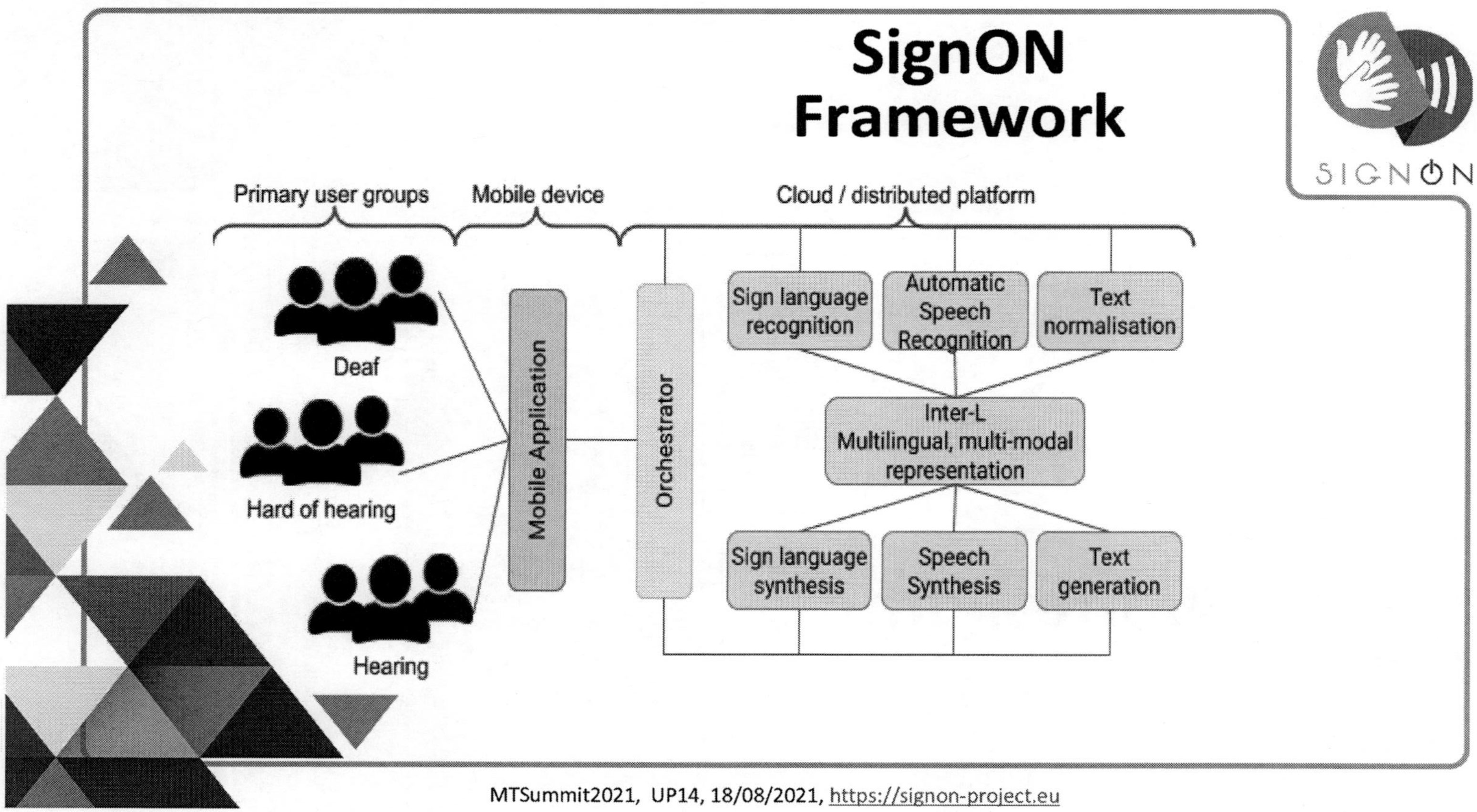
SignON
Framework
SIGNON
Primary user groups
Mobile device
Cloud / distributed platform
Deaf
Hard of hearing
Hearing
Mobile Application
Orchestrator
Sign language recognition
Automatic Speech Recognition
Text normalisation
Inter-L
Multilingual, multi-modal representation
Sign language synthesis
Speech Synthesis
Text generation
MTSummit2021, UP14, 18/08/2021, https://signon-project.eu

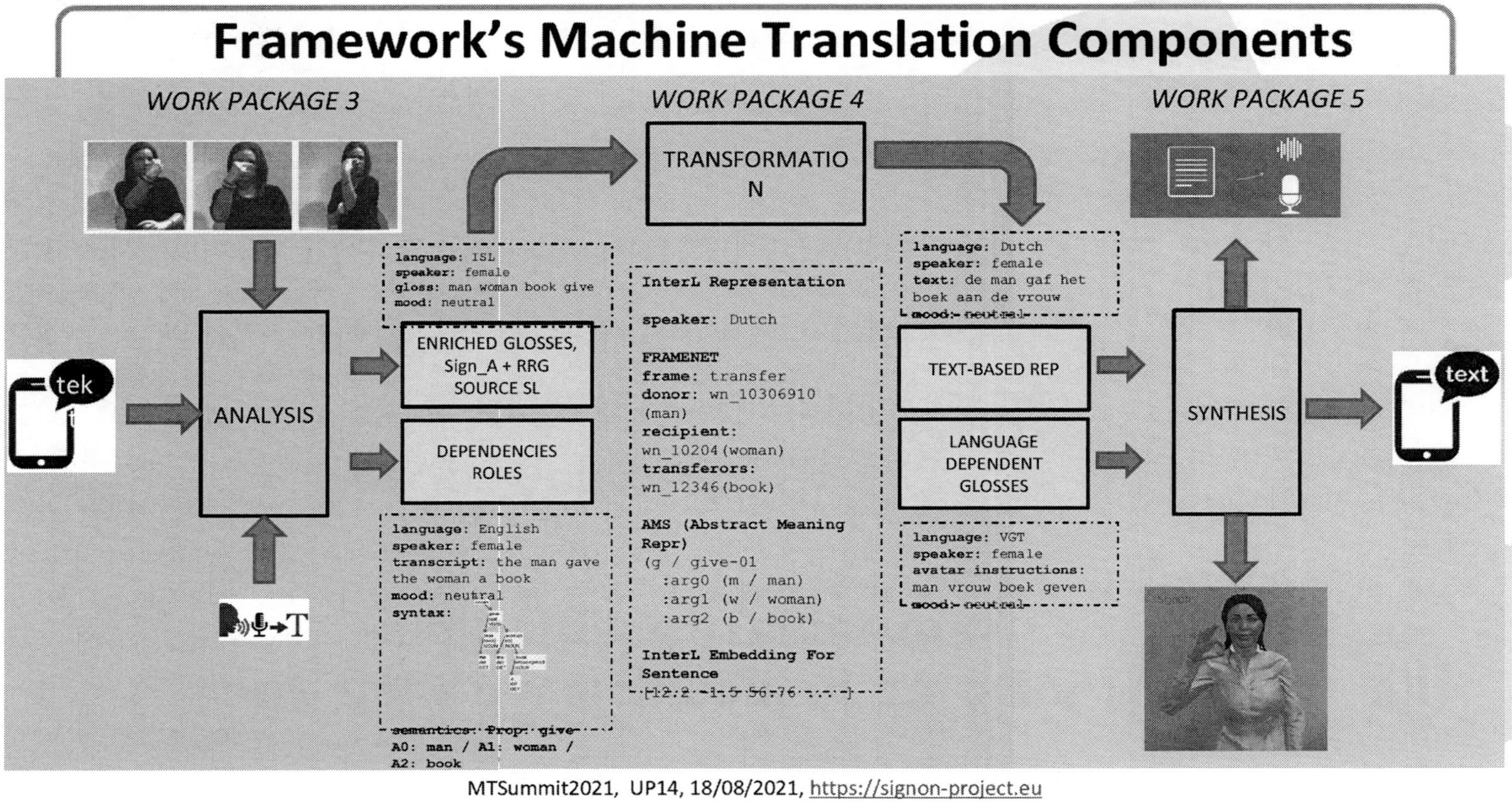
Framework's Machine Translation Components
WORK PACKAGE 3
WORK PACKAGE 4
WORK PACKAGE 5
tek
ANALYSIS
language: ISL
speaker: female
gloss: man woman book give
mood: neutral
ENRICHED GLOSSES, Sign_A + RRG SOURCE SL
DEPENDENCIES ROLES
language: English
speaker: female
transcript: the man gave the woman a book
mood: neutral
syntax:
semantics: Prop: give
A0: man / A1: woman /
A2: book
TRANSFORMATIO N
InterL Representation
speaker: Dutch
FRAMENET
frame: transfer
donor: wn_10306910 (man)
recipient: wn_10204(woman)
transferors: wn_12346(book)
AMS (Abstract Meaning Repr)
(g / give-01
:arg0 (m / man)
:arg1 (w / woman)
:arg2 (b / book)
InterL Embedding For Sentence
[12.2 -1.5 56.76 ...]
language: Dutch
speaker: female
text: de man gaf het boek aan de vrouw
mood: neutral
TEXT-BASED REP
LANGUAGE DEPENDENT GLOSSES
language: VGT
speaker: female
avatar instructions: man vrouw boek geven
mood: neutral
SYNTHESIS
text
MTSummit2021, UP14, 18/08/2021, https://signon-project.eu

Early-stage development of the SignON Application & Framework

SIGNON

- DevOps Approach
- Users' driven Co-Creation Cycle
- Early & many Fast Prototypes
- Iterative Evolution towards the final Service

MTSummit2021, UP14, 18/08/2021, https://signon-project.eu

Agile DevOps approach

- **User-driven Iterative co-creation evolution of the Application** until its final release at the end of the project - to ensure
  - wide uptake,
  - improved sign language detection &
  - multilingual speech processing on mobile devices for everyone
- An **initial fast prototype** to enable **users become actively involved** in the **Co-Creation Cycle** of its functional specification & its **co-development** from **start of project.**

MTSummit2021, UP14, 18/08/2021, https://signon-project.eu

Nothing about us without us
=> Co-Creation Cycle

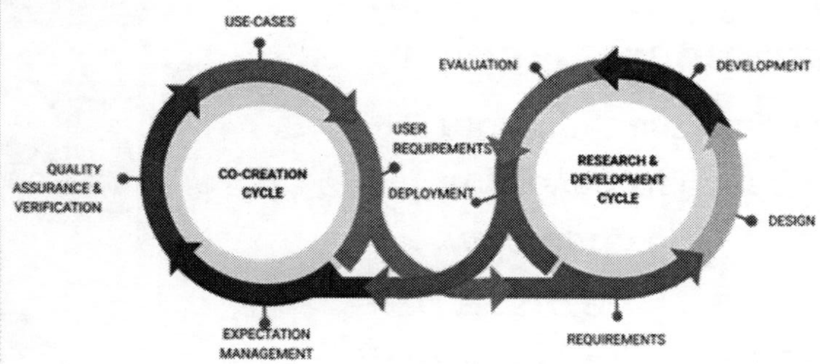

- **Expectation management**: SignON service (at its present stage) outline its intended use for defined use-cases & benefits for users.

This project has received funding from the European Union's Horizon 2020 research and innovation programme under grant agreement No 101017255

- **Quality assurance & verification**: Quality of the SignON service tested by the user community. Defined expectations are confirmed/discarded. QoS will re-evaluated & verified.
- **Use-cases**: Quality & functionality of SignON service considered in redefining currently addressed use-cases (if needed) & defining new ones.
- **User-requirements**: Collect evaluation metrics & statistics, reviews, & use case (re)definitions translated into user requirements drives development cycles.

MTSummit2021, UP14, 18/08/2021, https://signon-project.eu

Initial Fast Prototype

- **For Signed, Spoken & Text Languages**
  - SignON Mobile App Input Functions
  - SignON Platform & Framework Services
  - SignON Mobile App Output Functions
- Users start to **see, hold & feel** something tangible
  - to provide realistic inputs on what they need,
- Developers appreciate the realities of the mobile app & Framework platform & cloud requirements.

SIGNON

MTSummit2021, UP14, 18/08/2021, https://signon-project.eu

Initial Fast Prototype

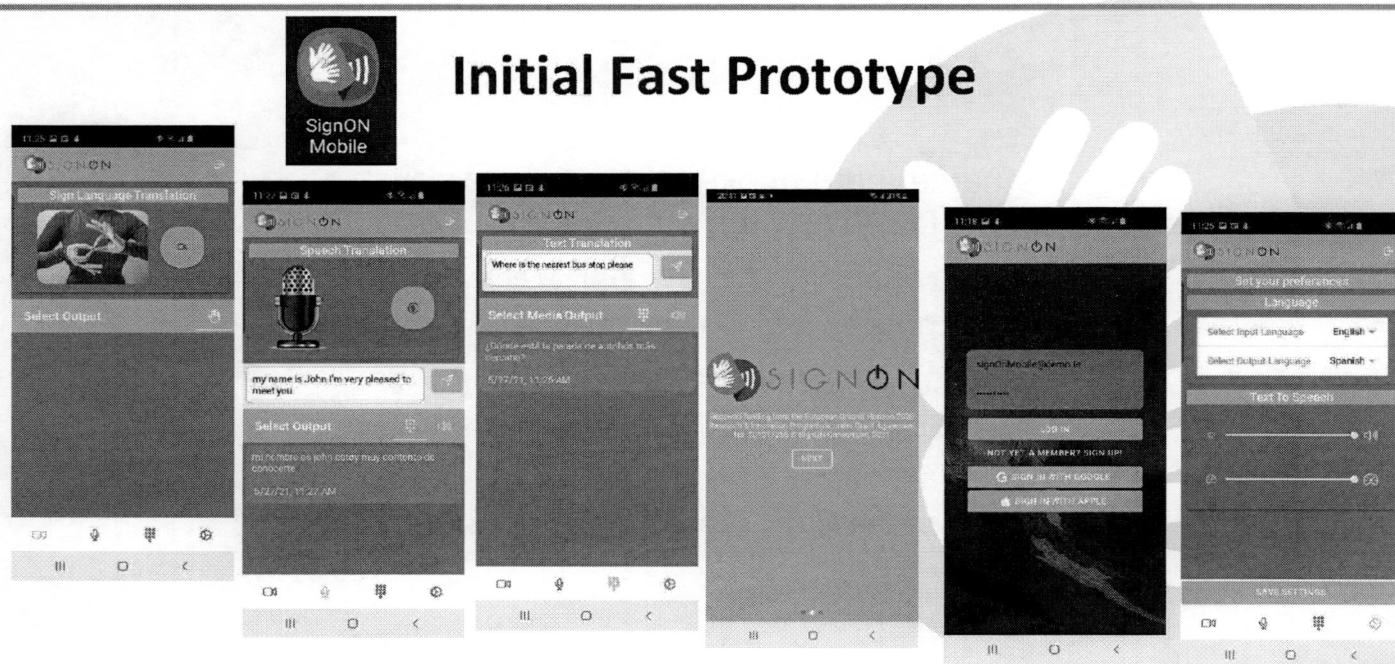

This project has received funding from the European Union's Horizon 2020 research and innovation programme under grant agreement No 101017255

Published on Google **Play Store** as closed/hidden, for "**Internal Testing**" by Authorised Testers, that the Partners' Users applied to join

MTSummit2021, UP14, 18/08/2021, https://signon-project.eu

Cognitive Walkthrough Evaluation Methodology

- Users' Use Case Tasks & Functions
- Scored the severity of any problems doing these
- System Usability Scale (SUS).
- User feedback suggestions

SignON Use Case Tasks / SignON Functions.	Functional App	SL input	SL output	Speech input	Speech output	Text input	Text output	Translate Mode	Translate Language
1. Install & run the SignON App on your Android mobile phone.	X								
2. Record a Video of yourself or another person Signing a message (in the Sign Language Translation screen).		X							
3. Display the Video – can you clearly see the Signing?			X						
4. Choose the Speaker's input language & your output language (English, Spanish or Dutch) in Setup screen.									X
5. Record an Audio of yourself or another person speaking a message (in the Speech Translation screen).				X					
6. Play the Audio & read its Text translated to your chosen output language (in the Speech Translation screen) – are they understandable?					X		X	X	X
7. Key in a Text message & translate to another language as text & speech. (in the Text Translation screen).					X	X	X	X	X

This project has received funding from the European Union's Horizon 2020 research and innovation programme under grant agreement No 101017255

MTSummit2021, UP14, 18/08/2021, https://signon-project.eu

Cognitive Walkthrough Results

- Users' overall severity score for the Walkthrough steps was "Low" & 79% (including 73% of sign language users) indicated they would recommend the App to a colleague
  - Indicating **a usable first prototype** & **good foundation for future** evolution of the App,
- **Users feedback** was over 70 suggestions that will now be addressed in the next iteration of the prototype
- Users' **SUS rating** for the SignON Mobile App was 80 overall
  - **Well above the SUS threshold** of acceptability of 68,
  - Indicating the **SignON App has started on the right track of what users need & want**.
- From the overall process the we **defined the User technical requirements** of the SignON Mobile App & Framework under the following features:
  - A. User's Mobile Device
  - B. System Performance
  - C. User Preferences
  - D. Sign Language Translation
  - E. Speech & Text Translation

MTSummit2021, UP14, 18/08/2021, https://signon-project.eu

Challenges, Opportunities & Lessons Learned

- **Challenges**
  - Creating a **genuinely useful SignON**
    Sign, Spoken & Text languages translation & communications Service.
- **Opportunities**
  - **Users' positive feedback**
    - They understand this is just the **first step**, but agree it has the **right look & feel**
    - **Text & speech translations are good** already, but **Sign Language translation functions need to be developed & be as simple**, & available soon.
  - Cognitive **Walkthrough** process facilitates the **Co-Creation Cycle.**
- **Lessons Learned**
  - **Co-Creation DevOps** process with a **proactive user community** & **fast prototype** App enables an iterative evolution towards an **excellent final Service**
  - As one user commented -
    "Keep working with end users & everything will be fine".

MTSummit2021, UP14, 18/08/2021, https://signon-project.eu

Thank you for your attention!
SIGNON
This project has received funding from the European Union's Horizon 2020 research and innovation programme under grant agreement No 101017255
MTSummit2021, UP14, 18/08/2021, https://signon-project.eu

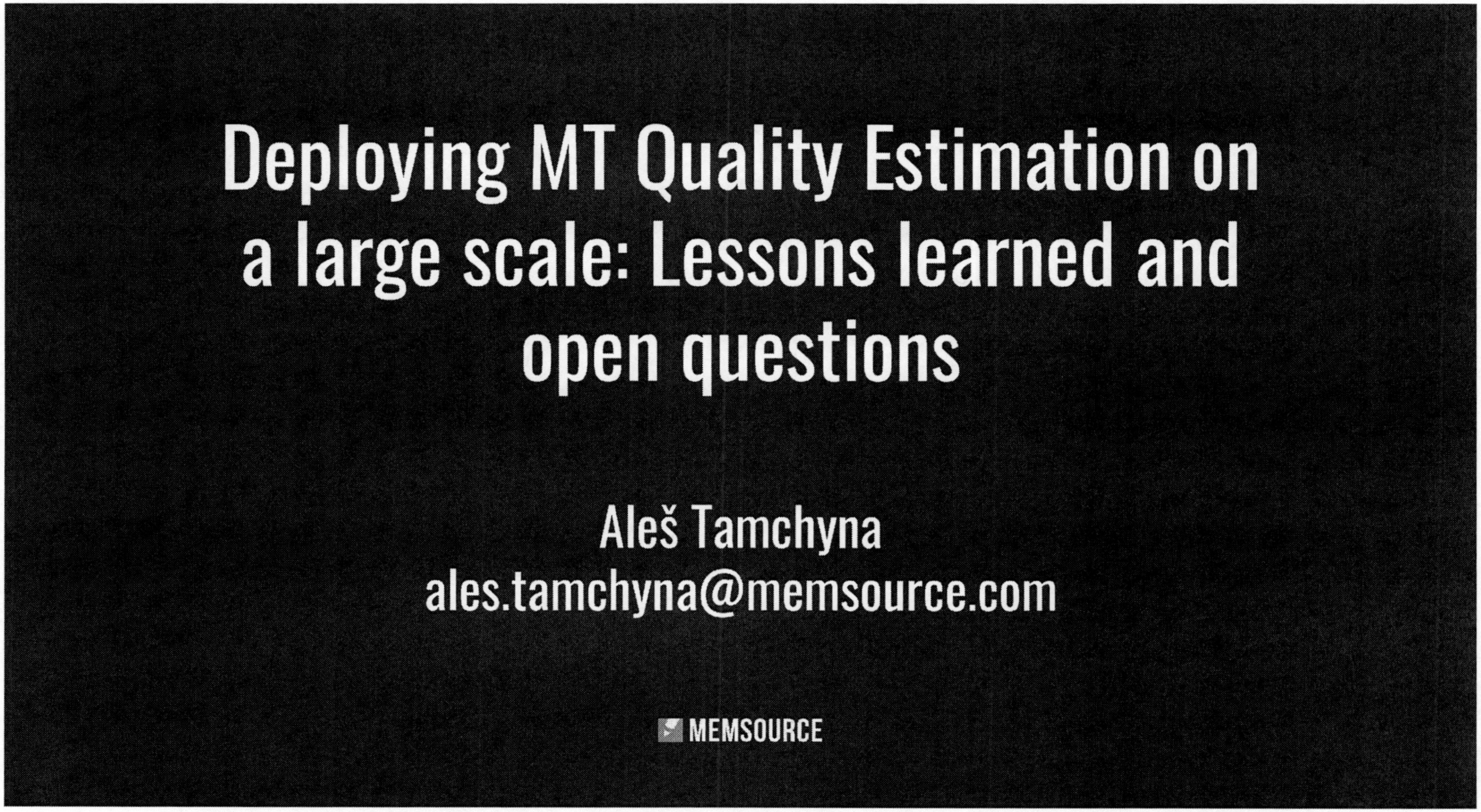
Deploying MT Quality Estimation on
a large scale: Lessons learned and
open questions
Aleš Tamchyna
ales.tamchyna@memsource.com
MEMSOURCE

OUTLINE

- MTQE in Memsource
- Defining “quality” in QE
- Academic tasks vs. applications
- Reference-free metrics for MTQE
- What factors affect post-editing effort?
- Conclusion

ABOUT MEMSOURCE

- Cloud-based translation management system (TMS).
- Includes translation editors (CAT tool).
- Diverse customer base:
  - Freelance translators.
  - Language service providers (LSPs).
  - Enterprises (Uber, Supercell, ...).

MTQE IN MEMSOURCE

Predict MT quality category for each input segment:

- **100** (perfect), **99** (near perfect), **75** (high quality) or **0** (low quality)

Source: Machine translation is hard.
MT: Strojový překlad je těžký.

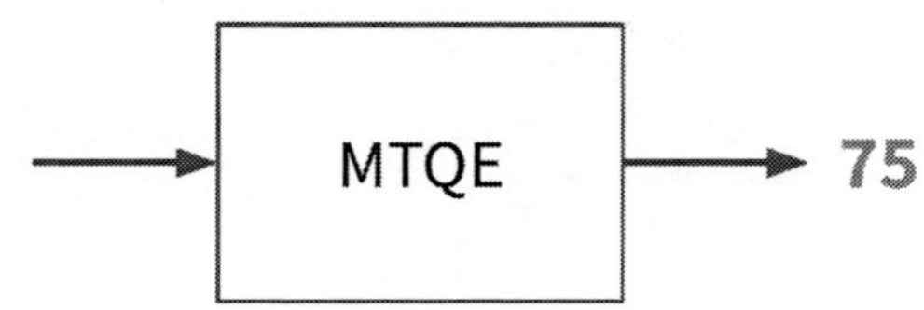

Internally, MTQE is a classifier based on a deep neural network, trained on large-scale datasets of MT outputs and their post-edits.

MTQE IN MEMSOURCE

Use cases:

- Predict overall savings thanks to MT before manual translation.
- Help translators choose when to start from scratch and when to post-edit the MT output.
- Routing: high-quality translations may even skip manual post-editing.
- Calculate translator compensation.

Interesting facts:

- First version deployed in 2018.
- We process around 10 million segments monthly.
- We support over 130 language pairs, models are updated every month with new data.

WHAT IS QUALITY?

- HTER represents the **amount of post-editing** required.
- Direct assessment (DA) represents overall **quality** as perceived by human annotators.

HTER and DA may not correlate very much and DA may be somewhat easier to predict, see Fomicheva et al. (2020) and Specia et al. (2020).

Which metric to choose probably depends on the use case.

At Memsource, we use a customized version of **(H)chrf3**.

- Essentially post-editing effort but more robust w.r.t. tokenization, morphology,...

ACADEMIC TASKS VS. REAL WORLD APPLICATIONS

WMT QE Shared tasks are a standard benchmark.

- How well do they capture realistic settings and challenges?
- Some doubts outlined by Sun et al. (2020) -- imbalanced score distributions, statistical artifacts, able to perform well when looking only at source or MT.

	WMT	**In practice**
Training data	$\sim 10^3$ sentences	$\sim 10^6$ sentences
Domains	Few	Many
Quality target	Fixed	Varied

Good systems for WMT may not necessarily perform well in practical settings.

- On our datasets, fine-tuned multilingual pre-trained models work comparably or better than QE-specific approaches.

REFERENCE-FREE METRICS FOR MTQE

Segment-level evaluation, Spearman correlation

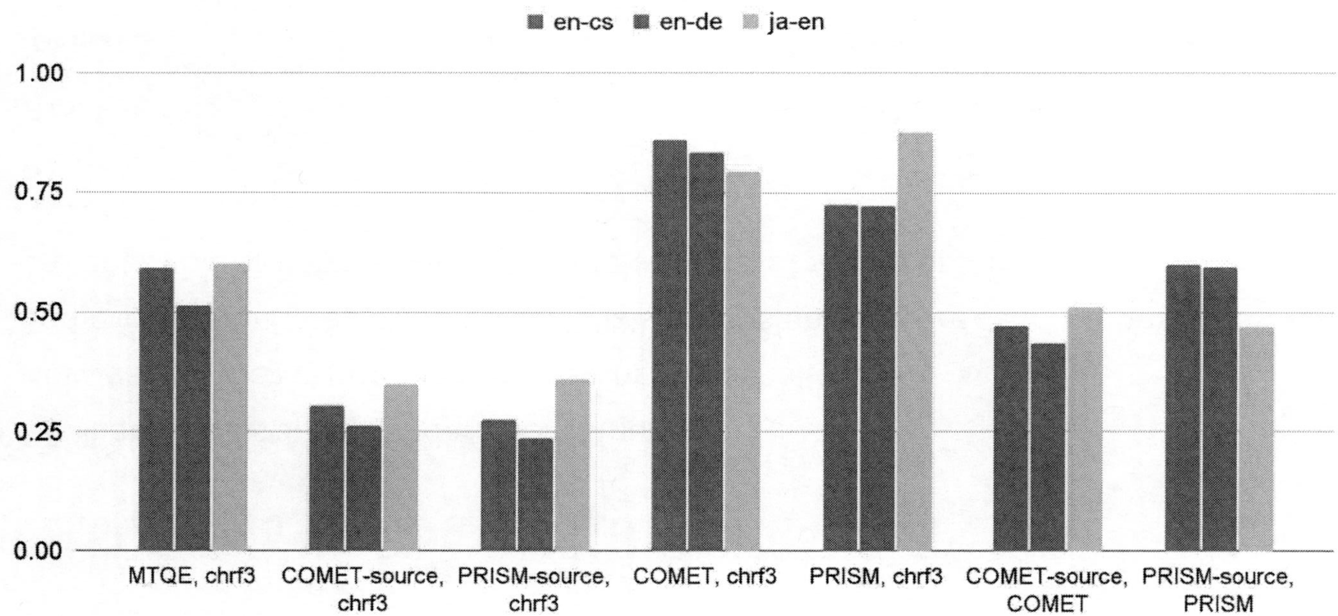

REFERENCE-FREE METRICS FOR MTQE

Document-level evaluation, Spearman correlation

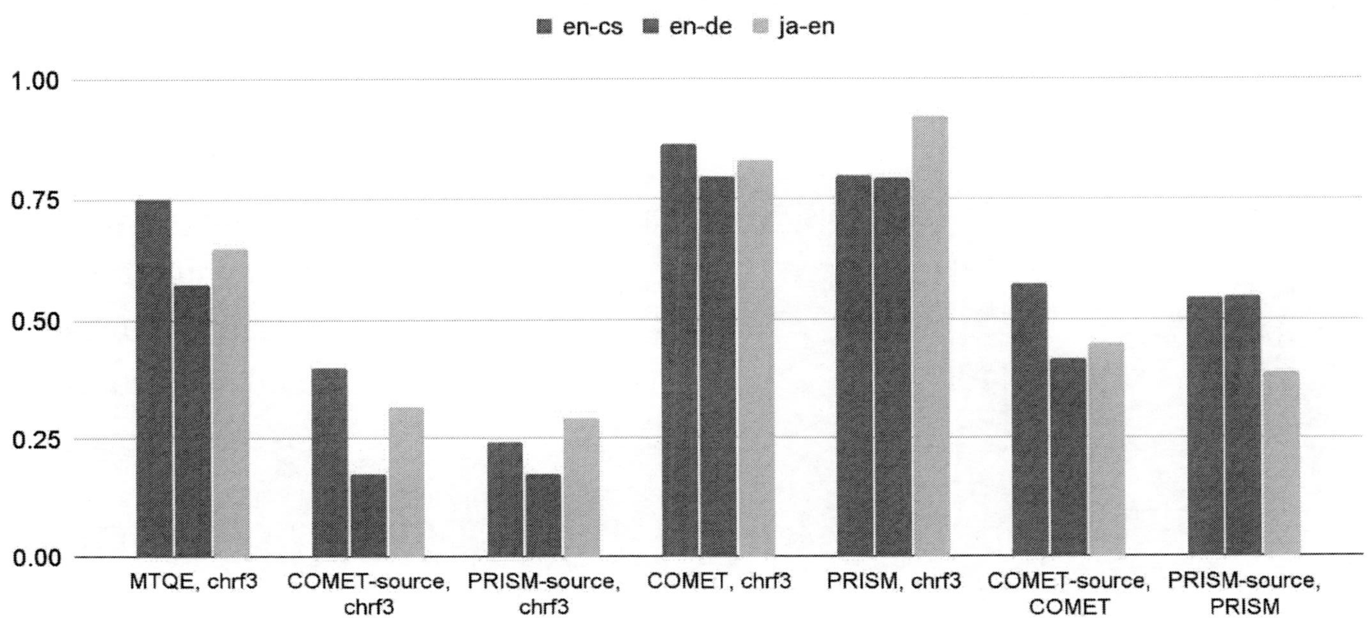

MT QUALITY IS NOT ONLY ABOUT MT

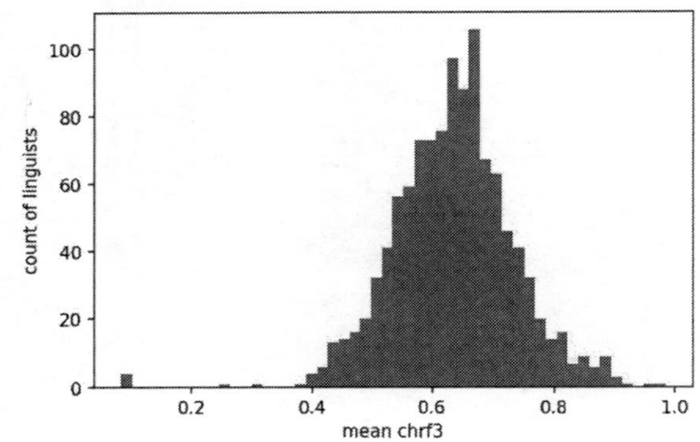

Various factors play a role:

- Customer and domain.
- Customer budget.
  - Is light post-editing okay?
  - Will there be (multiple rounds of) manual revisions?
- Translator attitude towards MT.
  - Some translators like to overedit, others like to underedit the MT outputs.

In a way, when we get a post-edited translation, we're really getting just a **random sample from some distribution of possible post-edits**. This distribution may have quite a large variance.

- Corollary: completely accurate MTQE is impossible.

EFFECT OF POST-EDITORS

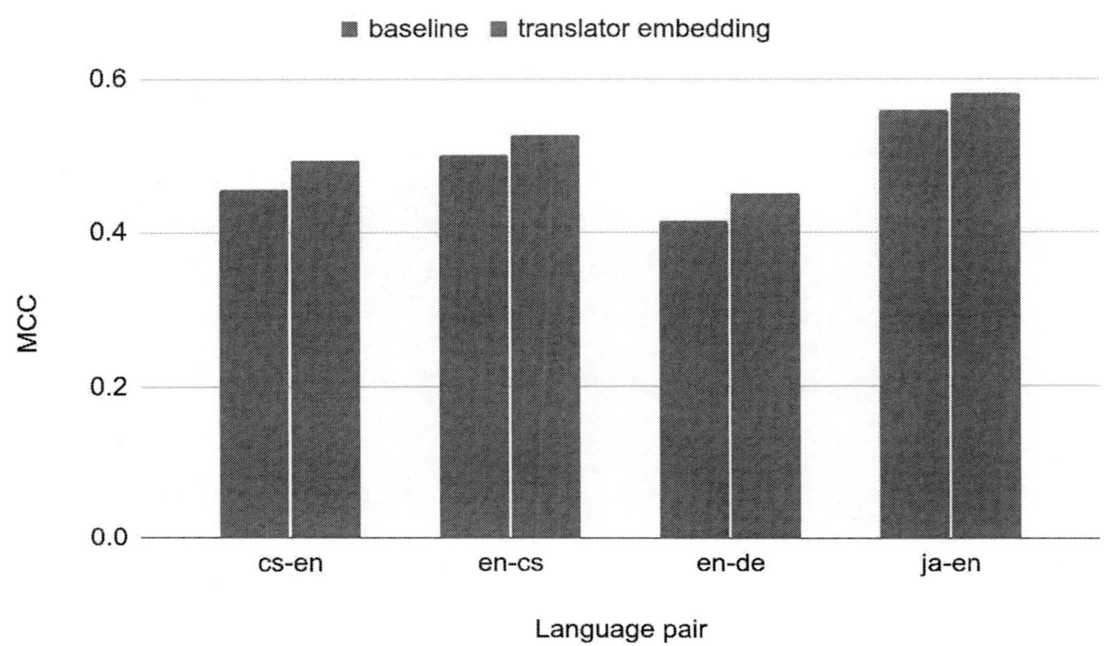

CONCLUSION

- MT quality has various definitions.
- Results on academic tasks do not always translate to real-world performance.
- Post-editing effort is influenced by various factors.
  - Translator attitude plays an important role.
- As MT systems approach human quality, we may need to revisit the definition of MTQE entirely.

REFERENCES

- Agrawal, S. et al. (2021). Assessing Reference-Free Peer Evaluation for Machine Translation. https://arxiv.org/abs/2104.05146
- Graham, Y. et al. (2016): Is all that Glitters in Machine Translation Quality Estimation really Gold? https://aclanthology.org/C16-1294/
- Fomicheva, M. et al. (2020). MLQE-PE: A multilingual quality estimation and post-editing dataset. https://arxiv.org/pdf/2010.04480.pdf
- Specia, L. et al. (2020). Findings of the WMT 2020 Shared Task on Quality Estimation. https://aclanthology.org/2020.wmt-1.79/
- Sun, S. et al. (2020). Are we Estimating or Guesstimating Translation Quality? https://aclanthology.org/2020.acl-main.558/

Q&A

MEMSOURCE

THANK YOU

MEMSOURCE

Validating Quality Estimation in a Computer-Aided Translation Workflow: Speed, Cost and Quality Trade-off

Fernando Alva-Manchego f.alva@sheffield.ac.uk
Department of Computer Science, University of Sheffield, UK

Lucia Specia l.specia@imperial.ac.uk
Department of Computing, Imperial College London, UK

Sara Szoc sara.szoc@crosslang.com
Tom Vanallemeersch tom.vanallemeersch@crosslang.com
Heidi Depraetere heidi.depraetere@crosslang.com
CrossLang, Kerkstraat 106, 9050 Gentbrugge, Belgium

Abstract

In modern computer-aided translation workflows, Machine Translation (MT) systems are used to produce a draft that is then checked and edited where needed by human translators. In this scenario, a Quality Estimation (QE) tool can be used to score MT outputs, and a threshold on the QE scores can be applied to decide whether an MT output can be used as-is or requires human post-edition. While this could reduce cost and turnaround times, it could harm translation quality, as QE models are not 100% accurate. In the framework of the APE-QUEST project (Automated Post-Editing and Quality Estimation), we set up a case-study on the trade-off between speed, cost and quality, investigating the benefits of QE models in a real-world scenario, where we rely on end-user acceptability as quality metric. Using data in the public administration domain for English-Dutch and English-French, we experimented with two use cases: assimilation and dissemination. Results shed some light on how QE scores can be explored to establish thresholds that suit each use case and target language, and demonstrate the potential benefits of adding QE to a translation workflow.

1 Introduction

Quality Estimation (QE) for Machine Translation (MT) predicts how good or reliable automatic translations are without access to gold-standard references (Specia et al., 2009; Fonseca et al., 2019; Specia et al., 2020). This is especially useful in real-world settings, such as within a translation company, where it can improve post-editing efficiency by filtering out segments that require more effort to correct than to translate from scratch (Specia, 2011; Martins et al., 2017), or select high-quality segments to be published as they are (Soricut and Echihabi, 2010). However, while the utility of MT is widely accepted nowadays, thus far no research has looked into validating the utility of QE in practice, in a realistic setting. To address this gap, in this paper we ask ourselves the following questions: 1) Can QE make the translation process more efficient (i.e. faster and cheaper)? 2) What is the impact of a QE-based filter on the quality of the final translations? and 3) How does varying the threshold for this filter affect these two competing goals (efficiency and quality)?

In the APE-QUEST project for Automated Post-Editing and Quality Estimation (Van den Bogaert et al., 2019; Depraetere et al., 2020),[1] we set up a proof-of-concept environment combining MT with QE. This Quality Gate was integrated within the workflow of the two companies in the consortium (CrossLang and Unbabel), specialized in computer-aided translation: predicted QE scores are used to decide whether an MT output can be used as-is (predicted as *acceptable* quality) or should be post-edited (predicted as *unacceptable* quality). It is expected that this Quality Gate speeds up the translation workflow and reduces costs since not all MT outputs would require human post-edition, but having humans read translations to make this decision is time-consuming. However, without a good understanding of the effects of QE-based filtering, there is a risk that the workflow becomes biased towards maximising throughput, i.e. towards selecting more low-quality translations as acceptable, and thus compromising the quality of the final translations. We propose a simple approach to studying the trade-off between speed, cost and quality, and show how important it is in allowing the Quality Gate to provide sufficiently-good MT while employing humans to only post-edit "difficult" sentences. We also show that this varies depending on the intended use of the translations.

Our experiments with the Quality Gate use state-of-the-art neural MT (NMT) and QE models with texts in the public administration domain, and translation use cases with different quality requirements (Section 3). To elaborate a realistic trade-off model, stakeholder input is important. As such, we collected human post-edits (along with post-editing time) and end-user acceptability judgements (binary scores) for two use cases (assimilation and dissemination) and two language pairs (English-Dutch and English-French) to evaluate the Quality Gate in different scenarios (Section 4). This data served to analyse how varying thresholds of QE scores affect post-editing time, overall cost and end-user acceptability, where we compare the Quality Gate against a human-only translation workflow (all MTs are checked and post-edited) and an MT-only translation workflow (all MTs are used as-is). Results (Section 5) show that QE scores can be used to establish thresholds that reduce cost and time, while maintaining similar quality levels as the human-only workflow, for all use cases and target languages. The gains are even greater when using oracle scores instead of predicted scores, signalling the benefits of improving this type of technology. This trade-off methodology for establishing QE thresholds proved helpful to demonstrate the benefits of incorporating QE in real-world computer-aided translation workflows (Section 6).

2 Related Work

Previous studies on the benefits of QE in translation workflows compared translators' productivity when post-editing selected MT outputs (based on QE scores) versus translating from scratch. Turchi et al. (2015) found that significant gains depend on the length of the source sentences and the quality of the MT output. Similarly, Parra Escartín et al. (2017) showed that translators spent less time post-editing sentences with "good" QE scores, i.e. scores that accurately predicted low PE effort. Different from these studies, we do not investigate impact on post-editor productivity, but rather whether it is possible to rely on QE scores to selectively bypass human post-edition and still achieve similar levels of translation quality. In addition, we experiment with state-of-the-art neural QE systems instead of feature-based ones.

The applicability of neural QE was investigated by Shterionov et al. (2019) when translating software UI strings from Microsoft products. The authors compared three systems in terms of business impact (using Microsoft's business metrics, such as throughput), model performance (using standard metrics, such as Pearson correlation), and cost (in terms of training and inference times). Different from theirs, our work relies on end-user translation acceptability as primary evaluation metric.

[1] `https://ape-quest.eu/`

Finally, some work attempted to determine thresholds for metrics' scores to identify ranges where post-editing productivity gains can be obtained (Parra Escartín and Arcedillo, 2015), or improvement in the quality of the raw MT output can be expected (Guerrero, 2020). However, they were based on post-hoc computations of TER (translation edit rate) or edit distance, respectively, instead of predicted QE scores as in our case. In addition, we experiment with thresholds of QE scores that benefit the overall translation workflow for different use cases and language pairs.

3 Quality Gate

We describe the technical components of the Quality Gate, the translation workflows that it compares to, and the translation use cases we considered.

3.1 Core Technologies

Machine Translation Module: The Quality Gate uses eTranslation[2] as backend NMT service. This service provides state-of-the-art NMT systems for more than 24 languages, and is targeted mainly at European public administrations and small and medium-sized enterprises.

Quality Estimation Module: The Quality Gate incorporates QE models built using TransQuest (Ranasinghe et al., 2020), the winning toolkit in the WMT20 Quality Estimation Shared Task for sentence-level QE (Specia et al., 2020). In these models, the original sentence and its translation are concatenated using the [SEP] token, and then passed through a pre-trained Transformer-based language model to obtain a joint representation via the [CLS] token. This serves as input to a softmax layer that predicts translation quality.

We trained language-specific models by fine-tuning Multilingual BERT (Devlin et al., 2019) with the dataset of Ive et al. (2020), which contains (source, MT output, human post-edition, target) tuples of sentences in the legal domain. We chose this data since it is the closest to our application domain, and contains instances in the language pairs of our interest: 11,249 for English-Dutch (EN-NL) and 9,989 for English-French (EN-FR). In order to obtain gold QE scores, we used `tercom` (Snover et al., 2006) to compute a TER value for each sentence. We trained our models using the same data splits as Ive et al. (2020), obtaining better results than the ones originally reported with ensembles of 5 models per language (Table 1).

	EN-NL		EN-FR	
Model	r	MAE	r	MAE
Ive et al. (2020)	0.38	0.14	0.58	0.14
Ours	**0.51**	**0.10**	**0.69**	**0.10**

Table 1: Performance of QE models in terms of Pearson's r correlation coefficient and Mean Absolute Error (MAE) in the test set of Ive et al. (2020).

Whilst the performance of the models is moderate according to Pearson, the error is relatively low (0.1 in a 0-1 range), and thus we believe the predictions can be useful to analyse the utility of current state-of-the-art QE in a real-word setting.

3.2 Workflows

In the **Quality Gate** workflow, given an automatic translation, the QE module provides a score that needs to be thresholded such that: (1) acceptable-quality MT will be left unchanged and

[2] https://ec.europa.eu/cefdigital/wiki/display/CEFDIGITAL/eTranslation

passed directly to the end-user; and (2) unacceptable-quality MT will be sent to a Human Post-Editing (HPE) pipeline. This workflow will be compared to a **Traditional** workflow, where all MT outputs are manually checked and edited as needed, as well as to an **MT-Only** workflow, where translations from MT are not checked/post-edited but used as-is.

3.3 Use Cases

In our experiments, we used source texts snippets composed by texts sampled from a European public administration handling consumer complaints.[3] We devised two use cases that correspond to two distinct well-established uses of MT:

Assimilation: Translations are to be used for internal communication purposes (e.g. emails) or for general text understanding. Translation quality is expected to be *good enough* to understand the main message of the text.

Dissemination: Translations are to be published in any form (online or in print), so they need to be of *very high* quality, only requiring final quality checks (i.e. proofreading).

The input to the workflows are individual sentences, but they are post-edited and assessed in the context of the surrounding sentences.

4 Evaluation Protocol

Our trade-off model should help to answer the following questions:

- When compared to the Traditional workflow, does the Quality Gate workflow help to improve speed (i.e. time to get to final translation) and reduce cost (how many translations need HPE), while maintaining translation quality?
- When compared to the MT-Only workflow, does the Quality Gate workflow help to improve translation quality?

In addition, we investigate how the answers to these questions vary for: (1) different thresholds on the predicted quality of translations; (2) each of the two use cases (assimilation and dissemination); (3) different target languages; and (4) different quality of the QE scores (predicted vs oracle).

4.1 Measurable Criteria

The measurable criteria we compute for each use case and target language are:

Quality: Percentage of sentences considered of acceptable quality by independent human raters.

Cost: Percentage of sentences that require HPE, versus being fit for purpose.

Speed: Time required for HPE. The time to predict QE scores is negligible so it is not considered.

4.2 Datasets

For our evaluation, we used English text snippets from the public administration for each use case and target language. This type of text is challenging for the Quality Gate since it is out-

[3]For reasons of confidentiality, we cannot disclose the name of this administration. Therefore, the examples provided in this paper are taken from a publicly available dataset provided by the U.S. government: `https://catalog.data.gov/dataset/consumer-complaint-database`.

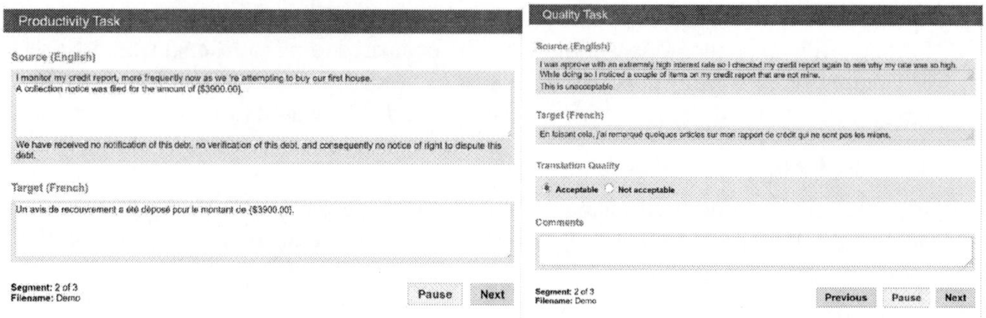

(a) Human post-edits

(b) Binary acceptability ratings

Figure 1: Screenshot of the MT Evaluation tool used to collect manual annotations.

of-domain compared to the texts used to train the NMT system (mainly general public administration) and the QE models (legal domain). The decision on the target languages – Dutch (NL) and French (FR) – is based on the availability of the human raters.

Assimilation Dataset: It consists of user complaints received by the public administration. This data is particularly interesting since it corresponds to conversational language. Sentence segmentation was applied before sending the texts to the MT system. After all preprocessing steps, we ended up with 25 complaints, totalling 966 English source sentences with an average length of 22.51 words per sentence.

Dissemination Dataset: Original texts were obtained from the website of the public administration. The data was segmented into sentences and then sent to the MT system. This resulted in 114 input sentences, with an average length of 18.32 words per sentence.

4.3 Human Annotations

We collected human annotations in two forms: **post-edits (HPE)** and **acceptability ratings**. While sentences that go through HPE are expected to have acceptable quality, we still collected human ratings for them to validate this assumption.

HPEs were obtained for all MT outputs available in each use case and target language. Post-editors were experienced professional translators in the domain of interest and for each use case. For each target language, three post-editors were hired, and each sentence was post-edited once.

Ratings were elicited for all MT outputs and their corresponding HPEs. Raters were professional translators that judged the quality of the sentences as Acceptable/Unacceptable for each use case. Raters were not informed of whether the sentences being judged were an MT output or HPE. For each target language and use case, two raters scored each translation (either MT or HPE) once.

HPEs and ratings were collected using the in-house MT Evaluation tool of one of the consortium's companies. Following recommended practice (Läubli et al., 2018; Toral et al., 2018), sentences were post-edited and rated within the document context of the source language, i.e. the preceding and the following sentences. For HPEs (Figure 1a) we also collected timestamps of when an editor started the editing job and of when the final job was delivered, at the sentence level. For collecting ratings (Figure 1b), the tool is flexible regarding the type of judgements that can be collected. In our case, we used binary ones for each use case.

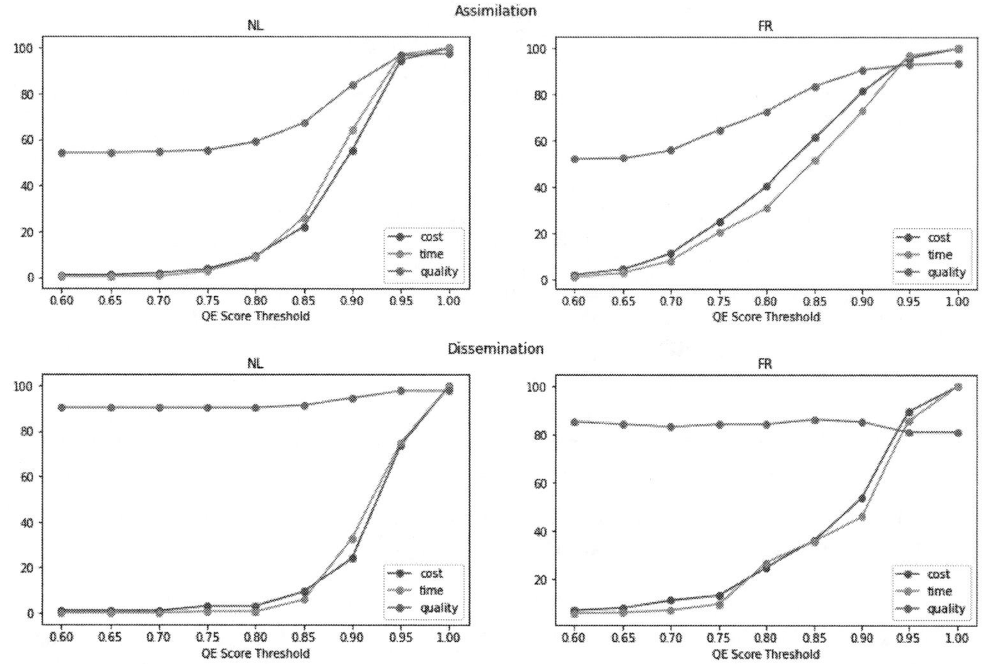

Figure 2: Variation of Cost, Time and Quality based on the QE score (**predicted**) threshold in the Quality Gate workflow for each use case and language (NL = English-Dutch; FR = English-French).

5 Experiments and Results

We evaluate the performance of the Quality Gate workflow depending on different values of QE score thresholds. We present the three evaluation metrics: Quality, Cost and Time. For better visualisation, we normalized Time as a percentage with respect to the Traditional workflow.

We set up thresholds from 0 to 1 in 0.05 increments, and computed the evaluation metrics under the assumption that sentences whose QE score was below the threshold required HPE. More specifically, for these sentences we took their post-editing time and quality judgement after HPE to calculate the metrics. For the rest (i.e. sentences not "requiring HPE") their time is 0 and their quality judgement is that of the MT output.

We first use the predicted QE scores to evaluate the current performance of the Quality Gate (Section 5.1). Then, we experiment with an oracle scenario where the QE scores are perfect, in order to measure the potential best-case-scenario performance of the Quality Gate workflow (Section 5.2).

5.1 Predicted QE Scores

Figure 2 shows how the three evaluation criteria vary depending on the threshold selected for the predicted QE score in the Quality Gate workflow. Table 2 details and compares the values to those from the Traditional (post-edit everything) and MT-only (do not post-edit anything) workflows.[4]

For all target languages and use cases, it is possible to set up a QE score threshold that allows the Quality Gate Workflow to obtain Quality with a value similar to the Traditional

[4]The QE < 1.0 threshold is excluded since no instance had a predicted QE score between 0.95 and 1.0.

Lang	Threshold	Assimilation			Dissemination		
		Cost	Time	Quality	Cost	Time	Quality
NL	Traditional	100.00	100.00	97.67	100.00	100.00	97.89
	QE < 0.95	94.77	97.24	96.80	73.68	74.98	97.89
	QE < 0.90	55.52	64.18	83.87	24.21	33.02	94.74
	QE < 0.85	22.24	26.17	67.30	9.47	5.87	91.58
	MT-Only	0.00	0.00	54.07	0.00	0.00	90.53
FR	Traditional	100.00	100.00	93.79	100.00	100.00	81.25
	QE < 0.95	95.86	97.02	93.10	89.58	85.64	81.25
	QE < 0.90	81.38	73.00	90.69	54.17	46.22	85.42
	QE < 0.85	61.38	51.54	83.79	36.46	36.11	86.40
	MT-Only	0.00	0.00	50.34	0.00	0.00	86.46

Table 2: Cost (% of sentences that need HPE), Time (% of HPE time with respect to Traditional) and Quality (% of acceptable translations) for varying thresholds of **predicted** QE scores in the Quality Gate compared to the Traditional and MT-only workflows.

Workflow, with reductions in Cost and Time. This QE score threshold is 0.95 for most cases. The gains in Time and Cost vary depending on the target language and use case.

For both use cases, the Quality Gate workflow achieves better results in NL than the MT-only one. The gains in Time and Cost vary according to the threshold selected. In the case of FR, the gains are evident for the Assimilation use case. However, MT-only obtains a better Quality score in the Dissemination use case, even superior to the Traditional workflow. This is because, for a few sentences, whilst one rater judged their MT outputs as acceptable, the other rater judged their HPE versions as unacceptable. We hypothesize that this is caused by disagreements in the human judgements rather than HPE being worse than MT. More analysis with multiple human ratings per translation would be needed to test this hypothesis.

5.2 Oracle QE Scores

Since we have HPEs for all MT outputs, we use them to compute oracle QE scores, that is, their "real" QE scores. This models an ideal scenario where the Quality Gate perfectly determines the QE score of an MT output. This could be seen as an upper bound of the potential benefits of the Quality Gate workflow. Figure 3 and Table 3 show our results in this setting.

In this ideal scenario, the gains are higher for all target languages in both use cases. This evidences the potential of the Quality Gate for reducing Cost and Time while preserving high Quality. We would expect the Quality Gate workflow to be able to move towards this ideal scenario as it is put in place and post-edits in the actual domain of interest are collected to better train the QE models.

6 Conclusions

In this paper, we provided evidence of the benefits of introducing QE into the computer-aided translation workflow of a company. In the framework of the APE-QUEST project, we implemented a Quality Gate that decides, based on predicted QE scores, whether MT outputs can be used as-is (acceptable quality) or if they require post-edition (unacceptable quality). We performed a trade-off study to establish thresholds on the QE scores that allow reducing time and cost, while keeping translation quality more or less stable. We collected human post-edits and acceptability ratings from real use case scenarios and real end-users, and demonstrated that the

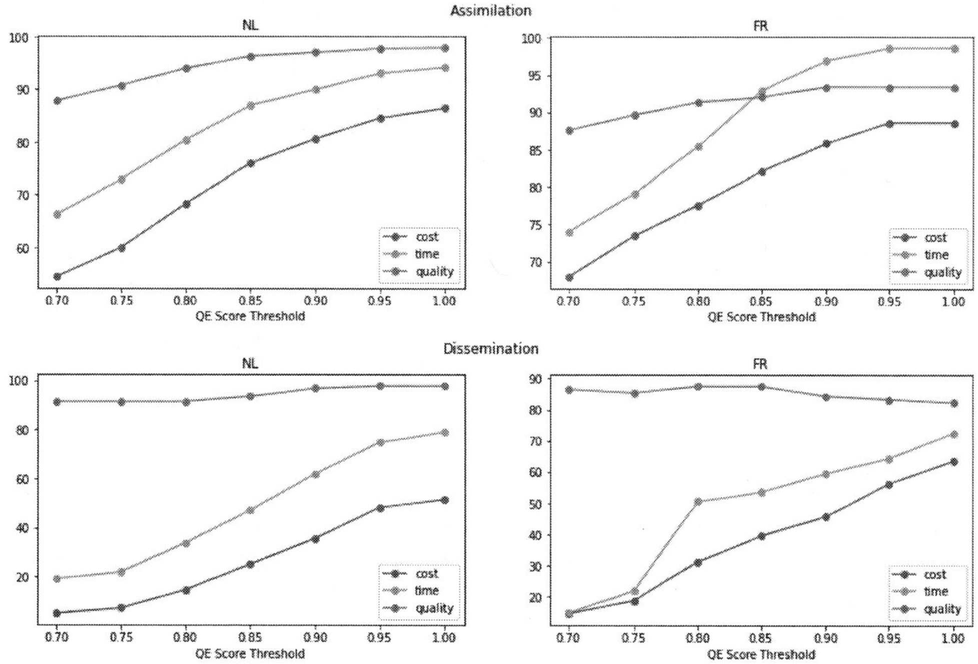

Figure 3: Variation of Cost, Time and Quality based on the QE score (**oracle**) threshold in the Quality Gate workflow for each use case and language (NL = English-Dutch; FR = English-French).

Lang	Threshold	Assimilation			Dissemination		
		Cost	Time	Quality	Cost	Time	Quality
NL	Traditional	100.00	100.00	97.67	100.00	100.00	97.89
	QE < 1.00	86.48	94.20	97.97	51.58	79.12	97.89
	QE < 0.95	84.59	93.12	97.82	48.42	74.89	97.89
	QE < 0.90	80.67	90.04	97.09	35.79	62.00	96.84
	MT-Only	0.00	0.00	54.07	0.00	0.00	90.53
FR	Traditional	100.00	100.00	93.79	100.00	100.00	81.25
	QE < 1.00	88.62	98.63	93.45	63.54	72.51	82.29
	QE < 0.95	88.62	98.63	93.45	56.25	64.37	83.33
	QE < 0.90	85.86	96.95	93.45	45.83	59.55	84.38
	MT-Only	0.00	0.00	50.34	0.00	0.00	86.46

Table 3: Cost (% of sentences that need HPE), Time (% of HPE time with respect to Traditional) and Quality (% of acceptable translations) for varying thresholds of **oracle** QE scores in the Quality Gate compared to the Traditional and MT-only workflows.

Quality Gate can obtain similar levels of quality to the current human-only workflow, for all use cases and target languages explored. In addition, when the predicted QE scores are changed to oracle ones, the gains are higher, illustrating the potential benefits of improving the predictive abilities of the QE models.

Acknowledgements

APE-QUEST was funded by the EC's CEF Telecom programme (project 2017-EU-IA-0151). The project ran from 2018 to 2020.

References

Depraetere, H., Van den Bogaert, J., Szoc, S., and Vanallemeersch, T. (2020). APE-QUEST: an MT quality gate. In *Proceedings of the 22nd Annual Conference of the European Association for Machine Translation*, pages 473–474, Lisboa, Portugal. European Association for Machine Translation.

Devlin, J., Chang, M.-W., Lee, K., and Toutanova, K. (2019). BERT: Pre-training of deep bidirectional transformers for language understanding. In *Proceedings of the 2019 Conference of the North American Chapter of the Association for Computational Linguistics: Human Language Technologies, Volume 1 (Long and Short Papers)*, pages 4171–4186, Minneapolis, Minnesota. Association for Computational Linguistics.

Fonseca, E., Yankovskaya, L., Martins, A. F. T., Fishel, M., and Federmann, C. (2019). Findings of the WMT 2019 shared tasks on quality estimation. In *Proceedings of the Fourth Conference on Machine Translation (Volume 3: Shared Task Papers, Day 2)*, pages 1–10, Florence, Italy. Association for Computational Linguistics.

Guerrero, L. (2020). In search of an acceptability/unacceptability threshold in machine translation post-editing automated metrics. In *Proceedings of the 14th Conference of the Association for Machine Translation in the Americas (Volume 2: User Track)*, pages 32–47, Virtual. Association for Machine Translation in the Americas.

Ive, J., Specia, L., Szoc, S., Vanallemeersch, T., Van den Bogaert, J., Farah, E., Maroti, C., Ventura, A., and Khalilov, M. (2020). A post-editing dataset in the legal domain: Do we underestimate neural machine translation quality? In *Proceedings of the 12th Language Resources and Evaluation Conference*, pages 3692–3697, Marseille, France. European Language Resources Association.

Läubli, S., Sennrich, R., and Volk, M. (2018). Has machine translation achieved human parity? a case for document-level evaluation. In *Proceedings of the 2018 Conference on Empirical Methods in Natural Language Processing*, pages 4791–4796, Brussels, Belgium. Association for Computational Linguistics.

Martins, A. F. T., Junczys-Dowmunt, M., Kepler, F. N., Astudillo, R., Hokamp, C., and Grundkiewicz, R. (2017). Pushing the limits of translation quality estimation. *Transactions of the Association for Computational Linguistics*, 5:205–218.

Parra Escartín, C. and Arcedillo, M. (2015). Living on the edge: productivity gain thresholds in machine translation evaluation metrics. In *Proceedings of 4th Workshop on Post-Editing Technology and Practice (WPTP4)*, pages 46–56, Miami.

Parra Escartín, C., Béchara, H., and Orasan, C. (2017). Questing for quality estimation a user study. *The Prague Bulletin of Mathematical Linguistics*, 108:343–354.

Ranasinghe, T., Orasan, C., and Mitkov, R. (2020). TransQuest: Translation quality estimation with cross-lingual transformers. In *Proceedings of the 28th International Conference on Computational Linguistics*, pages 5070–5081, Barcelona, Spain (Online). International Committee on Computational Linguistics.

Shterionov, D., Carmo, F. D., Moorkens, J., Paquin, E., Schmidtke, D., Groves, D., and Way, A. (2019). When less is more in neural quality estimation of machine translation. an industry case study. In *Proceedings of Machine Translation Summit XVII Volume 2: Translator, Project and User Tracks*, pages 228–235, Dublin, Ireland. European Association for Machine Translation.

Snover, M., Dorr, B., Schwartz, R., Micciulla, L., and Makhoul, J. (2006). A study of translation edit rate with targeted human annotation. In *Proceedings of 7th Biennial Conference of the Association for Machine Translation in the Americas*, pages 223–231, Cambridge, Massachusetts, USA.

Soricut, R. and Echihabi, A. (2010). TrustRank: Inducing trust in automatic translations via ranking. In *Proceedings of the 48th Annual Meeting of the Association for Computational Linguistics*, pages 612–621, Uppsala, Sweden. Association for Computational Linguistics.

Specia, L. (2011). Exploiting objective annotations for minimising translation post-editing effort. In *Proceedings of the 15th Annual conference of the European Association for Machine Translation*, pages 73–80, Leuven, Belgium. European Association for Machine Translation.

Specia, L., Blain, F., Fomicheva, M., Fonseca, E., Chaudhary, V., Guzmán, F., and Martins, A. F. T. (2020). Findings of the WMT 2020 shared task on quality estimation. In *Proceedings of the Fifth Conference on Machine Translation*, pages 743–764, Online. Association for Computational Linguistics.

Specia, L., Turchi, M., Cancedda, N., Cristianini, N., and Dymetman, M. (2009). Estimating the sentence-level quality of machine translation systems. In *Proceedings of the 13th Annual conference of the European Association for Machine Translation*, Barcelona, Spain. European Association for Machine Translation.

Toral, A., Castilho, S., Hu, K., and Way, A. (2018). Attaining the unattainable? reassessing claims of human parity in neural machine translation. In *Proceedings of the Third Conference on Machine Translation: Research Papers*, pages 113–123, Brussels, Belgium. Association for Computational Linguistics.

Turchi, M., Negri, M., and Federico, M. (2015). MT quality estimation for computer-assisted translation: Does it really help? In *Proceedings of the 53rd Annual Meeting of the Association for Computational Linguistics and the 7th International Joint Conference on Natural Language Processing (Volume 2: Short Papers)*, pages 530–535, Beijing, China. Association for Computational Linguistics.

Van den Bogaert, J., Depraetere, H., Szoc, S., Vanallemeersch, T., Van Winckel, K., Everaert, F., Specia, L., Ive, J., Khalilov, M., Maroti, C., Farah, E., and Ventura, A. (2019). APE-QUEST. In *Proceedings of Machine Translation Summit XVII Volume 2: Translator, Project and User Tracks*, pages 110–111, Dublin, Ireland. European Association for Machine Translation.

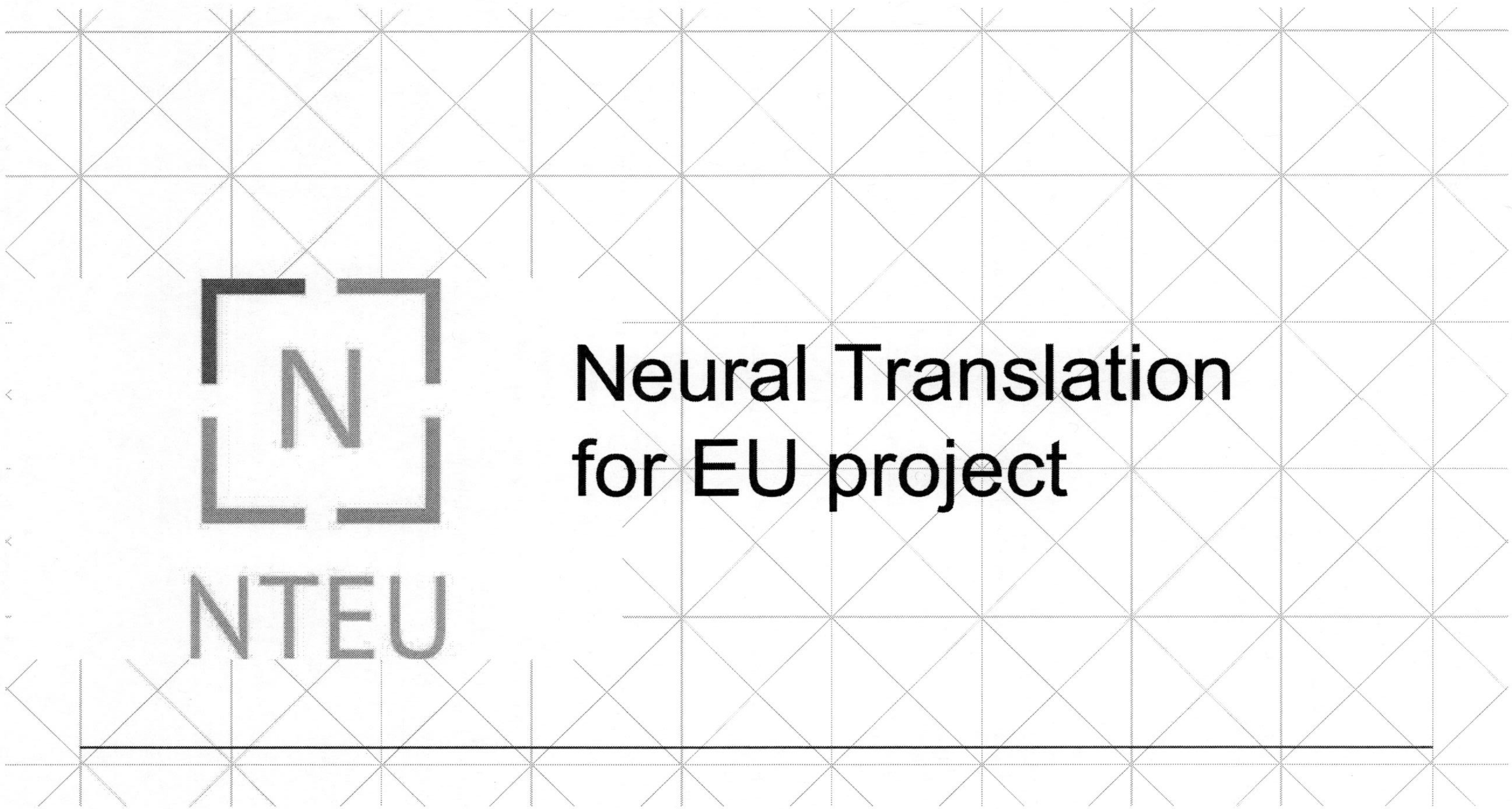
NTEU
Neural Translation
for EU project

Project Objectives
Sept.19 -Aug.21

- Build SOA NMT models for all EU official language combinations (24 languages, 552 combinations) without using a high-resourced language as pivot.

- Collect clean training data:
  - 15M segments 1-1 resourced languages
  - 10-12M segments under-resourced languages
  - 10M ultra-under-resourced (Maltese, Irish)

- Upload dockerised MT engines and collected data to ELRC-SHARE and European Language Grid, for use by Public Administrations

Language matrix (24 x 23=552 engines)

	BG	CS	DA	DE	EL	ES	ET	FI	FR	GA	HR	HU	IT	LT	LV	MT	NL	PL	PT	RO	SL	SK	SV
BG		-	-	-	-	-	-	-	-	-	-	-	-	-	-	-	-	-	-	-	-	-	-
CS	-		-	-	-	-	-	-	-	-	-	-	-	-	-	-	-	-	-	-	-	-	-
DA	-	-		-	-	-	-	-	-	-	-	-	-	-	-	-	-	-	-	-	-	-	-
DE	-	-	-		-	-	-	-	-	-	-	-	-	-	-	-	-	-	-	-	-	-	-
EL	-	-	-	-		-	-	-	-	-	-	-	-	-	-	-	-	-	-	-	-	-	-
ES	-	-	-	-	-		-	-	-	-	-	-	-	-	-	-	-	-	-	-	-	-	-
ET	-	-	-	-	-	-		-	-	-	-	-	-	-	-	-	-	-	-	-	-	-	-
FI	-	-	-	-	-	-	-		-	-	-	-	-	-	-	-	-	-	-	-	-	-	-
FR	-	-	-	-	-	-	-	-		-	-	-	-	-	-	-	-	-	-	-	-	-	-
GA	-	-	-	-	-	-	-	-	-		-	-	-	-	-	-	-	-	-	-	-	-	-
HR	-	-	-	-	-	-	-	-	-	-		-	-	-	-	-	-	-	-	-	-	-	-
HU	-	-	-	-	-	-	-	-	-	-	-		-	-	-	-	-	-	-	-	-	-	-
IT	-	-	-	-	-	-	-	-	-	-	-	-		-	-	-	-	-	-	-	-	-	-
LT	-	-	-	-	-	-	-	-	-	-	-	-	-		-	-	-	-	-	-	-	-	-
LV	-	-	-	-	-	-	-	-	-	-	-	-	-	-		-	-	-	-	-	-	-	-
MT	-	-	-	-	-	-	-	-	-	-	-	-	-	-	-		-	-	-	-	-	-	-
NL	-	-	-	-	-	-	-	-	-	-	-	-	-	-	-	-		-	-	-	-	-	-
PL	-	-	-	-	-	-	-	-	-	-	-	-	-	-	-	-	-		-	-	-	-	-
PT	-	-	-	-	-	-	-	-	-	-	-	-	-	-	-	-	-	-		-	-	-	-
RO	-	-	-	-	-	-	-	-	-	-	-	-	-	-	-	-	-	-	-		-	-	-
SL	-	-	-	-	-	-	-	-	-	-	-	-	-	-	-	-	-	-	-	-		-	-
SK	-	-	-	-	-	-	-	-	-	-	-	-	-	-	-	-	-	-	-	-	-		-
SV	-	-	-	-	-	-	-	-	-	-	-	-	-	-	-	-	-	-	-	-	-	-	

pangeanic: Spanish, Portuguese, Italian, Dutch, Maltese, Polish, Czech, **French**

KantanMT.com: Romanian, German, English, Bulgarian, Hungarian, Slovene, Greek, Irish

TILDE: Latvian, Estonian, Lithuanian, Finnish, Swedish, Danish, Croatian, Slovak

Evaluation in NTEU

- Domain: **administrative** language from the DGT.
- **Same test dataset** for all languages.
- Real documents, translated by humans into the 24 languages.
- Whole documents, not randomly extracted sentences

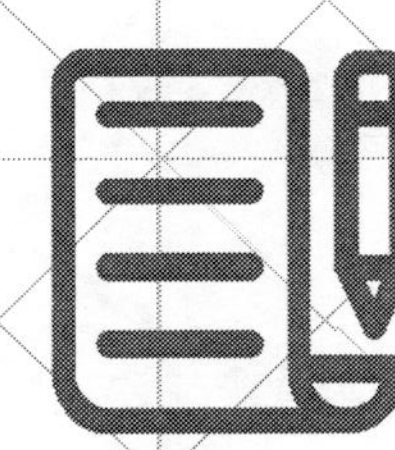

Automatic evaluation

- Test set consisting of 2000 sentences (one reference) from the selected evaluation dataset
- Isolated from the training and fine-tuning data.
- Metrics: BLEU, TER, F-Measure, Perplexity

Automatic evaluation. Example engines into Irish

	Word Count	Unique W/C	F-Measure	BLEU	TER	Perplexity
BG	78.512.192	231.082	75,00	69,00	37,00	1,72
CS	74.528.702	254.614	74,00	66,00	39,00	1,77
DA	95.973.362	321.335	74,00	65,00	39,00	1,84
DE	100.197.182	352.195	70,00	61,00	45,00	1,95
EL	111.930.392	310.248	74,00	66,00	39,00	1,82
EN	139.184.957	294.704	79,00	71,00	32,00	1,59
ES	116.138.462	237.159	73,00	65,00	41,00	1,91
ET	64.917.062	357.281	71,00	63,00	43,00	1,88
FI	70.093.082	447.897	71,00	63,00	43,00	1,87
FR	140.534.927	295.465	72,00	62,00	42,00	1,94
HR	125.199.272	3.488.938	60	40	59	3,21
HU	69.579.527	238.748	71	64	44	1,99
IT	110.602.172	145.378	73	64	41	1,95
LT	69.163.832	176.464	71	62	44	1,95
LV	70.926.452	177.535	73	65	41	1,86
MT	78.396.227	192.087	78	72	34	1,62
NL	112.834.022	183.141	72	63	42	1,91
PL	77.947.667	178.575	75	67	38	1,79
PT	117.879.917	142.278	73	65	40	1,91
RO	83.706.467	135.321	76	69	37	1,74
SK	75.441.647	177.666	75	68	37	1,77
SL	77.252.492	167.103	74	67	39	1,80
SV	89.511.137	190.720	74	65	40	1,85

Human evaluation

- We decided to use **native speakers of the target** language (difficult to find bilingual evaluators).
- We use Google translate as a benchmark.
- We have used a purpose-built evaluation platform, which will be published in GitHub at the end of the project as open-source code:

Machine **T**ranslation **E**valuation **T**ool (MTET).

Human evaluation

- In the evaluation platform, the evaluator is presented separately with:

  - the reference translation in the target language
  - the NTEU translation (unidentified)
  - the Google translation (unidentified)

  (NTEU and Google translations: in random order)

Blind evaluation

Human evaluation

- The evaluator is asked to assess each of the automatic translations (i.e. not just rank them).
- Assessment is performed through a slider that allows choosing a number in the range of 0 to 100.
- The number of sentences that has been evaluated for each engine is 500 (a subset of the validation set used for the automatic metrics).
- To mitigate human bias, each sentence has been evaluated by two evaluators.

MTET platform. Evaluator's view

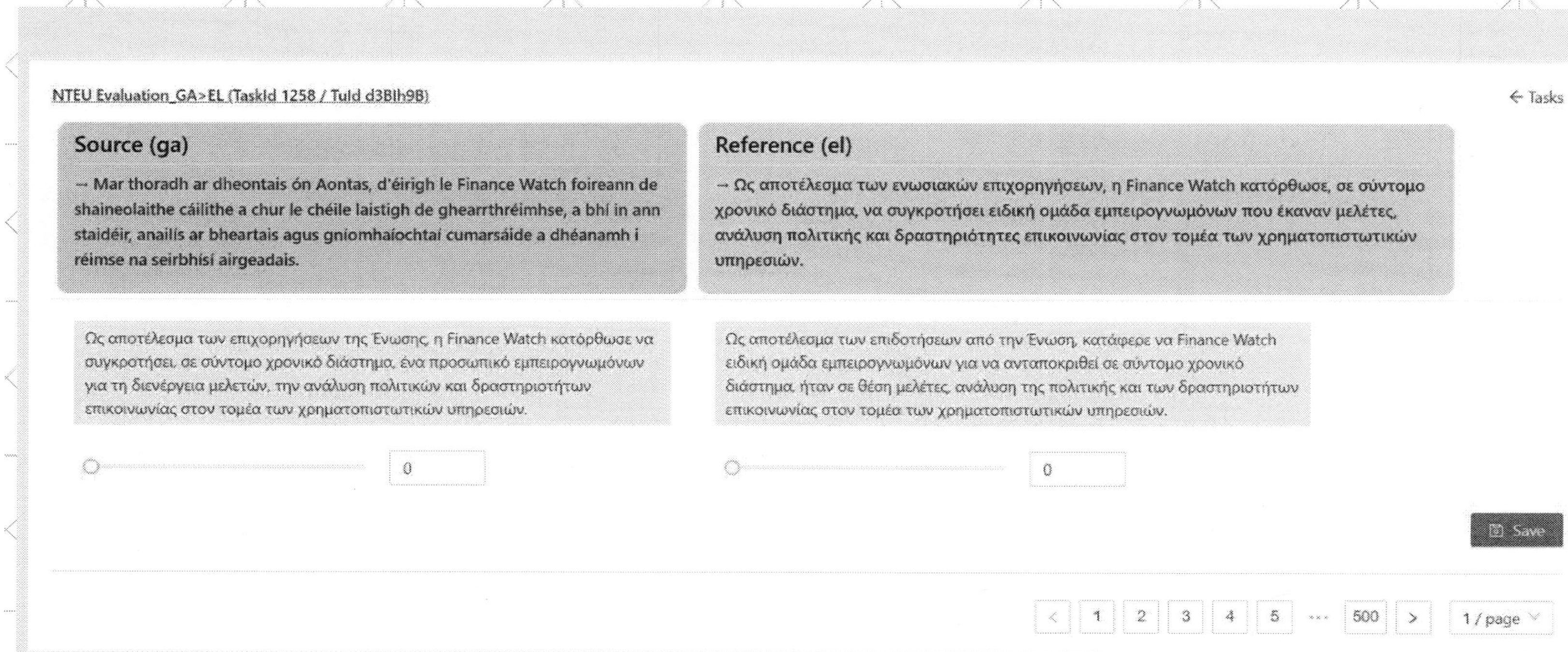

MTET platform. Evaluator’s view

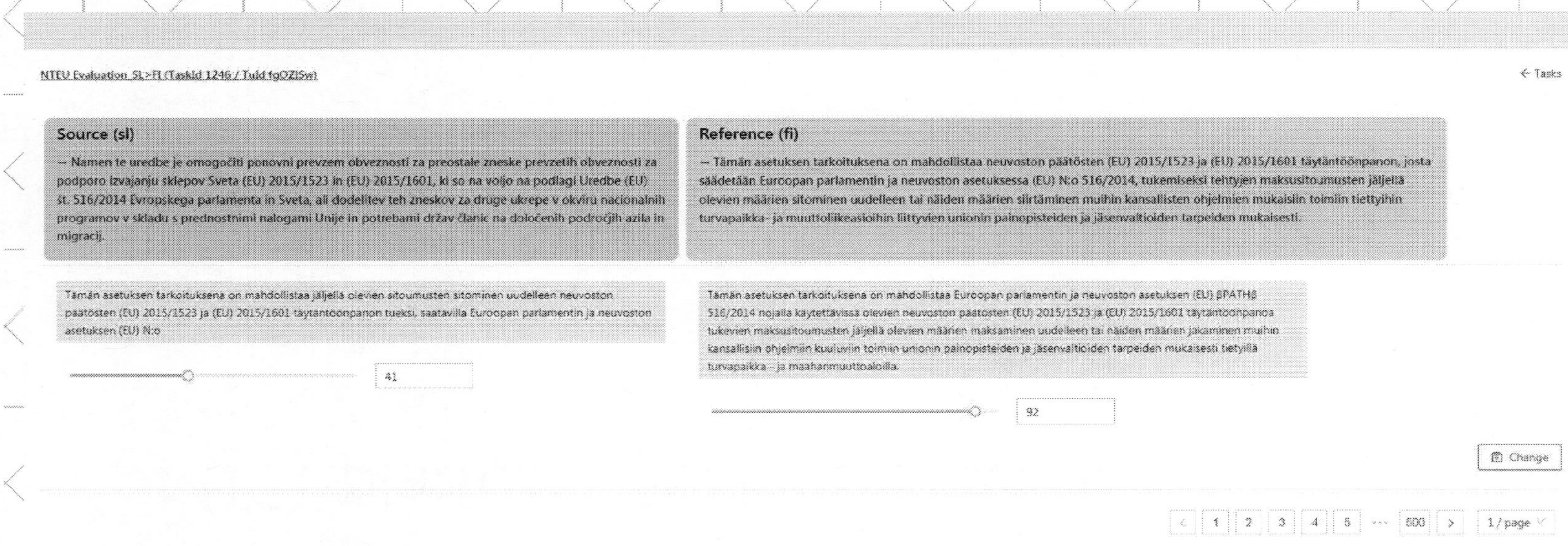

MTET platform. Administrator's view
Beneficiarii Tratatului de la Marrakesh sunt persoane nevăzătoare, persoane care au deficiențe de vedere ce nu pot fi corectate pentru a obține o funcție vizuală sensibil echivalentă cu cea a unei persoane fără astfel de deficiențe, persoane care au un handicap de percepție ori dificultăți de citire, inclusiv dislexie sau orice altă dizabilitate de învățare, care le împiedică să citească opere imprimate în aceeași măsură, în esență, ca persoanele fără astfel de dizabilități și persoane care suferă de o dizabilitate fizică ce le împiedică să țină în mână ori să manipuleze o carte sau să își concentreze privirea ori să își miște ochii astfel încât să poată citi, în măsura în care, ca urmare a acestor deficiențe sau dizabilități, acele persoane nu pot citi opere tipărite în aceeași măsură, în esență, ca o persoană care nu este afectată de astfel de deficiențe sau dizabilități.
asmenys, kurie yra akli, asmer
regos sutrikimą, kurio neįman
taip, kad jų rega iš esmės nesi
asmens, neturinčio tokio sutri
kurie turi suvokimo ar skaityn
įskaitant disleksiją ar bet kokį
sutrikimą, ir todėl negali skait
kūrinių iš esmės taip pat, kaip
neturintys asmenys, ir asmeny
fizinės negalios nepajėgia laik
knygos arba sutelkti žvilgsnio
taip, kaip to paprastai reikėtų
jei dėl tokių sutrikimų ar nega
nepajėgia skaityti spausdintų
taip, kaip tokio sutrikimo ar n
neturintys asmenys;
arties gavėjai yra aklieji, silpnaregiai žmonės, kurie negali būti ištaisyti gauti vizualiai funkciją iš esmės ly
, žmonės su regėjimo sutrikimais arba skaitymo sunkumų, įskaitant disleksija ar kitoje mokymosi negali
o spausdintus kūrinius tiek pat, kiek žmonių be tokių negalia ir žmonėms su fizine negalia, kurie neleidž

MTET platform. Administrator's view

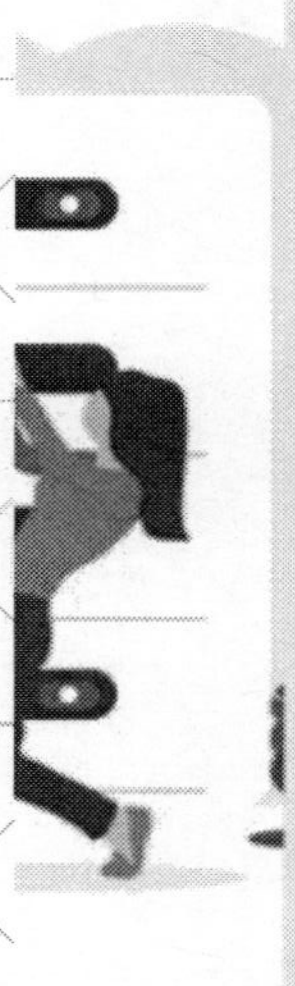

Projects

Id	Name	Source	Target	Type	#Tus	#Tuvs	Complete %
679	NTEU Evaluation_RO>LT	ro	lt	zero-to-one-hundred	500	2000	50.00
678	NTEU Evaluation_MT2>DE	mt	de	zero-to-one-hundred	500	2000	
675	NTEU Evaluation_MT>HU	mt	hu	zero-to-one-hundred	500	2000	55.50

So, how well have the NTEU engines fared?

NTEU engine is far better than Google in uncommon language combinations, where Google uses pivots

NTEU

	NTEU (Kantan)	Google
BG	51,72	27,49
CS	87,00	76,34
DA	50,30	14,95
DE	90,13	76,45
EL	46,52	9,84
EN	95,06	89,23
ES	92,23	77,56
ET	42,34	11,88
FI	88,94	75,81
FR	57,10	26,34
HU	87,89	75,06
LT	48,13	13,09
NL	33,16	14,10
PT	10,28	4,82

Target: Romanian

	NTEU (Kantan)	Google
BG	78,07	33,04
CS	89,85	44,81
DA	77,82	38,63
DE	47,23	13,11
EN	91,51	56,49
EL	89,92	46,26
ES	77,56	42,67
ET	88,30	43,30
FI	74,36	45,47
FR	79,66	42,30
LT	86,39	44,73
LV	76,83	46,09
NL	75,91	35,73
PL	77,98	46,52
PT	75,21	42,90

Target: Hungarian

But is also better in more common combinations

	NTEU	Google
Danish - German	80,33	60,96
English - German	76,77	48,57
Dutch - German	92,30	72, 28
English-French	83,01	67,11
Portuguese-Spanish	92,44	57,14
French-Spanish	91,33	62,86

Mostly for engines involving English the differences are less significant

	NTEU	Google
Spanish-English	91,44	88,71
Maltese - English	90,46	88,08
Irish - English	39,82	35,52
English - Bulgarian	92,41	84,42

Only two engines yield worse results than Google

	NTEU	Google
English - Maltese	82,52	88,41
Bulgarian - Maltese	77,56	80,74

Maltese as target.
English-Maltese Google Translate has quite good results.
These engines are being retrained to improve the metrics.

Results

- Around 90% of the NTEU engines are **better than Google** with statistical relevance.
- The other 10% are similar to Google or slightly better.

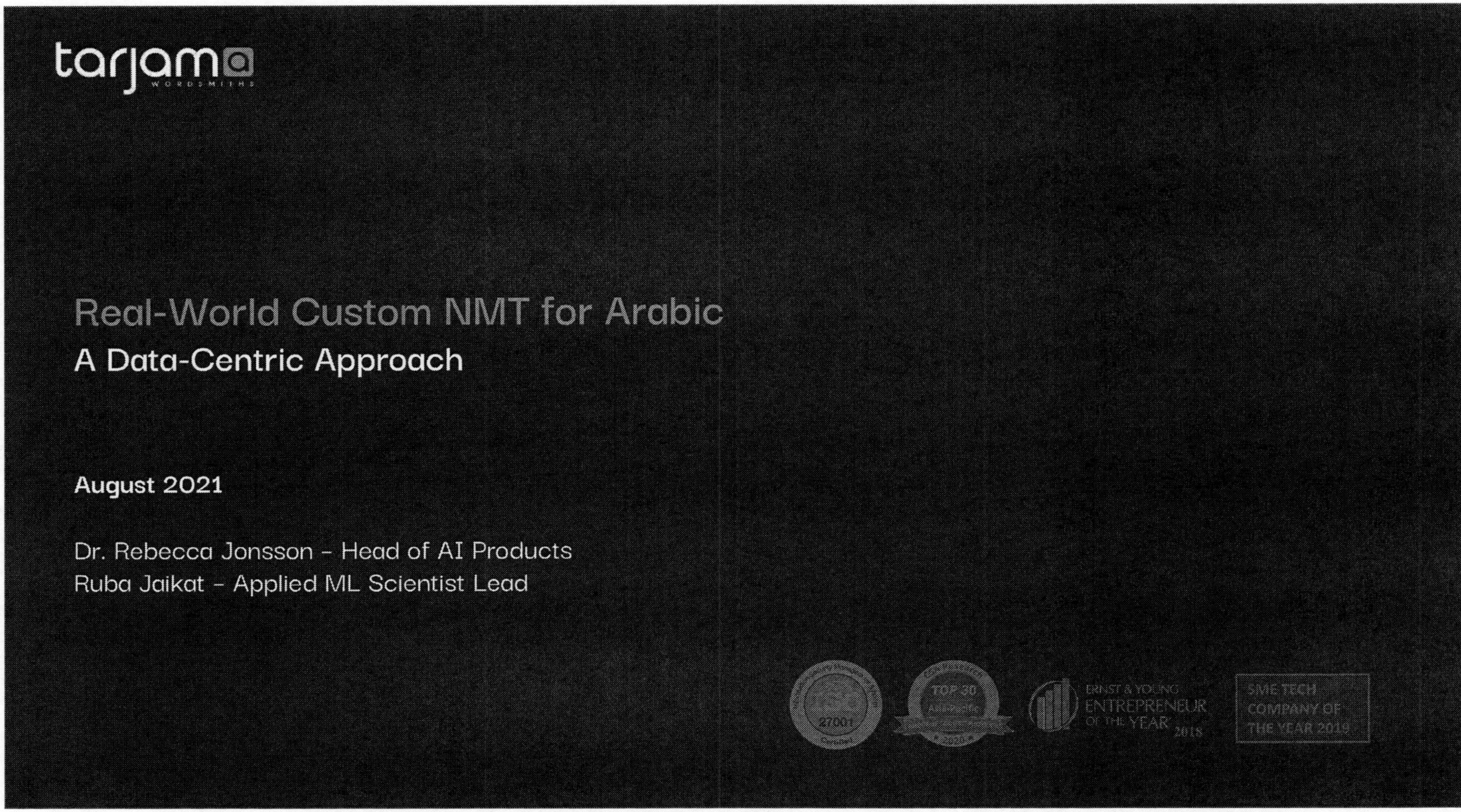
tarjama
Real-World Custom NMT for Arabic
A Data-Centric Approach
August 2021
Dr. Rebecca Jonsson - Head of AI Products
Ruba Jaikat - Applied ML Scientist Lead

12 Years of Innovation in Language Technology

A Language Service Provider in MENA region turning into a Language Tech Provider

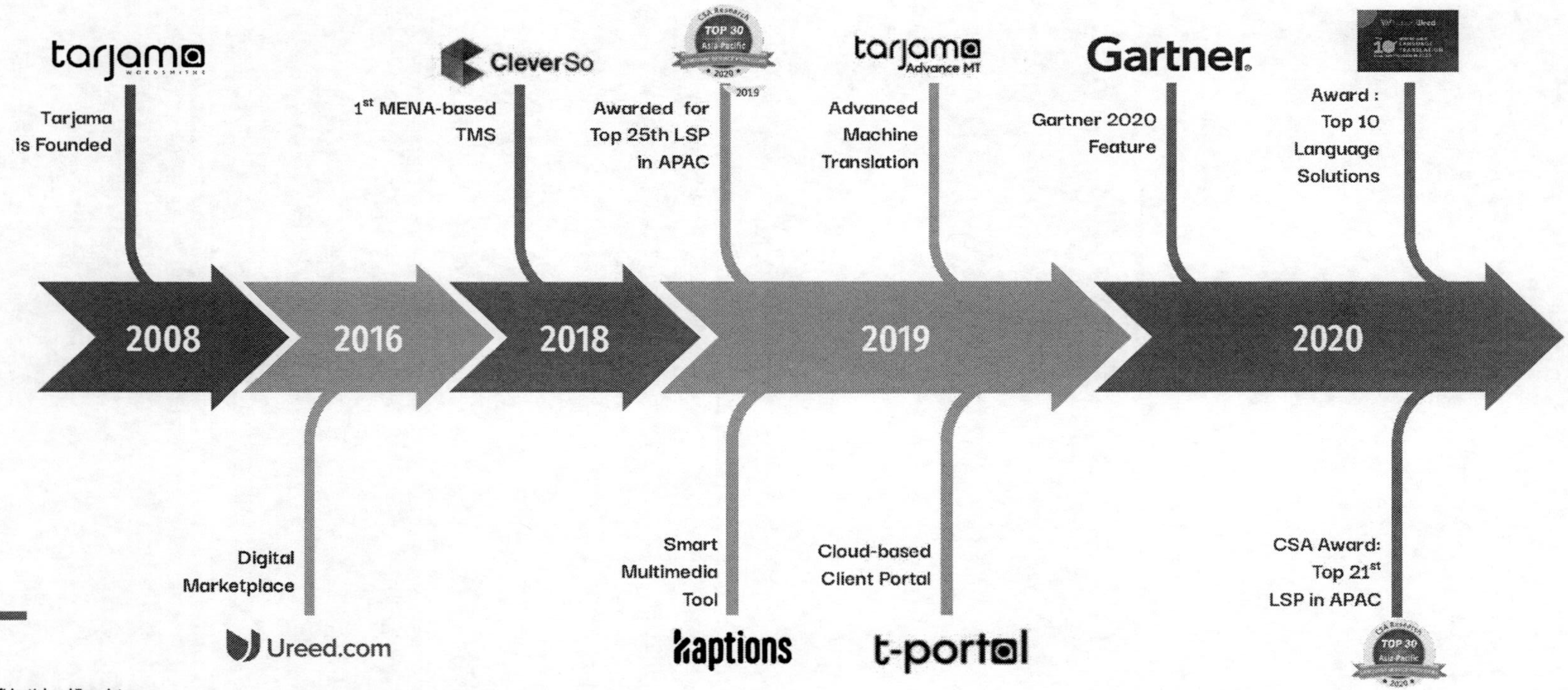

Confidential and Proprietary:

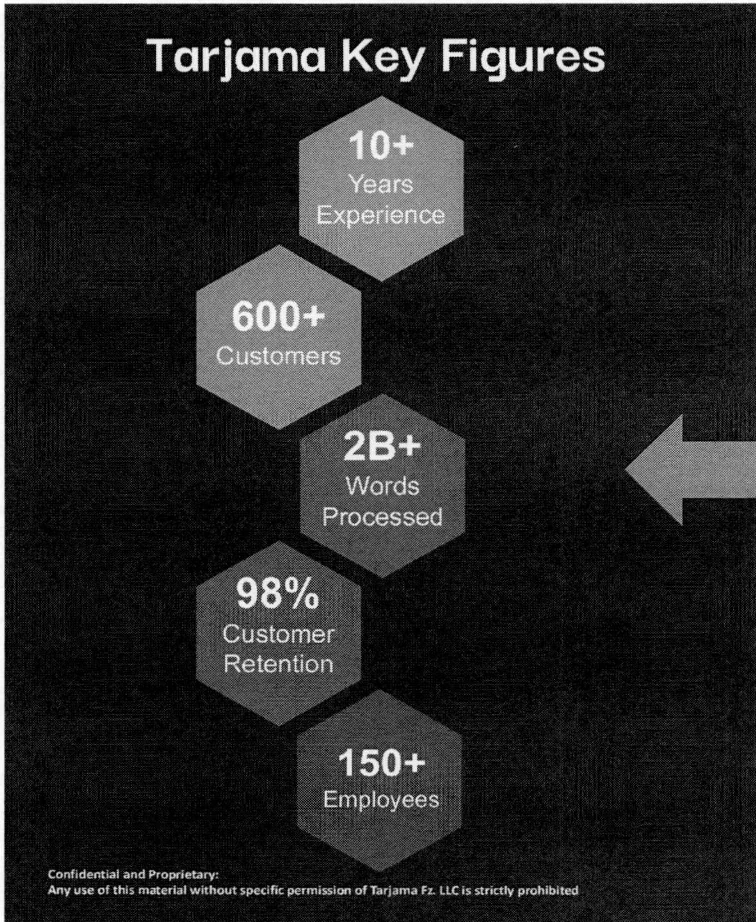

1. Female-led LSP transforming into a language technology company.
2. Localization, Translation, Interpreting, Subtitling and Content creation services.
3. Dominant in MENA region focusing on Arabic language and dialects.
4. Proprietary TMS system with focus on Arabic support.
5. Proprietary NMT system for EN-AR

Comparison Evaluation

(EN→ AR)

- Comparison Evaluation Set comprises of 120 segments with a total of 2.6k word count.
- Domain segments count is distributed as follows; Business: 38, Legal: 20, Health: 30, Finance: 40.
- Text is collected from online articles.

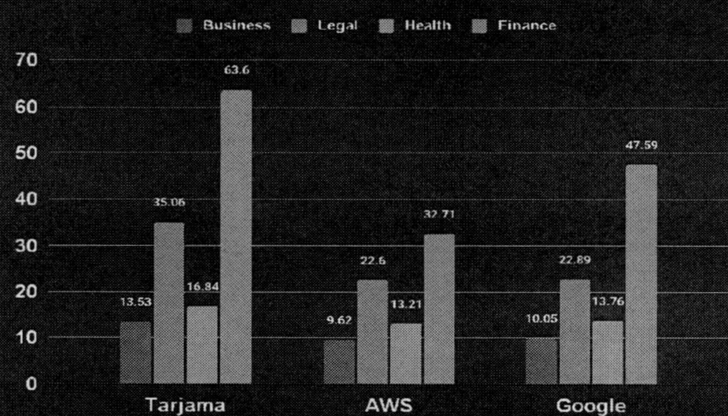

BLEU Scores on the Comparison Evaluation Set using Tarjama, AWS, and Google MT Engines.

Tarjama NMT Engine

- Tarjama NMT Engine development started late 2019.
- Tarjama NMT Engine is trained on high-quality Data translated by expert linguists.
- Tarjama Data covers various business domains, including: Legal, Consultancy, Health, Finance, Marketing, E-Commerce, Medical, Culture, News, Politics, Technology, Entertainment and more.
- Gold nuggets of external publicly available datasets are extracted and used to further enrich the engine.
- Currently, the use of Tarjama NMT within the Translation process reaches up to 35%.
- Productivity tests show that post-editing Tarjama NMT output saves at least 40% of the translator time.

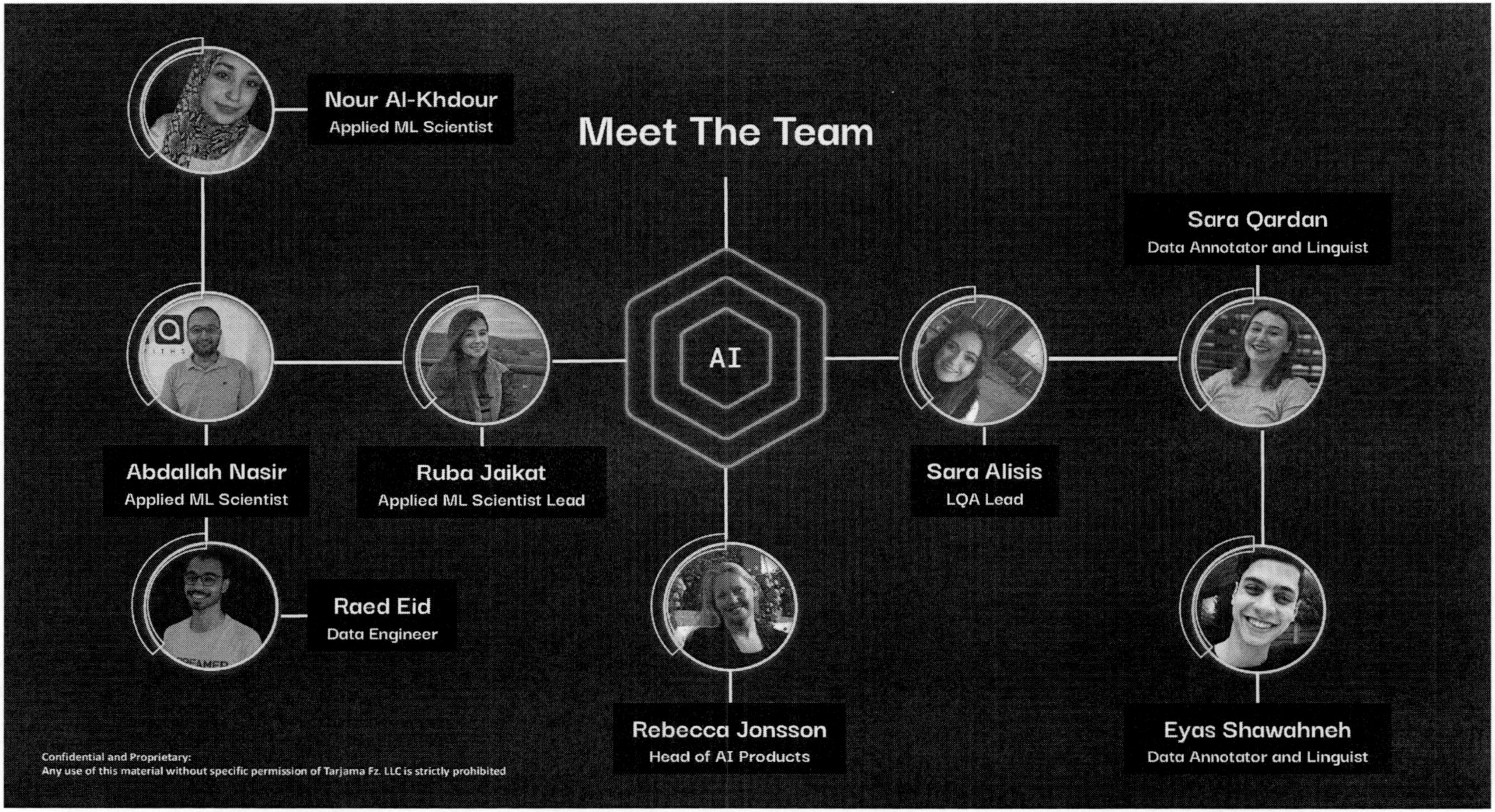
Meet The Team
AI
Nour Al-Khdour
Applied ML Scientist
Abdallah Nasir
Applied ML Scientist
Ruba Jaikat
Applied ML Scientist Lead
Raed Eid
Data Engineer
Rebecca Jonsson
Head of AI Products
Sara Alisis
LQA Lead
Sara Qardan
Data Annotator and Linguist
Eyas Shawahneh
Data Annotator and Linguist
Confidential and Proprietary:
Any use of this material without specific permission of Tarjama Fz. LLC is strictly prohibited

Tailored NMT models

- Going beyond Custom MT by tailoring a NMT model fit for the needs of a customer.
- Data-centric approach selecting the gold nuggets of their data and considering translation guidelines.
- Model that performs best-in-class on the customer data.
- Generalizes well on other data sets.
- Human Evaluation of candidate models to select a high-quality model.

Tailored NMT Development Cycle

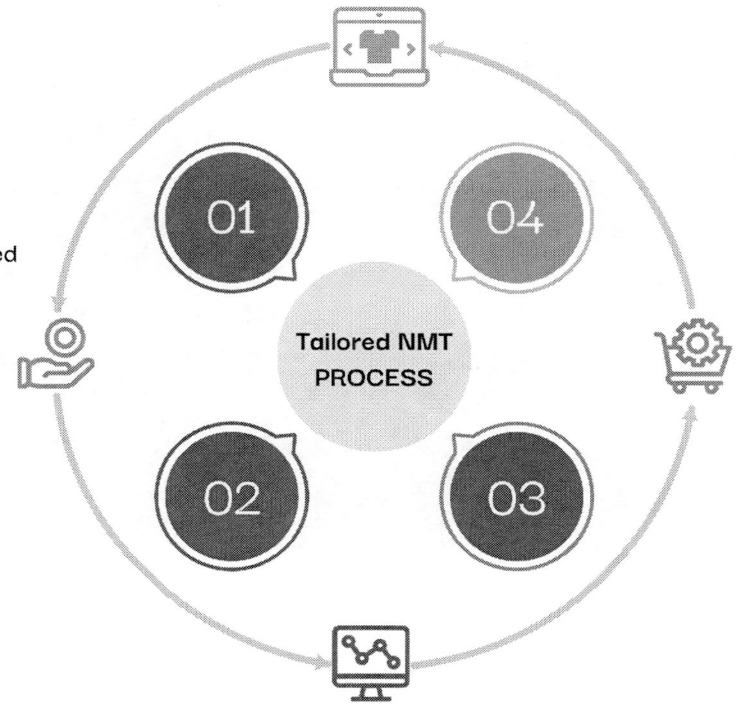

01

Data Acquisition & Analysis

Client Data received then analyzed by Linguistic QA Experts

02

Data Preprocessing & Filtering

Client Data run through Tarjama Data pipeline for preprocessing and filtering (selecting gold nuggets)

04

Model Adaptation

Experimenting, fine-tuning, analyzing, and evaluating the MT engine and its performance with client data

03

Add External Data

Carefully selecting out-of-domain data to add together with client data with the purpose of building a robust tailored MT engine that generalizes to other data

E-commerce data

"Stylized collectable stands 3 3/4 inches tall, perfect for any Harry Potter fan"

"The textured fabric truly brings this T-Rex to life"

"rectangular sunglasses ar 8069 5447/11"

"256GB NVMe SSD + 1TB (7200Rpm)"

"waterproof sun protection full car cover for gmc k15/k1500 pickup 1971-67"

"This Speed Cube Bundle (2x2x2 cube, 3x3x3 cube, pyramid 3x3x3 cube) is the classic color-matching puzzle, perfect for reducing stress & exercising your brain & improving memory & practicing hands-on dexterity skills"

"With the 144 Hz full HD, 1920 x 1080 display, on-screen action is incredibly smooth and fluid"

"2 in 1 ipad air case cover smart case cover with magnetic auto wake & sleep feature trifold stand for apple ipad air (ipad 5) tablet"

tarjama
Tailoring NMT for an e-commerce client
Dataset: 3M bilingual (EN→ AR) segments - high quality
Business
Legal
Health
Finance
70
60
50
40
30
20
10
0
13.53
35.06
16.84
63.6
9.62
22.6
13.21
32.71
10.05
22.89
13.76
47.59
8.56
28.99
14.53
45.29
Tarjama
AWS
Google
Client
BLEU Scores on the Comparison Evaluation Set using Tarjama, AWS, Google, and Tailored MT Engines.

tarjama
Tailoring NMT for an e-commerce client
Dataset: 3M bilingual (EN→ AR) segments - high quality
Tarjama Testset
Client Testset
40
30
20
10
0
26.44
20.91
25.46
32.86
Tarjama
Client
BLEU Scores on the Tarjama (5k) and Client (5k) Testing sets using Tarjama Generic and Client's Tailored MT engines.

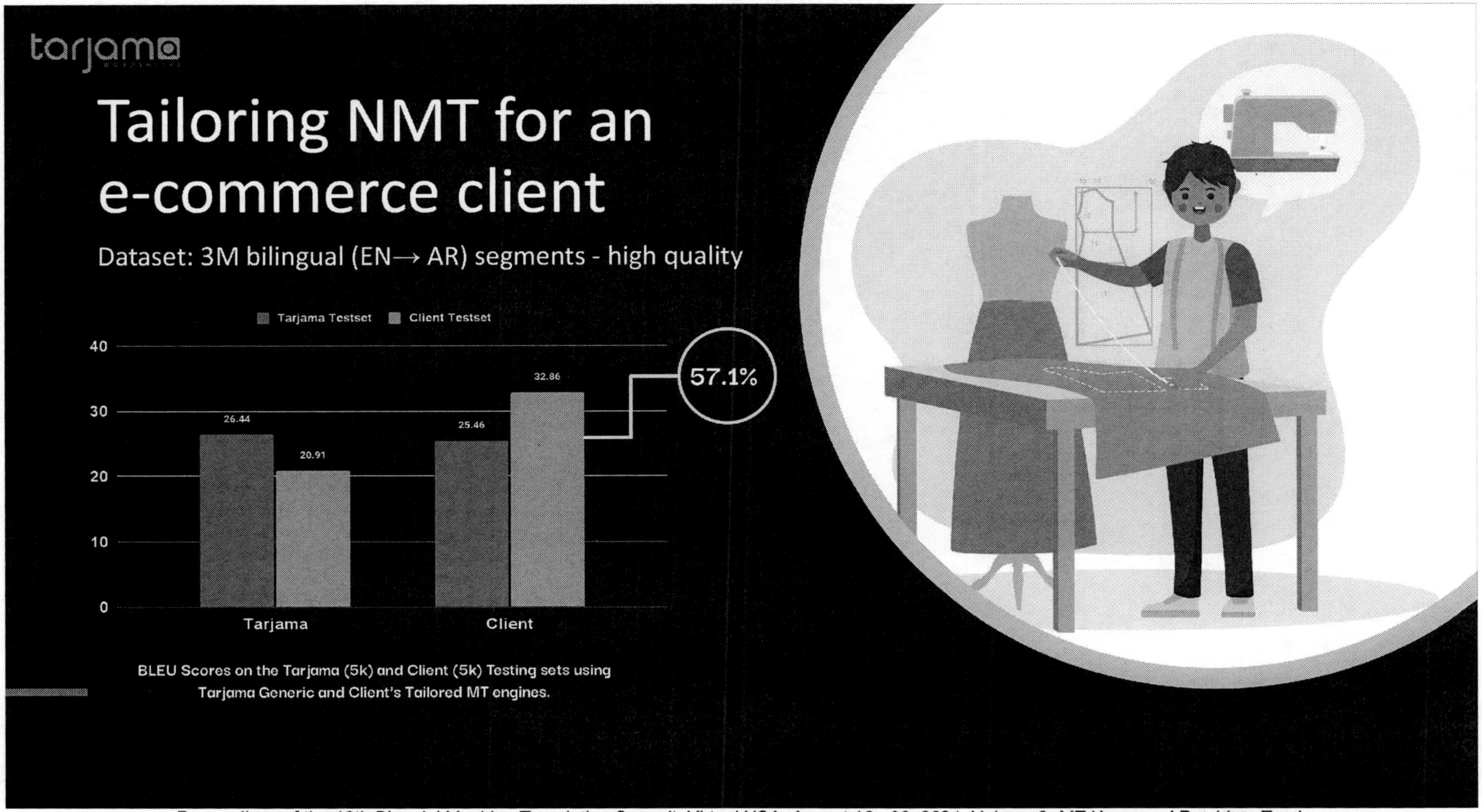
tarjama
Tailoring NMT for an
e-commerce client
Dataset: 3M bilingual (EN→ AR) segments - high quality
Tarjama Testset
Client Testset
40
30
20
10
0
26.44
20.91
25.46
32.86
57.1%
Tarjama
Client
BLEU Scores on the Tarjama (5k) and Client (5k) Testing sets using
Tarjama Generic and Client's Tailored MT engines.

tarjama
Tailoring NMT for an e-commerce client
Dataset: 3M bilingual (EN→ AR) segments - high quality
Tarjama Testset
Client Testset
40
30
20
10
0
26.44
20.91
25.46
32.86
Tarjama
Client
57.1%
-3.85%
BLEU Scores on the Tarjama (5k) and Client (5k) Testing sets using Tarjama Generic and Client's Tailored MT engines.

Manual Evaluation

Adapted MQM approach

- Manual Evaluation of 500 segments (4212 words) translated with the tailored NMT
  - 86% of the translations considered OK, Good or Perfect. Minor review.
  - Most common error: 4.5 % mistranslations

MT Quality	Distribution
Perfect MT translation	63%
Good MT translation (minor errors)	1.6%
OK translation (a few errors)	21.8%
Bad translation	11.8%
Nonsense translation	1.8%

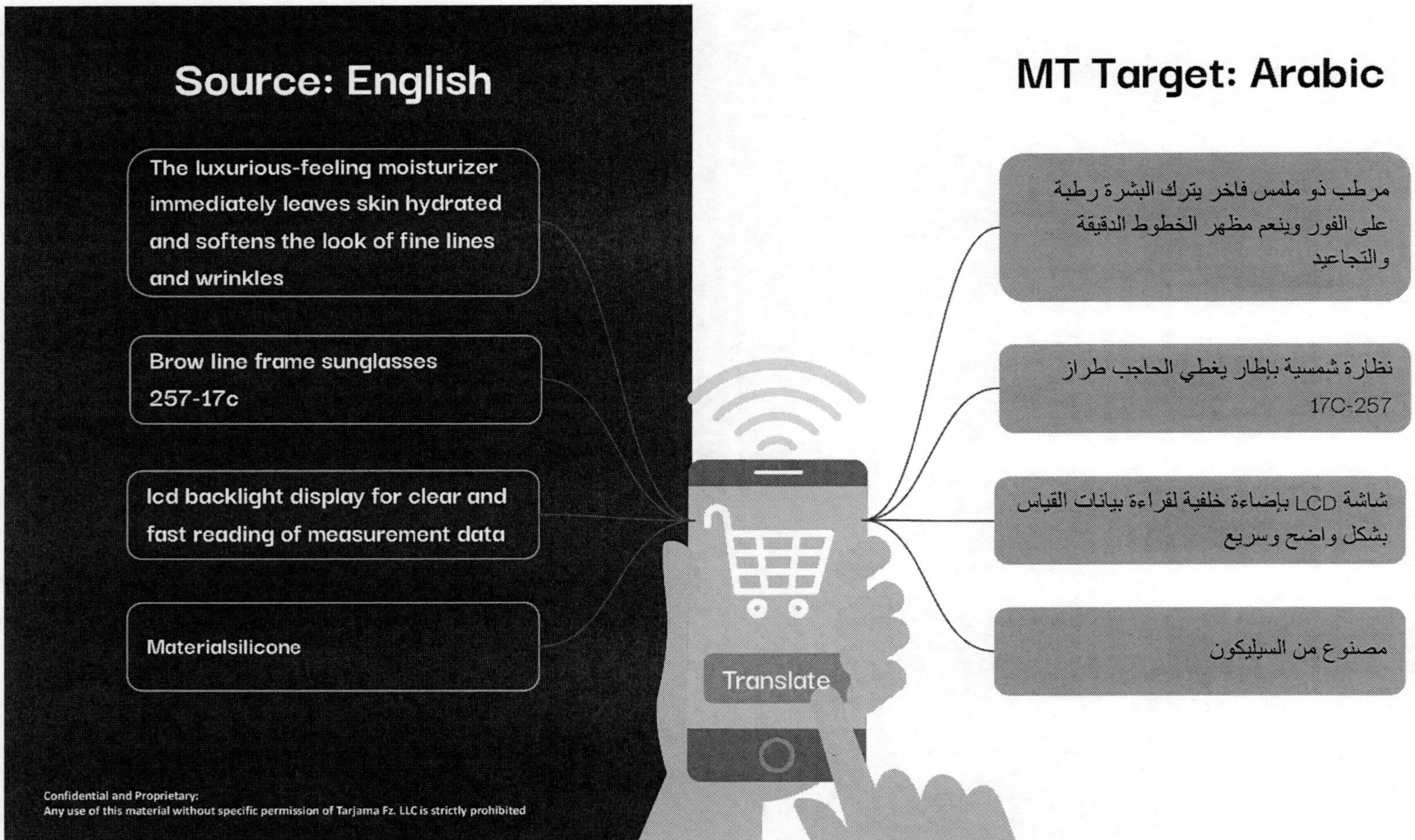
Source: English
The luxurious-feeling moisturizer immediately leaves skin hydrated and softens the look of fine lines and wrinkles
Brow line frame sunglasses 257-17c
lcd backlight display for clear and fast reading of measurement data
Materialsilicone
Confidential and Proprietary:
Any use of this material without specific permission of Tarjama Fz. LLC is strictly prohibited
Translate
MT Target: Arabic
مرطب ذو ملمس فاخر يترك البشرة رطبة على الفور وينعم مظهر الخطوط الدقيقة والتجاعيد
نظارة شمسية بإطار يغطي الحاجب طراز 17C-257
شاشة LCD بإضاءة خلفية لقراءة بيانات القياس بشكل واضح وسريع
مصنوع من السيليكون

tarjama

Real-world usage of a Tailored Model for e-commerce client

Translation of e-commerce data from English to Arabic using Tarjama's TMS system for an e-commerce client.

60-90 Translators (post-editors) in-house and freelancers.

Tailored NMT model used for pre-translation and translators performing post-editing and transcreation.

Real-world usage of a Tailored Model for e-commerce client

Productivity test: time saving of 38%
(Tailored NMT vs Generic Tarjama NMT)

Triple volume of translations delivered
to client and growing!

Translation Costs lowered by 50%!

Improved Consistency and Quality of translations

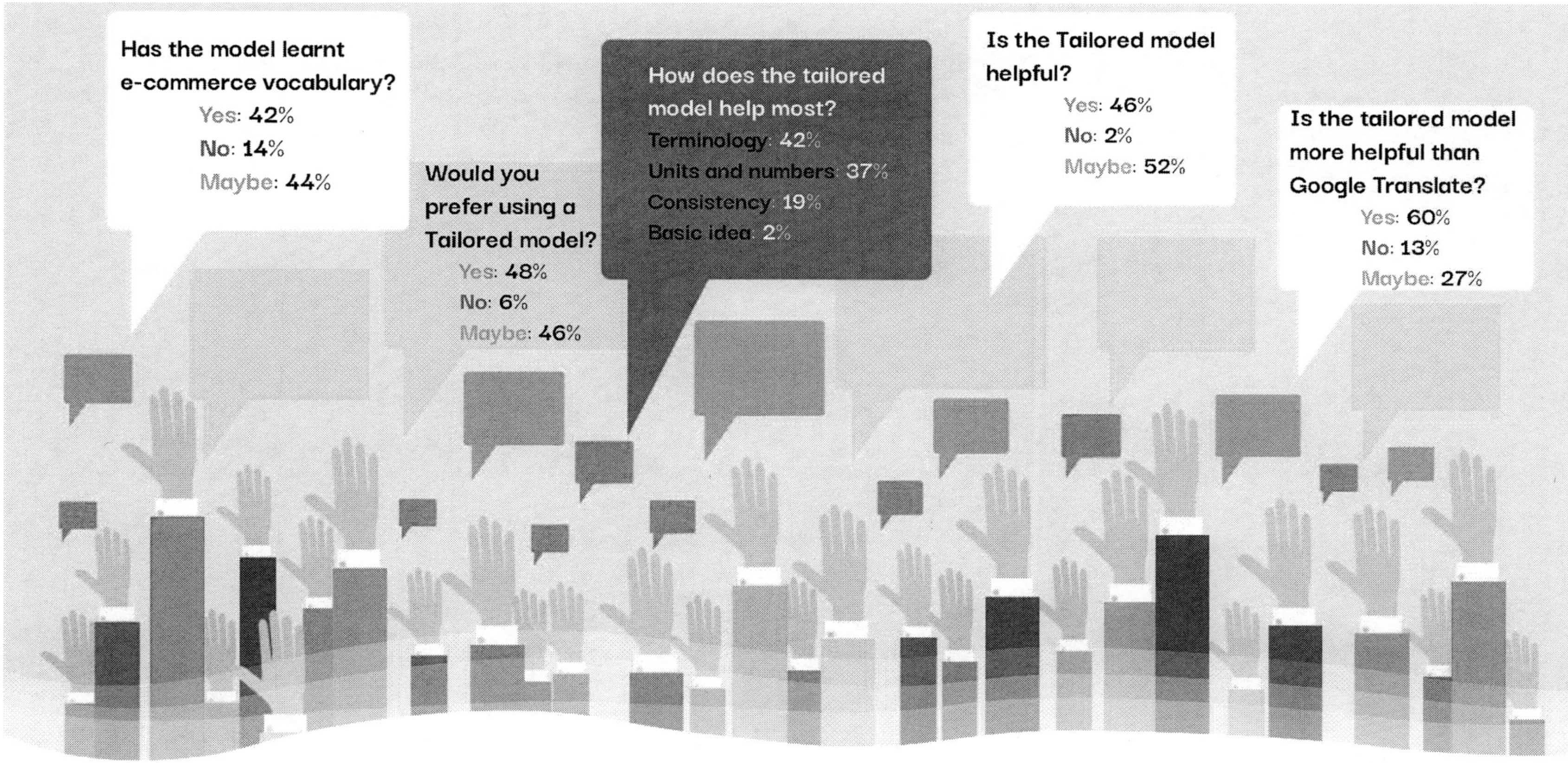

What did the translators think?

- ❑ Survey with 50 translators
- ❑ 65% has experience in post-editing

tarjama
WORDSMITHS
thank you
شكراً جزيلاً
Merci beaucoup
ありがとう
धन्यवाद
www.tarjama.com
Confidential and Proprietary:
Any use of this material without specific permission of Tarjama Fz. LLC is strictly prohibited

Building MT systems in low resourced EU languages for
Public Sector users in Croatia, Iceland, Ireland and Norway
Páraic Sheridan
MT Summit: August 2021
PRINCIPLE
The work presented here is co-financed by the
Connecting Europe Facility of the European Union
RWS

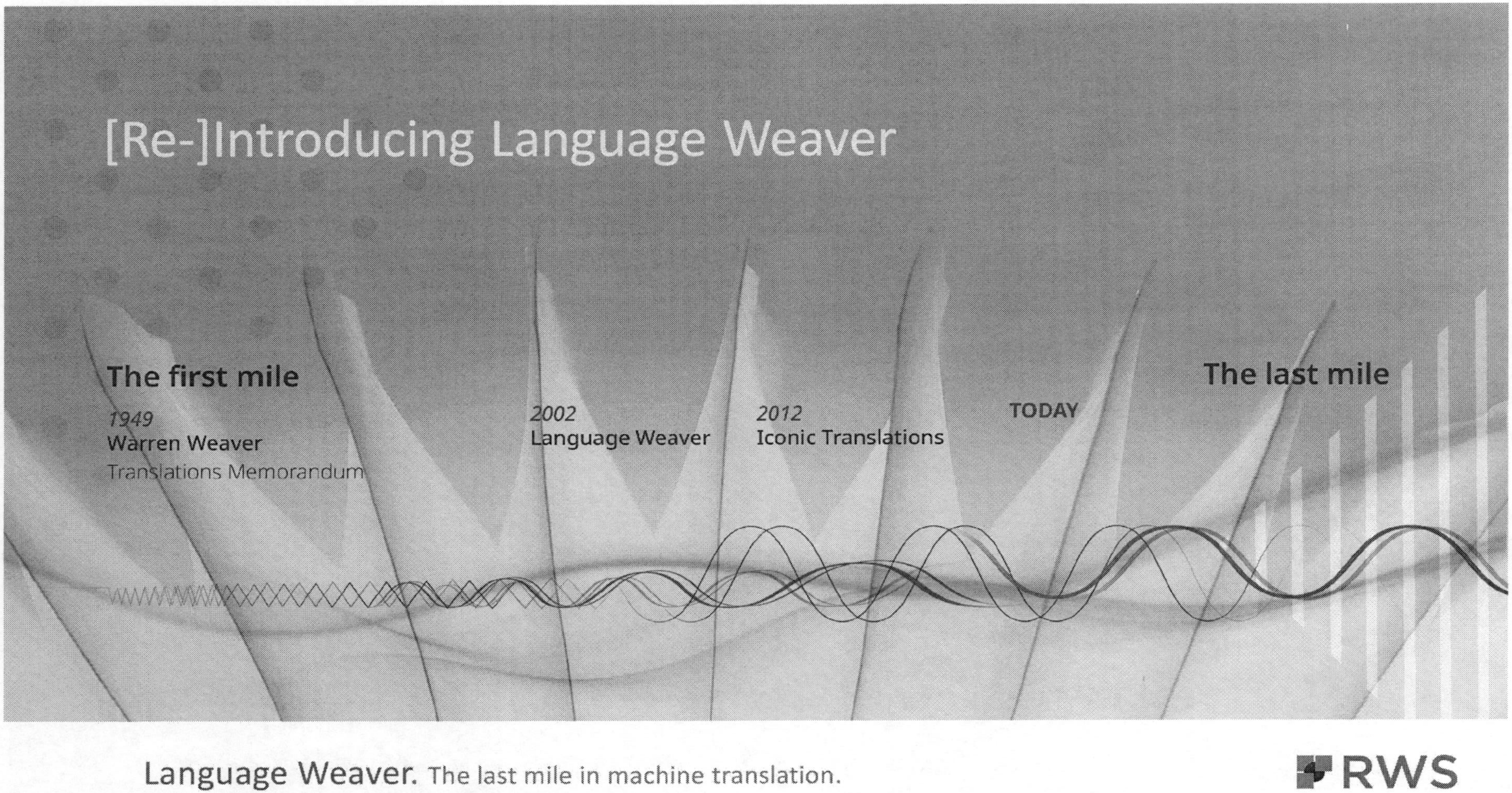
[Re-]Introducing Language Weaver
The first mile
1949
Warren Weaver
Translations Memorandum
2002
Language Weaver
2012
Iconic Translations
TODAY
The last mile
Language Weaver. The last mile in machine translation.
RWS

Introducing The PRINCIPLE Project

- A 2-year project funded by the Connecting Europe Facility (CEF)
- Focused on collecting data to improve translation quality in the EU Digital Services Infrastructures (DSIs) for prioritised low-resourced EU languages.
- The main aim of the project is to identify, collect and process high-quality Language Resources (LRs) for the following under-resourced European languages:
  - Croatian
  - Icelandic
  - Irish
  - Norwegian (Bokmål and Nynorsk)

Project Consortium: DCU, LANGUAGE BANK National Library of Norway, UNIVERSITY OF ICELAND, Iconic (Part of the RWS Group), Filozofski fakultet

PRINCIPLE

RWS

3

PRINCIPLE: The Role of Machine Translation

By building state-of-the-art Neural MT models with data collected in the PRINCIPLE project, two key objectives can be accomplished:

Benchmarking and evaluation of MT systems built using project data attests to the quality of data collected and its value for MT systems developed in Europe.

Granting free access and use of MT systems to Public Sector bodies during the course of the project provides an incentive for contributions of language data.

- Public sector bodies who participate in this incentive are labelled '**Early Adopters**' in the PRINCIPLE project.

PRINCIPLE

4

RWS

What Data Already Existed for These Languages?

Iconic completed a full search/download of existing resources from ELRC-Share*.

A quality review was conducted by PRINCIPLE project partners.

Language	# Resources	# Translation Units
Irish	41	901,421
Croatian	36	3,891,799
Icelandic	17	801,283
Norwegian	47	1,964,961
Norwegian (Nynorsk)	4	6,358

PRINCIPLE

5

* https://elrc-share.eu/

RWS

What Data Already Existed for These Languages?

Iconic completed a full search/download of existing resources from ELRC-Share.

A quality review was conducted by PRINCIPLE project partners.

Data was then cleaned/filtered for MT Baseline system development.

Language	# Resources	# Translation Units	#TU used in MT Baseline
Irish	41	901,421	588,663
Croatian	36	3,891,799	3,337,608
Icelandic	17	801,283	702,139
Norwegian	47	1,964,961	1,140,351
Norwegian (Nynorsk)	4	6,358	-

PRINCIPLE

6

* https://elrc-share.eu/

RWS

The PRINCIPLE Project then proceeded in Two Phases:

1

Data Provider	Country
National University of Ireland Galway (NUIG)	Ireland
CIKLOPEA D.O.O	Croatia
Icelandic Ministry of Foreign Affairs	Iceland
Standards Norway	Norway
Norwegian Ministry of Foreign Affairs	Norway

2

Data Provider	Country
Rannóg an Aistriúcháin	Ireland
Foras na Gaeilge	Ireland
CIKLOPEA D.O.O	Croatia
Ministry of Foreign and European Affairs	Croatia
Icelandic Standards	Iceland
Icelandic Met Office	Iceland

PRINCIPLE

7

RWS

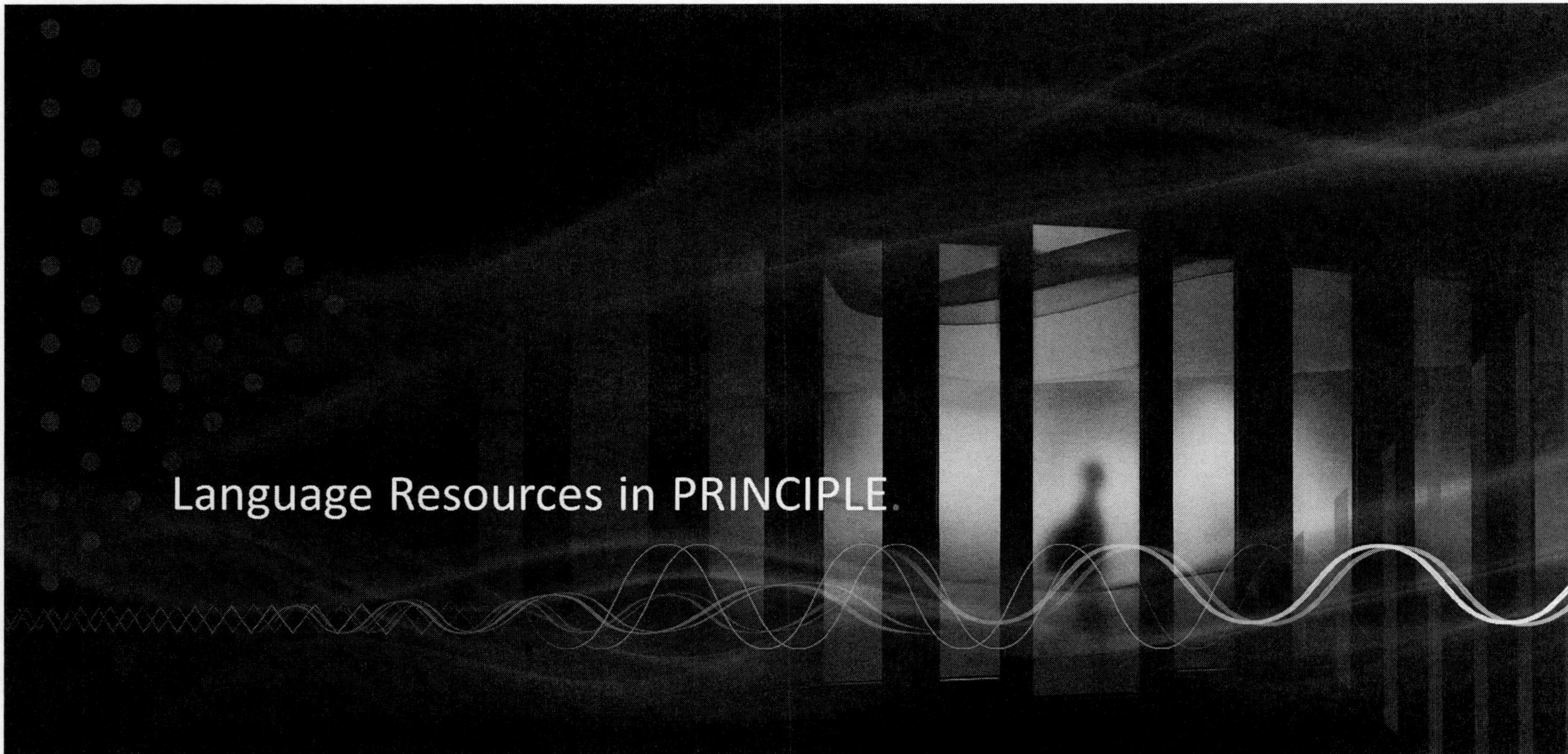

Language Weaver. The last mile in machine translation.

RWS

Language Resources collected in PRINCIPLE - Croatian

Dataset	TUs Collected	Data used in MT
EN>HR Baseline	3,891,799	3,708,493
MVEP Data	115,667	100,649
Other Data Providers	22,703	

REPUBLIC OF CROATIA
Ministry of Foreign and European Affairs

Dataset	TUs Collected	Data used in MT
HR>EN Baseline	3,891,799	3,708,493
Ciklopea Data (eProcurement)	36,634	47,135
Other Data Providers	22,703	

CIKLOPEA
eProcurement

Dataset	TUs Collected	Data used in MT
EN>HR Baseline	3,891,799	3,708,493
Ciklopea Data (eHealth)	76,108	72,455

CIKLOPEA
eHealth

PRINCIPLE

9

RWS

Language Resources collected in PRINCIPLE - Irish

Dataset	TUs Collected	Data used in MT
EN>GA Baseline	901,421	588,663
Foras na Gaeilge	60,443	54,141
Rannóg an Aistriúcháin	387,480	353,485
Dept. Culture… & Gaeltacht	64,694	58,057

Dataset	TUs Collected	Data used in MT
EN>GA Baseline	901,421	588,663
Rannóg an Aistriúcháin	387,480	353,485
Dept. of Justice	35,898	28,639
Dept. Culture… & Gaeltacht	64,694	58,057

Foras na Gaeilge

Tithe an Oireachtais Houses of the Oireachtas

An Roinn Dlí agus Cirt Department of Justice

PRINCIPLE

10

RWS

Language Resources collected in PRINCIPLE - Icelandic

Dataset [EN<>IS]	TUs Collected	Data used in MT
Ministry of Foreign Affairs Data	1,097,352	821,243

Note that the Icelandic Ministry of Foreign Affairs stipulated only their data to be used, no baseline/other data.

UTANRÍKISRÁÐUNEYTIÐ
Ministry for Foreign Affairs Iceland

Dataset	TUs Collected	Data used in MT
IS>EN Baseline	801,283	702,139
Icelandic Met Office Data	214,242	188,700

Veðurstofa Íslands
Icelandic Met Office

Dataset	TUs Collected	Data used in MT
EN>IS Baseline	801,283	702,139
Standards Iceland Data	16,590	16,423

Íslenskir staðlar

PRINCIPLE

11

RWS

Language Resources collected in PRINCIPLE – Norwegian [Bokmål]

Dataset [EN>NO]	TUs Collected	Data used in MT
Norwegian Ministry Foreign Affairs	1,757,609	1,616,568

NORWEGIAN MINISTRY OF FOREIGN AFFAIRS

Note that the Norwegian Ministry of Foreign Affairs stipulated only their data to be used, no baseline/other data.

Dataset	TUs Collected	Data used in MT
EN>NO Baseline	1,964,961	1,140,351
Standards Norway Data	132,360	77,664

standards norway

PRINCIPLE

12

RWS

Evaluating PRINCIPLE Engines vs. General Online Engines [Sanity Check]

Language Weaver. The last mile in machine translation.

RWS

An Overview of Automatic MT Evaluation in PRINCIPLE

For every MT model developed by Iconic, a sanity-check evaluation was conducted against freely available online MT Engines.

A test set of 2,000 segments is generally held out as a test from data provided by customers. In some cases with PRINCIPLE Early Adopters, where limited data was provided, a test set of 1,000 segments or 1,500 segments was used.

Test segments are run through multiple MT engines for comparison, with a range of metrics computed [SacreBLEU, TER, METEOR, chrF].

- Each data set (bar triplets) represents the evaluation on a held-out test set for that model, either a baseline model for the language (PRINCIPLE), or a model with Early Adopter data.

PRINCIPLE

14

RWS

Comparing PRINCIPLE Engines to Online MT - Croatian

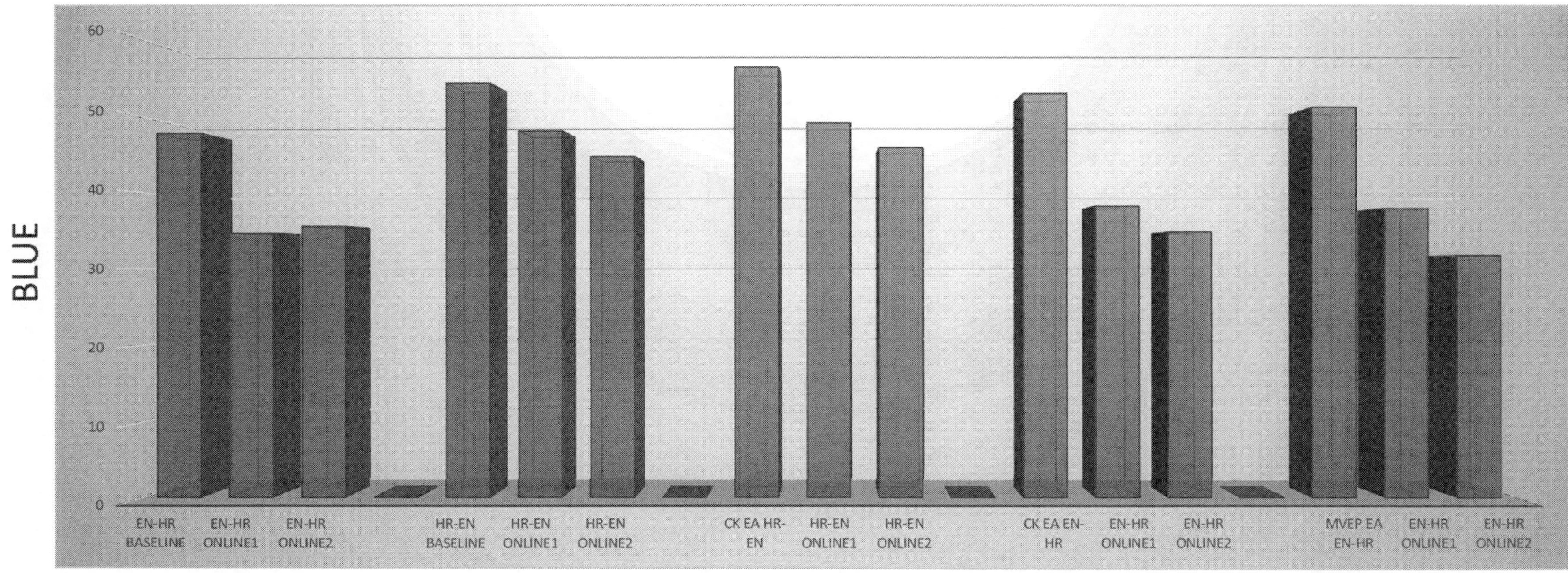

PRINCIPLE PRINCIPLE CIKLOPEA eProcurement CIKLOPEA eHealth

REPUBLIC OF CROATIA
Ministry of Foreign and European Affairs

PRINCIPLE

15

RWS

Comparing PRINCIPLE Engines to Online MT – Irish

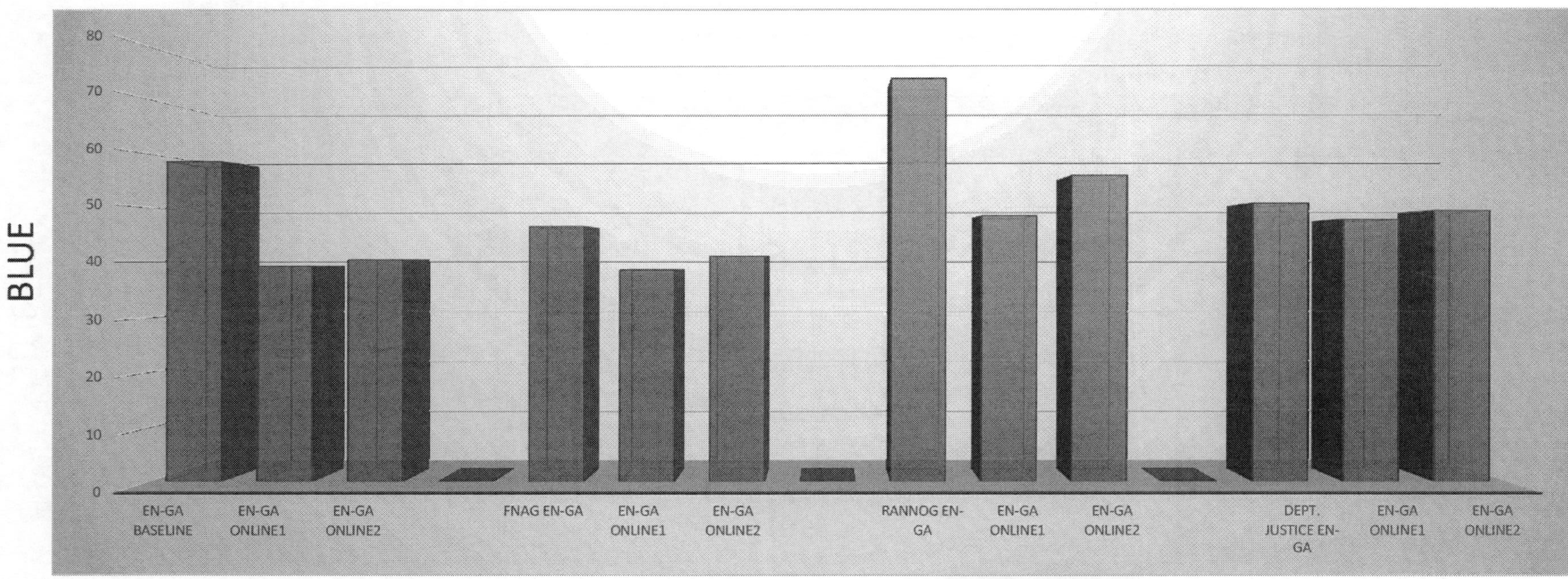

PRINCIPLE

Foras na Gaeilge

Tithe an Oireachtais Houses of the Oireachtas

An Roinn Dlí agus Cirt Department of Justice

PRINCIPLE

16

RWS

Comparing PRINCIPLE Engines to Online MT – Icelandic

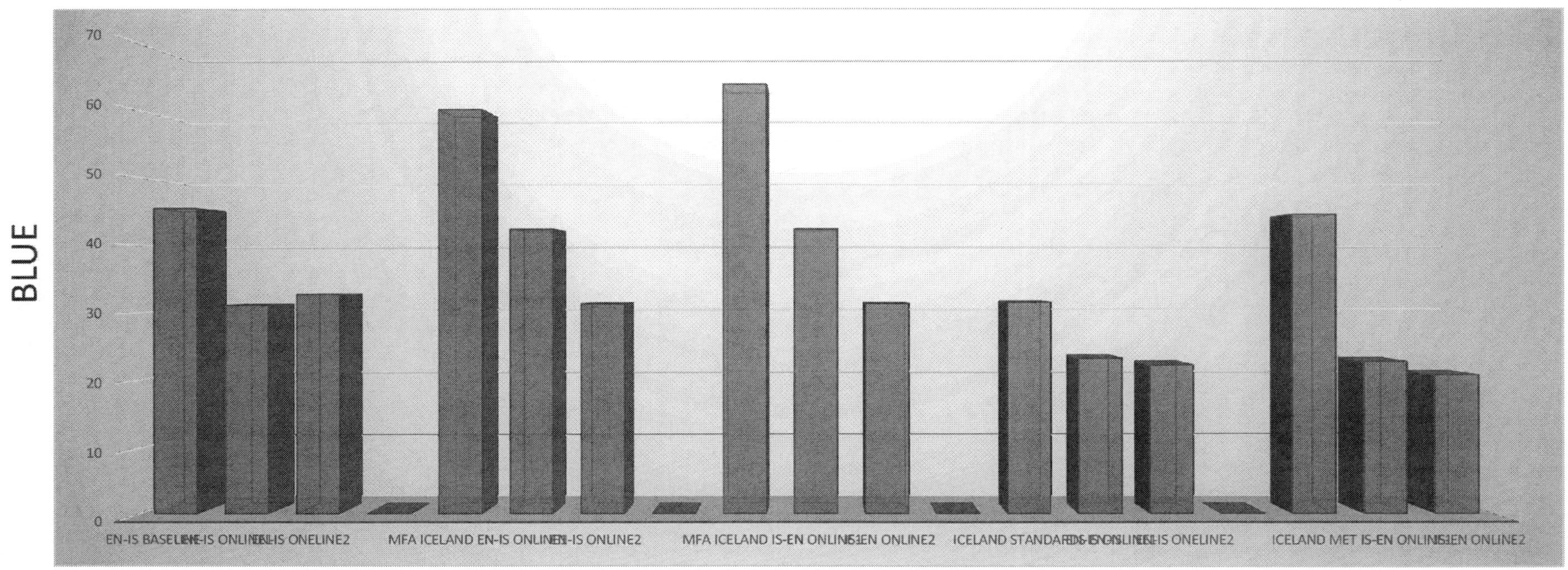

PRINCIPLE

UTANRÍKISRÁÐUNEYTIÐ
Ministry for Foreign Affairs Iceland

UTANRÍKISRÁÐUNEYTIÐ
Ministry for Foreign Affairs Iceland

Íslenskir staðlar

Icelandic Met Office

PRINCIPLE

17

RWS

Comparing PRINCIPLE Engines to Online MT – Norwegian

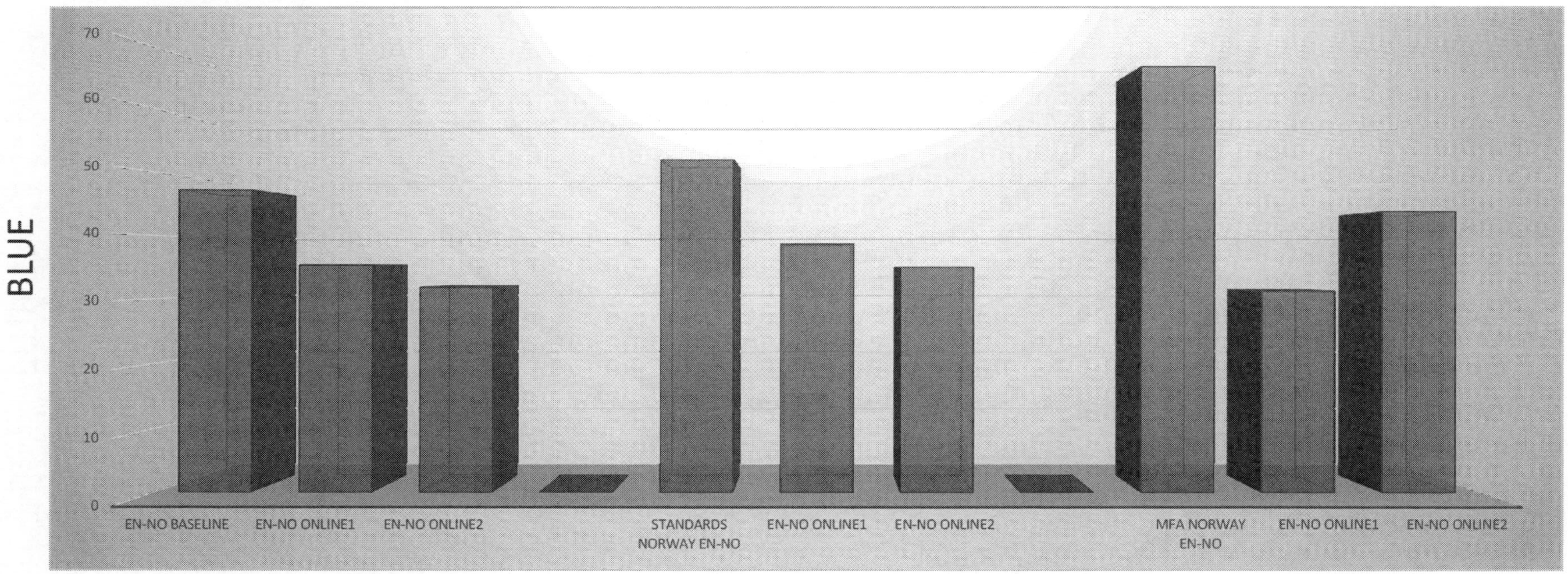

PRINCIPLE

standards norway

NORWEGIAN MINISTRY OF FOREIGN AFFAIRS

PRINCIPLE

RWS

18

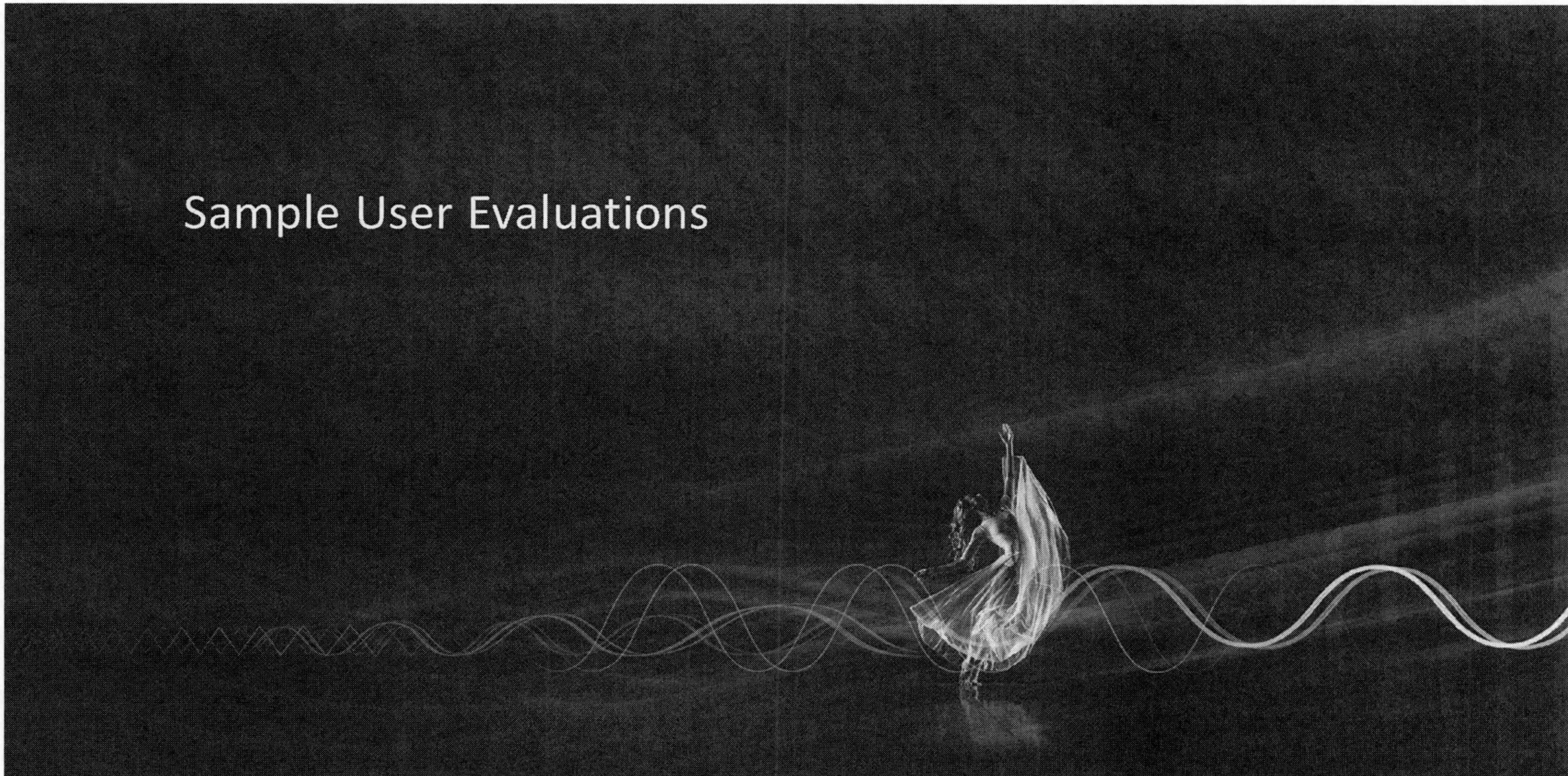

Language Weaver. The last mile in machine translation.

RWS

An Overview of User MT Evaluation in PRINCIPLE

Each PRINCIPLE 'Early Adopter' was invited to develop a test set to be used by DCU (Evaluation co-ordinator) to help evaluate MT both using automatic and manual means.

A test set was requested of 500 segment pairs that

- Had not already been provided to train the MT systems.
- Were representative of the texts intended to be translated with the MT system.
- The reference translation in the target language should not be obtained via MT/Post-edit.
- Did not contain any confidential material.

Early Adopters were offered a range of human evaluation protocols from which they could choose, depending on their preference and available resources.

- Comparative ranking, adequacy & fluency, direct assessment, comprehension, post-editing, or MT error analysis

PRINCIPLE

20

RWS

Comparison of MT Engines at Norwegian MFA [EN-NO]

NORWEGIAN MINISTRY OF FOREIGN AFFAIRS

A 500-segment Test Set was created by MFA Norway, separate from all training data.

An automatic evaluation was conducted independently by DCU of four MT engines.

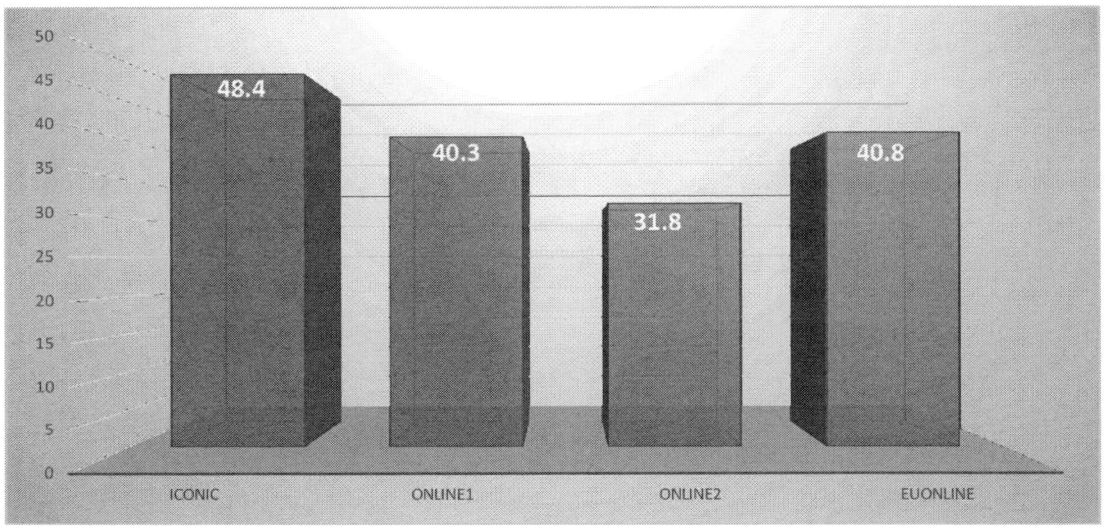

BLEU scores of four engines on a 500-segment test set provided by MFA Norway.

PRINCIPLE

21

RWS

Comparison of MT Engines at Norwegian MFA [EN-NO]

NORWEGIAN MINISTRY OF FOREIGN AFFAIRS

A direct comparison of two engines was conducted by three evaluators at MFA Norway across the 500-segment test set (one evaluator completed only half of the test set).

For 70% of segments, Iconic's MFA engine was equal to or better than the comparator.

	Evaluator 1 (500 Segments)		Evaluator 2 (500 Segments)		Evaluator 3 (250 Segments)		Total (1,250 Judgements)	
Iconic Best	229	45.8%	260	52.0%	94	37.6%	**583**	**46.6%**
Online Best	138	27.6%	127	25.4%	68	27.2%	**333**	**26.6%**
Equally Good	118	23.6%	84	16.8%	86	34.4%	**288**	**23.0%**
Equally Poor	14	2.8%	29	5.8%	1	0.4%	**44**	**3.5%**
Not Assigned	1	0.2%	0	0.0%	1	0.4%	**2**	**0.1%**
Total	500	100%	500	100%	250	100%	**1,250**	**99.8%**

PRINCIPLE

22

RWS

Comparison of MT Engines at Foras na Gaeilge [EN-GA]

Foras na Gaeilge

A 496-segment Test Set was created by Foras na Gaeilge, separate from all training data.

An automatic evaluation was conducted independently by DCU of four MT engines.

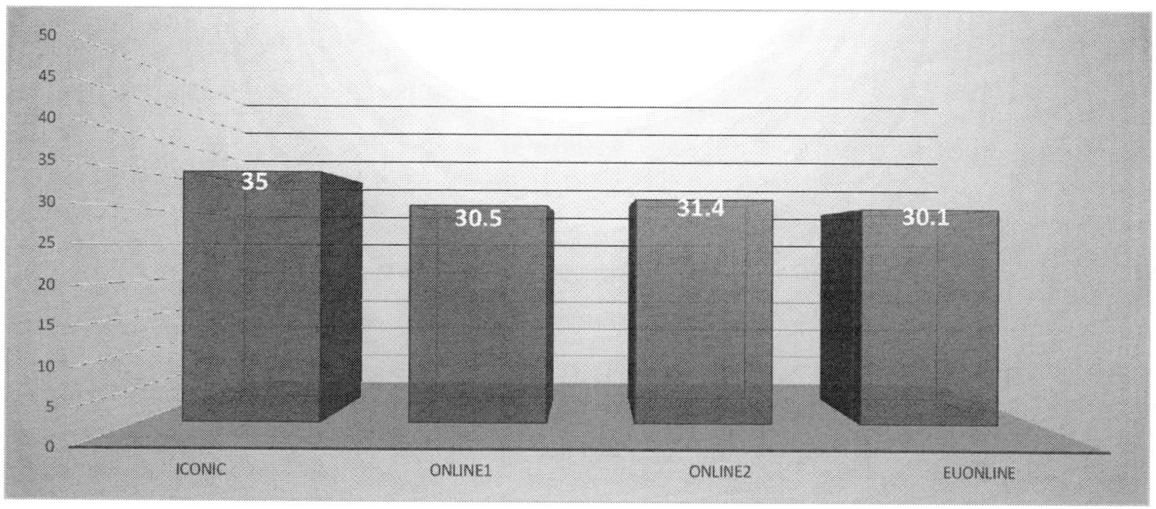

BLEU scores of four engines on a 496-segment test set provided by Foras na Gaeilge.

PRINCIPLE

23

RWS

Evaluation of MT Output at Foras na Gaeilge [EN-GA]

Foras na Gaeilge

Two FnaG translators undertook Adequacy and Fluency evaluation of Iconic MT output on the 496 test segments, using a 4-point Likert scale. The questions were

- *How much of the information and meaning expressed in the source is conveyed accurately in the translation?*
- *How fluent is the translation?*

Measurement of inter-translator agreement:

Cohen's Kappa	Adequacy	Fluency
Non-weighted	0.009	0.011
Weighted	0.031	0.026

- *Generally low agreement between translators*
- *Translator 2 more strict – ratings 2-3, not 4*

Translators' Rating of Adequacy and Fluency

	Adequacy	Fluency
Average	3.57	3.36
Mode	4	4

PRINCIPLE

24

RWS

Comparison of MT Engines at Met Office Iceland [IS-EN]

Veðurstofa Íslands

A 500-segment Test Set was created by Met Office Iceland, separate from all training data.

An automatic evaluation was conducted independently by DCU of four MT engines.

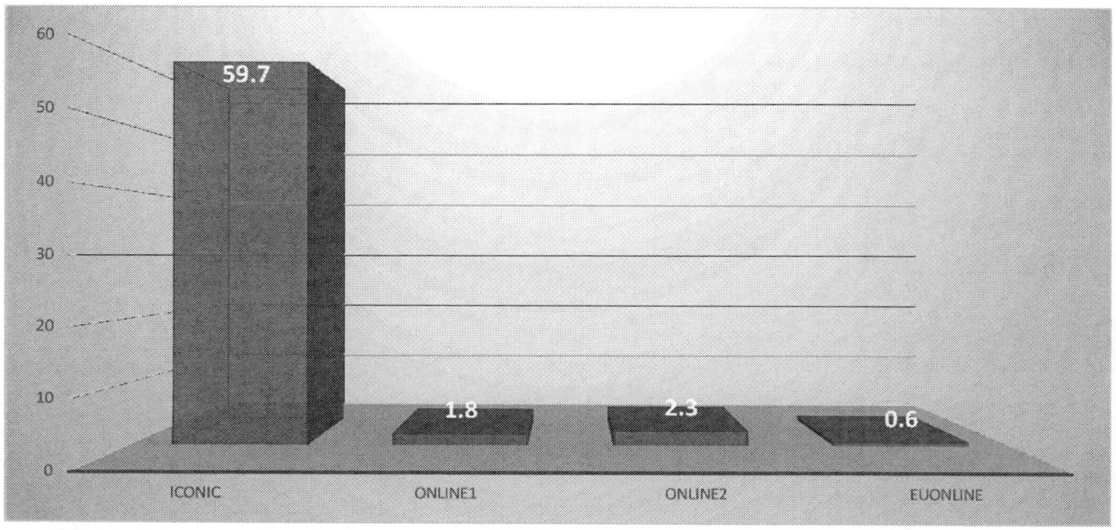

BLEU scores of four engines on a 500-segment test set provided by Met Office Iceland.

PRINCIPLE

25

RWS

MT Post-Editing at Met Office Iceland [EN-IS]

Veðurstofa Íslands

Two Met Office translators undertook a Post-Editing exercise, each translator post-editing the entire 500 segment test set.

	Total Time	Avg. per Sentence
Translator 1	00:48:04	00:05.7
Translator 2	00:39:51	00:04.7

TER scores were calculated to compare similarity of MT output and PE result to the original reference translation, and HTER measured how much post-editing was performed on the MT output.

TER (Reference)	Translator1	Translator2
Iconic MT	22.7	22.7
PE	20.1	21.8

hTER (PE)	Translator1	Translator2
Iconic MT	12.9	5.9

- *Translator 2 performed fewer post-edits*

PRINCIPLE

26

RWS

Deployment of MT to PRINCIPLE Early Adopter Users

Each PRINCIPLE 'Early Adopter' was set up with access to the MT model trained on their data for day-to-day use during the course of the project.

PRINCIPLE Early Adopters all work within the same use-case: MT to be used in conjunction with translator review / post-editing in the translation workflow.

Almost 1 million words have been processed through PRINCIPLE MT engines during the course of the project.

PRINCIPLE

27

RWS

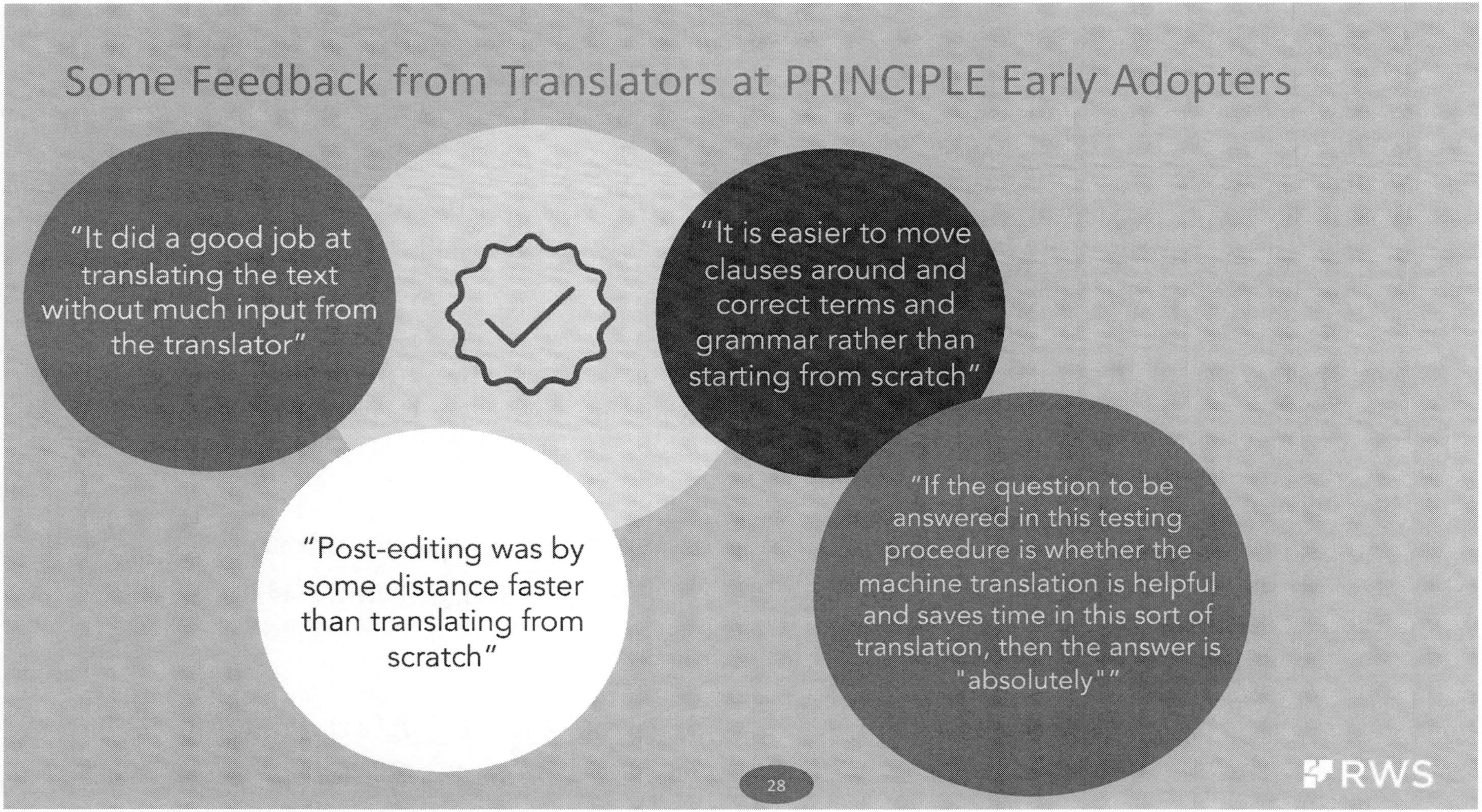
Some Feedback from Translators at PRINCIPLE Early Adopters
"It did a good job at translating the text without much input from the translator"
"It is easier to move clauses around and correct terms and grammar rather than starting from scratch"
"Post-editing was by some distance faster than translating from scratch"
"If the question to be answered in this testing procedure is whether the machine translation is helpful and saves time in this sort of translation, then the answer is "absolutely""
28
RWS

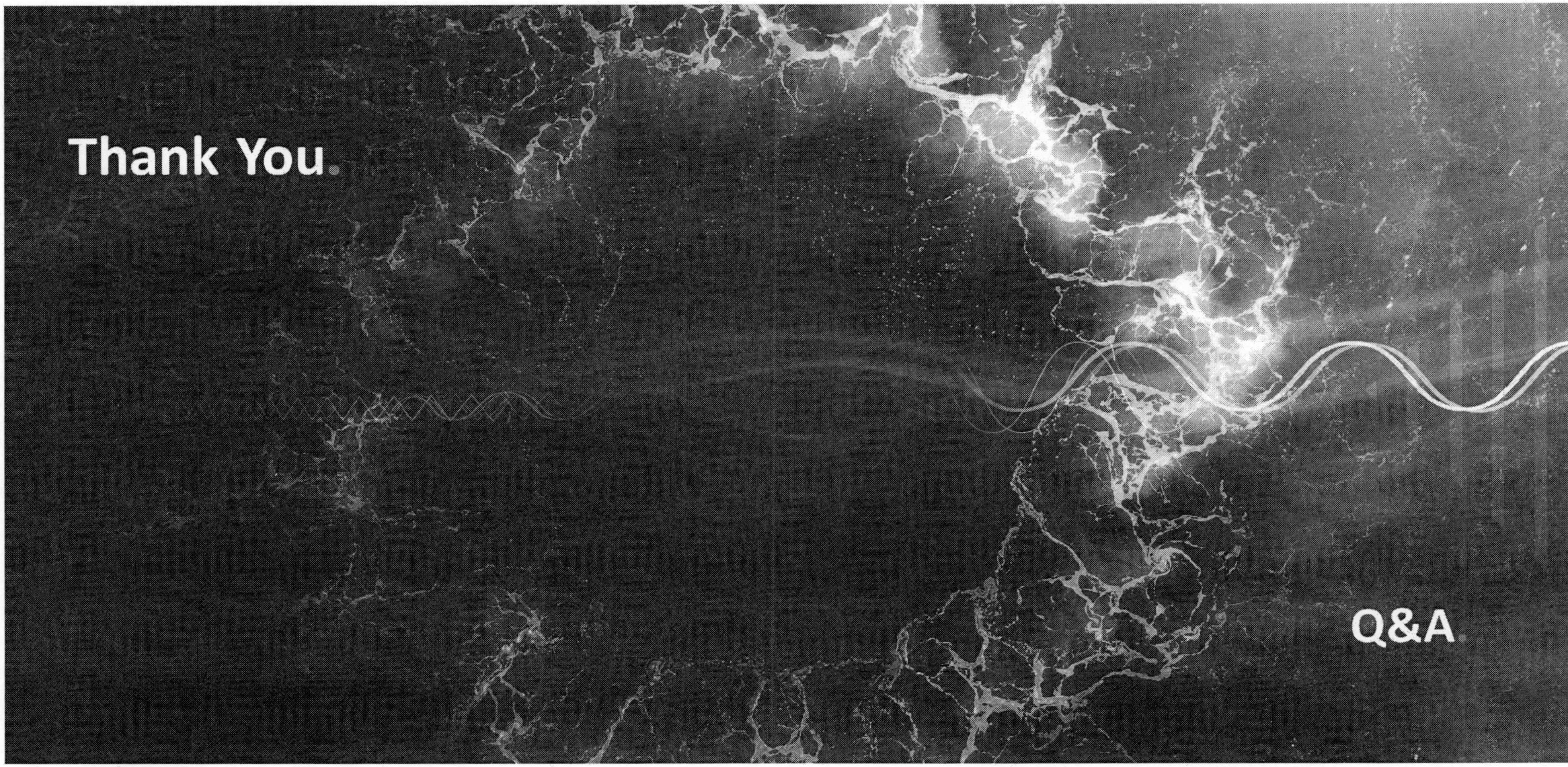

The work presented here is co-financed by the Connecting Europe Facility of the European Union

http://www.languageweaver.com
https://principleproject.eu

RWS

Using speech technology in the translation process workflow in international organizations: A quantitative and qualitative study

Jeevanthi Liyanapathirana, FTI, University of Geneva /WTO

Prof. Pierrette Bouillon, Faculty of Translation and Interpreting (FTI), University of Geneva

Background

- Automatic speech recognition (ASR) systems: contribute to ergonomics, productivity and quality of many situations in our daily lives

- Improvements in Machine Translation (MT) quality and the increasing demand for translations, post-editing has become a popular practice in the translation industry
  - Larger volumes of translations while saving time and costs

- Not many experiments have been conducted on how an interplay between ASR and MT fields can be used to improve translation process workflows within international organizations

Previous Work

Surveying the potential of using speech technologies for post-editing purposes in the context of international organizations: What do professional translators think?

Jeevanthi Liyanapathirana
World Trade Organization
Rue de Lausanne 154
Geneva, Switzerland
jeevanthi.liyana@wto.org

Bartolomé Mesa-Lao
Universitat Oberta de Catalunya Av. Tibidabo, 39-43
08035 Barcelona, Spain
bmesa@uoc.edu

Pierrette Bouillon
Fac. de traduction et d'interprétation
University of Geneva, 1211
Geneva, Switzerland
pierrette.bouillon@unige.ch

Attitude towards different methods of translation

- Research with 6 international organizations (5 in Geneva, 1 Luxembourg).

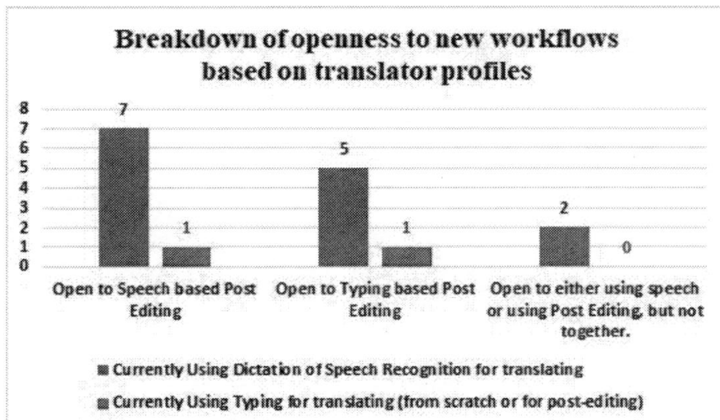

- **No previous quantitative experiments on speech based post-editing according to our knowledge**

Objective

- **Quantitative** and **Qualitative** research on the usage of speech and post-editing in the trade domain, in an international organization.
- Analysis on how different methods affect translation process
  - Post-editing using typing or speech
  - Speaking out the entire translation (while using MT as an inspiration)

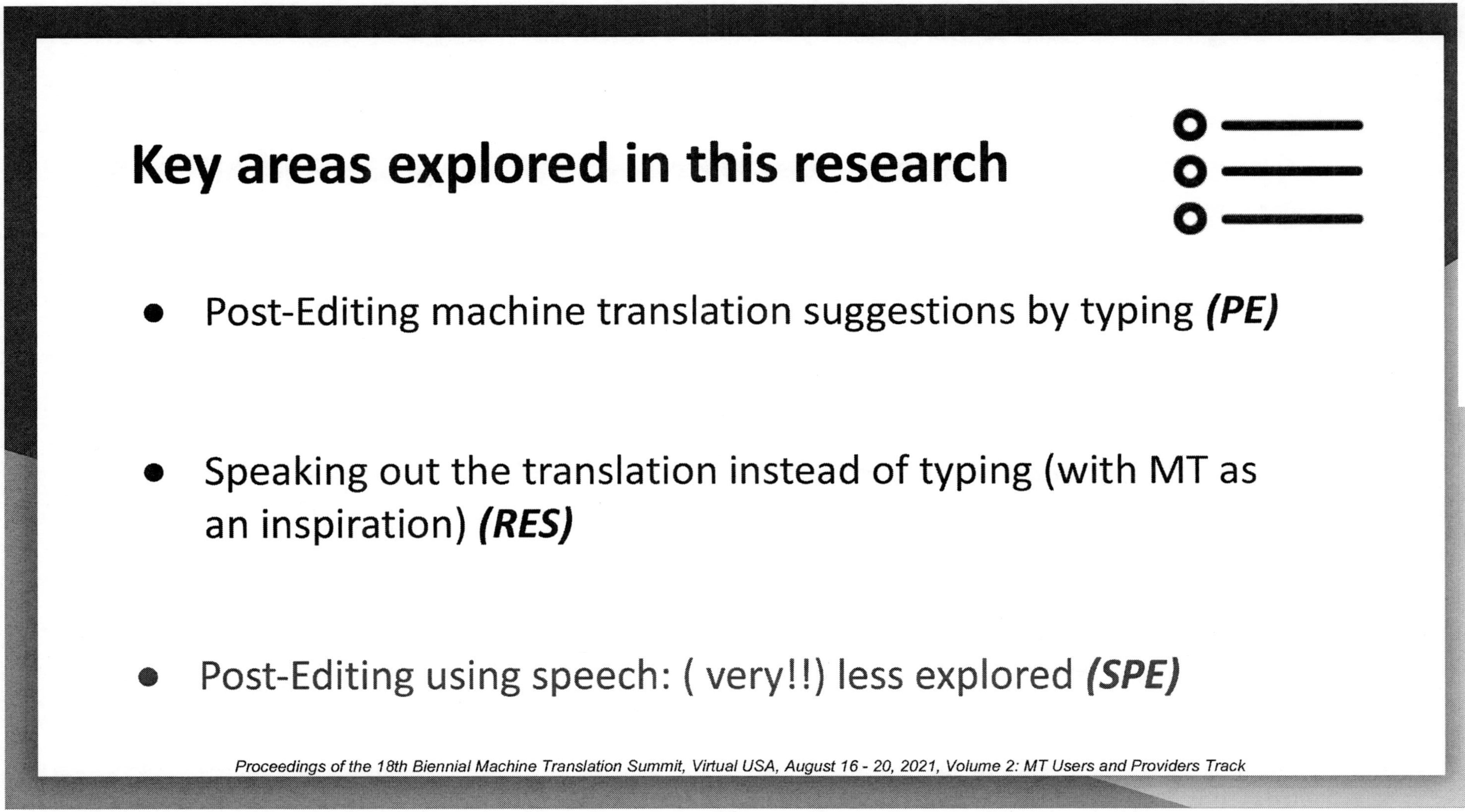
Key areas explored in this research
Post-Editing machine translation suggestions by typing (PE)
Speaking out the translation instead of typing (with MT as an inspiration) (RES)
Post-Editing using speech: (very!!) less explored (SPE)

Resources

- 3 professional translators from international organizations
- Trados Studio was used as the translation workbench
- Dragon Professional was integrated as the speech recognition support for the experiment
- Neural machine translation engines trained specifically using trade domain English and French parallel data were used as MT suggestions

Designing the experiment using Dragon and Trados

- ***Training translator profiles***, ***adding domain specific vocabulary***, ***using built-in commands*** as well as ***training new commands*** to navigate through Trados using Dragon speech

Action	commande vocale
sélectionner du texte	**sélectionner-ça**
désélectionner du texte	**désélectionner-ça**
annuler une action	**annuler-ça**
ouvrir la fenêtre de correction	**corriger-ça**
choisir une correction	**prendre -1|2|3...**
corriger soi-même	**épeler-ça**

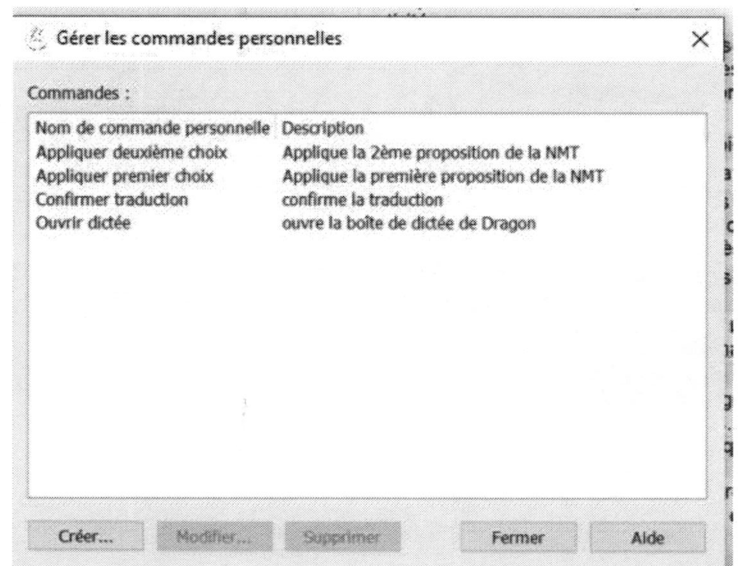

Trados setup

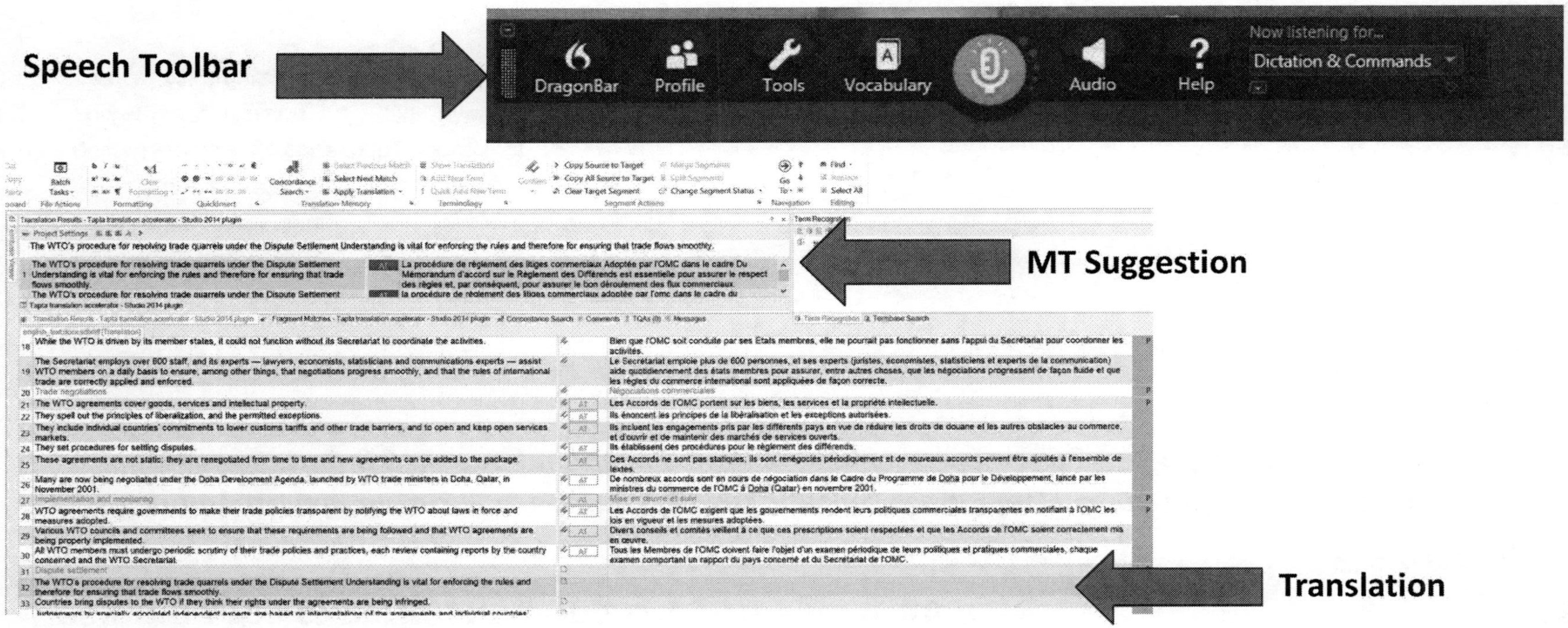

Experiment

DRAGON
NaturallySpeaking

- Three professional translators were asked to translate three different texts (average length of 180 words) of the trade domain using:
    - post-editing the MT suggestions by typing (PE)
    - speaking the translation with MT as an inspiration (RES)
    - editing the MT suggestion using speech (SPE)

- Translation performances of each of the three methods were compared against using BLEU and Translation Error Rate (HTER) scores

SDL* Trados Studio

Results

Method Used	Average BLEU score	Average HTER score	Average Time taken
Post-editing via typing (PE)	36.55	0.48	28 mins
Speaking the entire translation (RES)	28.19	0.55	35 mins
Speech based post-editing (SPE)	48.74	0.375	20 mins

Observations

- **Editing MT using speech (SPE) results in a better BLEU score with less edits made**, compared to the two other methods (**PE, RES**)

- **Respeaking the translation (RES) obtains the worst BLEU and TER scores**, suggesting that the changes do not improve the quality

- **Time used for translating is reduced when using speech based methods**, compared to typing

- Qualitative evaluation indicates that **translators prefer both methods using speech to typing**, since using speech allows them to translate longer segments faster and to think aloud while dictating

Conclusion and Future work

- With high quality ASR and MT support, ASR has the potential to increase the quality of the translation by optimally intermingling with machine translation support
- To the best of our knowledge, this is the first quantitative study conducted on using post-editing and speech together in large scale international organizations
- Future work
  - experimenting with more participants with written/spoken post-editing
  - evaluating temporal/technical effort, translator satisfaction

THANK YOU

Multi-Domain Adaptation in Neural Machine Translation Through Multidimensional Tagging

Emmanouil Stergiadis emmanouil.stergiadis@booking.com
Satendra Kumar satendra.kumar@booking.com
Fedor Kovalev fedor.kovalev@booking.com
Pavel Levin pavel.levin@booking.com

Abstract

While NMT has achieved remarkable results in the last 5 years, production systems come with strict quality requirements in arbitrarily niche domains that are not always adequately covered by readily available parallel corpora. This is typically addressed by training domain specific models, using fine-tuning methods and some variation of back-translation on top of in-domain monolingual corpora. However, industrial practitioners can rarely afford to focus on a single domain. A far more typical scenario includes a set of closely related, yet succinctly different sub-domains. At Booking.com, we need to translate property descriptions, user reviews, as well as messages, (for example those sent between a customer and an agent or property manager). An editor might need to translate articles across a set of different topics. An e-commerce platform would typically need to translate both the description of each item and the user generated content related to them. To this end, we propose MDT: a novel method to simultaneously fine-tune on several sub-domains by passing multidimensional sentence-level information to the model during training and inference. We show that MDT achieves results competitive to N specialist models each fine-tuned on a single constituent domain, while effectively serving all N sub-domains, therefore cutting development and maintenance costs by the same factor. Besides BLEU (industry standard automatic evaluation metric known to only weakly correlate with human judgement) we also report rigorous human evaluation results for all models and sub-domains as well as specific examples that better contextualise the performance of each model in terms of adequacy and fluency. To facilitate further research, we plan to make the code available upon acceptance.

1 Introduction

Neural machine translation (NMT) has achieved remarkable results in recent years. A strong testament to its success and efficacy is the increasingly widespread industrial adoption of NMT solutions Johnson et al. (2017); Levin et al. (2017a); Crego et al. (2016). Model parameter estimation in NMT architectures (Bahdanau et al., 2015; Gehring et al., 2017; Vaswani et al., 2017) is still largely a supervised learning problem which requires large amounts of translated sentence pairs (parallel data). Obviously, acquiring a sufficient number of high quality parallel sentences in order to train a functional domain-specific NMT system can be prohibitively expensive; especially, if one needs to develop such systems for several domains across different language pairs. On the other hand, large quantities of untranslated in-domain content (monolingual data) are often readily available.

Various domain adaptation strategies have been developed to address the low-resource setting of niche domains (Chu and Wang, 2018). Some of the more popular approaches involve

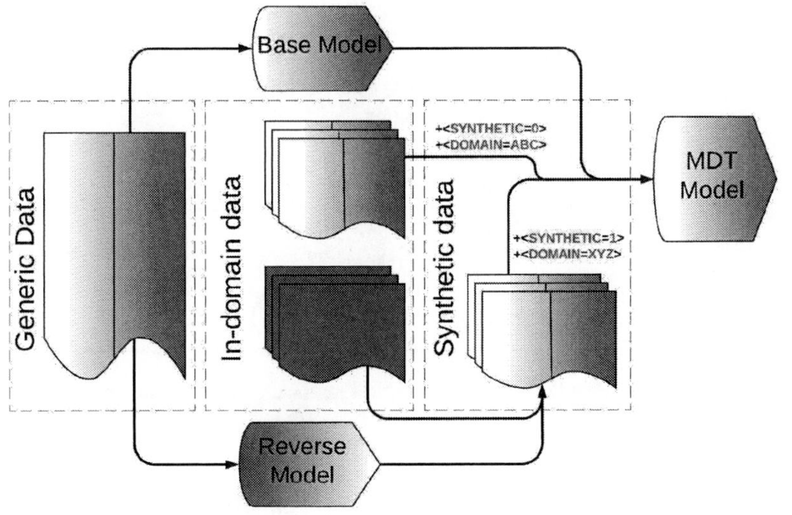

Figure 1: Schematic diagram of MDT in our setting. We use generic parallel data to train a base source-target and a reverse target-source models. We then back-translate target language monolingual in-domain data using the reverse model, and mix it with upsampled in-domain parallel data to fine-tune the base model. The data is tagged with two special tokens: <SYNTHETIC={0,1}>, and <DOMAIN={reviews,messaging,descriptions}>.

generating synthetic in-domain data with the help of existing monolingual corpora, and using that data to fine-tune the more general NMT systems Sennrich et al. (2016a).

In real-world scenarios practitioners often need to deploy translation engines for several closely related, yet different sub-domains. For example, an online travel marketplace needs to translate offering descriptions, user-generated reviews and customer service communications, all related to travel, but all having different linguistic nuances. This fragmentation is further compounded by the company's need to provide services across many distinct languages. It can be very expensive or outright impossible to develop and maintain separate translation pipelines for every combination of language and sub-domain.

We propose a new method for training models which are simultaneously fine-tuned on several closely related, yet succinctly different sub-domains. We show that those models achieve competitive (and often superior) results to single domain fine-tuned baselines while effectively serving N use cases, therefore cutting development and maintenance costs by a factor of N.

2 Related Work

Our work builds on a growing body of domain adaptation research, mainly related to fine-tuning through tagged back-translation.

2.1 Domain tagging

There are a number of research directions related to using tags (or special tokens) within NMT, primarily as a way to pass additional information to the model. Practically speaking, these are attractive approaches as they usually do not require any special modifications to off-the-shelf translation software. The majority of use cases tag sentences on the *source* side: Kobus et al. (2017) use them to control domain, Sennrich et al. (2016) the politeness, Yamagishi et al.

	Arabic	German	Russian
Parallel			
Generic	71M	92M	87M
Reviews	98k	63k	136k
Messaging	73k	76k	87k
Descriptions	60k	72k	80k
Monolingual			
Reviews	1M	1M	1M
Messaging	1M	1M	1M
Descriptions	1M	1M	1M

Table 1: Parallel and monolingual sentences used in our experiments.

(2016) the voice and Elaraby et al. (2018) the gender of translations. The idea also features in multilingual NMT models, for example Johnson et al. (2017) tag training examples according to which translation pair they belong to. An alternative approach by Britz et al. (2017) prepends the domain tag to the training input on the *target* side, thus forcing the decoder to predict the domain based on the source sentence alone.

2.2 Back-Translation for Domain Adaptation

Back-translation (BT) is a form of semi-supervised learning that can be used to fine-tune both statistical Bertoldi and Federico (2009); Bojar and Tamchyna (2011) and neural (Sennrich et al., 2016a) machine translation models to new domains. The idea behind this technique is to augment limited parallel in-domain data with a synthetic corpus produced by translating monolingual data from the *target* language using a *target-to-source* translation system. A synthetic corpus produced via back-translation will have machine-generated source sentences "translated to" human-written in-domain targets. BT model fine-tuning then becomes a three-stage process: first, genuine parallel data is used to train a reverse model in the target-to-source direction; second, that reverse model is used to translate target-side in-domain monolingual data into the source language; third, synthetic data is used in combination with few truly parallel in-domain samples to fine-tune the base source-to-target model. This simple approach works surprisingly well in practice Bojar et al. (2018); Barrault et al. (2019).

Recent research showed that the details of how we generate the synthetic BT data matter a lot (Edunov et al., 2018; Imamura et al., 2018). Specifically, the authors find that randomized sampling and noising is preferable to plain beam search. Edunov et al. (2018) hypothesise that the improvement is due to randomization contributing to the source-side diversification of the synthetic data. Caswell et al. (2019), on the other hand, suggest that synthetic data adds both helpful and harmful signals, which sampling and noising BT strategies help the model to separate. The TaggedBT technique which they introduce achieves competitive results by simply tagging synthetic data with a special token indicating that the data is machine-generated.

3 Multidimensional tagging

As discussed in Section 2, introducing special tokens in the training data has been independently useful at passing content-specific information (e.g. domain, voice, gender, etc.) and data-specific information (e.g. whether a given data point is synthetic). The current work extends this idea into the multidimensional setting. Whenever several meaningful dimensions describing the data are available at inference and training time, we can encode that information with special tokens indicating the values along each of the dimensions (Figure 1).

	Reviews			Messaging			Descriptions			Average		
	AR	DE	RU	AR	DE	RU	AR	DE	RU	AR	DE	RU
Human score												
Base model	3.65	3.73	3.50	3.27	3.44	3.18	2.67	3.28	2.95	3.20	3.48	3.21
+top10	**3.75 (+.10)**	3.80 (+.07)	3.57 (+.07)	3.36 (+.09)	3.65 (+.19)	3.53 (+.35)	3.02 (+.35)	3.70 (+.42)	2.95 (+.00)	3.38 (+.18)	3.71 (+.23)	3.47 (+.14)
+MDT	3.72 (+.07)	**3.88 (+.15)**	**3.62 (+.12)**	**3.49 (+.22)**	**3.78 (+.34)**	**3.53 (+.35)**	**3.20 (+.53)**	**3.73 (+.45)**	**3.04 (+.09)**	**3.47 (+.27)**	**3.80 (+.31)**	**3.40 (+.19)**
BLEU score												
Base model	42.95	43.63	38.25	39.01	44.18	41.18	45.00	45.97	38.92	42.32	44.60	39.45
+top10	**42.95 (+0.00)**	44.99 (+1.36)	38.35 (+0.10)	41.93 (+2.92)	**50.19 (+6.01)**	41.15 (-0.03)	45.35 (+0.35)	**50.98 (+5.01)**	37.84 (-1.08)	43.41 (+1.09)	48.72 (+4.13)	39.11 (-0.34)
+MDT	42.61 -0.34	**46.34 (+2.71)**	**41.12 (+2.87)**	**47.09 (+8.08)**	49.85 (+5.67)	**43.19 (+2.01)**	**46.54 (+1.54)**	50.84 (+4.87)	**39.14 (+0.22)**	**45.41 (+3.09)**	**49.01 (+4.41)**	**41.15 (+1.70)**

Table 2: Human evaluations and BLEU scores for the multi-domain adaptation experiments. MDT (our method) is competitive (and on average superior) against the strong fine-tuning baseline (*top10* from (Edunov et al., 2018)) despite having significantly lower training and deployment costs.

A real-world multi-domain adaptation setting lends itself very naturally to the MDT approach. For example, domain or topic is one such dimension, whether or not the data is synthetic is another. The definition of a synthetic sample may also differ between applications. Back-translation as used in this work is an obvious way of generating such samples, but so can be pseudo-alignment (Imankulova et al., 2017; Schwenk et al., 2019). A hybrid dataset may include samples from all three origins (genuine, machine translated and pseudo-aligned) and a tag can help the model differentiate between them. Lastly, multilingual models where the source languages are not trivially different, can be boosted with a language tag[1]. It is therefore clear that although our experiments only cover a two-dimensional setting with the attributes mentioned above (data domain and source), multidimensional tagging can be extended to cover other data aspects.

4 Experimental Setup

This section describes our data sources, model architecture, and synthetic data generation and mixing strategies that we employ in our experiments. Our principal goal is to evaluate MDT fine-tuning approach as a scalable alternative to state-of-the-art domain fine-tuning for NMT.

4.1 Data

We run our experiments on three language pairs (Arabic-English, German-English and Russian-English) which span three different scripts. Our parallel data sources include a large generic corpus which is a mixture of publicly available and in-house data[2], as well as three much smaller domain-specific parallel datasets (Table 1). The monolingual data which we use to create back-translated models contains 1M proprietary text segments for each language and domain. All three domains ("Reviews", "Messaging" and "Descriptions") are travel-related, and in fact could be considered as sub-domains of a more general "Travel" domain. Nevertheless, they all exhibit distinct linguistic characteristics which makes it challenging to treat them as a single domain. Appendix C provides examples of sentences from different data sources.

[1] Independent experiments (not shown in this work) have shown improved results when a Portuguese model is enhanced with a tag denoting a Brazilian versus a European Portuguese author.

[2] The publicly available portion of our data was sourced from `http://opus.nlpl.eu/` Tiedemann (2012)

4.2 Synthetic data generation

We generate all synthetic data using a target-source reverse model trained purely on the generic parallel corpus. According to prior experiments we found *top10*[3] method from Edunov et al. (2018) to be the best-performing domain adaptation method, and we use it as the main approach to benchmark against. Because we do have limited in-domain parallel data, our fine-tuning parallel data is not purely synthetic, but a mix of synthetic and genuine (which we upsample to reach 1:1 composition).

top10 Following Edunov et al. (2018) we use our reverse target-source models to translate monolingual data back to English, but at the generation stage we *sample* from the next token distribution instead of using beam search to approximate MAP translation. At each sampling step we only consider top 10 most probable candidates.

MDT As described in Section 3, we extend the idea of tagged BT Caswell et al. (2019) to multi-attribute setting by prepending source-side tags which qualify various aspects of the data. Specifically, in this experiment we tag the data according to two characteristics: (1) whether it is synthetically generated or genuine, (2) which sub-domain it belongs to. Both types of tags are treated just like any other tokens, i.e. their learned embeddings are stored in the shared source-side embeddings table.

4.3 Model architecture

Prior to feeding parallel data into the sequence-to-sequence models, all text is preprocessed using the byte-pair encoding (BPE) tokenization scheme (Sennrich et al., 2016b). Our models follow the transformer-base architecture from Vaswani et al. (2017) as implemented in OpenNMT-tf[4] v1.25 (Klein et al., 2017) with early stopping based on development sets of 5000 sentences per each use case.

4.4 Evaluation

The context of this work is a real-world industrial setting which involves translating large volumes of customer-facing text. Therefore our main evaluation criteria are human-based assessments. The human evaluation was performed by professional translators on a 4-point adequacy Likert scale using 250 samples per language, per domain. Appendix A provides details of the scoring guidelines that human evaluators follow. Additionally we report case-sensitive BLEU score (Papineni et al., 2002) as implemented by sacreBLEU[5] Post (2018).

5 Results

5.1 Multi-domain adaptation

Table 2 summarizes our multi-domain adaptation results. On average MDT does not only match, but in fact outperforms the strong *top10* (Edunov et al., 2018) baseline. As mentioned in Section 4.4, given the production quality requirement of our systems we consider human scoring the gold standard for evaluating translations, not the BLEU score alone. Most human and BLEU scores do rank-wise agree, but there are some exceptions. Specifically the German-English MDT model does better than the respective *top10* models on Messaging and Descriptions domains according to the human evaluators, however it is not reflected in the BLEU scores.

[3] Our fine-tuned *top10* baseline was actually our customer-facing production system at the time for several languages.

[4] https://github.com/OpenNMT/OpenNMT-tf

[5] https://github.com/mjpost/sacreBLEU

5.2 Ablation experiment

In order to assess the role of tags, we perform an ablation experiment for German language, in which we compare the MDT performance to that of a model trained without the tags (but on the same mix of training data). It appears that the tags indeed on average improve the performance (Table 3). The models without tags perform worse on "Reviews" and "Messaging" domains according to human evaluations, and on all three domains according to the BLEU score evaluations.

	Human score	BLEU score
Reviews		
MDT Model	3.88	46.34
(-tags)	3.82 (-.06)	44.24 (-2.10)
Messaging		
MDT Model	3.78	49.85
(-tags)	3.48 (-.30)	49.21 (-0.64)
Descriptions		
MDT Model	3.73	50.84
(-tags)	3.80 (+.07)	49.79 (-1.05)
Average	-.10	-1.26

Table 3: The effect of tags removal on human and BLEU score in German-English MDT model.

6 Conclusions

In this work we introduce multidimensional tagging and demonstrate that it can be a scalable solution for multi-domain adaptation in a realistic resource-constrained setting. Somewhat surprisingly we find that MDT models in fact outperform on average our best alternative fine-tuning technique (*top10* from Edunov et al. (2018)), even though the alternative method trains a custom model for each sub-topic. Although the present work offers limited empirical evaluations of MDT (two dimensions: 3 sub-domains and 2 data sources; three language pairs), we think that the technique can prove useful in a broader setting. We believe it to be particularly well suited to many real-world scenarios in which practitioners develop solutions for multiple related domains, while leveraging data from different sources, both genuine and synthetic. All experimental results reported in this work follow rigorous human evaluations in addition to the standard BLEU scores assessments.

References

Bahdanau, D., Cho, K., and Bengio, Y. (2015). Neural machine translation by jointly learning to align and translate. In *ICLR 2015 : International Conference on Learning Representations 2015.*

Barrault, L., Bojar, O., Costa-jussà, M. R., Federmann, C., Fishel, M., Graham, Y., Haddow, B., Huck, M., Koehn, P., Malmasi, S., Monz, C., Müller, M., Pal, S., Post, M., and Zampieri, M. (2019). Findings of the 2019 conference on machine translation (WMT19). In *Proceedings of the Fourth Conference on Machine Translation (Volume 2: Shared Task Papers, Day 1)*, pages 1–61, Florence, Italy. Association for Computational Linguistics.

Bertoldi, N. and Federico, M. (2009). Domain adaptation for statistical machine translation with monolingual resources. In *Proceedings of the fourth workshop on statistical machine translation*, pages 182–189.

Bojar, O., Federmann, C., Fishel, M., Graham, Y., Haddow, B., Koehn, P., and Monz, C. (2018). Findings of the 2018 conference on machine translation (WMT18). In *Proceedings of the Third Conference on Machine Translation: Shared Task Papers*, pages 272–303, Belgium, Brussels. Association for Computational Linguistics.

Bojar, O. and Tamchyna, A. (2011). Improving translation model by monolingual data. In *Proceedings of the Sixth Workshop on Statistical Machine Translation*, pages 330–336. Association for Computational Linguistics.

Britz, D., Le, Q., and Pryzant, R. (2017). Effective domain mixing for neural machine translation. In *Proceedings of the Second Conference on Machine Translation*, pages 118–126.

Callison-Burch, C., Fordyce, C., Koehn, P., Monz, C., and Schroeder, J. (2007). (meta-) evaluation of machine translation. In *Proceedings of the Second Workshop on Statistical Machine Translation*, pages 136–158. Association for Computational Linguistics.

Caswell, I., Chelba, C., and Grangier, D. (2019). Tagged back-translation. In *Proceedings of the Fourth Conference on Machine Translation (Volume 1: Research Papers)*, pages 53–63.

Chu, C. and Wang, R. (2018). A survey of domain adaptation for neural machine translation. In *Proceedings of the 27th International Conference on Computational Linguistics*, pages 1304–1319, Santa Fe, New Mexico, USA. Association for Computational Linguistics.

Crego, J., Kim, J., Klein, G., Rebollo, A., Yang, K., Senellart, J., Akhanov, E., Brunelle, P., Coquard, A., Deng, Y., et al. (2016). Systran's pure neural machine translation systems. *arXiv preprint arXiv:1610.05540*.

Edunov, S., Ott, M., Auli, M., and Grangier, D. (2018). Understanding back-translation at scale. In *EMNLP 2018: 2018 Conference on Empirical Methods in Natural Language Processing*, pages 489–500.

Elaraby, M., Tawfik, A. Y., Khaled, M., Hassan, H., and Osama, A. (2018). Gender aware spoken language translation applied to english-arabic. In *2018 2nd International Conference on Natural Language and Speech Processing (ICNLSP)*, pages 1–6. IEEE.

Gehring, J., Auli, M., Grangier, D., Yarats, D., and Dauphin, Y. N. (2017). Convolutional sequence to sequence learning. In *Proceedings of the 34th International Conference on Machine Learning-Volume 70*, pages 1243–1252. JMLR. org.

Imamura, K., Fujita, A., and Sumita, E. (2018). Enhancement of encoder and attention using target monolingual corpora in neural machine translation. In *Proceedings of the 2nd Workshop on Neural Machine Translation and Generation*, pages 55–63.

Imankulova, A., Sato, T., and Komachi, M. (2017). Improving low-resource neural machine translation with filtered pseudo-parallel corpus. In *Proceedings of the 4th Workshop on Asian Translation (WAT2017)*, pages 70–78.

Johnson, M., Schuster, M., Le, Q. V., Krikun, M., Wu, Y., Chen, Z., Thorat, N., Viégas, F., Wattenberg, M., Corrado, G., et al. (2017). Google's multilingual neural machine translation system: Enabling zero-shot translation. *Transactions of the Association for Computational Linguistics*, 5:339–351.

Kingma, D. P. and Ba, J. (2014). Adam: A method for stochastic optimization. In *Proceedings of the 3rd International Conference on Learning Representations (ICLR)*.

Klein, G., Kim, Y., Deng, Y., Senellart, J., and Rush, A. (2017). OpenNMT: Open-source toolkit for neural machine translation. In *Proceedings of ACL 2017, System Demonstrations*, pages 67–72, Vancouver, Canada. Association for Computational Linguistics.

Kobus, C., Crego, J., and Senellart, J. (2017). Domain control for neural machine translation. In *Proceedings of the International Conference Recent Advances in Natural Language Processing, RANLP 2017*, pages 372–378, Varna, Bulgaria. INCOMA Ltd.

Levin, P., Dhanuka, N., Khalil, T., Kovalev, F., and Khalilov, M. (2017a). Toward a full-scale neural machine translation in production: the booking.com use case. In *Proceedings of MT Summit XVI*, volume 2, pages 39–49.

Levin, P., Dhanuka, N., and Khalilov, M. (2017b). Machine translation at booking. com: Journey and lessons learned. In *Proceedings of the 20th International Conference of the European Association for Machine Translation (EAMT)*.

Papineni, K., Roukos, S., Ward, T., and Zhu, W.-J. (2002). Bleu: a method for automatic evaluation of machine translation. In *Proceedings of the 40th Annual Meeting of the Association for Computational Linguistics*, pages 311–318, Philadelphia, Pennsylvania, USA. Association for Computational Linguistics.

Post, M. (2018). A call for clarity in reporting BLEU scores. In *Proceedings of the Third Conference on Machine Translation: Research Papers*, pages 186–191, Belgium, Brussels. Association for Computational Linguistics.

Schwenk, H., Wenzek, G., Edunov, S., Grave, E., and Joulin, A. (2019). Ccmatrix: Mining billions of high-quality parallel sentences on the web. *arXiv preprint arXiv:1911.04944*.

Sennrich, R., Haddow, B., and Birch, A. (2016). Controlling politeness in neural machine translation via side constraints. In *Proceedings of the 2016 Conference of the North American Chapter of the Association for Computational Linguistics: Human Language Technologies*, pages 35–40, San Diego, California. Association for Computational Linguistics.

Sennrich, R., Haddow, B., and Birch, A. (2016a). Improving neural machine translation models with monolingual data. In *Proceedings of the 54th Annual Meeting of the Association for Computational Linguistics (Volume 1: Long Papers)*, volume 1, pages 86–96.

Sennrich, R., Haddow, B., and Birch, A. (2016b). Neural machine translation of rare words with subword units. In *Proceedings of the 54th Annual Meeting of the Association for Computational Linguistics (Volume 1: Long Papers)*, volume 1, pages 1715–1725.

Tiedemann, J. (2012). Parallel data, tools and interfaces in opus. In *Lrec*, volume 2012, pages 2214–2218.

Vaswani, A., Shazeer, N., Parmar, N., Uszkoreit, J., Jones, L., Gomez, A. N., Kaiser, L., and Polosukhin, I. (2017). Attention is all you need. In *Proceedings of the 31st International Conference on Neural Information Processing Systems*, pages 5998–6008.

White, J., O'Connell, T., and O'Mara, F. (1994). The arpa mt evaluation methodologies: evolution, lessons, and future approaches. In *Proceedings of the First Conference of the Association for Machine Translation in the Americas*, pages 193–205.

Yamagishi, H., Kanouchi, S., Sato, T., and Komachi, M. (2016). Controlling the voice of a sentence in Japanese-to-English neural machine translation. In *Proceedings of the 3rd Workshop on Asian Translation (WAT2016)*, pages 203–210, Osaka, Japan. The COLING 2016 Organizing Committee.

Supplementary Material

A Human evaluations criteria

Each reported human evaluation reading is based on a random test set of 250 text samples which are evaluated by professional translators. Even though all translators were aligned and calibrated during previous evaluations, all sentences from the sample are always sent to the same individual translator to preserve consistency. We use an internally built tool (Figure 2) which allows scoring on a four-point Likert scale, a modified version of the "Accuracy" dimension of the Fluency/Adequacy framework White et al. (1994); Callison-Burch et al. (2007); Levin et al. (2017b). We observed that fluency is almost never an issue in neural machine translation, so we do not score it explicitly. The following are the scoring guidelines for the four-point accuracy scale that are given to the translators:

4	All aspects of the review are comprehensible.
3	The fundamental information provided is accurately conveyed in the translation. Minor errors in non-essential supplementary information that are vague or obscured, but do not contend with the core of the meaning in the description, are allowed.
2	The fundamental information provided is obscured/distorted. The translation either indicates different factual information to what is present in the source, or the translation introduces incorrect information.
1	The translation does not make any sense, and/or does not even allude to the core of the source text.

B Reproducibility

Prior to feeding parallel data into the sequence-to-sequence models, all text is pre-processed using byte-pair encoding (BPE) tokenization scheme (Sennrich et al., 2016b). For all language pairs the BPE vocabulary size is set to 32k. For EN-DE language pair the vocabulary is learned jointly, while for EN-RU and EN-AR we use separate 32k vocabularies due to different alphabets in source and target. All our models follow the transformer-base architecture as described

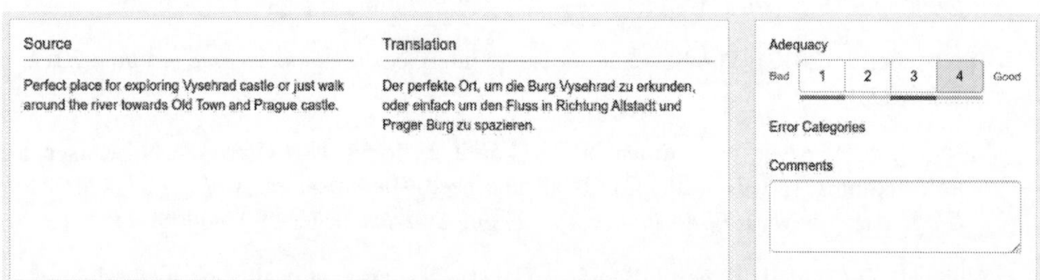

Figure 2: A screenshot of the internal human evaluation tool used by the language specialists.

in Vaswani et al. (2017) and implemented in OpenNMT-tf software (Klein et al., 2017)[6]. We trained the models using Adam Kingma and Ba (2014) optimizer with $\beta_1 = 0.9$ and $\beta_2 = 0.998$ with label smoothing set to 0.1 and noam decay with an initial learning rate of 2.0. While no hyper-parameter tuning is done, early stopping is based on a dev set of 5000 sentences. Furthermore, we use an effective batch size of 25,000 tokens accumulated over different GPUs and keep training until validation loss does not decrease for two consecutive steps. We select the checkpoint with minimum sentence level validation loss - therefore completely ignoring BLEU at model selection. We report both BLEU and human evaluation results using beam width equal to four on a separate test set.

Training our base models took around 5 days using 8 NVIDIA V100 GPUs. Fine-tuning (both the single-domain baseline and the multi-domain MDT variant) took around 16 hours on a single GPU of the same model showing that there is no noticeable difference in training time. Inference time is the same for all models and only depends on sequence length.

C Text samples

The table below provides a few typical text samples from each domain for each of the three source languages. We also show English reference (human) translation as well as translation outputs from each of the three engines: base model, domain fine-tuned model (top10) and MDT (our method).

Reviews

Source	Были всего одну ночь, поэтому в полной мере оценить не смогли.
Reference	We only stayed there for one night, so we couldn't fully appreciate it.
Base model	There was only one night, so we could not fully appreciate it.
top10	We were there only for one night, so we couldn't fully appreciate it.
MDT	We were only there for one night, so we could not fully appreciate it.
Source	die Abwesenheit von Personal der Raum lies sich nicht heizen
Reference	absence of staff the room could not be heated
Base model	the absence of personnel in the room could not be heated
top10	the absence of staff the room could not be heated
MDT	the absence of staff the room could not be heated
Source	مكانه فقط
Reference	Its location only
Base model	Just his place.
top10	Its location only
MDT	Its location only

[6]https://github.com/OpenNMT/OpenNMT-tf

Messaging

Source	если можно не выше второго этажа спасибо
Reference	If possible not higher than the second floor thank you.
Base model	If you can't go above the second floor thank you
top10	if possible not higher than the second floor thank you
MDT	if possible no higher than the second floor thank you
Source	wir möchten Elli, unsere Dalmatiner Hündin mitbringen.
Reference	we would like to bring Elli, our Dalmatian dog.
Base model	We'd like to bring Elli our Dalmatian bitch.
top10	we would like to bring Elli, our Dalmatian dog.
MDT	we would like to bring our Dalmatian dog Elli.
Source	مرحبا هل الدفع بالليرة ؟ وكم التكلفة لثلاث ليالي بالليرة
Reference	Hello, is the payment in Lira? What is the cost for three nights in Lira?
Base model	Hey. Is it a lira? How much for three nights a lira?
top10	Hello! Is the payment in pounds? And how much is it for 3 nights in lira
MDT	Hello Is the payment in lira? And how much it cost for 3 nights per lira.

Descriptions

Source	Просторные апартаменты обставленные в современном стиле, но при этом по домашнему уютные.
Reference	Spacious apartments are fitted in a modern style, but are still cosy like home.
Base model	Spacious apartment with modern furnishings and homelike interiors.
top10	Spacious apartments furnished in a modern style, but at the same time homely.
MDT	Spacious apartments furnished in a modern style, but at the same time homely.
Source	Feste und Kulinarik auf höchster Ebene garantieren Abwechslung das ganze Jahr!
Reference	Festivals and culinary delights of the highest standard guarantee variety all year round!
Base model	Festive and culinary cuisine at the highest level guarantees variety all year round!
top10	Festivals and culinary delights at the highest level guarantee variety all year round!
MDT	Festivals and culinary delights at the highest level guarantee variety all year round!
Source	مكان رائع لإقامه ممتعه يقع فى قرية بورتو ساوث بيتش بالعين السخنه حيث الجو الممتع والطبيعة الخلابة وحيث يتواصل البحر بالجبل والطبيعة الخلابة
Reference	A great place for a pleasant stay located in the village of Porto South Beach in Ain Sokhna, where the atmosphere is enjoyable and picturesque nature, and where the sea meets the mountain and picturesque nature
Base model	A great place for an enjoyable stay, located in the village of Porto South Beach with the hot eye, where the atmosphere is enjoyable and nature is picturesque and where the sea communicates with the mountain and picturesque nature
top10	A great place to stay, located in the village of Porto South Beach in Ain Sokhna, where the atmosphere is pleasant and the nature is wonderful and where the sea communicates with the mountain and the wonderful nature
MDT	A great place for a pleasant stay located in the village of Porto South Beach in Ain Sokhna, where the atmosphere is pleasant and the nature is picturesque and where the sea communicates with the mountain and the picturesque nature

Leave page blank due to pages 407-420 removed after publication

cushLEPOR uses LABSE distilled knowledge to improve correlation with human translation evaluations

Gleb Erofeev*, Irina Sorokina*, Lifeng Han^, Serge Gladkoff*

MT Summit 2021

* Logrus Global

^ ADAPT Centre, Dublin City University

The setting (data), and the metrics.
How to measure quality of MT engine candidate?

(And how can we obtain reference evaluation for reference-based metrics?)

Typical Data: TMs

Source	MT Proposal	TM Reference	Reference evaluation	Automated metrics
Lorem ipsum dolor..	...	HQ translation		
Ut enim ad minim..	...	HQ translation		
Duis aute irure dolor ..	...	HQ translation		

BLEU is grossly inaccurate, but readily available for free, e.g. in NLTK
Not much else is available for free
Human evaluations: costly, low agreement, may be biased, and mostly unavailable.
LABSE similarity is excellent proximity measure, but it is difficult to apply and computational-heavy
...we need accurate, simple, fast, free and easily available metrics... customise hLEPOR metric?

BLEU served well - now we need better tool

- Very rough measure.
- Inconsistent between implementations.
- Precision-only measure.
- Poor correlation with human judgment

(Was it used most often only because it was readily available for free in nltk?)

Little correlation with human judgment

A leap of imagination is required to draw a line here, a circle looks much more representative of this scatter.

(c) Diagram courtesy of Jay Marciano, Lengoo

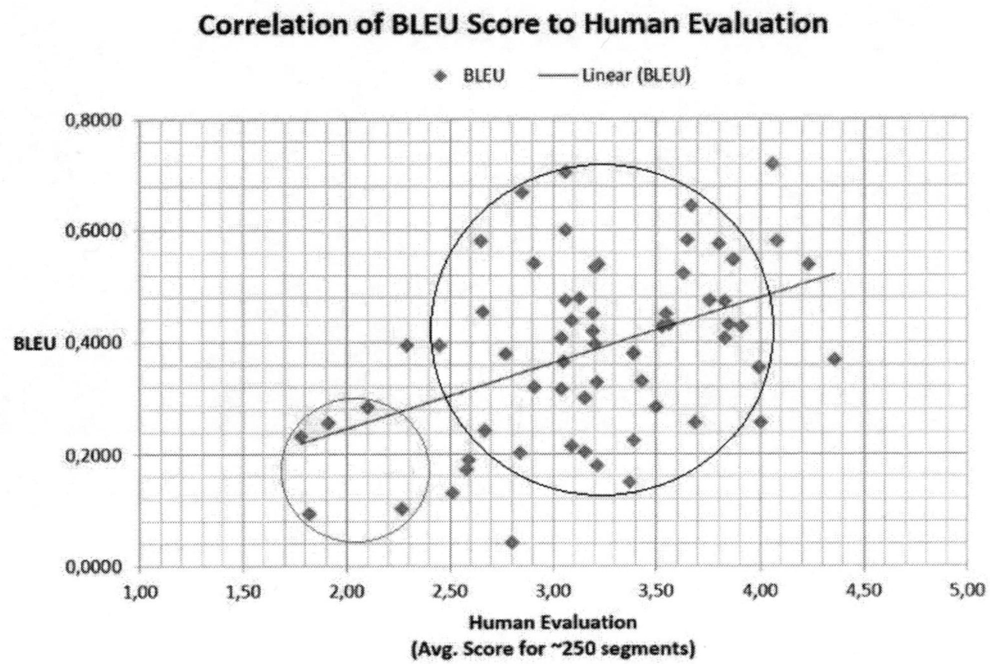

Sample: test set (outside of training set)
Human evaluation: 10% random sampling of test set

Accumulating the pitfalls: ACL2021 outstanding paper award winner

Scientific Credibility of Machine Translation Research: A Meta-Evaluation of 769 Papers

https://aclanthology.org/2021.acl-long.566.pdf

The paper presents the first large-scale metaevaluation of machine translation (MT). “We annotated MT evaluations conducted in 769 research papers published from 2010 to 2020.”

Killer question:

"Is a metric that better correlates with human judgment than BLEU used or is a human evaluation performed?"”

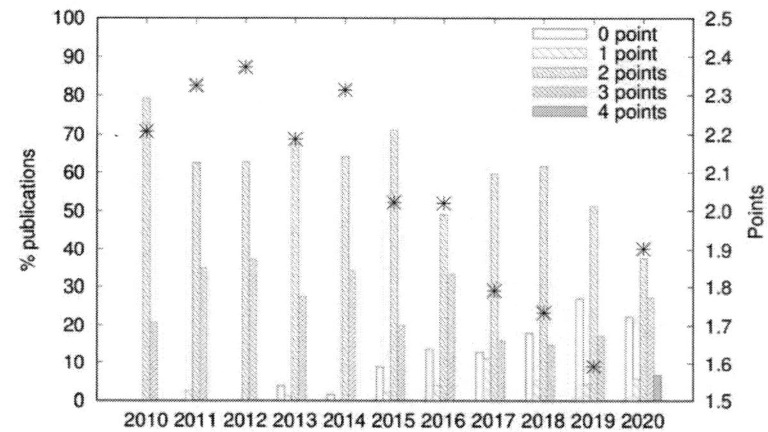

Average mate-eval score (Marie et al. 2021)
MT evaluation worsens.

hLEPOR: best correlation with human judgment

"A Description of Tunable Machine Translation Evaluation Systems in WMT13 Metrics Task" Han et al. 2013: www.statmt.org/wmt13/pdf/WMT53.pdf

hLEPOR includes broader evaluation factors (recall and position difference penalty) in addition to the factors used in BLEU (sentence length, precision), and demonstrated higher accuracy, but Python code was not available.

System	Correlation Score with Human Judgment								
	other-to-English				English-to-other				Mean
	CZ-EN	DE-EN	ES-EN	FR-EN	EN-CZ	EN-DE	EN-ES	EN-FR	score
LEPOR_v3.1	0.93	0.86	0.88	0.92	0.83	0.82	0.85	0.83	**0.87**
nLEPOR_baseline	0.95	0.61	0.96	0.88	0.68	0.35	0.89	0.83	0.77
METEOR	0.91	0.71	0.88	0.93	0.65	0.30	0.74	0.85	0.75
BLEU	0.88	0.48	0.90	0.85	0.65	0.44	0.87	0.86	0.74
TER	0.83	0.33	0.89	0.77	0.50	0.12	0.81	0.84	0.64

hLEPOR (v3.1) on system-level performance using WMT11 data

Directions	EN-FR	EN-DE	EN-ES	EN-CS	EN-RU	Av
LEPOR_v3.1	*.91*	*.94*	*.91*	*.76*	***.77***	***.86***
nLEPOR_baseline	*.92*	*.92*	*.90*	***.82***	*.68*	*.85*
SIMP-BLEU_RECALL	**.95**	.93	.90	**.82**	.63	.84
SIMP-BLEU_PREC	.94	.90	.89	**.82**	.65	.84
NIST-mteval-inter	.91	.83	.84	.79	.68	.81
Meteor	.91	.88	.88	**.82**	.55	.81
BLEU-mteval-inter	.89	.84	.88	.81	.61	.80
BLEU-moses	.90	.82	.88	.80	.62	.80
BLEU-mteval	.90	.82	.87	.80	.62	.80
CDER-moses	.91	.82	.88	.74	.63	.80
NIST-mteval	.91	.79	.83	.78	.68	.79
PER-moses	.88	.65	.88	.76	.62	.76
TER-moses	.91	.73	.78	.70	.61	.75
WER-moses	.92	.69	.77	.70	.61	.74
TerrorCat	.94	**.96**	**.95**	na	na	.95
SEMPOS	na	na	na	.72	na	.72
ACTa	.81	-.47	na	na	na	.17
ACTa5+6	.81	-.47	na	na	na	.17

hLEPOR (v3.1) on system-level using WMT13 data, Pearson correlation

under-utilized hLEPOR: we have done Python port:

hLEPOR was ported to Python and published on PyPi.org: https://pypi.org/project/hLepor/

Now it's available to all engineers and researchers for free!

This version of hLEPOR has 6 customizable parameters!

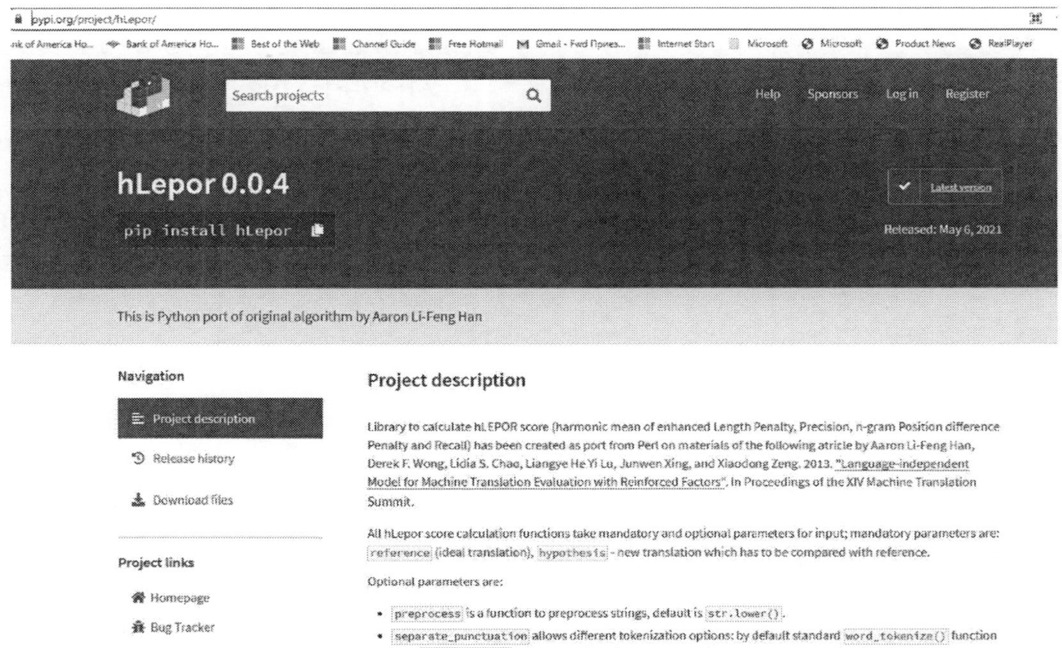

hLEPOR composition

alpha: the tunable weight for recall
beta: the tunable weight for precision
n: words count before and after matched word in npd calculation
weight_elp: tunable weight of enhanced length penalty
weight_pos: tunable weight of n-gram position difference penalty
weight_pr: tunable weight of harmonic mean of precision and recall

Original hLEPOR takes these parameters as certain suggested empirical values, but how good are they?

Now that we have hLEPOR code, we can try to optimize these parameters against certain data and criteria.

The next step: to fine-tune hLEPOR parameters

In the real world: we don't have human quality evaluations, but we will have TM at best.

How can we get by without the massive involvement of human evaluators, and only engage them for verification of small samples?

One way is to use LABSE similarity measure - Language Agnostic Bert Sentence Embedding by Feng et al. (2020). Its proximity measure shows syntactic similarity very well.

But it is computational-heavy.

Let's try to optimize hLEPOR parameters and see if we can improve hLEPOR performance!

(AND we can also try to optimize hLEPOR against human evaluations, too.)

OPTUNA : a hyperparameter optimization network

https://optuna.org/

Optuna is capable of finding the extremums in a seven-dimensional space of 6 parameters and the lowest RMSE (Root Mean Square Error) value.

CMA Evolution Strategy for Six-hemp camel function

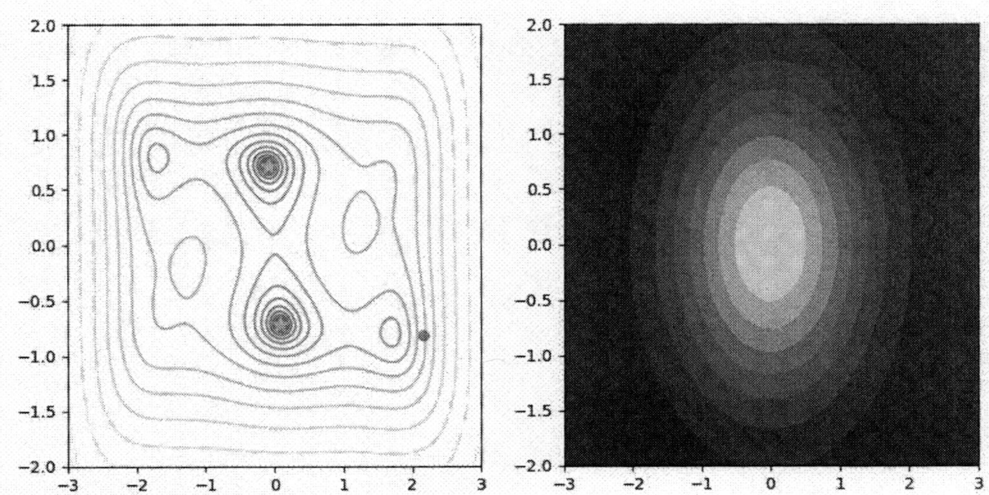

Left, the optimal solutions (yellow stars) and the solutions sampled by CMA-ES (red points); Right, the update process of the multivariate gaussian distribution.

(c) Image courtesy of Masashi SHIBATA

cushLEPOR: customized hLEPOR

1. We build LABSE similarity score on our data.
2. We use OPTUNA (https://optuna.org/, a hyperparameter optimization network) to get the lowest possible RMSE (Root Mean Square Error) between cushLEPOR and LABSE
3. The data is available on GitHub: https://github.com/poethan/cushLEPOR

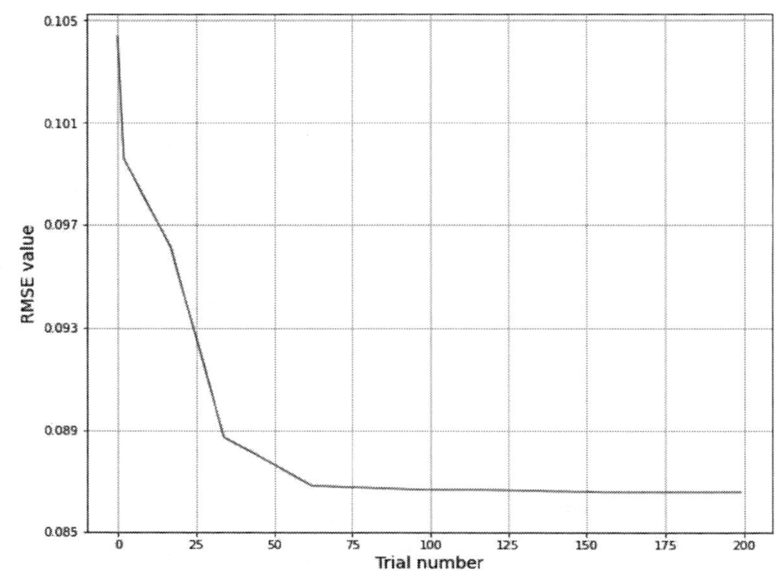

cushLEPOR now shows much better result

Before:

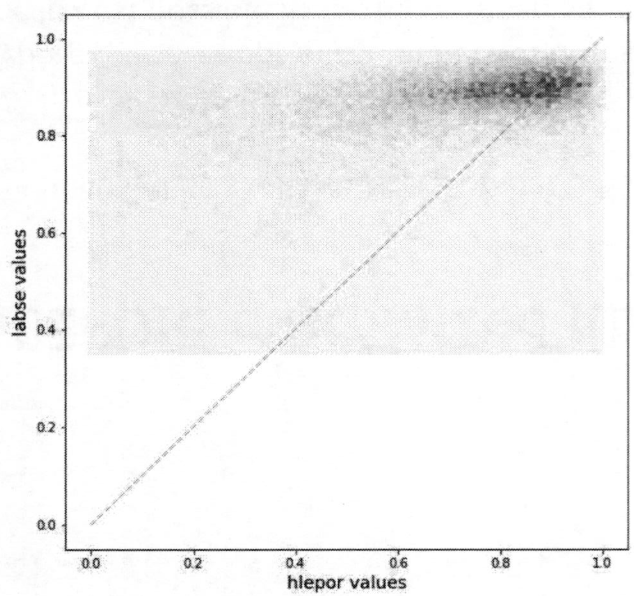

After:

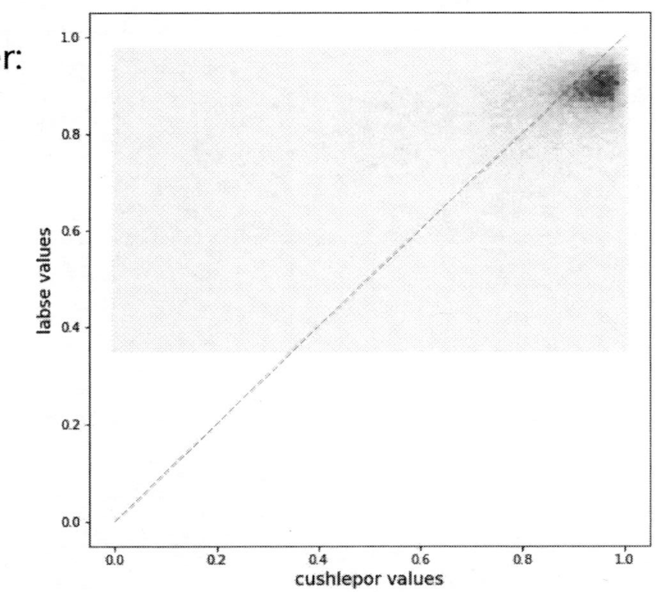

cushLEPOR(LABSE) has better RMSE than hLEPOR

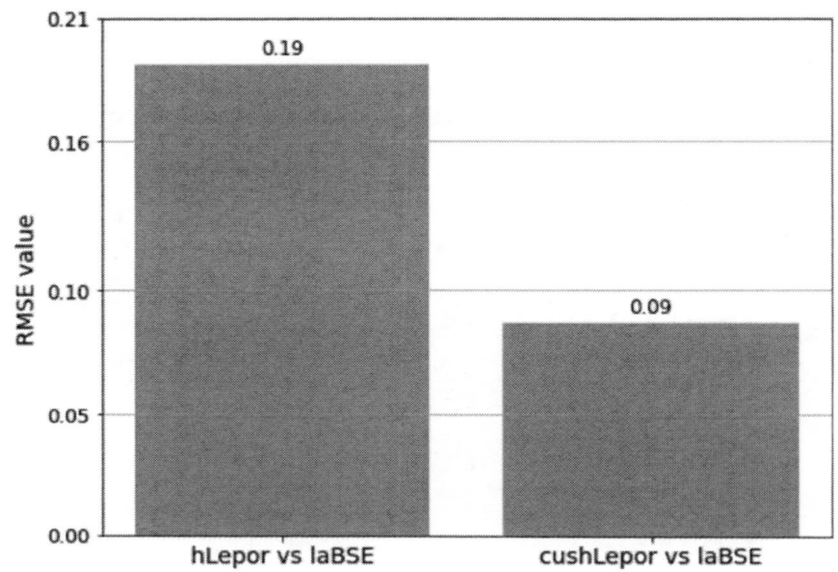

We have also tried to optimize cushLEPOR vs pSQM

WMT21 shared Metrics tasks suggest using Google Research experiment (with human translator annotated date using MQM and sPQM) for training.

"**Experts, Errors, and Context: A Large-Scale Study of Human Evaluation for Machine Translation**" by Marcus Freitag et.al. (2021) from Google Research: https://arxiv.org/abs/2104.14478

pSQM: professional translator annotated Scalar Quality Metrics
MQM: Multidimensional Quality Metrics (framework)

Features significant corpus of human annotated data with MQM and pSQM metrics.

Provides much better results for human judgment.

We have carried out cushLEPOR optimization against MQM and pSQM on En-De and Zh-En.

cushLEPOR(pSQM) gives better RMSE than BLEU

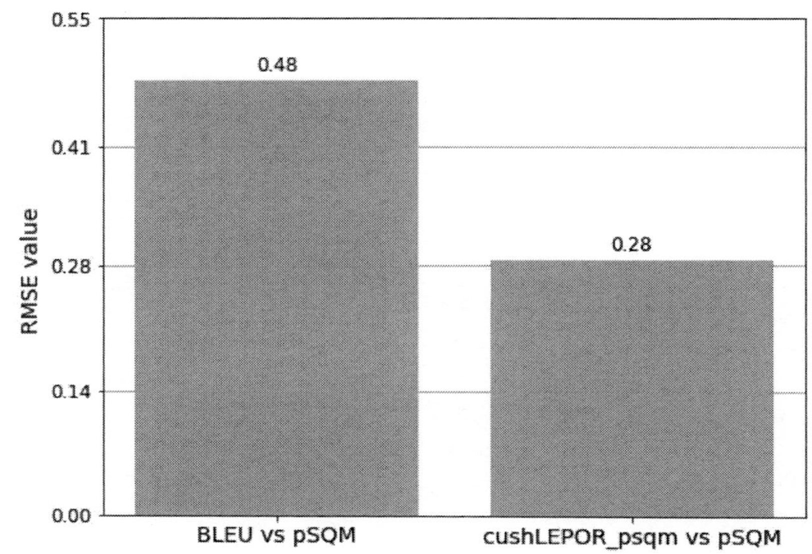

cushLEPOR(pSQM) performs better hLEPOR on pSQM

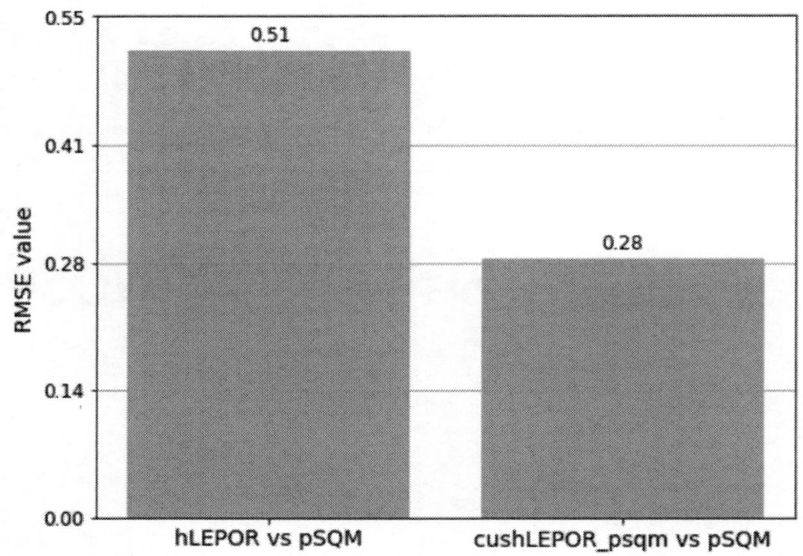

Conclusions: Advantages

- We now can use cushLEPOR for **target languages** as a light and fast similarity metrics.
- The same code that we have published on PyPi.org can be fine-tuned as cushLEPOR for your application.
- cushLEPOR can be trained on both human evaluations and LABSE similarity.
- N-gram metrics are sensitive to translation variants, but not cushLEPOR because it is optimized for correlation with LABSE (which takes many similar sentences into account as training data).
- LABSE transformer requires IT and ML skills and is computational-heavy. cushLEPOR is an instant light metric that produces the same result after similarity optimization for LABSE.
- Nice simplification of a very complex method.
- cushLEPOR better correlates with human judgment than BLEU, even without our optimization on them.

Conclusions: Drawbacks

LABSE and LABSE-optimized cushLEPOR undervalues the significance of errors, error types, showing grammatical syntactic similarity, instead of semantics. Top chart: pSQM human quality ratings distribution. Buttom chart: LABSE similarity measure distribution.

Future work will include semantic features.

In other words, small (from the post-editing point of view) errors may be significant from human perception, but cannot be captured automatically just yet. We plan to analyze different types of errors and assign them different significance (weights) during evaluations.

```
In [44]: 1 mean_df_final['u_score'].hist()
```

<AxesSubplot:>

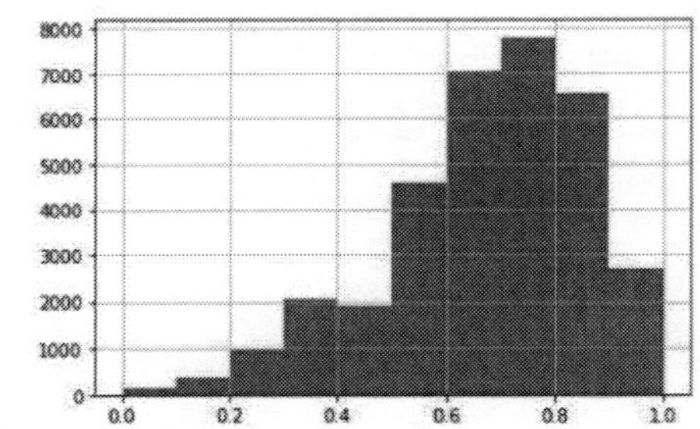

```
In [45]: 1 mean_df_final['labse'].hist()
```

<AxesSubplot:>

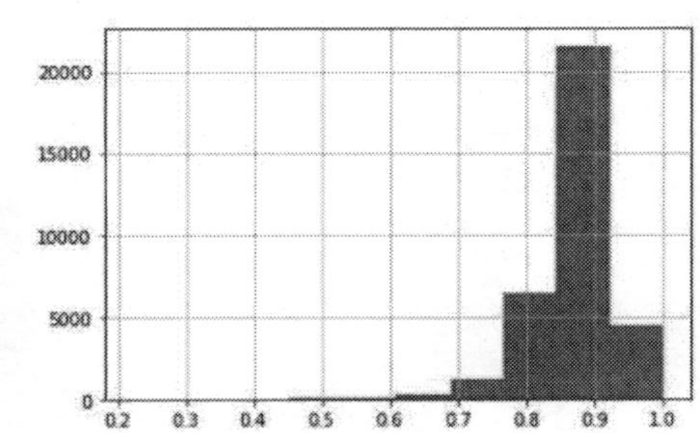

Conclusions: Practical outcome

You now can use cushLEPOR in actual product.

Do you want us to help you to train your own cushLEPOR for your data and your language pair?

You are welcome.

QUESTIONS?

rd@logrusglobal.com

welocalize

A SYNTHESIS OF HUMAN AND MACHINE

CORRELATING "NEW" AUTOMATIC EVALUATION METRICS WITH HUMAN ASSESSMENTS

Presenters: Andrea Alfieri, Mara Nunziatini

AGENDA

01 OBJECTIVES AND METHOD

02 RESULTS

03 CONCLUSIONS AND FURTHER RESEARCH

Objectives And Method

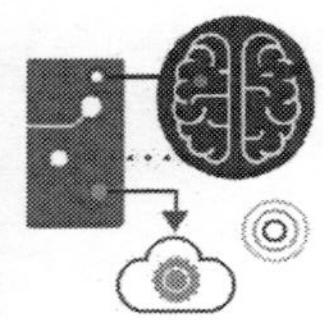

Objectives

- Provide an overview of new Machine Translation metrics: **characTER, chrF3, COMET, hLEPOR, Laser, Prism**.
- Analyze if and how these metrics correlate at a segment level to the results of Adequacy and Fluency **Human Assessments**.
- Analyze how they compare against **TER** scores and **Levenshtein Edit Distance** as well as against each of the other.

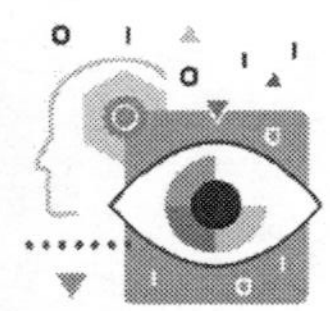

Method

1. **~500 segments** (~ 250 UI/UA + ~ 250 Marketing) selected for the experiment and scored for Adequacy and Fluency
    - Adequacy and Fluency: scores from 1 (lowest) to 5 (highest)
    - **3** experienced **linguists** per language (scores averaged)
    - Languages: **German, Hindi** (no model for Prism)**, Italian, Russian, Simplified Chinese**
2. The same segments were scored using characTER, chrF3, COMET, hLEPOR, Laser, Prism, TER and Levenshtein Edit Distance
3. Human Assessment scores and Automatic Scores aligned and analyzed (Pearson Correlation Coefficient)

Results

Pearson Correlation Coefficient per Metric and Language

German

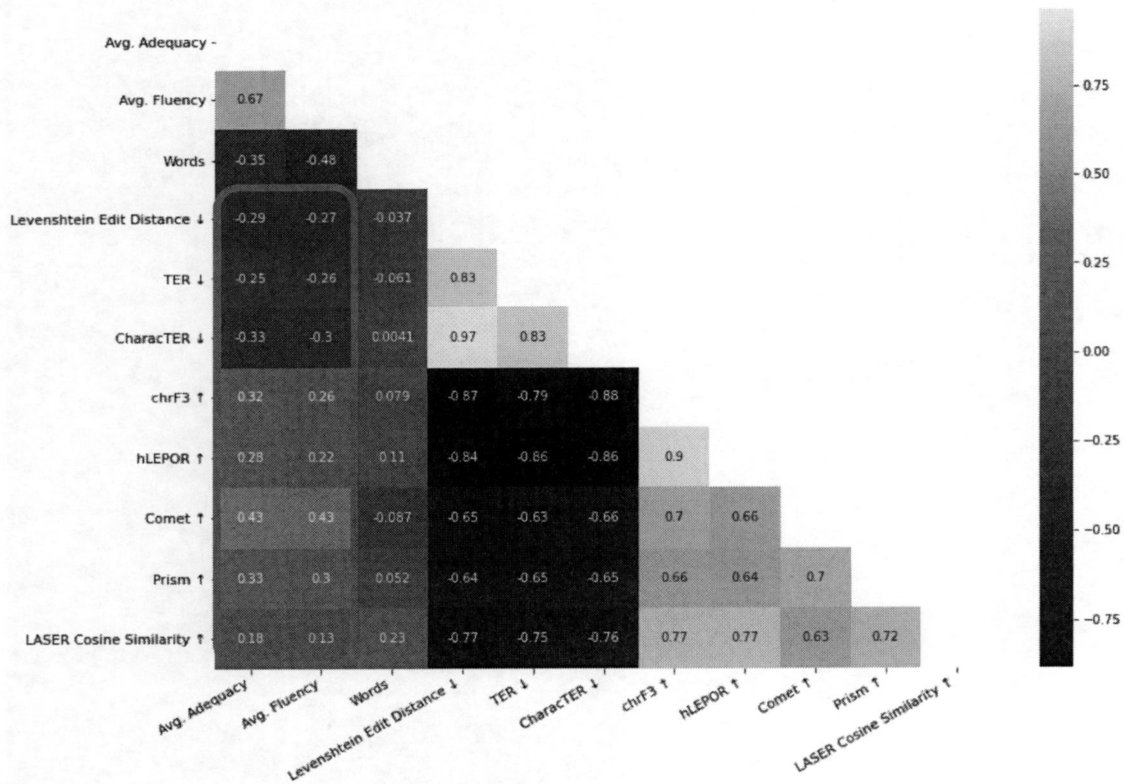

Insights

Pearson Correlation Coefficient calculated to analyze the correlation between Human Assessment and metrics, as well as between each one of the metrics included in the study.

- **COMET** is the metric that achieves the best correlation with Human Assessments.
- The second place goes to Prism and CharacTER, which show comparable results.
- The third place goes to chrF3.
- Levenshtein Edit Distance and TER show a worse correlation compared to the 3 new metrics mentioned above.

Hindi

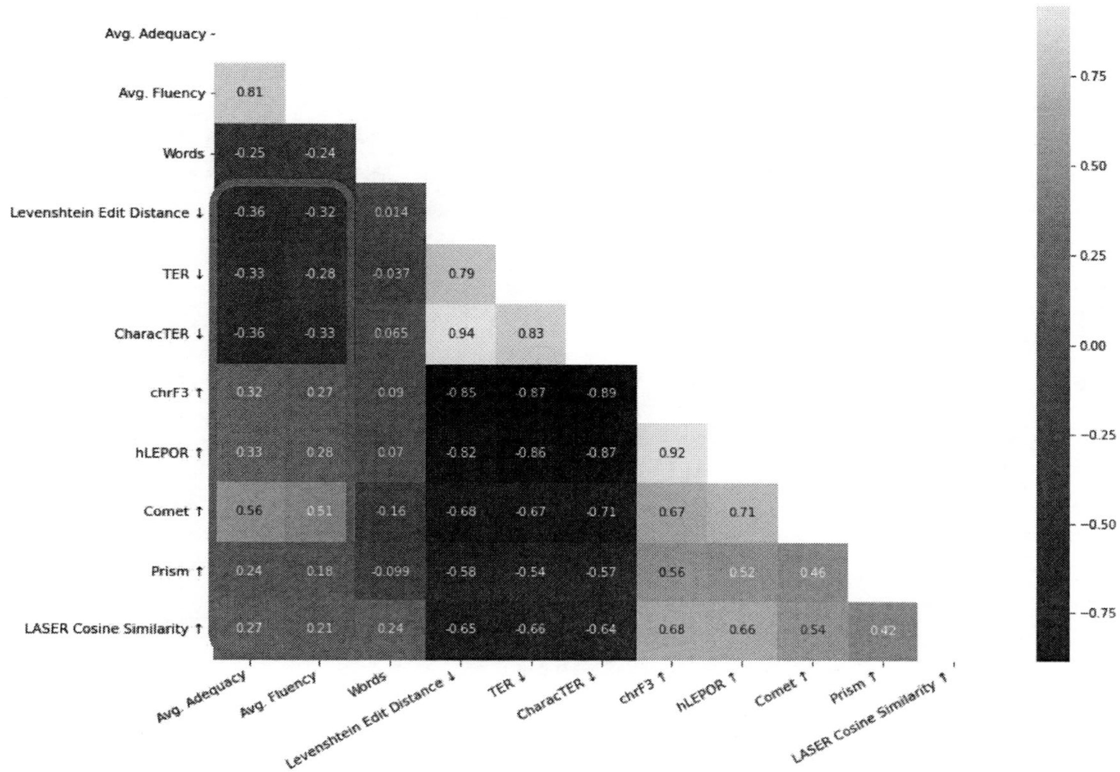

Insights

Pearson Correlation Coefficient calculated to analyze the correlation between Human Assessment and metrics, as well as between each one of the metrics included in the study.

- **COMET** is the metric that achieves the best correlation with Human Assessments. The coefficient is >0.50, this suggests that there is a **moderately high correlation**.
- The second place goes to CharacTER.
- The third place goes to Levenshtein Edit Distance.
- TER shows a worse correlation compared to the 3 new metrics mentioned above.

Italian

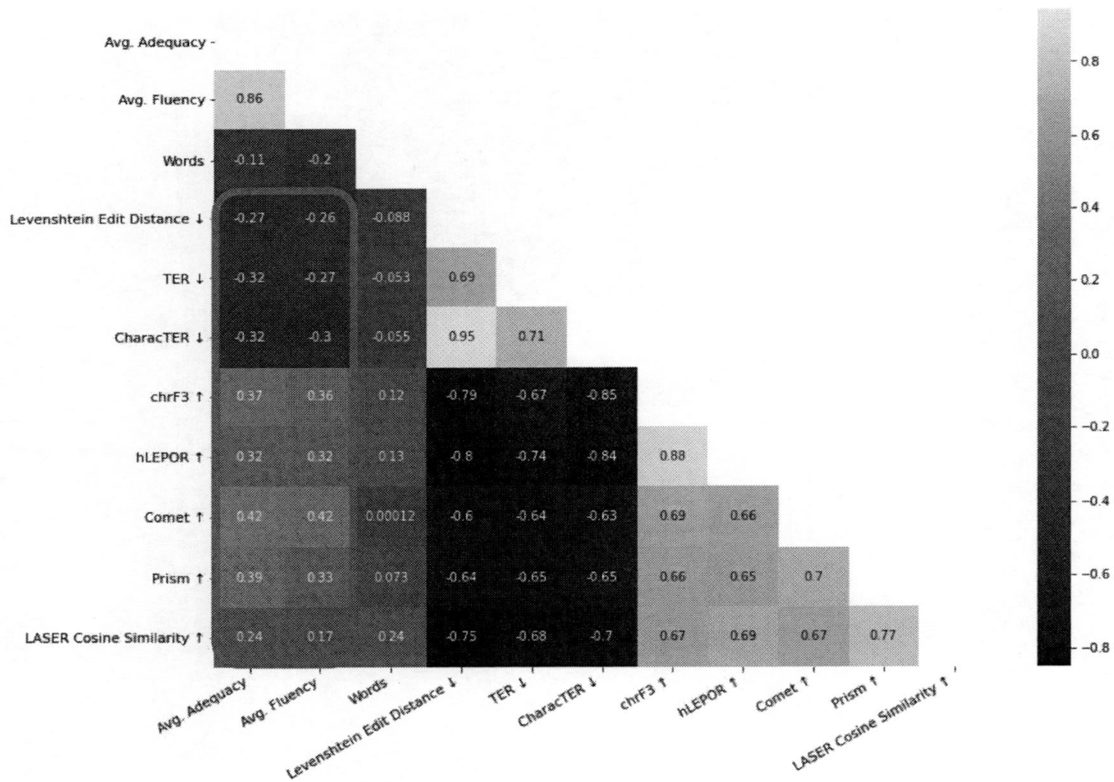

Insights

Pearson Correlation Coefficient calculated to analyze the correlation between Human Assessment and metrics, as well as between each one of the metrics included in the study.

- The best correlation between Human Assessments and metric is seen with **COMET**.
- The second place goes to chrF3 and Prism, which show comparable results (chrF3 better correlates with Fluency, compared to Prism).
- The third place goes to CharacTER and hLEPOR, which show comparable results.
- Levenshtein Edit Distance and TER show a worse correlation compared to the 3 new metrics mentioned above.

Russian

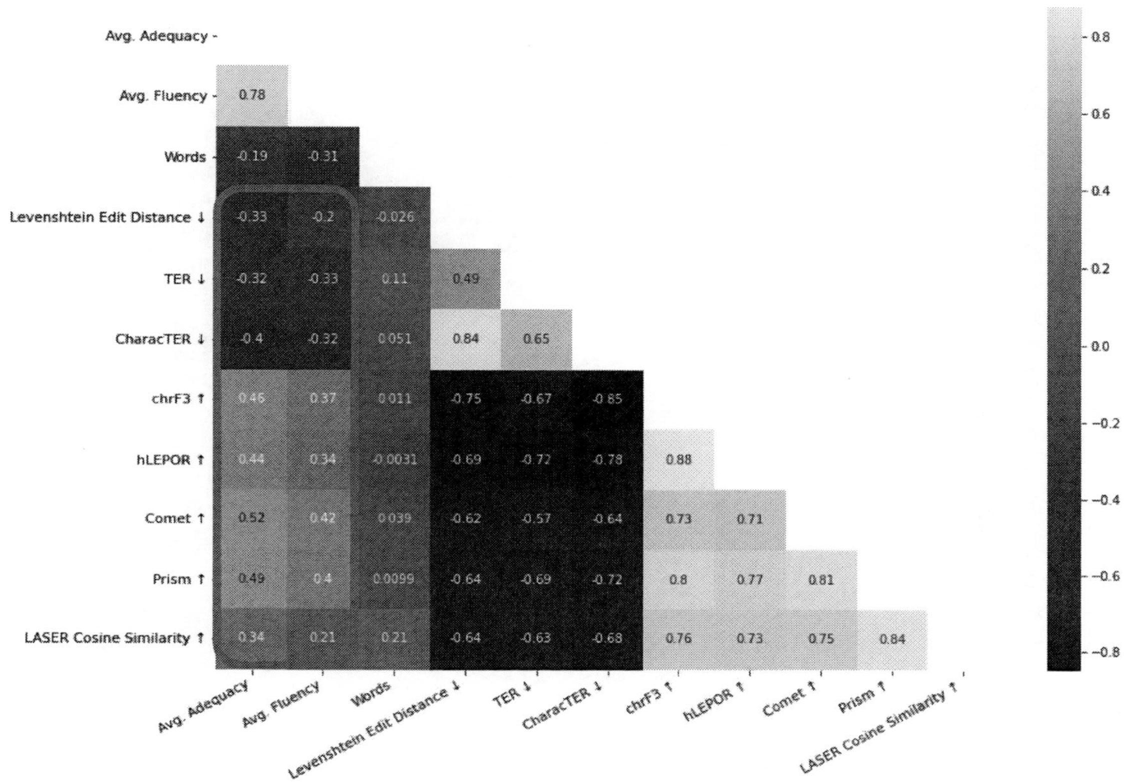

Insights

Pearson Correlation Coefficient calculated to analyze the correlation between Human Assessment and metrics, as well as between each one of the metrics included in the study.

- **COMET** is the metric that achieves the best correlation with Human Assessments. The coefficient is >0.50 with Accuracy, this suggests that there is a **moderately high correlation.**
- The second place goes to Prism, which also shows a high correlation, close to 0.50.
- The third place goes to chrF3 and hLEPOR which show comparable results.
- Levenshtein Edit Distance and TER show a significantly worse correlation compared to the 3 new metrics mentioned above.

Simplified Chinese

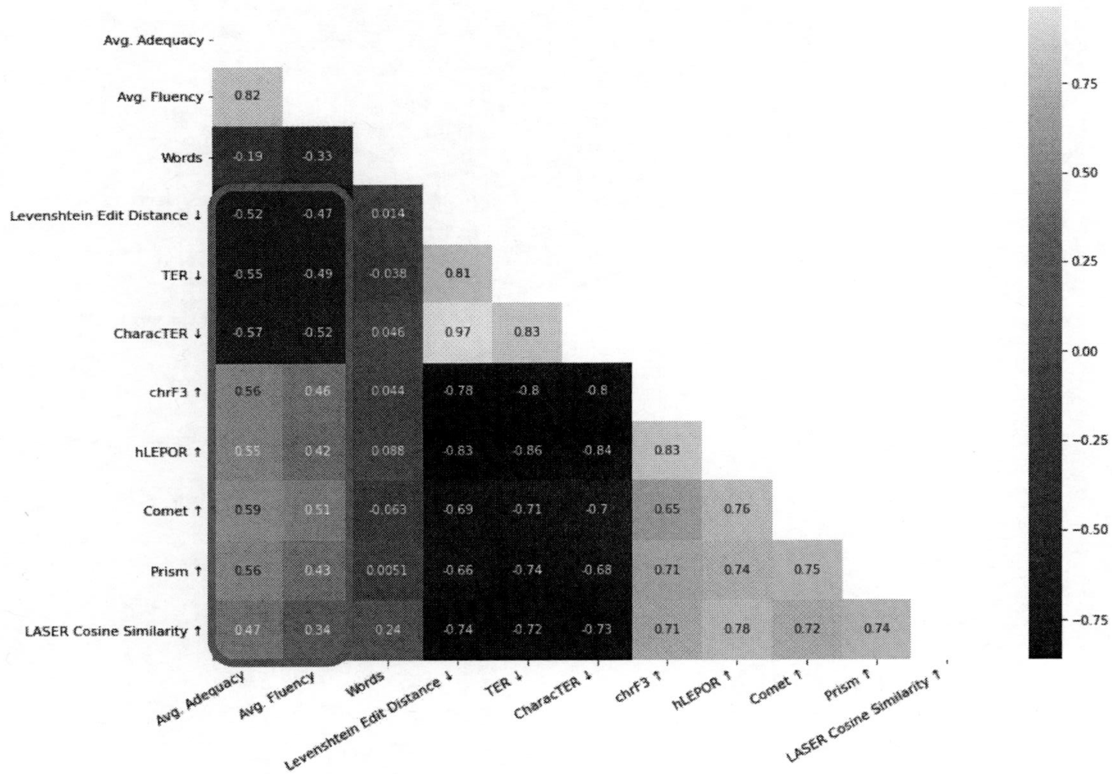

Insights

Pearson Correlation Coefficient calculated to analyze the correlation between Human Assessment and metrics, as well as between each one of the metrics included in the study.

- **COMET** is the metric that achieves the best correlation with Human Assessments. The coefficient is >0.50, this suggests that there is a **moderately high correlation**.
- The second place goes to CharacTER, which show comparable results.
- The third place goes to Prism and hLEPOR, which also show a high correlation with Accuracy.
- Levenshtein Edit Distance and TER also show a good correlation.
- **Need to investigate why correlations are overall better for Chinese.**

Conclusions

- Overall, **COMET achieves the highest correlation** with Human Assessment for each language (for some languages >0.50 Pearson correlation coefficient).
- **Prism, characTER and chrF3 also show good correlation** with Human Assessment across the board.
- **Laser Cosine Similarity score** is the only metric which shows a positive **correlation** (>0.20) **with the number of words** in the source segment for every language. This could suggest that Laser Cosine Similarity might does not perform well on shorter segments.
- **No significant differences were noticed in correlations based on the content type** (Product UI/UA vs Marketing). All metrics achieve at least moderate correlations ($\pm$ 0.30).
- **All the new metrics analyzed show a better correlation with Human Assessment** per language **compared to TER and Levenshtein Edit Distance**. Slightly different observation for Hindi.
- **Business implications**: ideally, the metric(s) with higher correlation should be used to evaluate the quality of the raw machine translation output, analyze the post-editing effort (which is closely related to MTPE discounts) and in quality estimation. Because we have seen that the preferred metric varies depending on the language, this could mean to have different "go-to" metrics in place, depending on the language in scope.

Further Research

1. Test the metrics on more languages – what is the best metric for every language and why? Is it possible and convenient for an LSP to use different preferred metrics for every language?
2. Establish the acceptability threshold for the most relevant metrics – what is a good score and what is a bad score?
3. Get a better understanding of the reasons underlying variance of the same metric across different languages.

Thank you
welocalize

And Special Thanks to...
Alex Yanishevsky
Anna Pizzolato
David Clarke
Elaine O'Curran
Jon Cambra
Lena Marg
welocalize

Appendix
welocalize

Metrics Definition

Levenshtein Edit Distance: The number of insertions, deletions, substitutions required to transform MT output to the human reference translation based on the Levenshtein algorithm. In our analysis, we normalize this value by the number of characters in the MT output.

TER (Translation Edit Rate): is a word-based error metric for machine translation that measures the number of edits (insertions, deletions, substitutions and shifts) required to change a system output into one of the human references.

$$\text{TER} = \frac{\text{\# of edits}}{\text{average \# of reference words}}$$

CharacTER: same as TER, but insertions, deletions, substitutions are calculated at the character level. The shift edit operation is still performed at word level. Unlike TER, the edit distance is normalized by the length of the MT output.

$$\text{CharacTER} = \frac{\text{shift cost} + \text{edit distance}}{\text{\#characters in the hypothesis sentence}} \quad (1)$$

chrF3: F3 score based on character n-grams of size 6. The F3 score can be defined as the harmonic mean of precision and recall, with recall having three times more weight than precision (β = 3)

$$\text{CHRF}\beta = (1+\beta^2)\frac{\text{CHRP} \cdot \text{CHRR}}{\beta^2 \cdot \text{CHRP} + \text{CHRR}} \quad (1)$$

Metrics Definition

hLEPOR: computes the similarity of n-grams between a MT output and a reference translation, taking into account a length penalty, an n-gram position difference penalty, and recall.

COMET: a framework to train multilingual MT evaluation models that can function as metrics. For our analysis, we used the publicly available wmt-large-da-estimator-1719 model, which is trained to predict human judgments from WMT by leveraging sentence embeddings extracted from the source, MT output and reference segment.

Prism: uses a multilingual NMT system to score MT outputs conditioned on their corresponding human references. The score is calculated by averaging the log-probability for each token in the output assigned by the model.

LASER cosine similarity: LASER is a neural model trained on parallel data from 93 languages open sourced by Facebook in 2019. Sentence embeddings produced by its encoder can be compared to measure intra or interlingual semantic similarity using cosine similarity.

CharacTER ↓

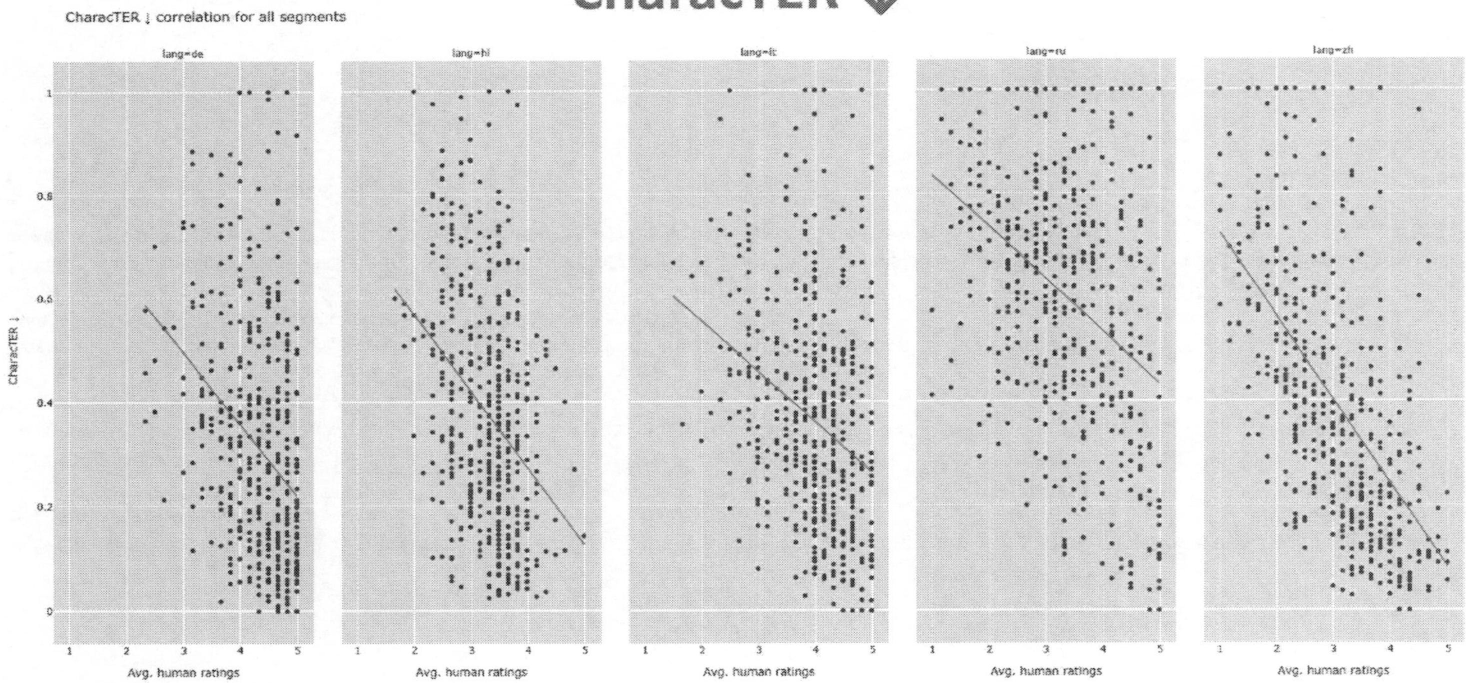

Key:

- ● Avg. Human ratings = Adequacy and Fluency ratings by 3 linguists averaged per segment
- — Trendline = the degree to which Avg. Human ratings and CharacTER scores are correlated. A diagonal line indicates a perfect correlation. The more points close to the line, the stronger the correlation.

CHRF3 ↑

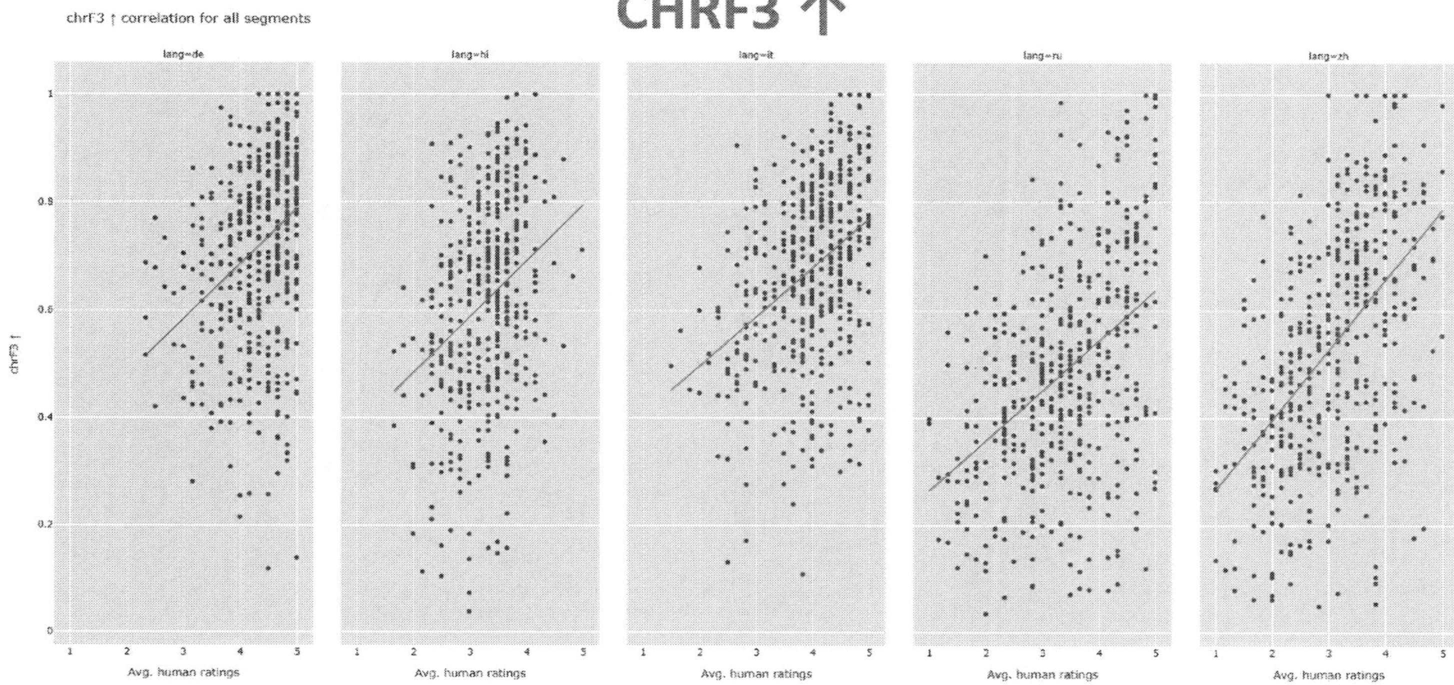

Key:

- ● Avg. Human ratings = Adequacy and Fluency ratings by 3 linguists averaged per segment
- ▬ Trendline = the degree to which Avg. Human ratings and chrF3 scores are correlated. A diagonal line indicates a perfect correlation. The more points close to the line, the stronger the correlation.

COMET ↑

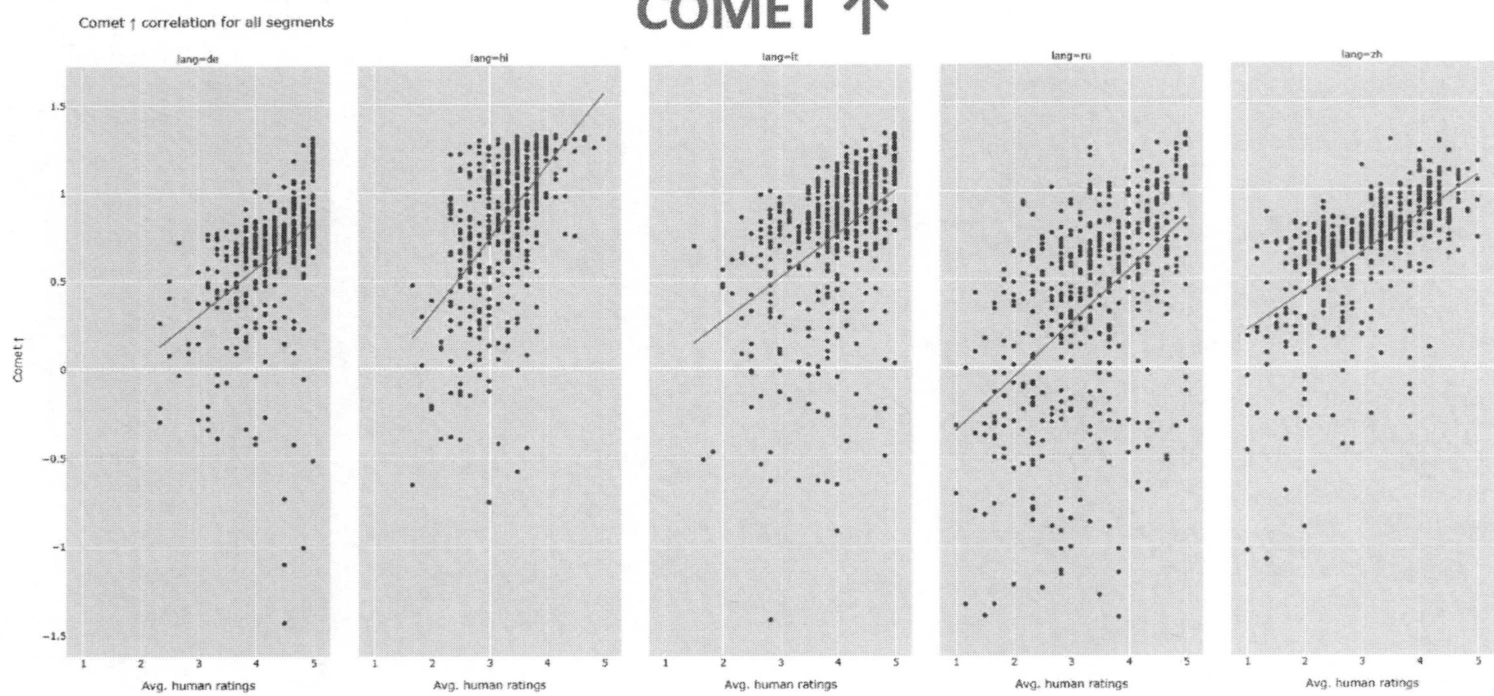

Key:

- ● Avg. Human ratings = Adequacy and Fluency ratings by 3 linguists averaged per segment
- — Trendline = the degree to which Avg. Human ratings and COMET scores are correlated. A diagonal line indicates a perfect correlation. The more points close to the line, the stronger the correlation.

hLEPOR ↑

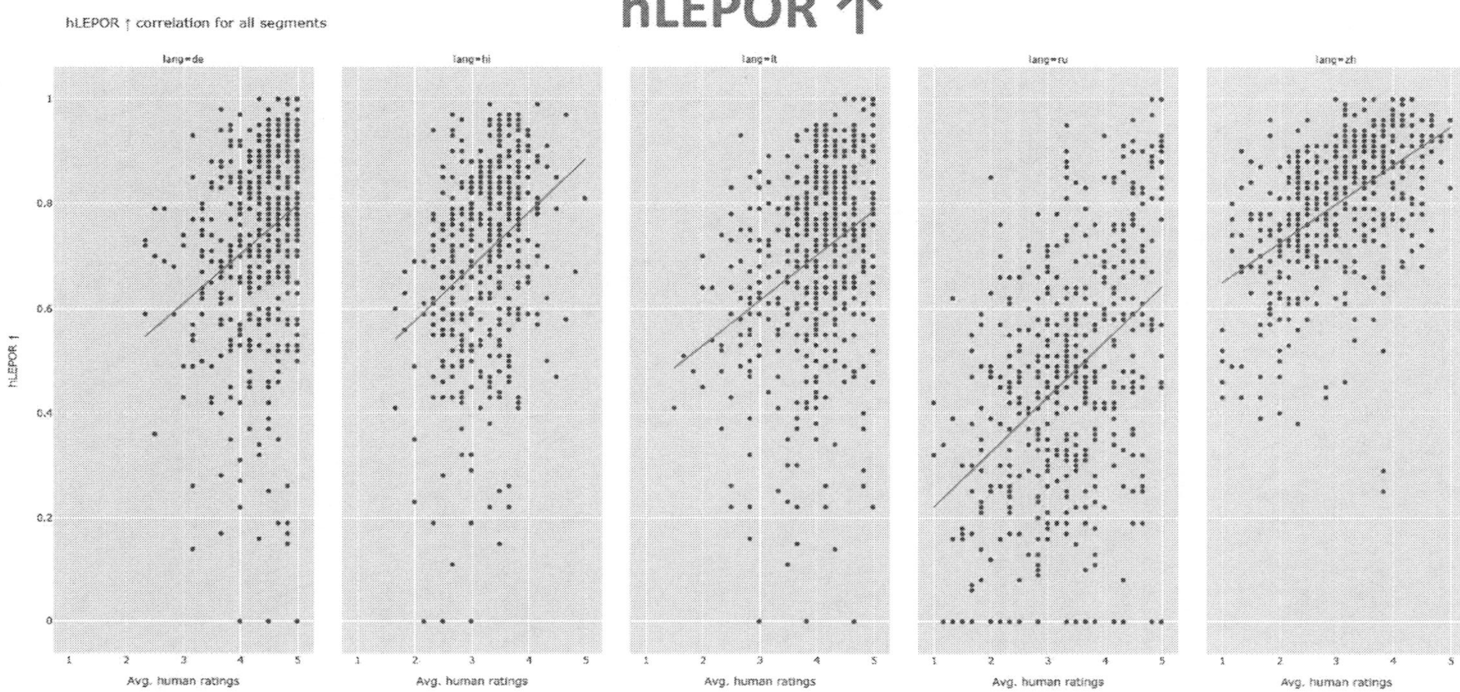

Key:

- ● Avg. Human ratings = Adequacy and Fluency ratings by 3 linguists averaged per segment
- ── Trendline = the degree to which Avg. Human ratings and hLEPOR scores are correlated. A diagonal line indicates a perfect correlation. The more points close to the line, the stronger the correlation.

LASER ↑

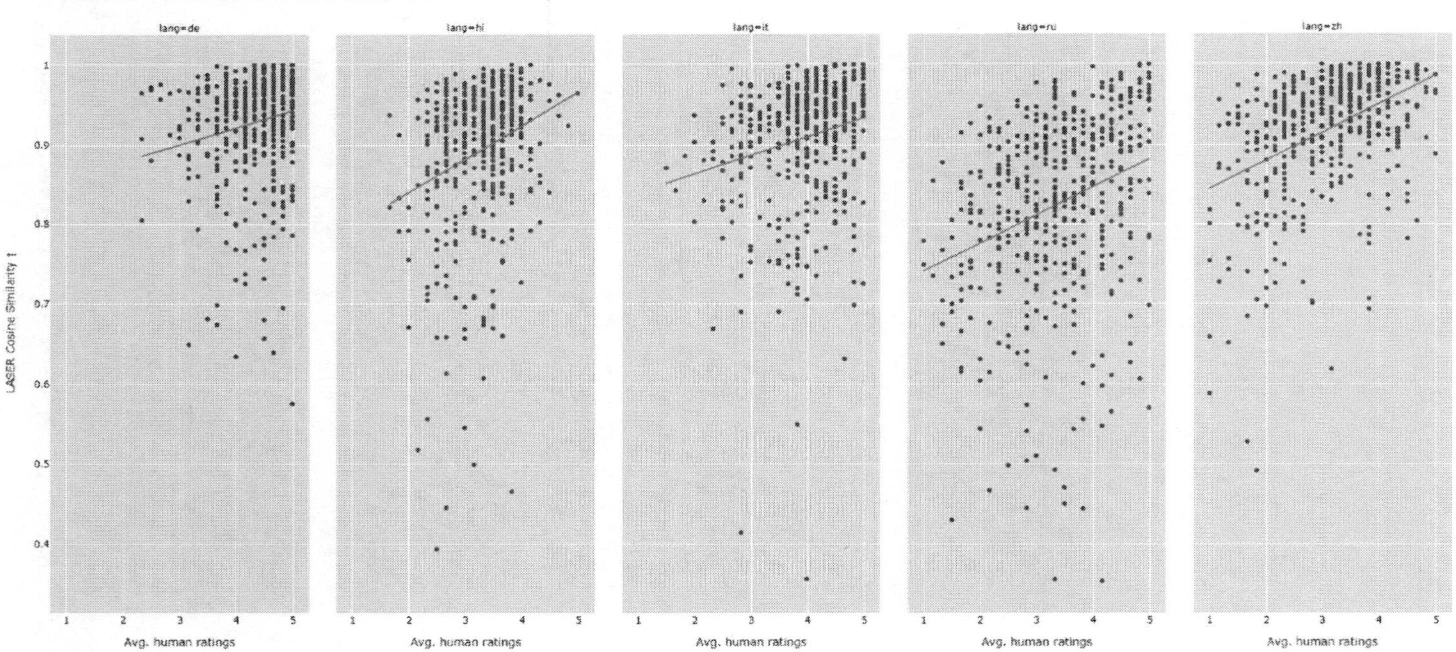

Key:

- ● Avg. Human ratings = Adequacy and Fluency ratings by 3 linguists averaged per segment
- — Trendline = the degree to which Avg. Human ratings and LASER cosine similarity scores are correlated. A diagonal line indicates a perfect correlation. The more points close to the line, the stronger the correlation.

Levenshtein ED ↓

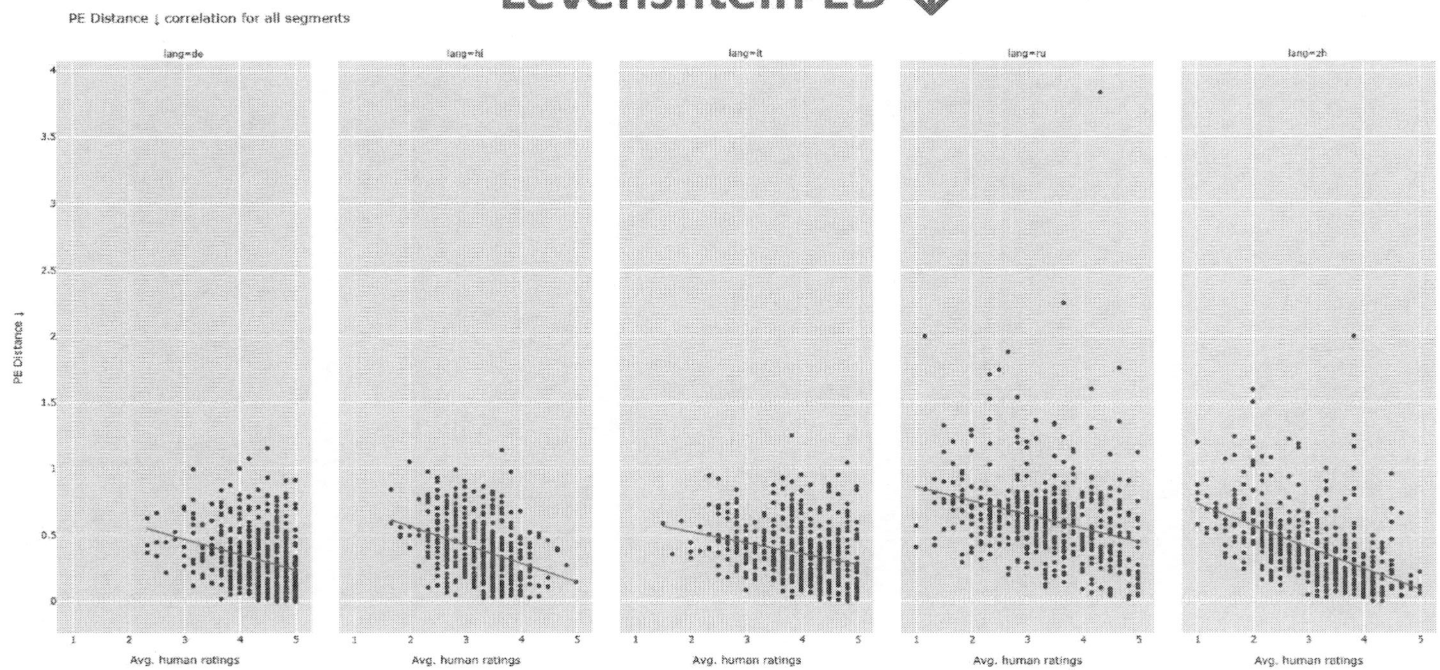

Key:

● Avg. Human ratings = Adequacy and Fluency ratings by 3 linguists averaged per segment

— Trendline = the degree to which Avg. Human ratings and Levenshtein Edit Distance scores are correlated. A diagonal line indicates a perfect correlation. The more points close to the line, the stronger the correlation.

PRISM ↑

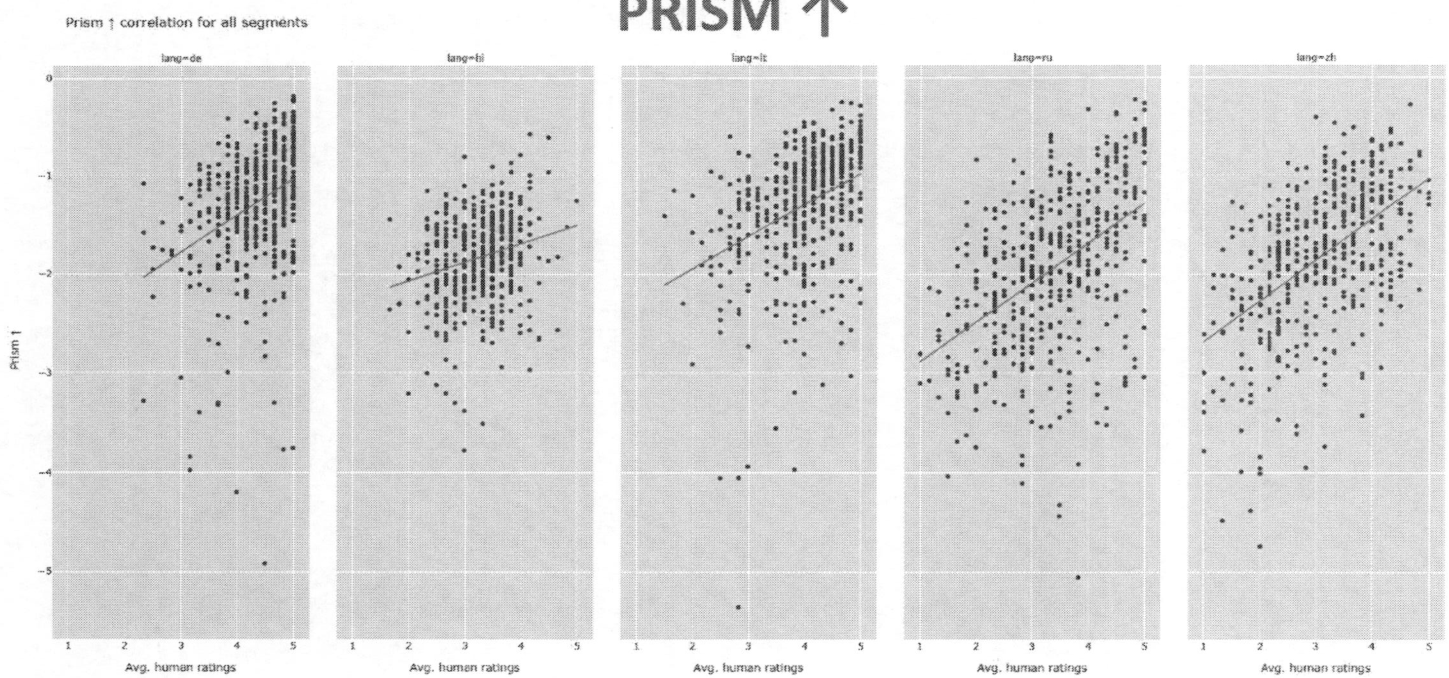

Key:

- ● Avg. Human ratings = Adequacy and Fluency ratings by 3 linguists averaged per segment
- — Trendline = the degree to which Avg. Human ratings and PRISM scores are correlated. A diagonal line indicates a perfect correlation. The more points close to the line, the stronger the correlation.

TER ↓

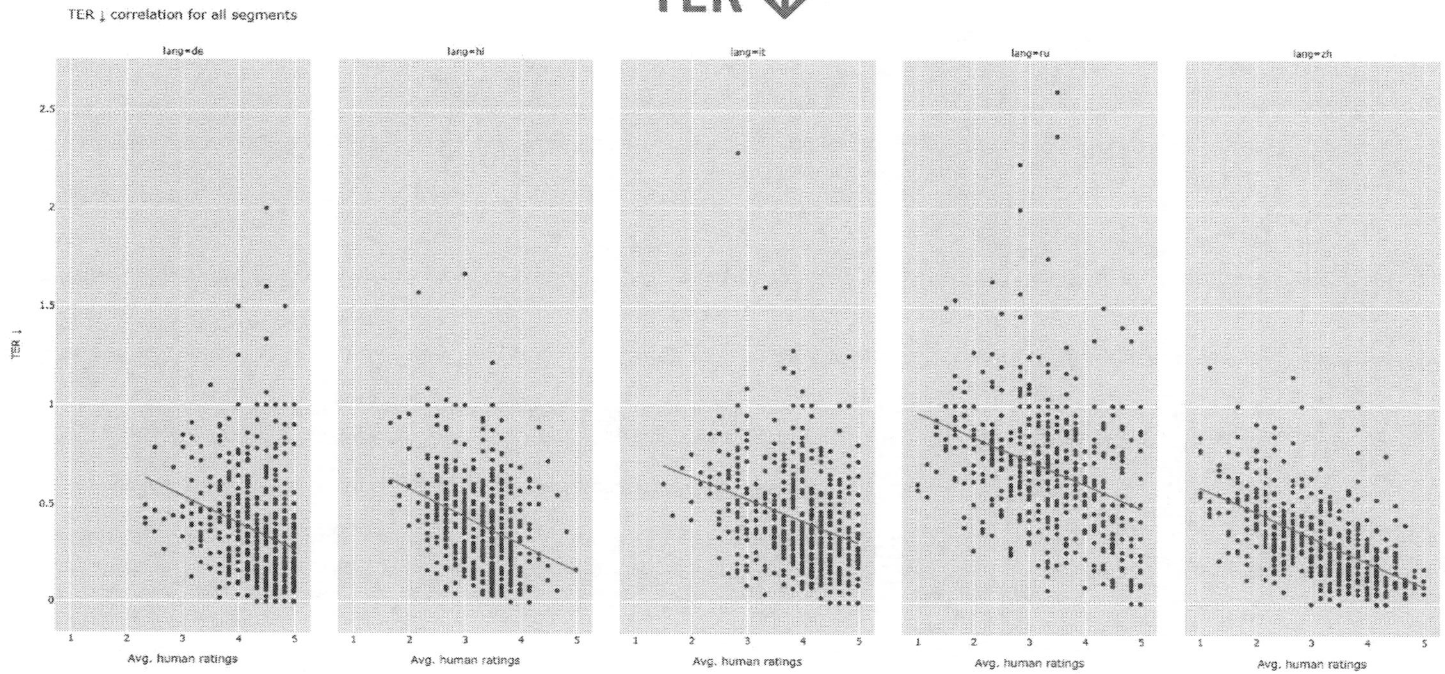

Key:

- ● Avg. Human ratings = Adequacy and Fluency ratings by 3 linguists averaged per segment
- — Trendline = the degree to which Avg. Human ratings and TER scores are correlated. A diagonal line indicates a perfect correlation. The more points close to the line, the stronger the correlation.

References

Artetxe, Mikel and Holger Schwenk. 2019. Massively Multilingual Sentence Embeddings for Zero-Shot Cross-Lingual Transfer and Beyond. *arXiv:1812.10464 [cs]*

Banerjee, S. and Lavie, A., 2005. METEOR: An Automatic Metric for MT Evaluation with Improved Correlation with Human Judgments. Proceedings of the ACL Workshop on Intrinsic and Extrinsic Evaluation Measures for Machine Translation and/or Summarization, 65–72.

Coughlin, D., 2001. Correlating Automated and Human Assessments of Machine Translation Quality.

Doddington, G., 2002. Automatic Evaluation of Machine Translation Quality Using N-gram Co-Occurrence Statistics. *HLT '02: Proceedings of the second international conference on Human Language Technology Research*, 138–145.

Han, Lifeng, Derek F. Wong, Lidia S. Chao, Liangye He, Yi Lu, Junwen Xing, and Xiaodong Zeng. 2013. Language-independent Model for Machine Translation Evaluation with Reinforced Factors.

Popović, Maja. 2015. chrF: character n-gram F-score for automatic MT evaluation. *Proceedings of the Tenth Workshop on Statistical Machine Translation,* 392–395.

Proceedings of the 5th Conference on Machine Translation (WMT), pages 1–55, November 19–20, 2020.

Rei, Ricardo, Craig Stewart, Ana C. Farinha, and Alon Lavie. 2020. COMET: A Neural Framework for MT Evaluation. *Proceedings of the 2020 Conference on Empirical Methods in Natural Language Processing (EMNLP)*, 2685–2702.

Snover, Matthew, Bonnie Dorr, Richard Schwartz, Linnea Micciulla, and John Makhoul. 2006. A Study of Translation Edit Rate with Targeted Human Annotation. *Proceedings of the 7th Conference of the Association for Machine Translation in the Americas: Technical Papers,* 223–231.

References

Snover, Matthew, Bonnie Dorr, Richard Schwartz, Linnea Micciulla, and John Makhoul. 2006. A Study of Translation Edit Rate with Targeted Human Annotation. *Proceedings of the 7th Conference of the Association for Machine Translation in the Americas: Technical Papers,* 223–231.

Thompson, Brian and Matt Post. 2020. Automatic Machine Translation Evaluation in Many Languages via Zero-Shot Paraphrasing. *arXiv:2004.14564 [cs]*

Wang, Weiyue, Jan-Thorsten Peter, Hendrik Rosendahl, and Hermann Ney. 2016. CharacTer: Translation Edit Rate on Character Level. *Proceedings of the First Conference on Machine Translation: Volume 2, Shared Task Papers*. 505–510.

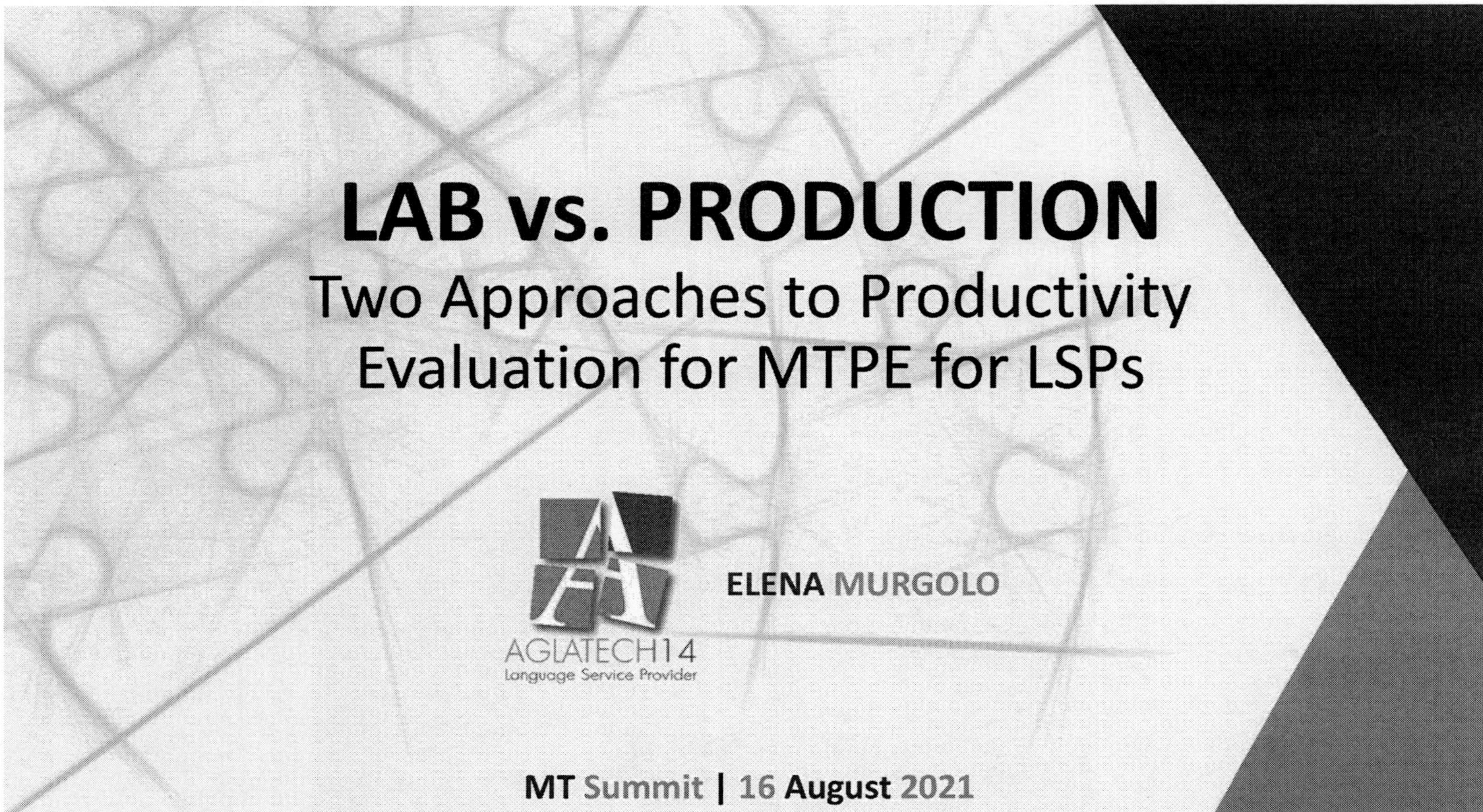
LAB vs. PRODUCTION
Two Approaches to Productivity
Evaluation for MTPE for LSPs
AGLATECH14
Language Service Provider
ELENA MURGOLO
MT Summit | 16 August 2021

ABOUT US
LSP
AGLATECH14

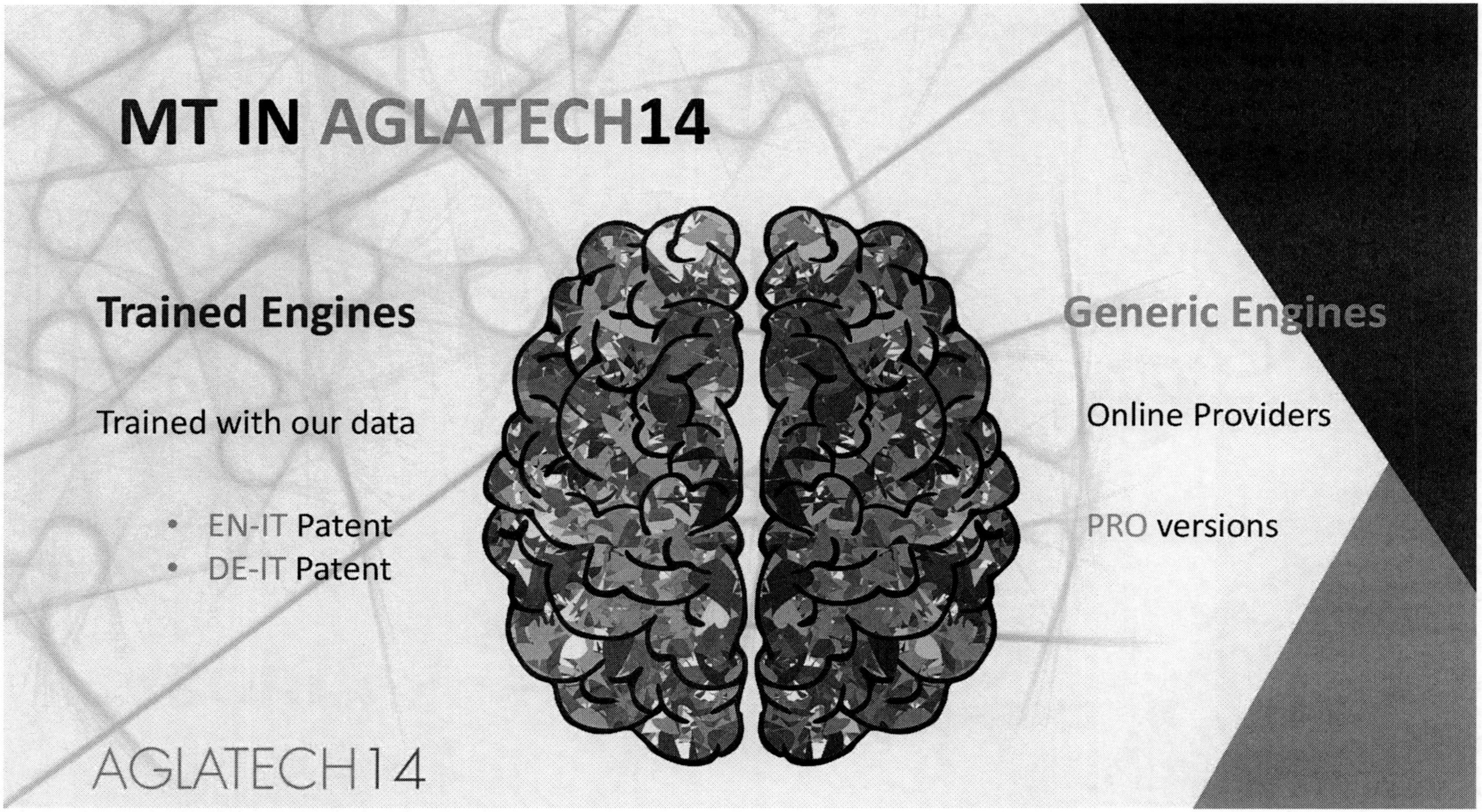
MT IN AGLATECH14
Trained Engines
Trained with our data
• EN-IT Patent
• DE-IT Patent
Generic Engines
Online Providers
PRO versions
AGLATECH14

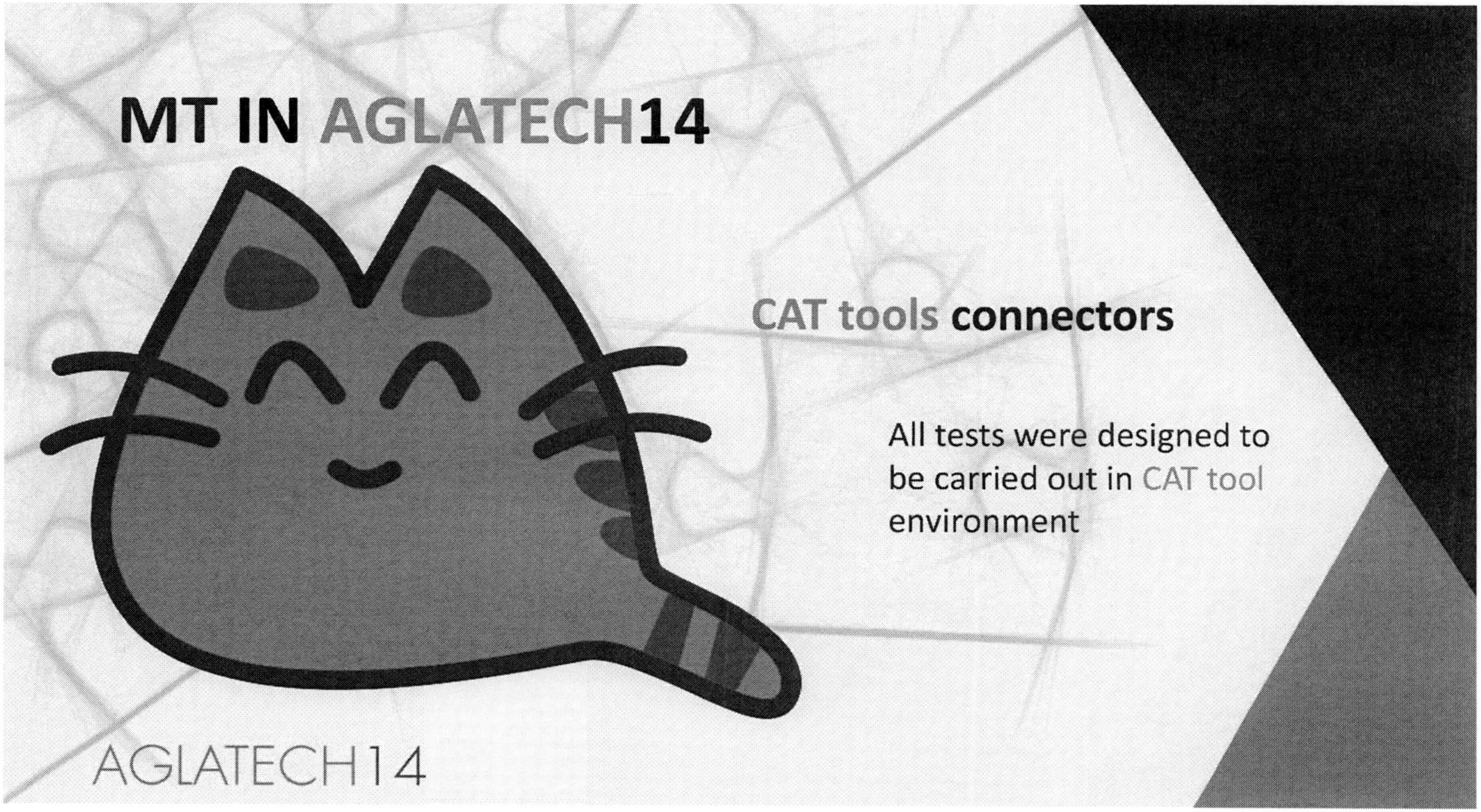
MT IN AGLATECH14
CAT tools connectors
All tests were designed to be carried out in CAT tool environment
AGLATECH14

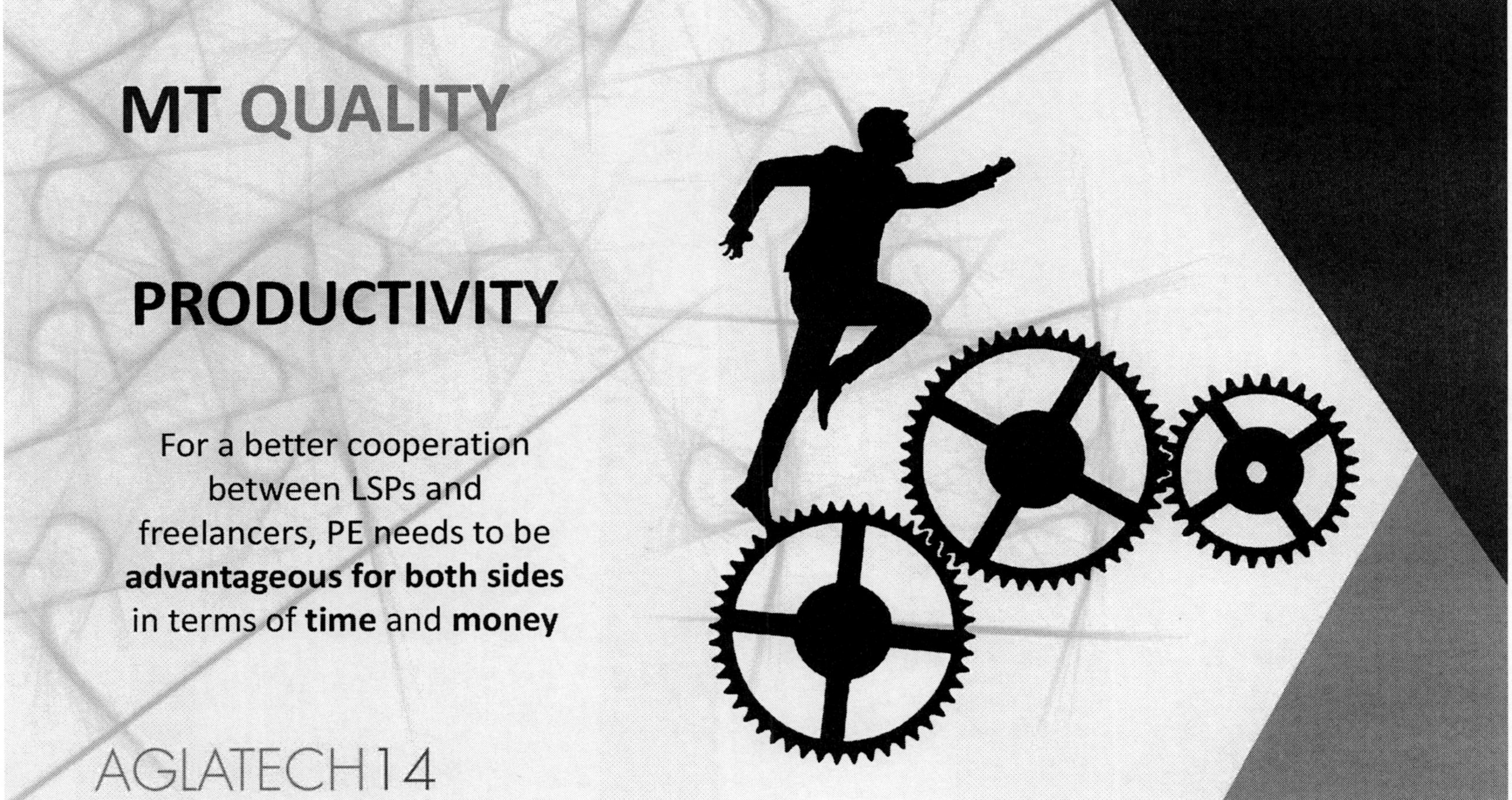
MT QUALITY
PRODUCTIVITY
For a better cooperation between LSPs and freelancers, PE needs to be **advantageous for both sides** in terms of **time** and **money**
AGLATECH14

PT TESTS
1. Lab Tests
2. Production Tests
Trados
AGLATECH14
Qualitivity

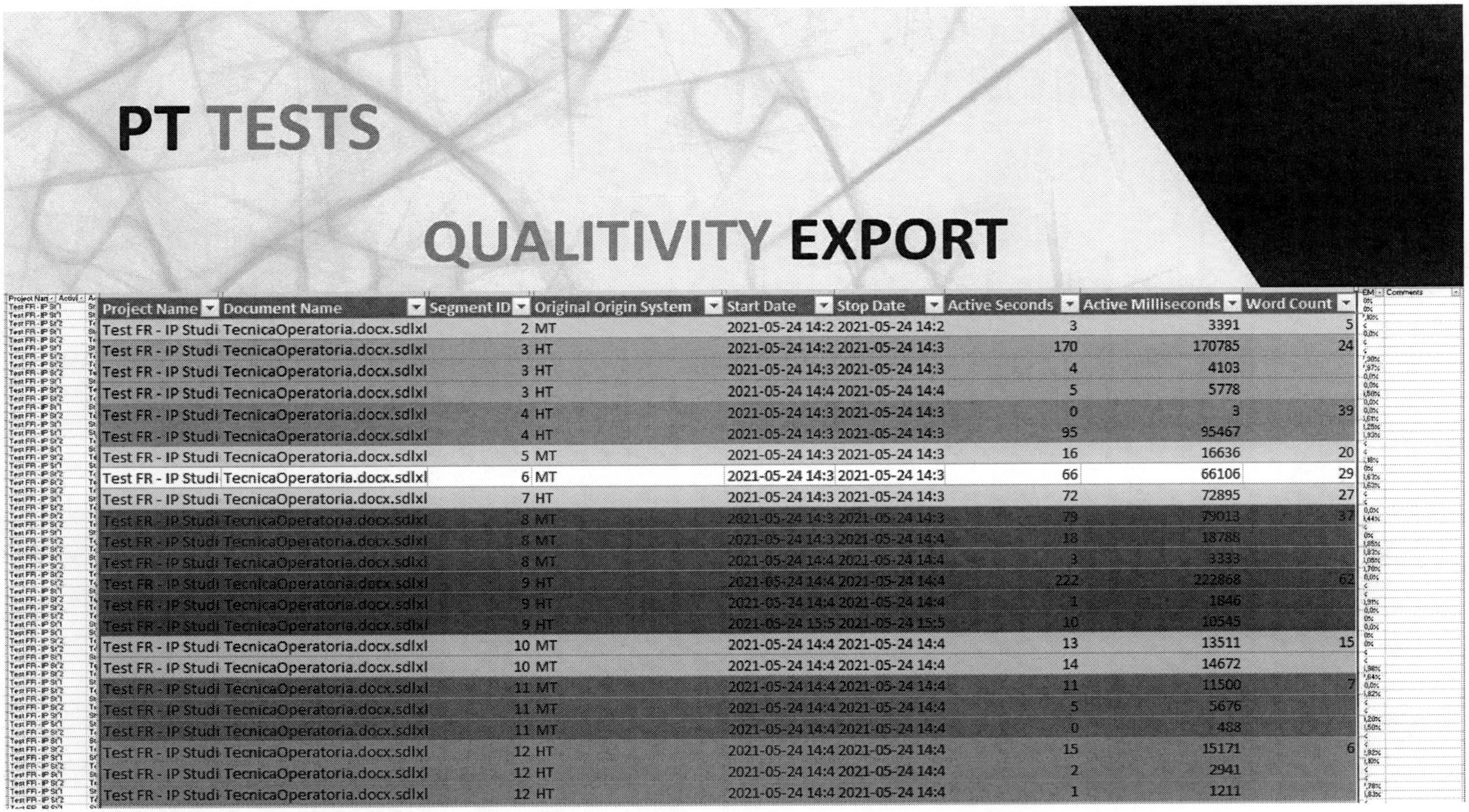

Project Name	Document Name	Segment ID	Original Origin System	Start Date	Stop Date	Active Seconds	Active Milliseconds	Word Count
Test FR - IP Studi	TecnicaOperatoria.docx.sdlxl	2	MT	2021-05-24 14:2	2021-05-24 14:2	3	3391	5
Test FR - IP Studi	TecnicaOperatoria.docx.sdlxl	3	HT	2021-05-24 14:2	2021-05-24 14:3	170	170785	24
Test FR - IP Studi	TecnicaOperatoria.docx.sdlxl	3	HT	2021-05-24 14:3	2021-05-24 14:3	4	4103	
Test FR - IP Studi	TecnicaOperatoria.docx.sdlxl	3	HT	2021-05-24 14:4	2021-05-24 14:4	5	5778	
Test FR - IP Studi	TecnicaOperatoria.docx.sdlxl	4	HT	2021-05-24 14:3	2021-05-24 14:3	0	3	39
Test FR - IP Studi	TecnicaOperatoria.docx.sdlxl	4	HT	2021-05-24 14:3	2021-05-24 14:3	95	95467	
Test FR - IP Studi	TecnicaOperatoria.docx.sdlxl	5	MT	2021-05-24 14:3	2021-05-24 14:3	16	16636	20
Test FR - IP Studi	TecnicaOperatoria.docx.sdlxl	6	MT	2021-05-24 14:3	2021-05-24 14:3	66	66106	29
Test FR - IP Studi	TecnicaOperatoria.docx.sdlxl	7	HT	2021-05-24 14:3	2021-05-24 14:3	72	72895	27
Test FR - IP Studi	TecnicaOperatoria.docx.sdlxl	8	MT	2021-05-24 14:3	2021-05-24 14:3	79	79013	37
Test FR - IP Studi	TecnicaOperatoria.docx.sdlxl	8	MT	2021-05-24 14:3	2021-05-24 14:4	18	18788	
Test FR - IP Studi	TecnicaOperatoria.docx.sdlxl	8	MT	2021-05-24 14:4	2021-05-24 14:4	3	3333	
Test FR - IP Studi	TecnicaOperatoria.docx.sdlxl	9	HT	2021-05-24 14:4	2021-05-24 14:4	222	222868	62
Test FR - IP Studi	TecnicaOperatoria.docx.sdlxl	9	HT	2021-05-24 14:4	2021-05-24 14:4	1	1846	
Test FR - IP Studi	TecnicaOperatoria.docx.sdlxl	9	HT	2021-05-24 15:5	2021-05-24 15:5	10	10545	
Test FR - IP Studi	TecnicaOperatoria.docx.sdlxl	10	MT	2021-05-24 14:4	2021-05-24 14:4	13	13511	15
Test FR - IP Studi	TecnicaOperatoria.docx.sdlxl	10	MT	2021-05-24 14:4	2021-05-24 14:4	14	14672	
Test FR - IP Studi	TecnicaOperatoria.docx.sdlxl	11	MT	2021-05-24 14:4	2021-05-24 14:4	11	11500	7
Test FR - IP Studi	TecnicaOperatoria.docx.sdlxl	11	MT	2021-05-24 14:4	2021-05-24 14:4	5	5676	
Test FR - IP Studi	TecnicaOperatoria.docx.sdlxl	11	MT	2021-05-24 14:4	2021-05-24 14:4	0	488	
Test FR - IP Studi	TecnicaOperatoria.docx.sdlxl	12	HT	2021-05-24 14:4	2021-05-24 14:4	15	15171	6
Test FR - IP Studi	TecnicaOperatoria.docx.sdlxl	12	HT	2021-05-24 14:4	2021-05-24 14:4	2	2941	
Test FR - IP Studi	TecnicaOperatoria.docx.sdlxl	12	HT	2021-05-24 14:4	2021-05-24 14:4	1	1211	

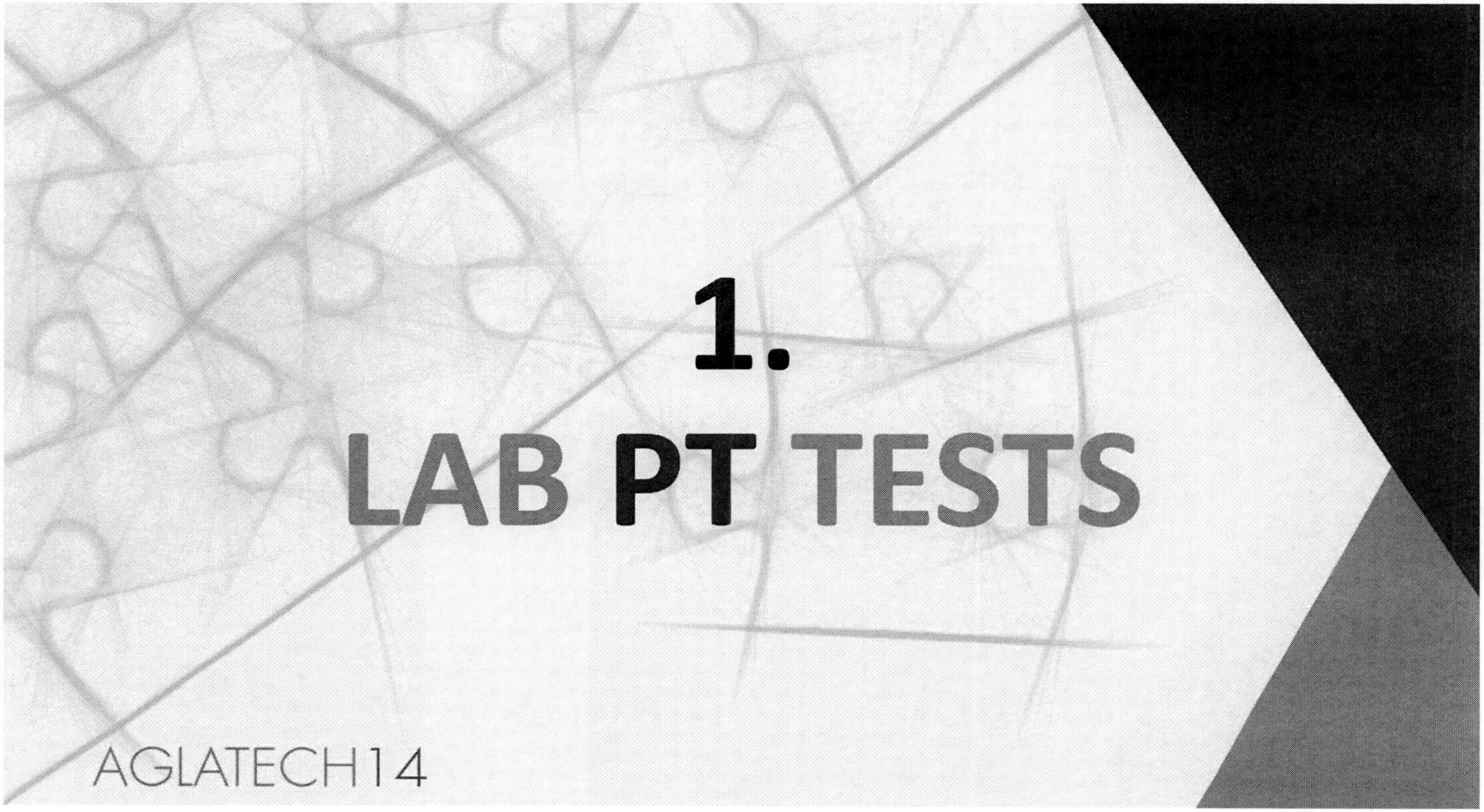
1.
LAB PT TESTS
AGLATECH14

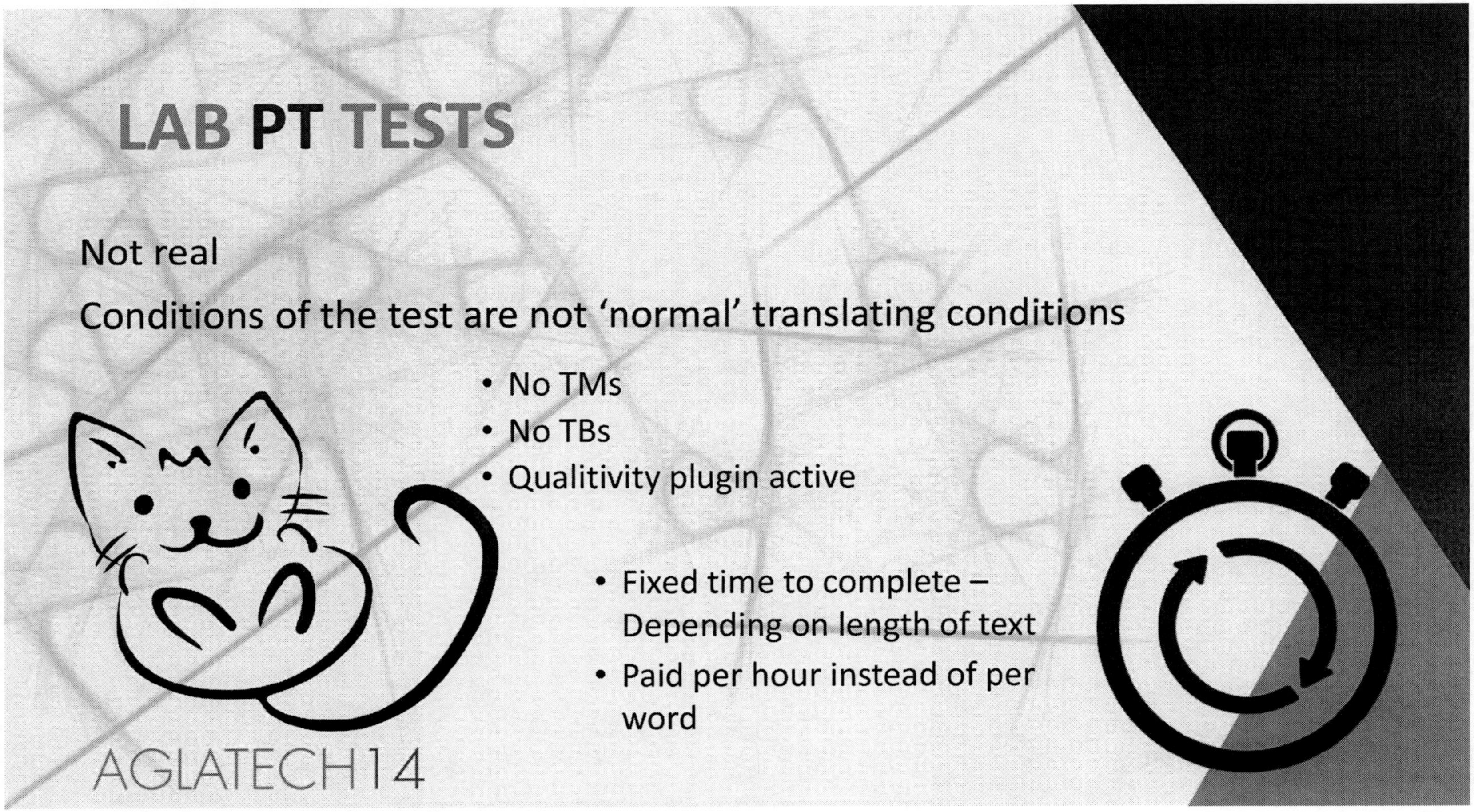
LAB PT TESTS
Not real
Conditions of the test are not ‘normal’ translating conditions
• No TMs
• No TBs
• Qualitivity plugin active
• Fixed time to complete – Depending on length of text
• Paid per hour instead of per word
AGLATECH14

LAB PT TESTS

Not real

Conditions of the test are not ‘normal’ translating conditions

- Text(s) created ad hoc – Combination of subject matters and characteristics needing testing
- 3000 to 4000 words

AGLATECH14

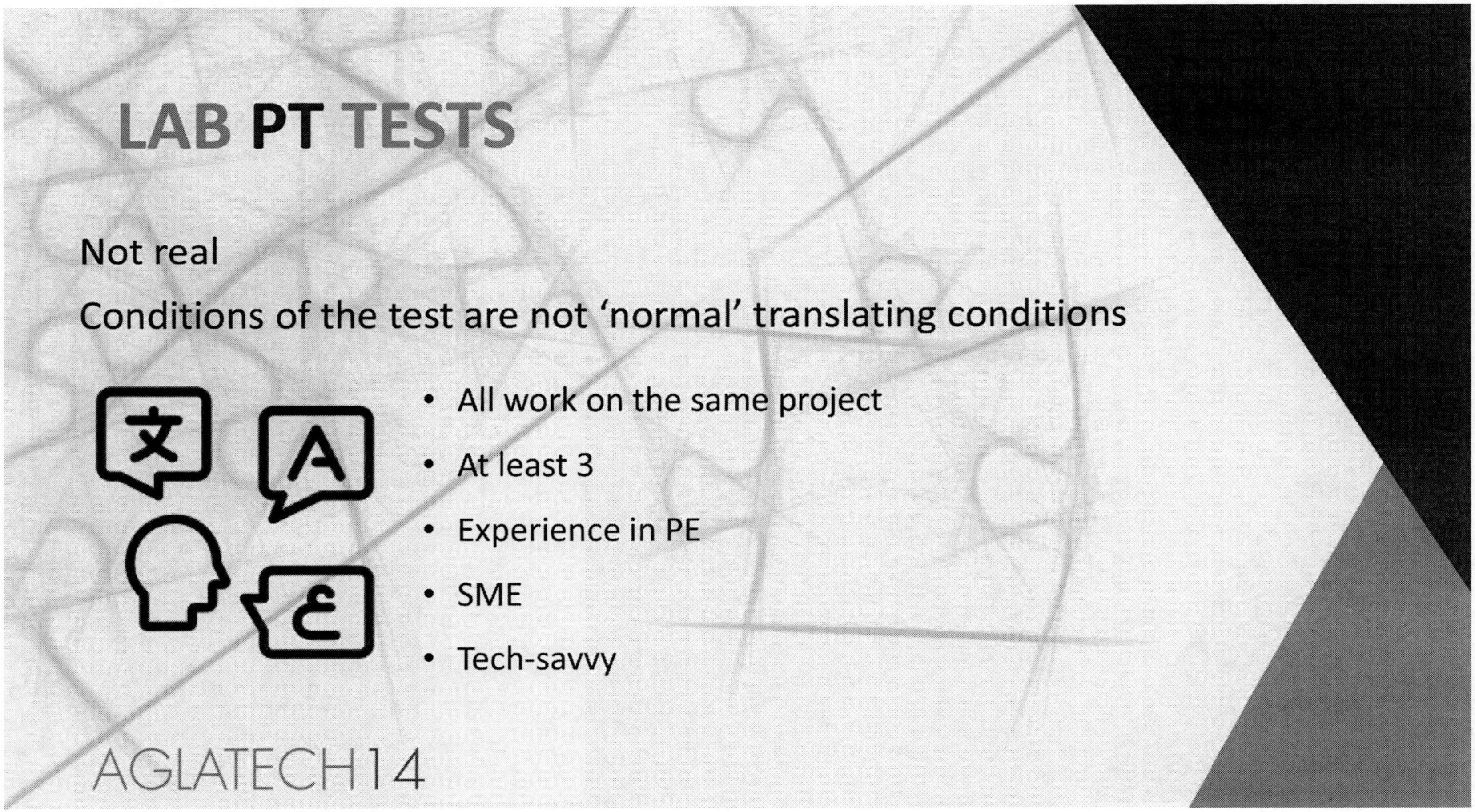
LAB PT TESTS
Not real
Conditions of the test are not 'normal' translating conditions
All work on the same project
At least 3
Experience in PE
SME
Tech-savvy
AGLATECH14

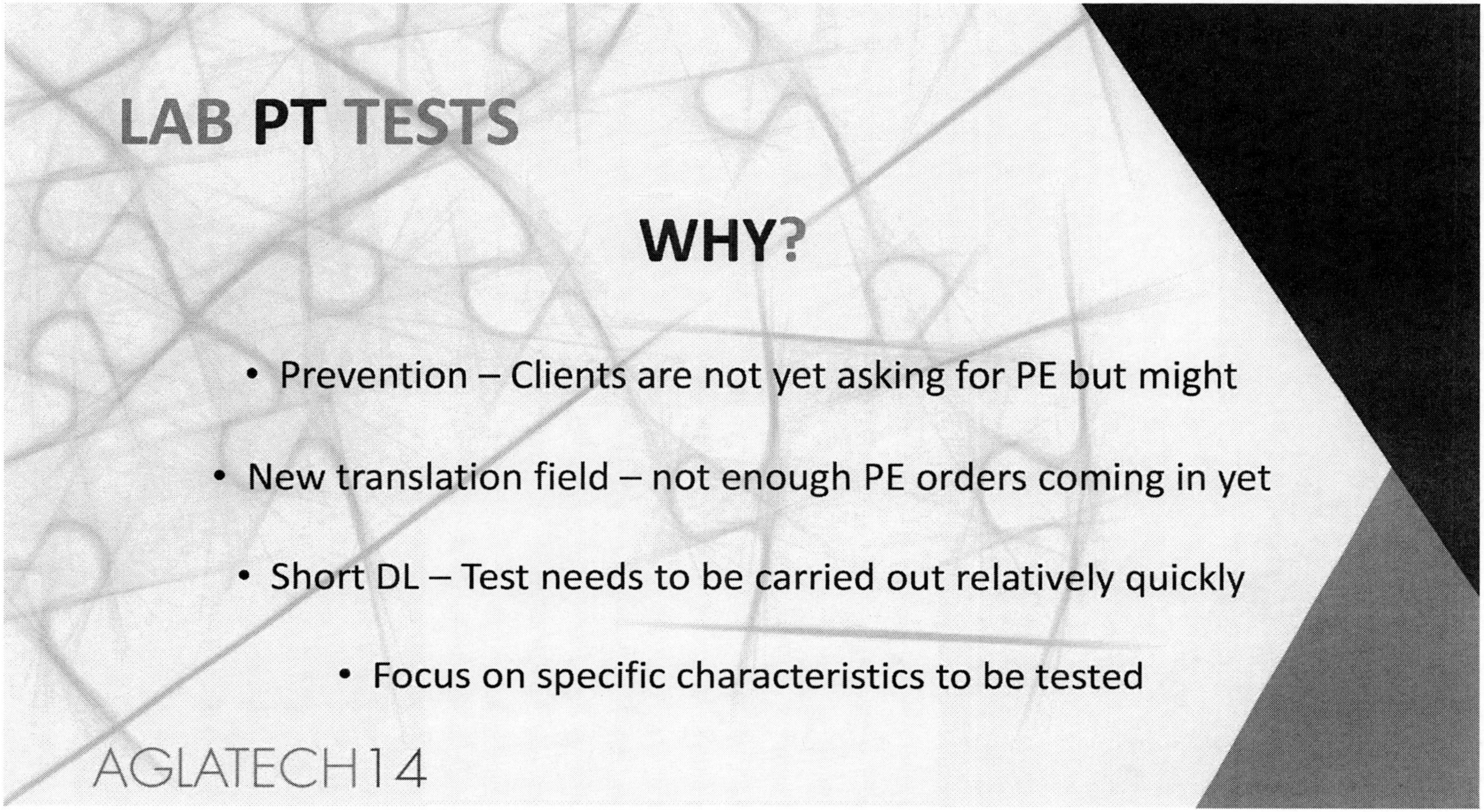
LAB PT TESTS
WHY?
• Prevention – Clients are not yet asking for PE but might
• New translation field – not enough PE orders coming in yet
• Short DL – Test needs to be carried out relatively quickly
• Focus on specific characteristics to be tested
AGLATECH14

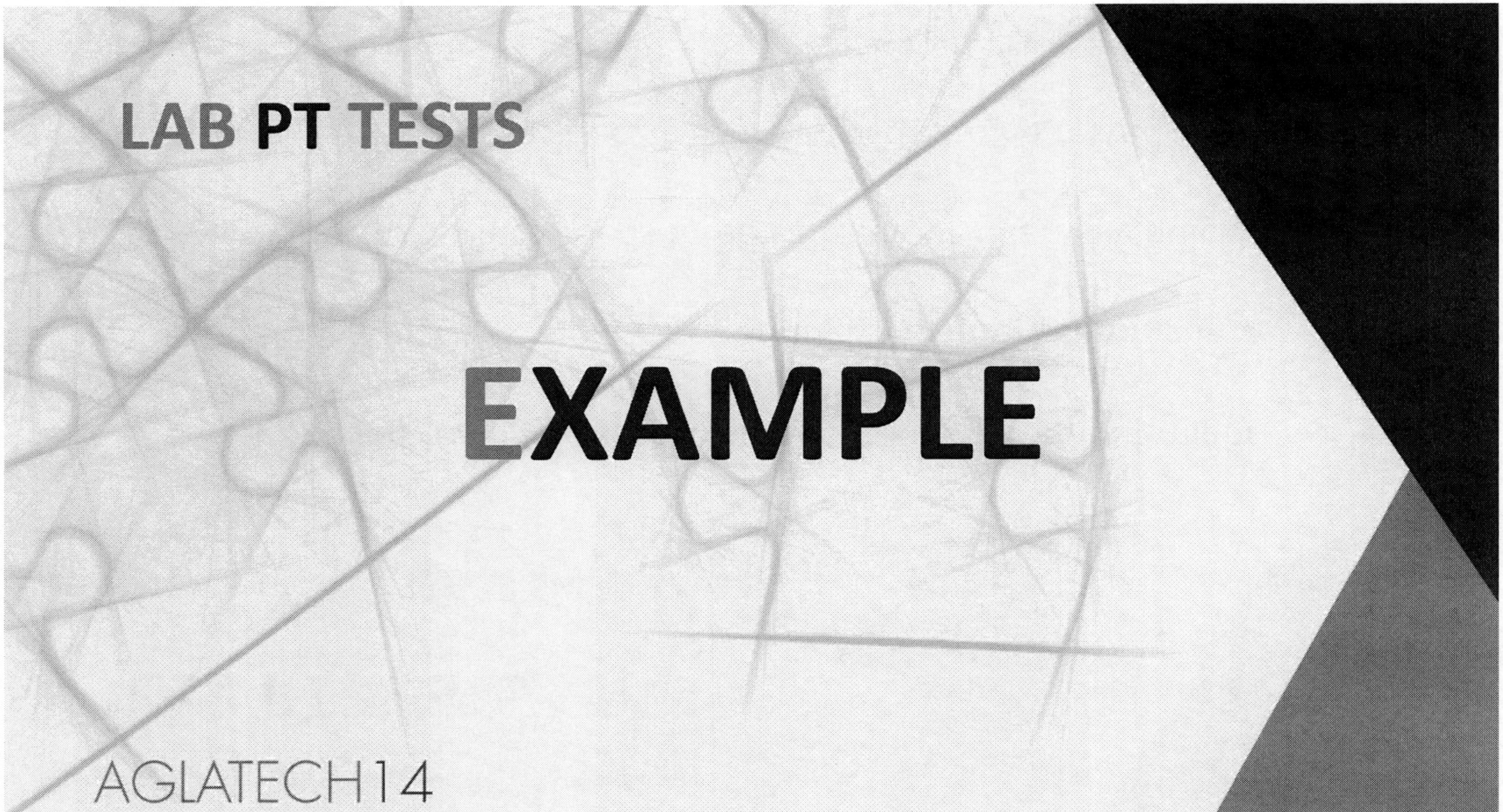
LAB PT TESTS
EXAMPLE
AGLATECH14

LAB PT TESTS

TEST SETUP

Testing data	
Total test hours	12
Hours each PE	4
Total Words	3.632
MT Engine(s)	Generic MT

	Subject Matters	# words	Total # words
Total words	Surgical Instruction	823	3.632
	Clinical Study	2.809	
HT words	Surgical Instruction	418	1.825
	Clinical Study	1.407	
MT words	Surgical Instruction	405	1.807
	Clinical Study	1.402	

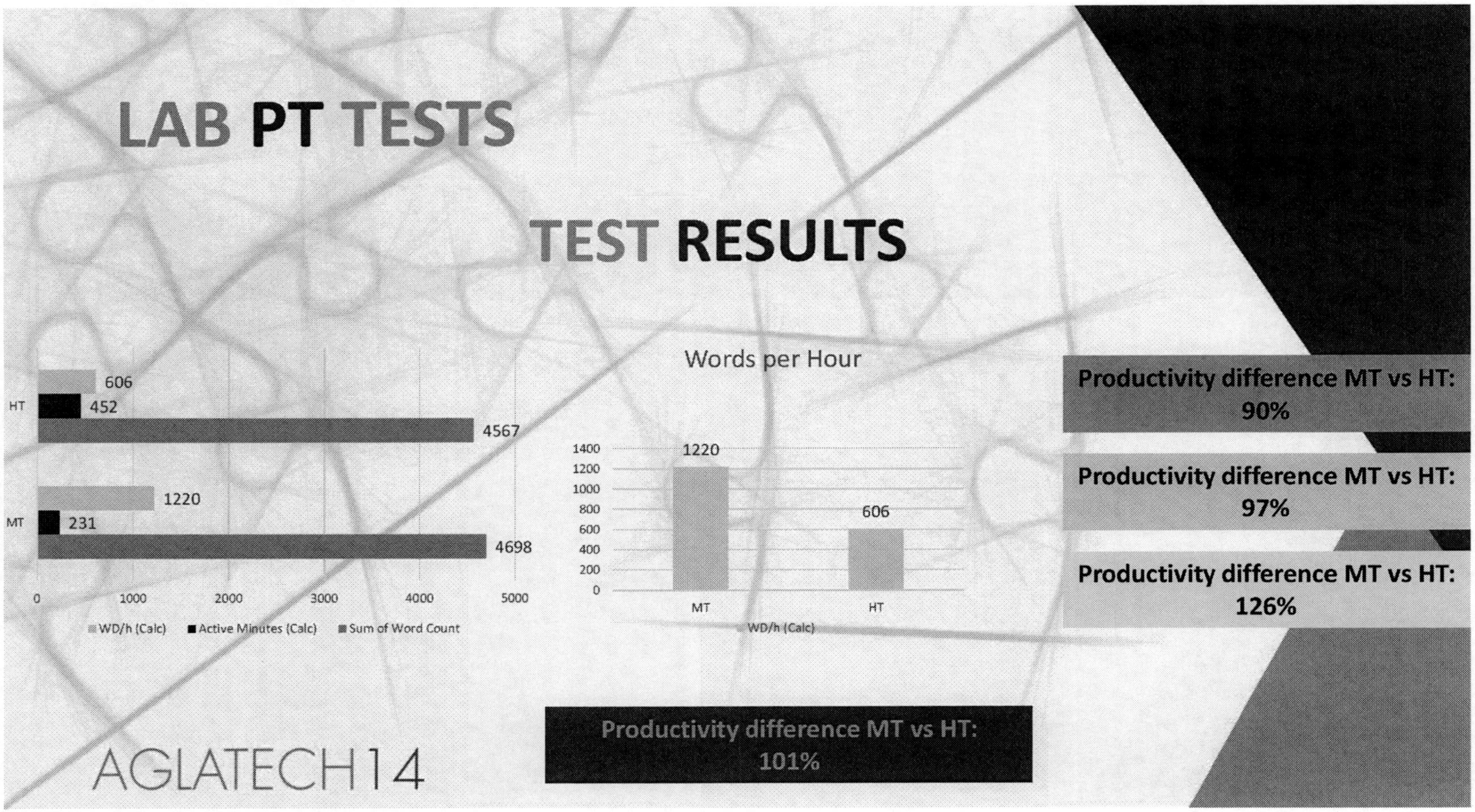
LAB PT TESTS
TEST RESULTS
HT
606
452
4567
MT
1220
231
4698
0
1000
2000
3000
4000
5000
WD/h (Calc)
Active Minutes (Calc)
Sum of Word Count
Words per Hour
1400
1200
1000
800
600
400
200
0
1220
606
MT
HT
WD/h (Calc)
Productivity difference MT vs HT: 90%
Productivity difference MT vs HT: 97%
Productivity difference MT vs HT: 126%
Productivity difference MT vs HT: 101%
AGLATECH14

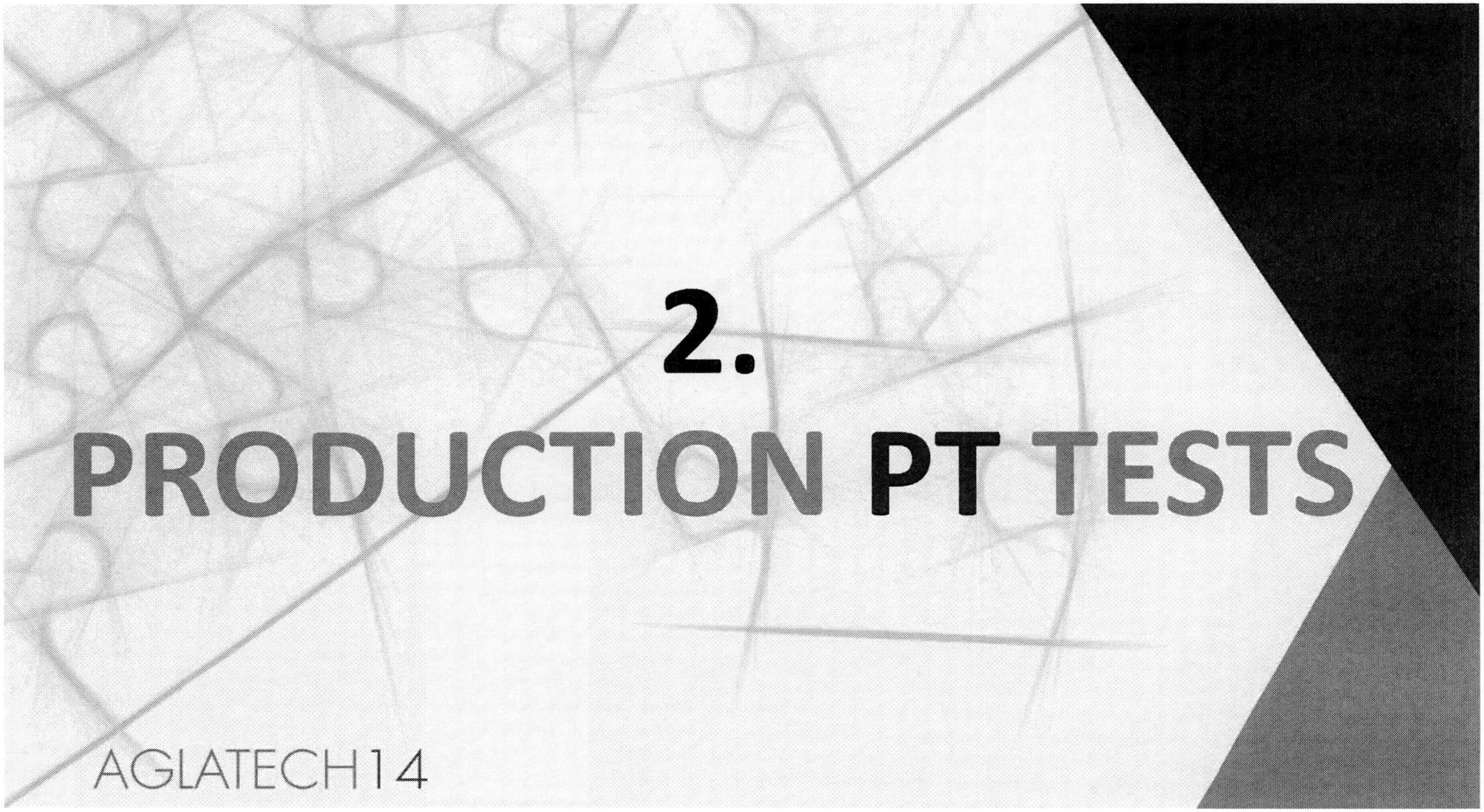
2.
PRODUCTION PT TESTS
AGLATECH14

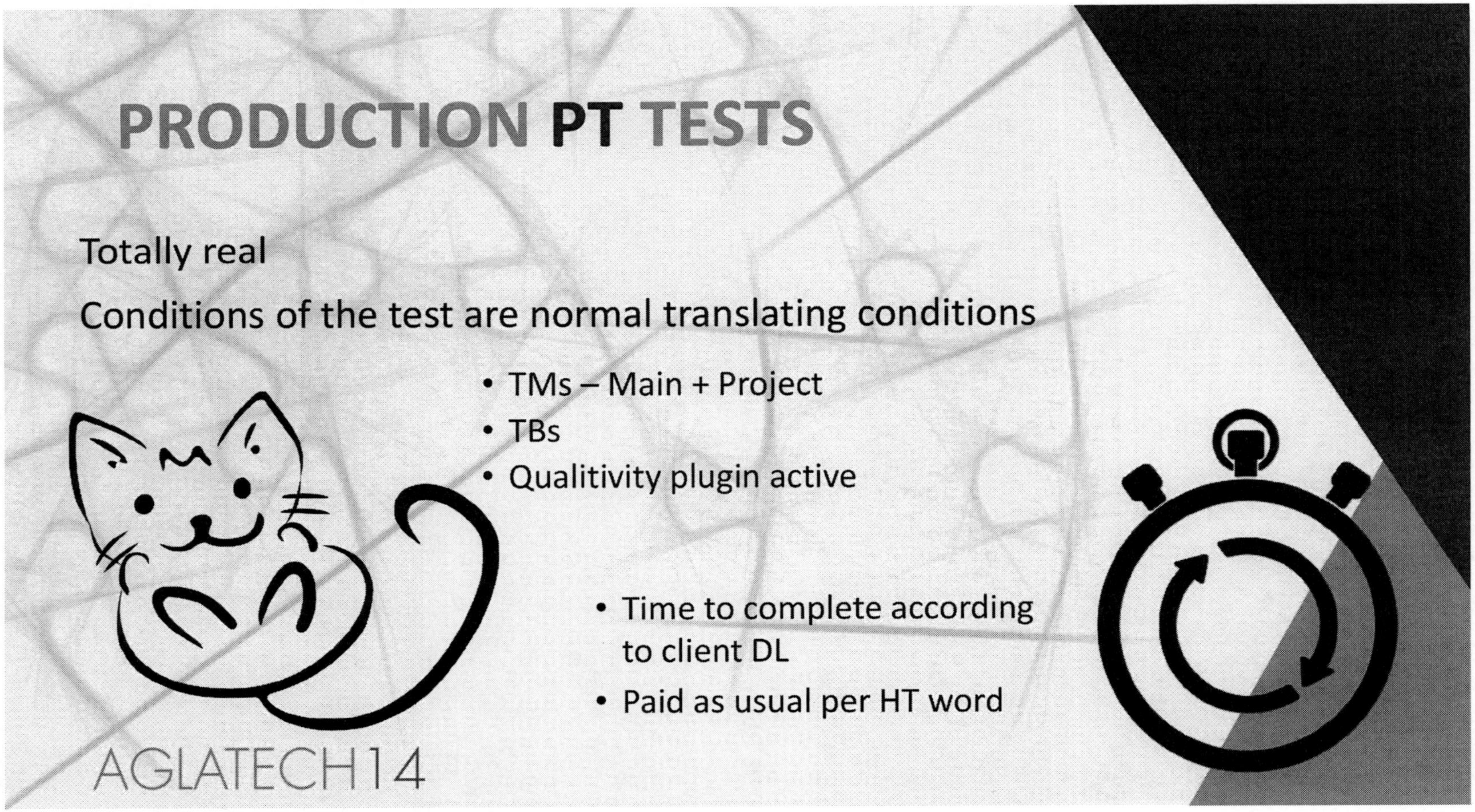
PRODUCTION PT TESTS
Totally real
Conditions of the test are normal translating conditions
• TMs – Main + Project
• TBs
• Qualitivity plugin active
• Time to complete according to client DL
• Paid as usual per HT word
AGLATECH14

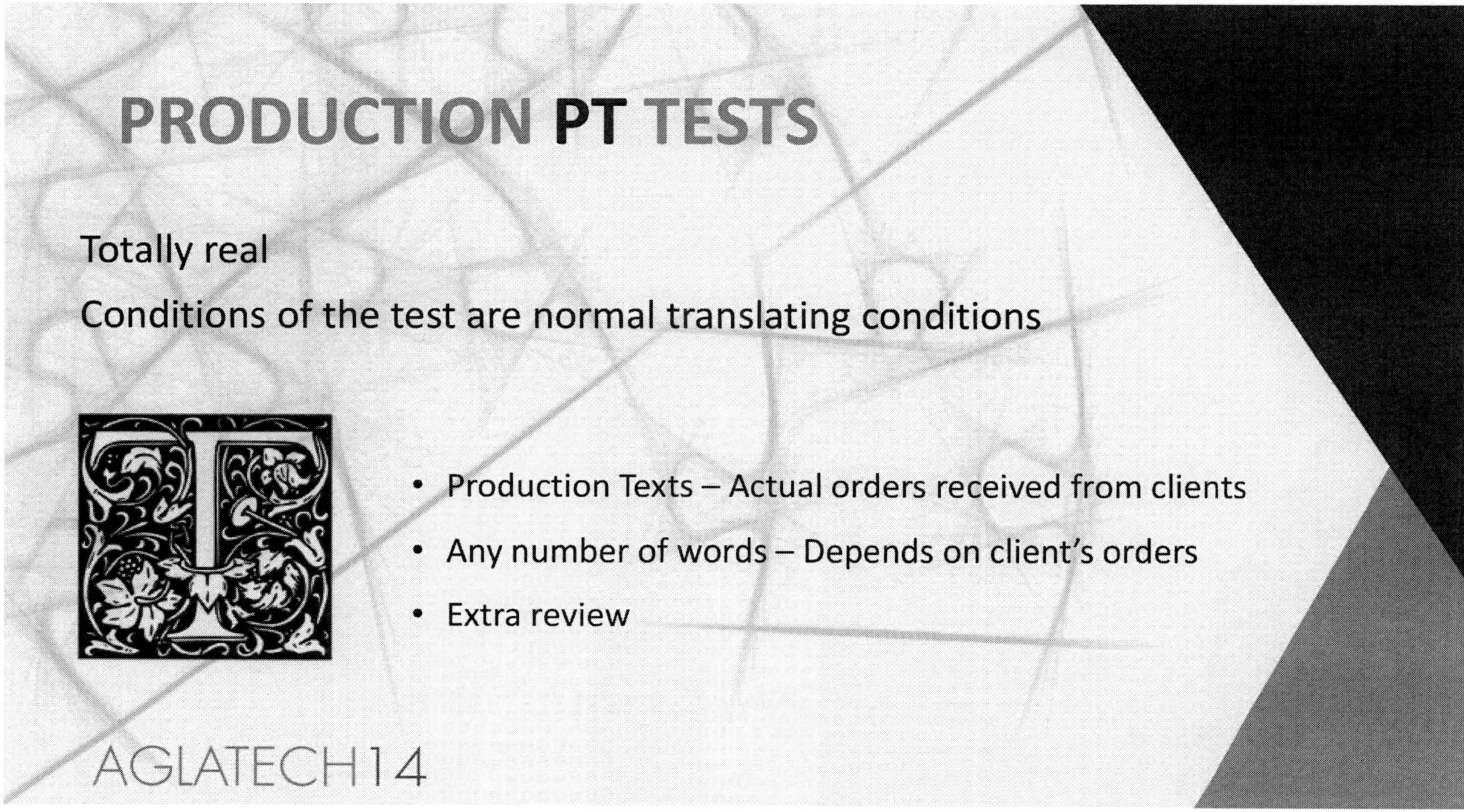
PRODUCTION PT TESTS
Totally real
Conditions of the test are normal translating conditions
• Production Texts – Actual orders received from clients
• Any number of words – Depends on client's orders
• Extra review
AGLATECH14

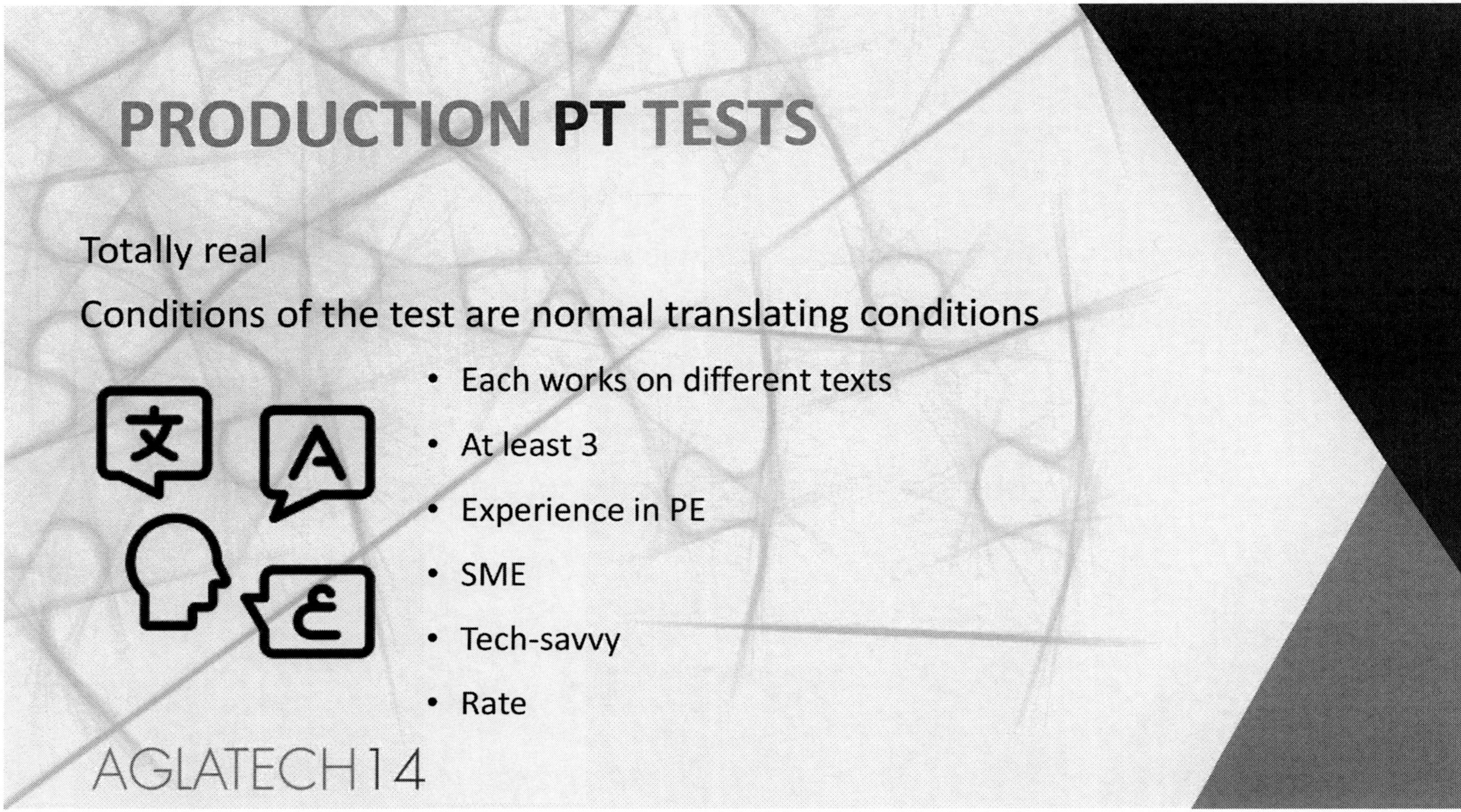
PRODUCTION PT TESTS
Totally real
Conditions of the test are normal translating conditions
• Each works on different texts
• At least 3
• Experience in PE
• SME
• Tech-savvy
• Rate
AGLATECH14

PRODUCTION PT TESTS

WHY?

- Response – Clients asking for PE in new domains/languages
- Accurate representation – On actual texts in real conditions
- Broader Spectrum – More varied cases
- Budget saving

AGLATECH14

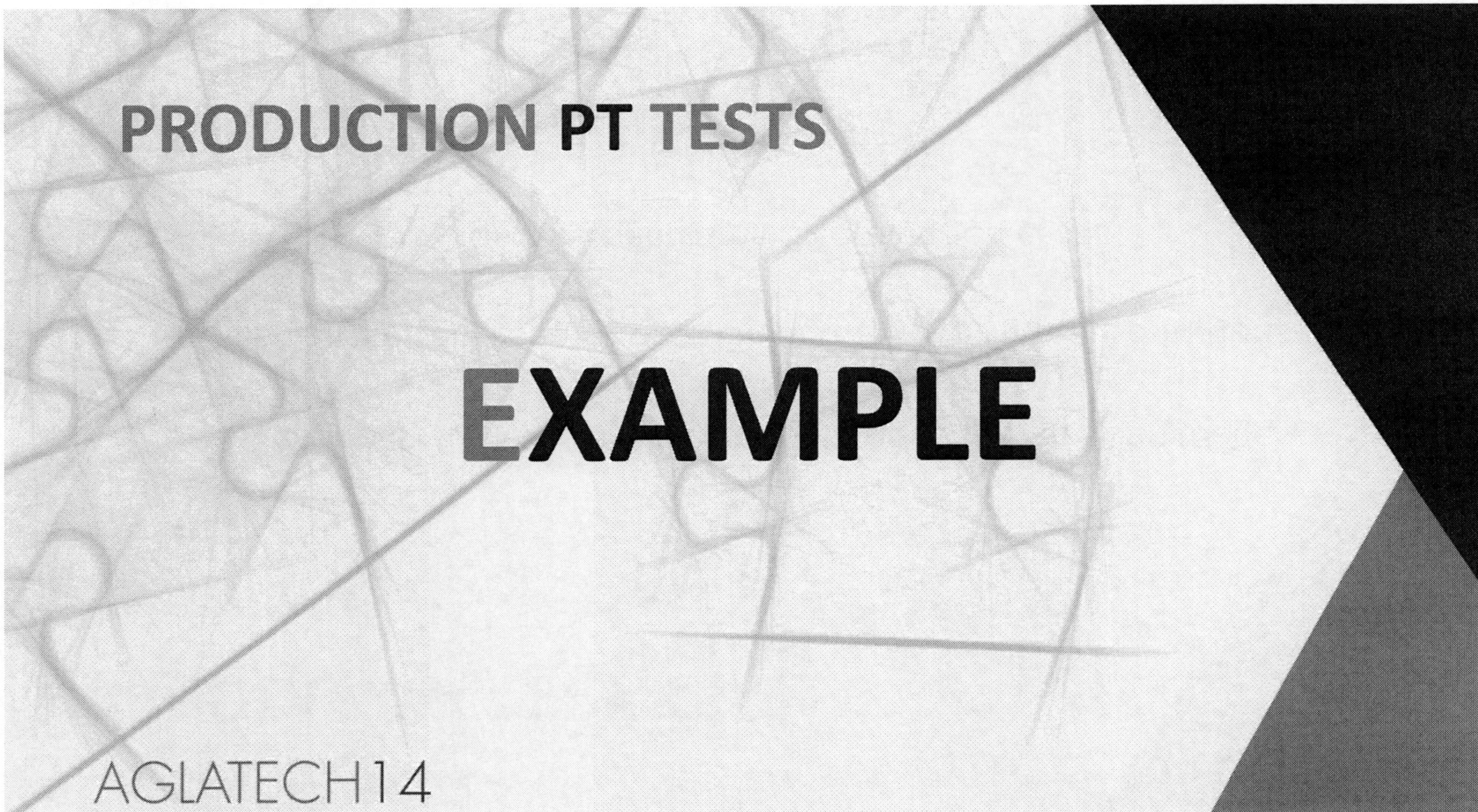
PRODUCTION PT TESTS
EXAMPLE
AGLATECH14

PRODUCTION PT TESTS

TEST SETUP

Subject Matters	
Materials Science	3
Industrial Processes	2
Medical Devices	1
Pharmaceutics	2
Chemistry	1
Mechanics	1
Electronics and Electrotechnics	2

	Total	Scientific	Mechanics
Orders	12	7	5
Word count	89.465	58.176	31.289
Post-editors	6		
MT Engine(s)	1 Generic + 2 Trained		

Post-Editor	# texts	# words
PE1	2	12.785
PE2	1	4.992
PE3	2	10.543
PE4	1	11.725
PE5	3	33.330
PE6	3	16.090

AGLATECH14

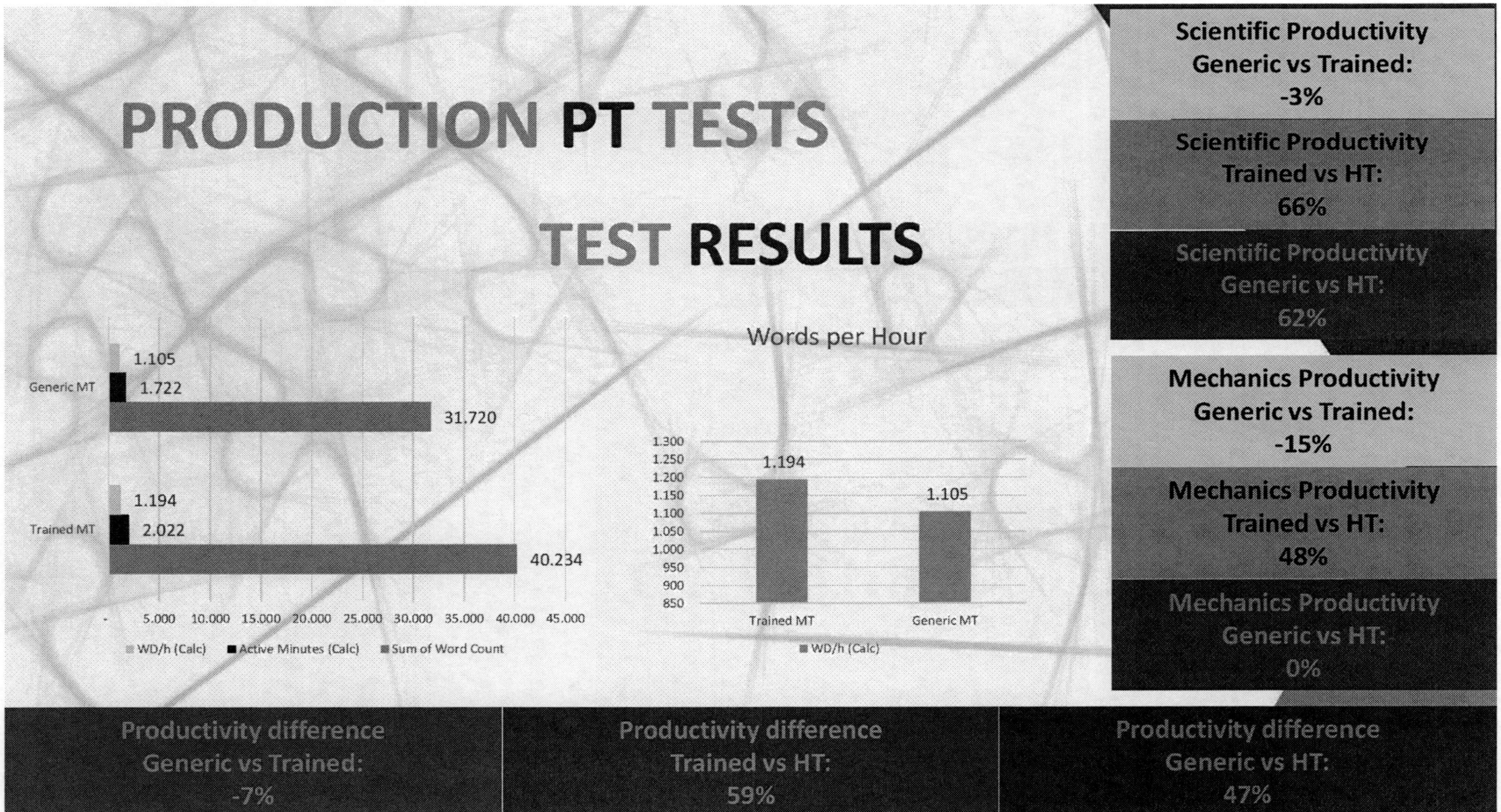
PRODUCTION PT TESTS
TEST RESULTS
Generic MT
Trained MT
1.105
1.722
31.720
1.194
2.022
40.234
-
5.000
10.000
15.000
20.000
25.000
30.000
35.000
40.000
45.000
WD/h (Calc)
Active Minutes (Calc)
Sum of Word Count
Words per Hour
1.300
1.250
1.200
1.150
1.100
1.050
1.000
950
900
850
1.194
1.105
Trained MT
Generic MT
WD/h (Calc)
Scientific Productivity Generic vs Trained: -3%
Scientific Productivity Trained vs HT: 66%
Scientific Productivity Generic vs HT: 62%
Mechanics Productivity Generic vs Trained: -15%
Mechanics Productivity Trained vs HT: 48%
Mechanics Productivity Generic vs HT: 0%
Productivity difference Generic vs Trained: -7%
Productivity difference Trained vs HT: 59%
Productivity difference Generic vs HT: 47%

QUESTIONS?
AGLATECH14

GRAZIE
emurgolo@aglatech14.it

Association for Computational Linguistics
209 N. Eighth Street
Stroudsburg, Pennsylvania 18360

ISBN 978-1-7138-3920-0

9 781713 839200

CURRAN ASSOCIATES INC.
proceedings.com